TOURING SHAKESPEARE

Drawing on a wealth of archival material, *Touring Shakespeare* reveals how English Shakespeare companies were deployed overseas in service to British diplomatic interests at the end of Empire and the start of the Cold War. In exploring the politics behind the global dissemination of Shakespeare performed by prominent English theatre companies like the Old Vic and the Shakespeare Memorial Theatre, Jim Taylor examines whether tours supported, contradicted, or ran adjacent to the broader diplomatic objectives they served. Peeling back layers of production and reception history in such diverse locations as Egypt, India, Nigeria, and Australia, his study discloses how the British state came to regard Shakespeare tours as an effective compensatory device for its loss of economic and political power overseas, and how the global Shakespeare myth was driven by British cultural institutions between 1939 and 1965.

DR JIM TAYLOR is an independent scholar. He has taught at Université Jean Moulin and Université Lumière in Lyon and held a Visiting Research Fellowship at the Open University, UK, where he received the Chancellor Lord Asa Briggs Award. His work has previously been published in *Shakespeare* and *The Palgrave Encyclopedia of Global Shakespeare*.

TOURING SHAKESPEARE

Theatre and Post-War Cultural Diplomacy

JIM TAYLOR

CAMBRIDGE
UNIVERSITY PRESS

CAMBRIDGE
UNIVERSITY PRESS

Shaftesbury Road, Cambridge CB2 8EA, United Kingdom

One Liberty Plaza, 20th Floor, New York, NY 10006, USA

477 Williamstown Road, Port Melbourne, VIC 3207, Australia

314–321, 3rd Floor, Plot 3, Splendor Forum, Jasola District Centre, New Delhi – 110025, India

103 Penang Road, #05-06/07, Visioncrest Commercial, Singapore 238467

Cambridge University Press is part of Cambridge University Press & Assessment, a department of the University of Cambridge.

We share the University's mission to contribute to society through the pursuit of education, learning and research at the highest international levels of excellence.

www.cambridge.org
Information on this title: www.cambridge.org/9781009381314

DOI: 10.1017/9781009381284

© Jim Taylor 2024

This publication is in copyright. Subject to statutory exception and to the provisions of relevant collective licensing agreements, no reproduction of any part may take place without the written permission of Cambridge University Press & Assessment.

When citing this work, please include a reference to the DOI 10.1017/9781009381284

First published 2024

A catalogue record for this publication is available from the British Library.

Library of Congress Cataloging-in-Publication Data
NAMES: Taylor, Jim, 1971- author.
TITLE: Touring Shakespeare : theatre and post-war cultural diplomacy / Jim Taylor.
DESCRIPTION: Cambridge ; New York, NY : Cambridge University Press, 2024. | Includes bibliographical references and index.
IDENTIFIERS: LCCN 2023058637 (print) | LCCN 2023058638 (ebook) | ISBN 9781009381314 (hardback) | ISBN 9781009381277 (paperback) | ISBN 9781009381284 (epub)
SUBJECTS: LCSH: Shakespeare, William, 1564-1616–Stage history–Foreign countries. | Shakespeare, William, 1564-1616–Appreciation–Foreign countries. | Cold War. | Politics and literature. | National characteristics, British.
CLASSIFICATION: LCC PR3091 .T39 2024 (print) | LCC PR3091 (ebook) | DDC 792.9/5–dc23/eng/20240123
LC record available at https://lccn.loc.gov/2023058637
LC ebook record available at https://lccn.loc.gov/2023058638

ISBN 978-1-009-38131-4 Hardback

Cambridge University Press & Assessment has no responsibility for the persistence or accuracy of URLs for external or third-party internet websites referred to in this publication and does not guarantee that any content on such websites is, or will remain, accurate or appropriate.

For Aya and Elliot

Contents

List of Figures		*page* viii
Acknowledgements		x
List of Abbreviations		xii
	Introduction	1
1	Cultural Diplomacy in the Mediterranean (1939–1946): *Hamlet*	15
2	Recolonisation in Australia (1948, 1953): *Richard III* and *Othello*	51
3	The Cultural Cold War in Eastern Europe (1955, 1957): *Titus Andronicus*	86
4	Decolonisation in Nigeria (1963): *Macbeth*	118
5	Globalisation in South and Southeast Asia (1964–1965): *The Tempest*, *Richard II*, and *The Taming of the Shrew*	143
	Conclusion	177
Notes		188
Bibliography		226
Index		247

Figures

1.1 Alec Guinness in *Hamlet*. The Old Vic Theatre Company, 1938. Directed by Tyrone Guthrie. Photo by Gordon Anthony. © Getty Images/Hulton Archive. — page 23

2.1 Laurence Olivier in *Richard III*. Old Vic Theatre Company's 1948–1949 tour of Australia and New Zealand. Directed by Laurence Olivier. Photo by John Vickers. © ArenaPAL. Used by permission of University of Bristol Theatre Collection. — 60

2.2 Laurence Olivier and Vivien Leigh arriving at Mascot Airport, Sydney, 1948. Photo by Fairfax Media. © Getty Images. — 63

3.1 Ernest Thesiger, Mary Ure, Paul Schofield, Diana Wynyard, and Alec Clunes (The Peter Brook Company) in Moscow, 1955. Photo by Reg Burkett. © Getty Images/Hulton Archive. — 96

3.2 Laurence Olivier as Titus Andronicus, backstage at the Théâtre Sarah-Bernhardt, Paris, 1957. Photo by Gamma-Keystone. © Getty Images. — 104

4.1 James Cairncross as Banquo in the Nottingham Playhouse *Macbeth*, 1963. Directed by Frank Dunlop. Photo by Allan Hurst. Image held by Nottinghamshire Archives, DD/NP/2/2/10/3. Used by permission of Nottingham Playhouse and Nottinghamshire Archives. — 131

4.2 John Neville and Judi Dench as Macbeth and Lady Macbeth in the Nottingham Playhouse *Macbeth*, 1963. Directed by Frank Dunlop. Photo by Allan Hurst. Image held by Nottinghamshire Archives,

List of Figures

	DD/NP/2/2/10/2. Used by permission of Nottingham Playhouse and Nottinghamshire Archives.	135
5.1	Mary Steele rehearsing *Love's Labour's Lost*. Directed by David William. Regent's Park Open Air Theatre, 1962. Photo by Kent Gavin. © Getty Images/Corbis Historical.	148
5.2	David William rehearsing as Richard II for the BBC Television Drama *The Age of Kings*, 1960. © Keystone/Hulton Archive/Getty Images.	154
5.3	The banquet scene from *The Tempest*, III. 3. The New Shakespeare Company, Regent's Park Theatre Company, 1964. Directed by David William. Photo by David Mordecai. Images held by the Shakespeare Institute, University of Birmingham DSH1/11/1/7/8. Used by permission of Regent's Park Theatre/Shakespeare Institute, University of Birmingham/Estate of David Mordecai.	166

Acknowledgements

This book began life at the Open University's Department of English and Creative Writing and would not have been written without the support and encouragement of my doctoral supervisors David Johnson and Edmund King. I owe them both a great debt of gratitude for sharing their expert knowledge from the outset, for providing detailed guidance throughout, and for their steadfast commitment to this project over many years. My heartfelt thanks also go to Shafquat Towheed, Anthony Howell, Susheila Nasta, Caroline Davis, Anne Wetherilt, and to other staff members and students at the Open University who offered valuable words of advice, friendship, and encouragement at various stages. I would especially like to thank Sara Haslam, Alex Tickell, and Andrew Murphy for their incisive and generous comments on the manuscript's earliest draft, and for encouraging me to see this project through to publication. Thanks are also due to several friends and colleagues who have helped along the way, especially Maud Perez and Damien Bidolet who read the typescript with such care and precision, Ivan Tacey and Robert Sherratt who advised on my initial book proposal, and Benjamin Broadribb for his generous help with indexing.

    The initial inspiration for this book came from working as a voluntary archivist at the Shakespeare Birthplace Trust. Special thanks to Amy Hurst, Madeleine Cox, and Victoria Jones for inviting me to work alongside them in the stacks, and to the late Roger Howell whose wonderful tales of touring behind the Iron Curtain first alerted me to this topic. I am sincerely grateful for the assistance that I received from numerous librarians and archivists who provided me with access to documents held at the British Library, the National Archives, the Shakespeare Birthplace Trust, and Birmingham University's Shakespeare Institute. For their help in obtaining permission to reproduce several of the photographs included in this book, I would like to thank Alice Gordon at Regent's Park Open Air Theatre, Biddy Hayward at ArenaPal, Lauren Eaton at the

Shakespeare Institute Archives, Anita Blackman and the Estate of David Mordecai, and Alexa Rees at Nottinghamshire Archives.

Some of the material in Chapter 2 was first aired at the Shakespeare Institute's Britgrad conference of 2020. I am grateful to Jodie Smith, Laryssa Schoeck, and the whole Britgrad team for kindly inviting me to present my work at this event. Warm thanks to Maria Shmygol, Kat Hipkiss, and everyone at the British Shakespeare Association for inviting me to share material from Chapter 3 at their 'Shakespeare In/Action' conference in 2021. The lively discussions at each gathering provided valuable feedback and prompted me to think through some of the key ideas underpinning this study. The warm and collegial atmosphere at both conferences was truly inspiring, and I would especially like to thank the regular 'Lava Party' attendees: Gemma Allred, Thea Buckley, Eleanor Rycroft, Andrea Smith, and many others, for their ongoing friendship and support.

This book has found a perfect home at Cambridge University Press, and I am immensely grateful to Emily Hockley, George Paul Laver, Balamuthukumaran Pasupathy, and all the editorial and project management teams for guiding me through the publishing process with such care, patience, and efficiency. I am greatly indebted to the anonymous readers who supported the publication of *Touring Shakespeare*, and whose generous feedback and detailed suggestions helped improve it immeasurably. All of these readers and editors have provided invaluable advice and assistance along the way, and any mistakes that remain are entirely my own.

I owe the greatest thanks to my old family back in Wales, and to my new family here in France. To Aya and Elliot especially, for their steadfast love and support.

Abbreviations

ABC	Australian Broadcasting Corporation
AETTF	Australian Elizabethan Theatre Trust Fund
ASIO	Australian Security Intelligence Organisation
BFBS	British Forces Broadcasting Service
BIS	British Information Services
CCF	Congress for Cultural Freedom
CEMA	Council for the Encouragement of Music and the Arts
CRD	Cultural Relations Department (UK Foreign Office)
DAC	Drama Advisory Committee (British Council Dance and Drama Department)
ELT	English Language Teaching
EMB	Empire Marketing Board
ENSA	Entertainment National Services Association
IRD	Information Research Department (UK Foreign Office)
LOP	Laurence Olivier Productions
NSC	New Shakespeare Company
RSC	Royal Shakespeare Company, Stratford-upon-Avon
SMT	Shakespeare Memorial Theatre, Stratford-upon-Avon
SRC	Soviet Relations Committee (UK Foreign Office/British Council)
USIS	United States Information Services

Introduction

Speaking at the inauguration of the British Institute in Lisbon on 23 November 1938, the British Council Chairman Lord Lloyd acknowledged the 'accusation' frequently levelled against the British that they were 'too proud, or too indifferent, or perhaps too lazy, to make available, even to their friends, the riches of their civilisation'.[1] Lloyd assured his audience that such misconceptions were due to Britain's 'reluctance to advertise'; a national temperament 'born of the age of laissez-faire' that had earned the British a reputation for being 'cold commercial Philistines, interested only in trade, finance, and sport'.[2] With the establishment of a British Institute in Lisbon, however, Portuguese students would be invited to study Britain's 'literature and our language, or science or industry; or those problems which, as the inheritors and administrators of huge African territories, we are jointly interested to examine and to solve'.[3] Lloyd urged his Portuguese hosts to keep in mind 'the things that really unite us so closely':

> we are both Empires fashioned in the same manner and founded upon the seas by the adventurous and daring spirit of our two Races. Both of us possess a great Colonial Empire discovered, occupied, and civilised by our sons, of which we are not only rightly proud, but strongly tenacious.[4]

In accepting a copy of Luís de Camões' *The Lusiads* (1572) from the Portuguese Minister of National Education, Lloyd declared that he

> could not do better than present to Your Excellency the works of our greatest national poet, in a form representative of the best in modern Shakespeare scholarship and of the best in modern English book production.[5]

With both writers functioning as exemplars of their respective national cultures rooted in the early maritime history of European colonial expansion, Shakespeare and Luís de Camões were evidently considered apt literary figures for sealing the new diplomatic entente between Britain and Portugal.

Characterised as an imperialist 'of the Curzon type' who believed in 'the inscrutable decrees of Providence' placed upon 'the shoulders of the British race', Lloyd is credited with ensuring the 'permanent recognition' of cultural propaganda's value to British foreign policy.[6] Indeed, behind the high-imperial language of Lloyd's speech lay immediate and pressing concerns over the competing colonial ambitions of fascist Italy and Germany within Europe itself. In a further countermeasure to the steady stream of virulent anti-British propaganda flowing throughout the Mediterranean region from Italy's Radio Bari, the Old Vic Theatre Company disembarked at Lisbon docks on 6 February 1939 at the start of a lengthy tour of Portugal, Italy, Egypt, Greece, and Malta, locations where Lloyd had recently established an extensive network of British Institutes. The company's tour of *Hamlet* and *Henry V* was to be one of the British Council's earliest successes, a venture that demonstrated how staged Shakespeare could be utilised to help Britain achieve a range of cultural diplomatic objectives overseas; from building friendly relations with decision-making elites in order to guarantee their neutrality in the event of any future conflict with Germany, to maintaining Egypt's loyalty and support while reassuring the British colony of London's continuing presence and protection. All of the above were objectives that cultural diplomacy was particularly well-suited to securing and, though their aims were broad, each had significant implications for imperial defence and security. Delaying Italy's entrance into the war, for instance, bought Britain valuable time to secure its military position in Egypt, which, in 1939, was the strategic heart of its vast and highly integrated imperial world system.[7]

In sum, Lloyd's speech signalled Britain's acceptance that it could no longer rely exclusively upon its material wealth and military strength to guarantee power and prestige overseas, that henceforth Britain would be more proactive in projecting a positive image of itself throughout the world, and that it would be calling upon Shakespeare to help it do so. For its rulers, the overarching challenge that Britain faced over the next twenty-five years was the transition from Empire to Commonwealth within the context of the Cold War. Throughout this period Britain would call repeatedly upon touring Shakespeare companies to serve the national interest, helping it: counter the threat of fascism and maintain its imperial presence within an increasingly restive Empire (Chapter 1); strengthen the shared identity of the white-settler Commonwealth along ethnocultural lines (Chapter 2); fight communism at home and abroad during the cultural Cold War (Chapter 3); manage the process of decolonisation in West Africa (Chapter 4); and maintain England's prominent cultural status within an increasingly globalised postcolonial world (Chapter 5). In providing a cultural panacea for the numerous political challenges that the post-war era presented, Shakespeare proved to be an effective compensatory device for shoring up Britain's dwindling reserves of power and prestige overseas. Overall, it is no coincidence that Britain came to view Shakespeare tours as an effective means for securing its diplomatic objectives abroad during the mid-twentieth century because, as the historian J. M. Lee asserts, Britain's increasing reliance upon 'the insubstantiality of cultural diplomacy' was 'part of the trauma of losing great-power status'.[8]

Brief Overview

Touring Shakespeare surveys a wide range of Shakespeare productions that travelled overseas in service to British cultural diplomacy between 1939 and 1965. The principal tours are Tyrone Guthrie's 1939 Old Vic tour of *Hamlet* to Portugal, Italy, Egypt, and Malta; The Donald Wolfit Shakespearean Company's *Hamlet* in Egypt, 1945; The John Gielgud Company's *Hamlet* in Egypt, 1946; the Australian leg of the Old Vic's 1948 Commonwealth Tour of *Richard III*; The Shakespeare Memorial Theatre's Coronation Tour of *Othello* in Australia, 1953; The Peter Brook Company's 1955 *Hamlet* in Moscow; The Shakespeare Memorial Theatre's 1957 tour of *Titus Andronicus* to Poland, Austria, and Yugoslavia; The Nottingham Playhouse's 1963 tour of Nigeria with *Macbeth*; and the New Shakespeare Company's 1964–65 Shakespeare Quatercentenary circuit of Pakistan, India, Bangladesh, Sri Lanka, Hong Kong, the Philippines, Malaysia, and Singapore with *The Tempest, Richard II*, and *The Taming of the Shrew*.

Touring Shakespeare provides a detailed historical account of the material practices that underpinned the global circulation of English Shakespeare between 1939 and 1965, a formative period when Empire came to an end and the Cold War fuelled intense transnational theatrical rivalries. This book discloses how Britain's investment in the myth of its national poet provided effective cover for the pursuit of its political agendas overseas and considers how such forays out into the wider world impacted the development of the British Shakespearean theatre itself. In disclosing the overseas reception of English productions that are mostly absent from the performance histories of the plays themselves, *Touring Shakespeare* maps the evolving history of diplomatic touring practices during the mid-twentieth century.

Though a common-enough theatrical activity, touring is a challenging practice to study, one that demands a shift in focus away from famous actors, influential productions, individual plays, or prominent theatre companies, and towards an extensive network of overlapping creative and administrative practices that make up its social, political, and institutional formation.[9] Consequently, this book employs the term 'touring Shakespeare' or 'Shakespeare tours' as shorthand for complex cultural practices. While the phrase explicitly refers to English productions that performed overseas in service to British cultural diplomacy, it aims to demonstrate that touring was a demanding material practice only made possible by the economic support and political will of closely intertwined state, private, and institutional interests whose primary objective was the achievement of specific outcomes and benefits for Britain itself.

Touring Shakespeare has several areas of concern that overlap in practice but can, for the sake of clarity, be parsed into three distinct lines of inquiry. The first is the historical and political evolution of touring practices, the second is the performance and reception of individual Shakespeare productions, and the third concerns the institutional and state–private relations that enabled touring practices in the first place. On the first point, the overall aim of this book is to provide a coherent (though far from comprehensive) account of the initial twenty-six-year period, between 1939 and 1965, when Shakespeare tours ceased to be merely commercial ventures and came to be seen as effective vehicles for promoting British state interests overseas. How did English Shakespeare productions become an instrument of British state diplomacy, and how did such practices change and evolve over time? The second point considers why certain theatre companies were selected for touring and whether the choice of individual plays, or their adaptation to the stage, were determined by their cultural mission. It asks whether the productions themselves supported, contradicted, or ran adjacent to the diplomatic objectives of the tours they were undertaking? My third and final concern is with the state–private networks and institutional formations that encouraged and enabled the projection of Shakespeare tours in the first place. This line of inquiry seeks to disclose the close working relationship that existed between key individuals within the UK theatre industry and arm's-length governmental bodies like the British Council. It considers the role that state–private networks played in commissioning tours, selecting theatre companies, supporting them overseas, and commemorating their endeavours back in the UK. Though the separate areas of interest outlined above overlap considerably, we will return to our guiding concerns on the evolution of touring practices, the performance and reception of individual English productions overseas, and the state–private networks and institutional formations that enabled Shakespeare tours within each chapter.

The content and structure of *Touring Shakespeare* is dictated by the evolving history of touring practices as evidenced by the archive itself. Its primary geographical and thematic concerns are: the rise of cultural diplomacy in the Mediterranean region, recolonisation in Australia, the cultural Cold War in Eastern Europe, decolonisation in Nigeria, and postcolonial globalisation in South and Southeast Asia. This chronological, though geographically diverse, narrative reflects the evolving history of cultural diplomatic touring practices that moved through national, transnational, and global stages of world history during the mid-twentieth century.[10]

The Archive

My initial interest in touring Shakespeare came from surveying the audio collection held at the Shakespeare Birthplace Trust, Stratford-upon-Avon. Amongst the stacks, I came across 78 rpm acetate discs of the incidental music and sound effects used on various mid-century tours to Canada, Australia, New Zealand, Continental Europe, the United States, and the Soviet Union; mute and fragile ephemera that evinced a significant though long-forgotten history of extensive touring practices. Searching for further information, I was disappointed to discover that the annual souvenir programmes from the period were as slight and evasive in content as they were proud and celebratory in tone. The *Shakespeare Memorial Theatre Annual Programme, 1957*, for instance, merely provides a map of *Titus Andronicus*'s route across 'the Continent and London' accompanied by a selection of Angus McBean's glamorous production photographs of the initial Stratford staging taken two years previously.[11] Though tours 'Behind the Iron Curtain' were certainly no state secret, their exploits and reception overseas were left entirely to the readers' imagination. Annual programmes seemed to perpetuate the discreet, deferential, and carefully polished front common to diplomatic events themselves, with major touring endeavours compressed into clipped celebratory remarks upon their successful completion. From our own historical perspective then, they appear to collude in a deeper silence that have led us to forget significant theatrical events that were a relatively common practice throughout the period.

Thankfully, theatre practitioners rely upon more informal channels to record their own version of history. Comparing *Titus Andronicus*'s cast list against published autobiographies led to Michael Blakemore's *Arguments With England* (2005), a vivid first-hand account that discloses how the Memorial Theatre actors viewed themselves as cultural ambassadors undertaking an important mission behind the Iron Curtain.[12] Despite the diplomatic sensitivities surrounding tours to the Eastern bloc following the Hungarian uprising, or Nigeria in the wake of independence, actors' biographies have provided an indispensable source for leavening the official archive with telling details, revealing stories, and indiscreet gossip. In providing such rich and compelling commentary, biographical accounts have been invaluable in fleshing out the bare outline provided in official commemorations, confirming Paul Menzer's assertion that 'the history of theatre told *by* the theatre is an anecdotal one'.[13] Despite being informal, and even unverifiable, actors' memoirs, anecdotes, and travelogues constitute an important repository for this study, disclosing the ways in which actors apprehended their own experience of touring overseas, and providing insights into how company members fashioned themselves into the role of Shakespearean cultural ambassadors whilst on tour.[14]

An important breakthrough that brought these diverse performance documents together was the realisation that they all had one administrative element in common: each tour travelled under the auspices of the British Council, an organisation whose declared mission is to 'create friendly knowledge and understanding between the people of the UK and other countries' through 'cultural relations and educational opportunities'.[15] Although the British Council's current activities centre primarily around the provision of English language training, it is also active in promoting the UK through a wide range of cultural practices including dance, drama, music, literature, and fine art. Recorded interviews with retired British Council personnel undertaken by the British Library's Theatre Archive Project led to the realisation that, beyond supplying essential financial support by guaranteeing overseas ventures against loss, the organisation actively commissioned Shakespeare tours in direct response to requests from various Departments of State such as the Foreign Office, the Colonial Office, and the Commonwealth Relations Office.[16] With representatives stationed throughout the world, and with an advisory panel made up of prominent figures from within the UK theatre industry, the organisation was instrumental in facilitating the projection of English staged Shakespeare overseas.

This discovery prompted a necessary shift in focus towards the British Council's institutional history, and led to further inquiries into their records held by the National Archives, Kew.[17] Within these extensive holdings, the records of the Drama Advisory Committee (DAC), Regional Reports, and Annual Reports have been especially germane. The DAC, for instance, acted as a conduit between nominally separate arenas of civic and political life, with the minutes of its meetings providing detailed insight into the close working relationship that existed between the semi-governmental cultural bodies that instigated overseas tours and Britain's post-war theatre establishment.[18] Given the ways in which it linked artistic, academic, commercial, and governmental spheres, the DAC afforded the British Council an extraordinary degree of access and flexibility in its dealings with Britain's creative industries. In Robert Phillipson's assessment, committees made up of such 'eminent professionals' ensured that the organisation enjoyed access to 'key people and developments in the relevant field':

> It guarantees that the Council is sensitive to a considerable range of pressures from both governmental and private interests. It is relatively autonomous on the executive level but could not function effectively unless it was attuned to the needs of government and to relevant sectors of private business.[19]

The DAC's minutes reveal the decision-making process behind each tour, divulging the initial proposal, early assessment, on-going planning, and subsequent reception of each cultural mission. More detailed accounts recounting how tours faired closer to the ground can be found in the relevant Representative Reports from each country visited. As internal documents circulating back to London from overseas, such dispatches provide comprehensive and occasionally unguarded insights into the challenges and opportunities that each touring venture presented. Furthermore, the voice of higher officialdom – expressing the views of the Foreign Office, High Commissioners, and Colonial and Commonwealth Offices – can be heard in amendments attached to Annual Reports. Overall, the rich cultural history lying dormant within the British Council's extensive administrative archives has helped contextualise the fragments of performance and reception materials I have discovered in more conventional theatrical archives and has inadvertently prompted the partial recovery of the cultural organisation's own institutional memory.

As *Touring Shakespeare* concerns the activities of prominent English companies representing British theatrical culture overseas, the book inevitably adopts a transnational rather than global perspective. There are inherent limits and ethical dangers to such an approach, primarily the privileging of a metropolitan-periphery model. However, treating the British nation-state and its prominent theatrical and cultural institutions as discreet units of national affiliation reflects the imperatives and worldview of the diplomatic touring practices under discussion. In this sense, *Touring Shakespeare* deliberately follows the archive's Anglo-centric iteration of imperial power relations; that is to say, of Shakespeare being domestically validated and then officially deployed 'out' to foreign audiences for specific political purposes and commercial gains. It simultaneously reads against the grain of such assumptions, however, placing English narratives in dialogue with extant local accounts that contest and contradict them. Where the evidence is available, I deliberately juxtapose the perspectives of the British tourists against opposite local reports in the hope of bringing previously submerged, silenced, and redacted narratives to bear as fully as possible against contradictory, and often self-serving, British accounts. Hopefully, such proximate tensions bring the expansionist, proselytising, and homogenising intentions behind each tour into sharp relief. Overall, by bringing together archival materials from several countries and from nominally separate disciplinary fields, *Touring Shakespeare* aims to provide a 'thick historical description' of English Shakespeare productions that performed overseas, situating the micro-narratives of individual tours within the broader history of British diplomacy between 1939 and 1965.[20]

Decolonisation and the Cold War

As *Touring Shakespeare* situates a series of Shakespeare performance case studies within the larger narrative of decolonisation and the Cold War, it is germane to briefly map out some of the historical terrain here at the outset. I use the term decolonisation to indicate the fraught historical period immediately following the Second World War that witnessed the rapid demise of Britain's formal Empire and its transition towards Commonwealth and other forms of post-imperial settlement.[21] Reflecting the more variegated realities of Britain's ever-adaptable imperial system, *Touring Shakespeare* covers a range of specific imperial relations: from informal rule in Egypt, recolonisation in Australia, the adaptation of non-aligned positions in response to the Cold War throughout the Third World, Nigeria's earliest encounters with Anglo-American neo-colonialism following independence, and finally the new international dispensation of independent but highly networked postcolonial nation-states that we will, for the sake of simplicity, term globalisation.[22] All of these late-imperial developments were impacted by the Cold War, a global political contestation that gave rise to a surge in national-cultural competition and transnational theatrical exchanges that sought to establish, negotiate, and overcome entrenched ideological differences.

In February 1946, US diplomat George F. Kennan called for the containment of the Soviet Union in response to Stalin's statement that the world now held only 'two centres of world significance' between whom there could be no 'permanent *modus vivendi*'.[23] Although Kennan's 'Long Telegram' is often hailed as signalling the formal start of the Cold War, *Touring Shakespeare* begins in 1939 to show how by 1946 both the United States and Soviet Russia had reached a shared belief in the universal applicability of their competing world systems. Following Kennan's advice, President Truman sought to challenge the expansion of Soviet influence at its geographical boundaries. Beginning in the ruins of post-war Germany and Europe in the second half of the 1940s, the conflict spread to Asia following Mao Zedong's establishment of the People's Republic of China in 1949, and continued to expand throughout the decolonising Third World during the 1950s and 1960s. As the sudden retreat of Europe's global empires exposed new terrain to advancing US–Soviet competition, each power bloc sought to influence newly independent nations and replicate their respective political systems throughout the postcolonial world. As a battle fought by means other than direct military conflict, the overt and covert projections of competing ideological worldviews were constitutive characteristics of the Cold War and so, from the 1930s onwards, Shakespeare became a prize of world-historical significance as liberal-democratic, communist, and fascist ideologies fought to assert themselves as the rightful inheritors of Europe's enlightenment tradition.[24]

Current Debates

To date only a handful of books and articles take Shakespeare tours as their primary topic of concern and very few consider them in relation to cultural diplomacy. That said, *Touring Shakespeare* shares research interests with the closely related disciplinary fields of theatre and the cultural Cold War, and Shakespeare and globalisation. *Theatre, Globalization, and the Cold War* (2017) edited by Christopher B. Balme and Berenika Szymanski-Düll addresses the 'mutual imbrication of Cold War politics and theatre' with sections dedicated to touring, institutional, and postcolonial perspectives. The collection confirms this study's premise that governments began to take 'the performing arts very seriously' during the early Cold War, and that 'theatres, groups and even individual artists could stand in for a country, an ideology, a way of life' when travelling overseas.[25] In terms of the broader ideological uses of twentieth-century Shakespeare, a substantial amount of scholarship exists on Soviet appropriations of the playwright, such as the essay collections, Alexandr Parfenov and Joseph G. Price, eds., *Russian Essays on Shakespeare and His Contemporaries* (1998), and Irena R. Makaryk and Joseph G. Price, eds., *Shakespeare in the Worlds of Communism and Socialism* (2006).[26] Debates on fascist Shakespeare can be found in Irena R. Makaryk and Marissa McHugh, eds., *Shakespeare and the Second World War: Theatre, Culture and Identity* (2012), and Keith Gregor, ed., *Shakespeare and Tyranny: Regimes of Reading in Europe and Beyond* (2014).[27] Little in this area of scholarship has been written on Britain's own use of Shakespeare as a countermeasure against such fascist and communist appropriations, or as a means of sustaining the antithetical ideological position of Europe's liberal democracy in an era of imperial decline.[28] Countering any assumption that liberal democracy is somehow beyond ideology itself, *Touring Shakespeare* shows how English productions were deployed to counter fascist and communist claims over a period of decades, and that many productions bear traces of such instrumental usage in their performance and reception histories. Erica Sheen and Isabel Karremann, eds., *Shakespeare in Cold War Europe* (2016) addresses areas of concern similar to mine, though examining different productions and locations.[29] The collection contributes a great deal to our knowledge of communist Shakespeares but does not provide sustained consideration on how fighting the Cold War shaped Britain's own practices, or the broader institutional implications for Shakespearean soft power that ensued from the creation of state–private networks. Furthermore, it is not concerned with the role that Shakespeare played in sites beyond Europe or the part it played in superpower contestations taking place in countries such as Egypt, Nigeria, and Australia.

Since the 2016 quatercentenary of Shakespeare's death, there has been growing interest in the political instrumentalisation of Shakespeare within global Shakespeare studies.[30] The essay collection *Local and Global Myths in Shakespearean Performance* (2018) edited by Aneta Mancewicz and Alexa Alice Joubin sets out many of the contradictory and foundational myths that make Shakespeare useful in 'so many different cultural contexts', and investigates some of the 'values and ideas' that 'sustain or undermine' Shakespeare's cultural work overseas.[31] An important distinction is that none of the essays in *Local and Global Myths in Shakespearean Performance* touch upon touring practices and all are concerned with productions dating from the end of the Cold War era in 1989. In terms of the myth of Shakespeare's political relevance, however, *Touring Shakespeare* provides numerous examples of Shakespeare being 'deployed for interventionist purposes in significant historical moments and political turning points', while several other Shakespearean myths (of timelessness, authenticity, universality, moral authority, and political relevance, for instance) can be seen fading in and out of differing touring contexts depending on historical circumstances and political expediency.[32] Overall, *Touring Shakespeare* brings to light new historical evidence of extensive material practices that helped cultivate the foundational myth of the canon's utilitarian value to the state, detailing the deliberate and extraordinary lengths to which Britain went to project its own preferred version of Shakespeare overseas in the mid-twentieth century, and revealing how politically motivated touring practices have played a constitutive role of keeping English Shakespeare in global circulation.

Outline

Chapter 1 provides three case studies of Mediterranean tours of *Hamlet* that took place in 1939, 1945, and 1946. The chapter maps some of the earliest instances where Shakespeare tours were deployed overseas in service to British state interests, contests the common notion that Britain's earliest forays into cultural diplomacy were merely enemy-led anti-fascist measures, and demonstrates how long-held imperial and anti-communist concerns occupied official minds from the outset. Actors undertaking the Old Vic's 1939 Mediterranean Tour were confronted with a range of political compromises in the field. In attempting to appease Portuguese and Italian decision-making elites, the company came to realise that England's national poet had been successfully recruited to the fascist cause they sought to oppose, while occupied Egypt brought the actors face to face with the grotesque inequalities of British imperial rule overseas, prompting them to reflect unhappily on the class hierarchies and commercial pressures constraining the UK's own theatrical landscape. The demoralising effects of Britain's cultural blackout during the early stages of the Second World War led to the formation of the Council for the Encouragement of Music and the Arts (CEMA) and the Entertainment National Services Association (ENSA), organisations that eventually came to view Shakespeare tours as an indispensable engine for national morale at home and abroad. The provision of Shakespeare for the troops brought the Donald Wolfit Company to Egypt for the 1945 Cairo and Alexandria

Drama Festival. There, the actor-manager's popularity with Egyptian royalty and Commonwealth military audiences marked a brief cultural entente that soon sank beneath the waves of nationalist student uprisings opposing Britain's continuing occupation. The final Cairo and Alexandria Drama Festival of 1946 saw the John Gielgud Company attempt a return to pre-war cultural practices by supporting elite British schooling in the face of mounting local resistance. Overall, Chapter 1 shows how the earliest experiments in touring Shakespeare that began on the eve of the Second World War had become regular practices by the end of it. With the creation of the Cultural Relations Department (CRD) in 1943, touring had become part of a newly politicised cultural strategy aimed at helping Britain maintain control within increasingly contested colonial spaces at the start of the Cold War.

Chapter 2 illustrates how Shakespeare tours served Britain's diplomatic interests more effectively within the white-settler Commonwealth. With Laurence Olivier and Vivienne Leigh at the helm, the Old Vic's 1948 Commonwealth Tour of Australia and New Zealand secured a variety of strategic goals for Britain: from the importation of essential material aid to the 'mother country' during its post-war recovery to the establishment of a new intelligence network demonstrating the Empire-Commonwealth's value to America at the start of the Cold War. Overall, the Old Vic tour of *Richard III* confirmed that Shakespeare could play an important role in strengthening the sense of a Greater-British identity that underpinned essential trade and security links. The Shakespeare Memorial Theatre's 1953 Coronation Tour of *Othello* helped the regional company vie for the role of National Theatre, presenting itself as a locus of 'deep England' and Shakespeare as a nativist cultural symbol capable of drawing together a globally dispersed Greater-British community. In constructing a shared settler-Commonwealth identity represented as linguistically English and racially white, the Memorial Theatre tour aligned itself with reactionary New Elizabethan ideas that reflected metropolitan anxieties over the collapse of formal Empire and increasing non-white Commonwealth migration into Britain itself. Both tours exploited Australia's sense of cultural inferiority (a phenomenon since dubbed 'the cultural cringe') and used Shakespeare to perpetuate 'complex patterns of symbolic and cultural connection' between the Dominion and the UK.[33]

Following the death of Stalin, military stalemate on the continent led to a significant thaw in East–West relations with culture becoming a new front in Europe's Cold War. Chapter 3 discloses how anti-Communist bodies such as the Soviet Relations Committee (SRC) provided political direction to the British Council's touring activities; disrupting ties between British communists and the Soviet bloc, regaining control of cultural exchanges between Britain and the Soviet Union, and gradually exposing the Soviet world to Western ideas.[34] After considering Peter Brook's 1955 tour of Russia with *Hamlet*, the chapter focuses on the Shakespeare Memorial Theatre's 1957 touring production of *Titus Andronicus* that visited France, Austria, Yugoslavia, and Poland. Chapter 3 reconsiders Brook's assertion that *Titus Andronicus* provided timely insights into the nature of totalitarianism within the context of the cultural Cold War, disclosing how the production's touring mission led to the rehabilitation of a previously marginalised text back into the Shakespearean canon via performance. The consequent UK publication of *Shakespeare Our Contemporary* (1964) by the Polish émigré academic Jan Kott is examined as an accompanying critical legacy in the tour's overall objective of countering communist political influence at home and abroad.

Chapter 4 provides a detailed account of the Nottingham Playhouse's 1963 tour of *Macbeth* to Nigeria. It finds that the venture was a direct intervention in the country's post-independence cultural renaissance, and that the tour's initial reception evidenced considerable local resistance to the return of colonial-era assumptions and cultural practices. Extensive British and American philanthropic investment in the key developmental areas that supported Nigeria's nascent theatre industries following independence meant that Nigerian artists found themselves receiving support and validation from wealthy institutions harbouring powerful and controlling neo-colonial agendas. As the Nottingham Playhouse tour followed in the immediate wake of local Yoruba-style adaptations of Shakespeare undertaken by the University of Ibadan's Travelling Theatre, the chapter argues that the Nottingham Playhouse venture helped Britain secure valuable cultural capital for the advancement of its own commercial interests in West Africa following decolonisation, especially in the field of educational publishing.

In examining the New Shakespeare Company's 1964–65 Quatercentenary tour of South and Southeast Asia, Chapter 5 finds that English companies struggled to maintain their exclusive claim on the playwright in the era of postcolonial globalisation. Self-determination and developmentalism prompted newly independent nations to celebrate Shakespeare as a global cultural commodity, strengthening a plurality of local claims upon it and thus encouraging more searching critiques of the visiting English productions themselves. The British Council's efforts to ensure that the Shakespeare quatercentenary of 1964 was celebrated on a truly global in scale resulted in the projection of threadbare and uneven productions of *Richard II*, *The Tempest*, and *The Taming of the Shrew* to South and Southeast Asia, shows that reflected sharp disagreements between the British Council and the NSC over what kind of staged Shakespeare productions best represented British culture overseas. Enabling myths that had made Shakespeare an ideal tool for British cultural diplomacy – myths such as the authority of the absent author, for instance – came under scrutiny when brought to bear on unruly texts like *The Taming of the Shrew*; while the association of Shakespeare with heritage notions of English cultural identity were challenged and undermined by more political approaches to history plays like *Richard II*. The sense that Shakespeare was taking on new radical meanings and political resonances at home spilt out into reviews overseas, while internal disputes over the unreasonable working conditions that the NSC actors endured whilst on tour indicated that the conservative cultural consensus that had held sway since the war was coming to an end by the mid-1960s.

After summarising the most prominent features and contradictions inherent to the practice of touring Shakespeare in service to British cultural diplomacy, the book concludes by considering the current and emerging myth of Shakespearean soft power. It asks whether the kinds of instrumental approaches outlined in this historical survey can square with widespread demands to decolonise Shakespeare coming from within the theatre industry today.

CHAPTER I

Cultural Diplomacy in the Mediterranean (1939–1946)
Hamlet

This chapter surveys three touring productions of *Hamlet* that supported British diplomatic objectives in the Mediterranean region immediately prior to, and following, the Second World War. Firstly, it considers the Old Vic company's pro-appeasement engagement with Portuguese, Italian, and Egyptian decision-making elites in 1939; secondly, the Donald Wolfit Company's provision of Shakespeare for the troops as part of the Allied forces' victory celebrations in Egypt, 1945; and finally, the John Gielgud Company's attempt to repair strained Anglo-Egyptian relations and support elite British schooling against a backdrop of anti-British protests in Egypt, 1946. Though not the first time that Shakespeare had been mobilised into the service of British state power, the prelude to the Second World War pioneered the deployment of touring productions overseas in service to diplomatic objectives.[1] This chapter shows how, between 1939 and 1946, tours undertaken by Britain's most prominent Shakespeare companies evolved from being unprecedented cultural endeavours performed in exceptional political circumstances, to becoming frequent, urgent, and necessary vehicles for the dissemination of British culture overseas in the face of mounting international challenges.

Imperial Decline and the Rise of Cultural Diplomacy

In most accounts, the British Council's initial support of British imperial interests is obscured by a more idealised narrative emphasising its role in countering fascism.[2] Philip M. Taylor summarises this prevailing view of the cultural organisation's projection of 'British democratic institutions' and 'all that was considered best in the British way of life' as a[3]

> democratic response to the new and urgent problems caused by the emergence of the totalitarian state in Europe ... powerfully and deliberately

directed against British interests abroad [that] forced Britain onto the defensive by offering foreign audiences an alternative ideology.[4]

This chapter seeks to emphasise the imperial character of Britain's overseas 'interests', stressing how some of the earliest propaganda advertising Britain's 'democratic institutions' and 'way of life' sought to appease pro-fascist European states with comparable imperial status. As these initial deployments laid the foundation for touring practices that became more urgent and necessary as the Cold War advanced and the British Empire collapsed, it is important to acknowledge how pro-imperial concerns and anti-communist sentiments constituted the ideological seedbed from which British cultural-diplomatic initiatives would continue to flourish long after the Second World War. Whatever the diplomatic battle of the day, post-war cultural propaganda was primarily geared towards securing and maintaining the vestiges of a global status which rested upon Britain's long imperial history.

Britain's initial response to the imperial crises that emerged prior to the Second World War laid the foundations for later cultural-diplomatic practices. Commercial losses resulting from increasing global competition, as outlined in the 1930 D'Abernon 'Report on a British Economic Mission to South America', finally persuaded the Treasury that culture and commerce had become 'mutually complementary'.[5] The D'Abernon Report led to the removal of an eleven-year financial embargo against cultural-diplomatic activities, instigating a series of initiatives including the establishment of English language libraries and some of the earliest state-supported deployments of theatrical companies overseas. The broad intention was to raise Britain's cultural profile to help shore up its global commercial interests. As early as 1931, Rex Leeper, the founder of the British Council, stated that he had 'taken over a new sphere of activity – known, for want of a better name, as "cultural propaganda"'.[6] Alongside increased international competition from France, Italy, Germany, America, and many others, the 1930s brought the British Empire face to face with a range of depression-era challenges such as soaring domestic unemployment, falling commodity prices, contracting world trade, and widespread anti-imperial protests. In its earliest incarnation as 'British Committee for Relations with Other Countries' (1934–36), the British Council sought to use culture to lessen the impact of these multiple dilemmas. Though its original intention was to raise private funds for independent commercial interests, the state was prompted into taking more direct control of cultural diplomacy as the decade's global economic crisis evolved into a political confrontation that threatened Liberal Democracy itself.[7]

With stiffening international competition and a deepening economic depression undermining the Empire's free-market principles, modern advertising methods were introduced to publicise and promote the mutual benefits of a 'Third British Empire' of closely integrated world trade.[8] The Empire Marketing Board (EMB, 1926–33) deployed striking visual media to advertise the 'virtues and values' of imperial commerce to the British public. Views differed, however, on the EMB's attempt to shape patterns of domestic consumption by fostering greater Empire consciousness. *The Times*' criticism that it was a 'futile and wasteful institution', for instance, was publicly rebuffed by the South African Prime Minister Jan Smuts, who hailed it as 'the one bright spot in recent Empire policy'.[9]

Following the EMB's disbandment, its outgoing Secretary Stephen Tallents provided the blueprint for a new cultural organisation that laid the foundations for the eventual establishment of the British Council. Tallents' influential pamphlet *The Projection of England* (1933) argued:

> No civilised country can today afford either to neglect the projection of its national personality, or to resign its projection to others ... peace itself may at any time depend upon a clear understanding abroad of her actions and motives.

Tallents proposed 'a school in national projection' established 'in the borderland which lies between Government and private enterprise'.[10] The project sanitised its advocacy for propaganda by employing the American term 'public relations', a rhetorical move necessitated by the common perception that the British press had indulged in excessive and damaging propaganda activities during the First World War, as well as the word's close association with the Communist International or Comintern (1919–43), and the disinformation campaigns of fascist Italy and Germany. Though hailed as a necessary liberal-democratic counterbalance, Tallents' ideas were freighted with problematic political and institutional implications from the outset.[11] His vision of an orchestrated and interconnecting 'borderland' of public bodies including the press, the BBC, and Britain's film and theatre industries could have led to more centralised control that strengthened the political intelligentsia's hold on the nation's culture industries. Consequently, the potential for replicating the kinds of state-directed propaganda apparatus enjoyed by more autocratic regimes is one of British cultural diplomacy's most dubious attributes, though the generally decentralised institutional structure of Britain's Information Services is often hailed as an important formal distinction.[12]

A third technologically driven cultural initiative can be seen in the formation of the BBC's Empire Service (1932–39), the precursor to its Overseas Service (1939–65) and today's World Service (1965–present). Although initially aimed at strengthening links throughout the British Dominions and Dependencies through the provision of English language content, the Empire Service branched out into foreign-language broadcasting from 1938 onwards. The original intention of enhancing cultural exchange expanded to include international security concerns, with the launch of counterpropaganda initiatives within imperial territories agitating for independence such as India, and against hostile European powers. In a move aimed at countering Italy's anti-British broadcasts following its invasion of Ethiopia (then Abyssinia) in October 1935, the Empire Service began to broadcast pro-British material throughout the Middle East in Arabic from 3 January 1938, in Spanish and Portuguese across South America from April 1938, and in a variety of languages across Europe from September 1938 onwards.[13] A number of prominent left-wing writers and intellectuals such as George Orwell worked in the Overseas Service at the time, illustrating how anti-imperial sympathies were often subordinated to anti-totalitarian concerns.[14]

The D'Abernon Report, the EMB, and the BBC's Empire Service illustrate how Britain's earliest forays into cultural diplomacy sprang from imperial concerns. Over time, however, the notion of a Britishness that defined itself against continental fascism would replace initial attempts at establishing one based on overt Empire consciousness. Britain's domestic wealth and security had long been indivisibly linked to its status as a global Empire and, between 1939 and 1946, Britain would discover the important role that cultural-diplomatic initiatives such as Shakespeare tours could play in protecting these interests overseas.

Elite Diplomacy versus Mass Propaganda: Lord Lloyd and Lord Beaverbrook

Lord Lloyd, whose career bridged colonial administration and the birth of the British Council, provides a compelling portrait of the pro-imperial and anti-communist political figures who presided over the emerging field of cultural propaganda in the late 1930s. As its second Chairman from 1937 to 1941, Lloyd came to the British Council following a long and controversial career in colonial administration.[15] Following an authoritarian governorship of Bombay between 1918 and 1923 during which he imprisoned Mahatma Gandhi, Lloyd was promoted to High

Commissioner of Egypt in 1925 where his intransigence alienated the Wafd Nationalist Party to the point that the Foreign Office were forced to negotiate behind Lloyd's back, prompting his early resignation in 1929.[16] As Frances Donaldson notes, establishing the importance of cultural propaganda through his work at the British Council was a return from the political wilderness for Lloyd, providing an outlet for his 'energy and talents' whilst appealing to his 'romantic imperialism' and 'intolerance of radical philosophy'.[17]

Unlike Tallents and subsequent British Council chairmen, Lloyd was not afraid of describing the organisation's work as propaganda. He is credited, however, with giving the British variation a more respectable gloss by defining it against the Nazi German and Fascist Italian varieties. In a speech delivered to the House of Commons, Lloyd assured Members of Parliament that

> everywhere we find people turning in relief from the harshly dominant tones of totalitarian propaganda to the less insistent but more reasonable cadences of Britain. We do not force them to 'think British'; we offer them the opportunity to learn what the British think.[18]

Lloyd's emphasis on 'reasonable cadence' helped define Britain's more magnanimous, take-it-or-leave-it, brand of propaganda. He espoused a long historical view that interpreted culture as heritage at home and civilisation abroad, conservative notions which would help align the Shakespearean theatre with traditional structures of state power. From the outset, Lloyd emphasised the provision of English language teaching as an effective strategy for attracting the best foreign students to Britain and thus improving cultural relations throughout the non-Anglophone world. Taken together, such initiatives prompt Lloyd's biographer to credit him with laying the foundations for British cultural diplomacy in the post-war era.[19]

As the first foreign visitor to be received at Spain's Royal Palace towards the end of the Spanish Civil War (1936–39), Lloyd met General Franco officially to push for the British Council to start work in Madrid, but informally to persuade him to keep out of any future European conflict.[20] Their strong personal friendship and shared antagonism towards communist socialism resulted in Lloyd being offered the position of Ambassador to Spain, a reciprocal gesture to the French sending Marshal Pétain (later Chief of State for Vichy France) to Madrid as Special Ambassador. During several overseas visits setting up British Institutes across Mediterranean Europe, the Near East, and the Baltic states, Lloyd found that the cultural organisation's 'semi-official' status provided effective cover for establishing private channels of communication between Churchill and a range of prominent continental leaders.[21]

When war broke out, Lloyd came to represent the more right-wing elements of Churchill's coalition government, serving as Secretary of State for the Colonies whilst maintaining direct influence over the British Council.[22] Following Lloyd's untimely death in 1941, Churchill had to be dissuaded from shutting the fledgling cultural organisation down altogether, indicating perhaps that the British Council's overt cultural activities were considered less important than its covert political uses.[23] With his broad political connections and ability to secure treasury funding (under Lloyd's tenure the British Council's grant rose from £5,000 in 1935/36 to £330,249 by 1939/40), Lloyd ensured the organisation's survival and the 'permanent recognition' of 'cultural propaganda' in British foreign policy.[24] Lloyd's career as an imperial administrator in India and Egypt, however, not to mention his enduring personal friendship with autocratic dictators like General Franco, undermines the common assertion that Britain's initial forays into cultural projection were predominantly anti-fascist in character.

Before moving on to discuss the Old Vic's 1939 production of *Hamlet*, it is important to note the strength of domestic feeling against the British Council's earliest cultural activities. Britain's previous Minister of Information during the First World War, Lord Beaverbrook, launched frequent broadsides against Shakespeare tours in the popular press. A later, though typical, Beaverbrook editorial fumed:

> Which is the best propaganda for us – the roar of ... British bombers and fighters, or the melody of madrigals broadcast by the British Council? If we saved the money we wasted by the council, we could have three extra squadrons of fighters to join the display.[25]

British Council staff endured Beaverbrook's portrayal of them in the popular press as privileged hobbyists, 'effete and ineffectual amateurs', and 'precious cultural dilettantes' bringing untold damage to 'Britain's robust picture of itself abroad' as a nation of 'tough, no-nonsense islanders'.[26] Though uncertainty remains over the motives behind Beaverbrook's blistering attacks (speculations range from obscure personal vindictiveness to disappointment that he did not get Lloyd's job himself), such tirades exacerbated entrenched class-cultural schisms and prompted public debates on whether, in an age of mass politics, wooing foreign elites with theatrical productions wasn't simply a waste of time and resources.[27] In the initial stages of the First World War, British propaganda had followed the typical Foreign Office strategy of being qualitative rather than quantitative, aiming to 'influence those who can influence others' rather than attempting 'a direct appeal to the mass of the population'.[28] As these early endeavours failed to avert conflict, Lloyd George established the Enemy Propaganda Department in February 1918 under the direction of Lord Northcliffe (owner of *The Daily Mail* and *The Daily Mirror*) whilst promoting Lord Beaverbrook (owner the *Daily Express* and the *Evening Standard*) to the position of Minister of Information. Taylor concludes that, in muzzling domestic news outlets and fabricating stories of German atrocities, this 'Press Gang' inadvertently damaged British foreign policy after the war.[29] Though this was true of public perceptions in the late 1930s, more recent studies have led historians to reassess such claims.[30]

In 1939, rather than simply marshalling Shakespeare as England's national poet (a role it had played during the First World War), the British Council hailed the playwright as a transnational literary figure representing high-cultural values shared by all civilised and peace-loving European nation-states. In effect, a return to the older and preferred Foreign Office strategy that Beaverbrook's 'Press Gang' had replaced in 1918. Consequently, as the British Council mobilised the best available English Shakespeare productions to win over foreign decision-making elites, Beaverbrook lambasted their endeavours as a waste of taxpayers' money and exposed such activities to unwanted scrutiny in the national press back home.[31]

Tyrone Guthrie's Old Vic *Hamlet* (1938–1939)

The Old Vic's 1939 Mediterranean tour of Portugal, Italy, Egypt, Greece, and Malta was one of the British Council's earliest successes.[32] The circuit was planned by the organisation's honorary dramatic advisor William Bridges-Adams, an experienced theatre director whose New Shakespeare Company toured uncut productions throughout interwar Britain in an attempt to cultivate the popular audiences needed to establish an English National Theatre; an endeavour that earned him the nickname 'Un-a-Bridged' Adams.[33] The Old Vic tour comprised eight productions, the flagship being Tyrone Guthrie's modern-dress *Hamlet* starring Alec Guinness, with Anthony Quayle in *Henry V* providing the other half of the tour's Shakespeare programme.[34] Guthrie's staging was viewed as a bold and stylish attempt at contemporising *Hamlet* by setting it in the 1930s.[35] Guinness was a relatively unknown actor at the time, following tentatively in the footsteps of John Gielgud and Laurence Olivier's acclaimed portrayals of 1936 and 1937. The most significant precursor to Guthrie's production, however, was Barry Jackson's Birmingham Repertory staging from 1925. As the first modern-dress production of the play, Jackson's '*Hamlet* in plus-fours' had generated global publicity from Canada to India, demonstrating how interpretations that set *Hamlet* in the interwar period could appeal to a diverse range of international audiences.[36]

As it entered a crowded field of competing international claims upon Shakespeare, Guthrie's *Hamlet* sought to define itself as a distinctly English production. Modern dress suited the ensemble playing style then favoured by the Old Vic company, with the approach bringing 'minor' characters to life and affording them a subtlety and complexity than was not easily achieved when the play was staged in Elizabethan costume or as a 'star' vehicle. A surface resemblance to West End drawing-room dramas legitimised a faster and more naturalistic form of verse speaking then championed by modernist reformers like William Poel and Harley Granville-Barker. Furthermore, the production presented audiences with a flawed and psychologically complex Prince who displayed a violent temper, especially towards Gertrude and Ophelia. Guinness's remarkably understated and naturalistic performance was enhanced by a gift for stillness punctuated by moments of explosive rage and anger: a decidedly Freudian display rarely seen in more conventional and romantic portrayals.[37] Guinness's performance divided the London critics. Writing for *The Observer*, Harold Hobson enthused that he had 'never seen a better young Hamlet', whilst James Agate, writing for *The Sunday Times*, dismissed Guinness's interpretation as 'non-acting', complaining that 'this young actor is obviously not trying any of the things in *Hamlet* which are the ABC of the part. He attempts neither play of feature nor gesture. He rejects mordancy'.[38] Kenneth Tynan later concluded that in eschewing 'conventional flourishes' the 'whole production' bestowed 'an aura of civilised controversy' upon Guinness's name that 'marked his independence from the past' (Figure 1.1).[39]

Guthrie's production insisted on the relevance of the play, presenting audiences with a young prince who was recognisable in his complexity and concerns. Its emphasis on domesticity within the setting of naturalistically rendered drawing rooms helped contemporise the play further, evoking a familiar interwar context that chimed with the popular theme of generational conflict. Likewise, the production made tentative nods towards the political concerns of continental interpretations. In the graveyard scene for instance, Hamlet wore a sweater and workman's boots, an echo of Karel

Figure 1.1 Alec Guinness in *Hamlet*. The Old Vic Theatre Company, 1938.
Directed by Tyrone Guthrie. Photo by Gordon Anthony. © Getty Images/Hulton Archive.

Hilar and Vlatislav Hofman's Prague production that played down the character's princely stature and emphasised his distance and alienation from the centres of power.[40] In other scenes, Guinness wore his father-in-law's First World War dress uniform, evoking the memory of that tragic conflict and troubling audiences with the notion that the sins of their fathers' 'lost' generation threatened to bear down on them all once again.

The Old Vic Company in Portugal (1939)

The Old Vic's modern-dress *Hamlet* sought to promote the London theatre scene as young, vibrant, and unostentatious. In stark contrast to a British theatrical culture predominantly shaped by cut-throat commercial competition, continental productions could be the result of generous state funding and often became monumental in effect. In Italy for instance, Shakespeare's *Julius Caesar* had become part of Mussolini's ideological appropriation of the Caesar myth.[41] The far-right's embrace of Shakespeare saw Mussolini debuting as a dramatist himself, with his state-supported productions undertaking international tours of their own.[42] *Cesare* (1939), the final instalment of Mussolini's trilogy, was a biased revision of Shakespeare's complex historical perspective that portrayed Brutus as immature, dithering, and confused; a rather Hamlet-esque presentation of vacillating youth that paled in comparison to Mussolini's depiction of Caesar as the archetypal fascist man of action.[43] As it premiered in April 1939, *Cesare* may well have played a part in prompting the Old Vic to include Italy on its tour itinerary. Certainly, its absorbing spectacle of charismatic despotic power betrayed by treasonous intellectualism could not have been more different from Guthrie's *Hamlet*.

The publicity campaign that surrounded the Old Vic tour emphasised 'youth' as the defining characteristic of London's vibrant theatrical culture. Defending the upcoming expedition on the BBC, Lewis Casson – actor, tour leader, and then Chairman of the British Council's Drama Advisory Committee (DAC) – asserted that it was good for other nations to 'see that we have a new generation of ... vigorous youngsters who are going to carry on the theatre tradition'.[44] Merula Guinness's personal diary of the tour noted that 'Guthrie is becoming quite a God: they ... are amazed he is so young. They are amazed at the youthfulness of the company altogether'.[45] Continental audiences seemed responsive to the pathos that such an emphasis on youthful innocence could evoke. Contessa Marcella Pavolini, for instance, wrote a personal letter to Guinness confessing that she found his performance in Rome a marvellous experience, a revelation of the real, human, intelligent, and immensely unhappy Prince. You were so young, so helpless, so lost, among those worldly, stupid, and selfish people, it made my heart ache to see you and to listen to you; I could not even get up from my seat, during the intervals, I trembled so much – and I was not a sensitive, emotional girl, but a woman forty years old.[46]

The emotional charge contained in such fan mail suggests that the anti-war theme of 'doomed youth' shined through in Guthrie's production.

Although an impending sense of conflict coloured the Old Vic's reception, hindsight allowed accounts to overstate the war's inevitability. Anthony Quayle's autobiography is particularly bullish in this regard, asserting that none of the company members 'doubted that war was coming; our anxiety was to get *Hamlet* on before the bombs fell'.[47] Guinness recalled the immediate antagonism the company faced in fascist Europe. Along with forty-two cast members, twelve tons of stage material required transportation. Arriving in Lisbon aboard the *Alcantara* on 23 January, Guinness recounted how the company

> watched in horror as all our scenery was carefully lowered into the Tagus ... It was probably a genuine error on the part of the crane workers, but the British were far from popular in Portugal.[48]

The company soon found themselves immersed in pro-Franco celebrations following the fall of Barcelona:

> Lisbon went mad with joy. We found it very depressing. Even more depressing was seeing the grander makes of British cars displaying the Union Jack flanked by the Swastika, the Rising Sun of Japan, as well as the flags of Nationalist Spain and Portugal.[49]

While Casson recalled that almost everyone they met was happy that the 'red menace' had been crushed, Guinness admitted that the company felt 'small, alien, lonely and threatened' when caught up in the nationalist celebrations.[50] In marked contrast to Lloyd's warm friendship with Franco, or Casson's officious belief in the tour's mission of appeasement, Guinness remembered the company feeling 'not a little suspicious of our fellow countrymen in Lisbon'.[51]

The enthusiasm that many English residents in Portugal displayed for the nationalist cause troubled the visiting company and complicated their role as cultural propagandists. Merula Guinness's memoir describes in lively and unguarded terms how a mental distance was maintained between the company, their propaganda mission, and the tour's administrators. Following a performance of *Henry V* when speeches were given before the Portuguese President and an assembly of international ambassadors, Merula noted that 'Alec [was] extremely good, Tony very charming' but 'Casson made an embarrassing speech'.[52] She found the atmosphere at the British Institute in Lisbon

> very proud. V. Serious about it all, and serious about Lisbon. They are giving lectures on the plays we are doing. Place plastered in Old Vic propaganda... We do not like the B.I. Boys. Little scruffy one... a fascist, awfully proud of his superiors – wears pork pie hat, thinks he owns Lisbon, very self-important. The other one very ponderous and pompous... we do not like Lisbon, we do not like the Portuguese, and we do not like the British people in Portugal.[53]

Merula Guinness's private diary provides a frank and unguarded account of what it meant to be embroiled in the twilight world of cultural propaganda just prior to the outbreak of the Second World War. The development of her thoughts and feelings in response to the experience of touring Shakespeare illustrates the personal jeopardy involved in taking on the role of cultural ambassador. As such, it is worth sketching out a little of her background here to better understand the impact of the tour upon herself and other company members.

Merula Guinness's cultural and political sensibility could be described as disenchanted bohemianism. Though not politically active, she looked to art, in a typical iconoclastic gesture of the time, to provide strategic refuge from the mounting crises and challenges of life during the interwar years. The Salamans, her British South African Jewish family, were a lively example of upper-class eccentricity, with a country estate near Essex where her father was chief of the hunt and a close friend of the painter Augustus John. Merula's mother enjoyed civilised controversy by being widely regarded as a drawing room Communist and fellow traveller.[54] Despite her privileged class position, Merula's Jewish background barred her from the very top enclaves of British society, with establishment anti-Semitism ensuring that she was denied access to the most exclusive girls' school of the day, Hayes Court.[55] In classic bohemian fashion, Merula was independently wealthy enough to survive on a young actress's salary, yet dissenting enough to resent the patronage required to protect her chosen profession from the vicissitudes of the open market. In contrast, Alec Guinness came from a lower-middle-class background and had no independent income beyond the little money that acting work paid at the time. Guinness rehearsed *Hamlet* in the only suit he owned, the one he wore at their wedding just prior to the tour (which also served as an unconventional honeymoon for the young couple). Despite his modest income, class anxiety got the better of Guinness when he blew an entire month's salary on a Savile Row suit just in time for *Hamlet*'s opening night. Merula Guinness's belief that art could dignify poverty, form a spiritual bulwark against the uncultured consumption habits of the wealthy, and shelter the practitioner from the political extremes of the period, would be called into question by the experience of touring the Mediterranean with *Hamlet*.[56] The muted rage Merula felt towards the vulgar elites the company were underpaid to entice towards more democratic and civic responsibility through Shakespearean performance, found regular outlet in the pages of her remarkable tour diary.

The Old Vic Company in Italy (1939)

With evident relief, Merula Guinness discovered that Italian audiences were 'tremendously fond of the theatre – refreshingly enthusiastic' and showed 'genuine appreciation' for the Old Vic's work.[57] On 6 February 1939, the company were officially welcomed by the President of the Federazione Nazionale Fascista, a prominent political figure whose speech displayed a clear understanding of the British Council's propagandist intentions in bringing the Old Vic to Italy, congratulated them on doing so, and then proceeded to make a startling array of fascist counterclaims. The President stressed for instance how Italian theatre had progressed well beyond traditional habits of cultural elitism and was successfully appealing to the masses directly:

> It was one of the first points to be considered by the fascist government, as soon as it took the lead of the nation, to find in the theatre a foundational element for the spiritual education of the people, and it has established a Ministry for Popular Culture ... thus we have arranged great representations for audiences of over 20,000 ... 'Carri di Tespi' ... [who] do what your ancient companies of 'strollers' did, but with modern direction and perfectly equipped, which have caused wonder and cheers everywhere amongst the peasantry ... [at] seeing a show which formerly was a privilege of the high classes.[58]

Lloyd's emphasis on the difference in cadence and tone between British and Italian propaganda is evident here, and yet so too is Beaverbrook's scepticism as to whether cultural-diplomatic initiatives targeting foreign elites was really effective in an era of mass politics. While Britain, with its antiquated class system that aligned classical culture with high social standing, was hoping to influence key decision-makers through Shakespeare, Italy could boast of mobilising 'the peasantry' through the mass dissemination of an artform that was no longer considered 'a privilege of the high classes'.[59] In response, the Old Vic cast adopted a typically British front, mixing polite embarrassment with a blatant disregard towards all forms of political grandstanding:

> Casson read his [speech], only ¼ hour long but most embarrassing, luckily the Italians did not understand a word, then it got quite gay ... a very strange performance. Most of them had just finished playing *Hamlet* here, very badly I believe.[60]

Though the English actors were aware that there had been a recent Italian production of the same play, they brushed aside any hints of competition with studied indifference. Italy was full of such mirroring cultural encounters. During the company's residence in Florence, Guinness's scheduled rendezvous to take tea with Mussolini was cancelled after Pope Pius XI died. Rome was in official mourning by the time the company reached the Valle Theatre, with Guinness later recalling that 'it was a curious experience playing *Hamlet*, in conventional 'nighted colours' in spite of the modern dress, before an audience entirely swathed in black'.[61] Invited to a Rome production of *Macbeth* performed by Ruggero Ruggeri, Casson was taken aback by how the Italian actor had managed to underplay the villainous aspects of the character, adopting a 'solemn and serious' approach that succeeded in portraying Macbeth in a sympathetic fascist mode as 'a sort of troubled Saint'.[62] Such different though plausible interpretations provided clear instances of Shakespeare in performance being shaped to promote an alternative world view. Indeed, as Richard Halpern notes, Shakespeare was a firm favourite 'of both left and right in the age of mass politics' and became the most frequently produced foreign playwright by both Soviet Russia and Nazi Germany in the 1930s and 1940s.[63] Rather than inducing a sense of unease over his own culpability in leading a counter-propagandist Shakespeare tour, however, Casson merely viewed such alternative interpretations as unorthodox curiosities.[64]

In the twilight world of diplomatic cultural exchange, it was difficult for the actors to gauge how much genuine feeling lay behind the warm approval the company receive in Italy. Although Alec and Merula Guinness were convinced that the Italian passion for Shakespeare was sincere, Quayle insisted that the tour's social reception was itself a piece of carefully managed political theatre. He noted for instance, how tables of diners would habitually stand up and clap whenever the company entered a restaurant. Though they were 'feted and entertained', and though 'the intelligentsia coo[ed]' the company 'like doves', the atmosphere felt 'forced', especially with 'the ever-growing strains' of the fascist hymn *Giovinezza* playing in the background.[65] While the British Council interpreted such public endorsements as proof of the cultural-diplomatic mission's success, Quayle refuted any notion that the tour helped dampen the simmering political tensions that lay beneath the surface. In comparison to the firm belief in the virtues of cultural exchange conveyed by Lloyd during the inauguration of new British Institutes throughout Europe, Quayle felt his ears being 'stuffed with hot air' at a reception at the PEN club in Milan when the 'hosts expressed their horror at the very thought that the country of Michelangelo and the nation that had given birth to Shakespeare should ever confront one another in enmity'.[66]

In Portugal and Italy, a sense of unreality and even personal jeopardy coloured the actors' experience of touring Shakespeare in service to British diplomacy. The strategy of appeasing foreign elites brought the company into unwanted association with celebrations over the fall of the Spanish Republic, a forced and unwanted political affiliation that compromised most of the actors' personal values and beliefs. Within a context of mass mobilisation, strident nationalism, and committed militarism, the tour's message of appeasement seemed disingenuous, not least when the company witnessed their fellow countrymen applauding fascist advances on the continent. Furthermore, the Old Vic's cultural mission was ineffective because Shakespeare had already been appropriated and recruited into the very cause that the English visitors were hoping to deploy it against. While Britain was just starting to mobilise its national theatrical culture for propaganda purposes, Italy had long been doing so to level Europe's class-based cultural divisions and establish a theatre for the 'spiritual education' of the masses. In 1939, a pro-British *Hamlet* confronted a range of Mediterranean pro-fascist Shakespeares and history suggests that, in Portugal and Italy at least, the latter prevailed.

Anglo-Egyptian Relations

In 1939 Egypt was the strategic centre of Britain's imperial world system, linking the various spheres of its sprawling global Empire to the advantage of British economic interests.[67] Late Victorian expansion had led to massive infrastructural investment in the region, including the construction of the Suez Canal in 1869 and, as an attendant cultural symbol, Cairo's Khedivial Opera House. During the ensuing economic boom, Egypt enjoyed the reputation of being a dynamic satellite economy on the periphery of Europe, while the bust of 1876 provided Britain with an excuse to place the country under a 'temporary occupation' that lasted over seventy years. This period of informal rule met immediate local resistance, with the revolution of 1881 giving rise to Egypt's first Nationalist Party, Wafd, and the establishment of nominal independence in 1922 following the revolution of 1919.[68] As James Whidden notes, 'British government policy and the interests of the British business community' began to diverge around 1918, with London officially prioritising imperial strategy over the rights of its resident British community with the Anglo-Egyptian Treaty of 1936. In exchange for ongoing access to military bases in and around Suez the treaty abolished the British colony's longstanding financial advantages in Egypt (known as the Capitulations) effectively stripping the resident British community of their historical privileges.[69] In part the Old Vic tour of 1939 helped support this British colony (also made up of 'out-land' Jewish and Christian Levantines, British Maltese, and British Cypriots) who, at the onset of war, occupied an ever-diminishing colonial status.

For Egyptians themselves, ensuing industrialisation fostered a growing working and middle class that anticipated the constitutional and material advantages of modernisation.[70] In order to contain Egyptian nationalism and growing resistance against Britain's informal occupation, colonial administrators had become adept at orchestrating political tensions between Egypt's Palace and Parliament through a 'veiled protectorate' based at the High Commissioner's residence. By the mid-1930s however, Britain's divide and rule tactics had become transparent to the Egyptian population and to the world at large, dangerously exposing the country to the influence of other national actors in the region.[71] Following Mussolini's invasion and occupation of Ethiopia in 1935 Axis propaganda began advertising the illegality of Britain's occupation, thus posing a direct threat to the Suez Canal and British imperial communications spreading as far as India, Australia, and the Far East. Despite its vital strategic importance, Britain was ill prepared to defend Egypt militarily in 1939. The broad diplomatic objective when the Old Vic arrived therefore, was to delay Italy's entrance into the conflict, reassure the colony of Britain's continuing presence and protection, and maintain local Egyptian loyalty and support; all aims that cultural diplomacy could play an effective role in securing.[72]

The Old Vic Company in Egypt (1939)

Anthony Quayle's autobiography recalls the bitter irony of confronting the imminent Axis invasion of Egypt with a threadbare touring production of

Henry V. Thanks to the antics of the Lisbon dock workers Quayle inadvertently ruined *Hamlet*'s opening night in Cairo when he fell through the water-damaged stage floor. Following another show he discovered Hans Beckhoff, a Nazi enthusiast he had previously met in London, waiting for him in the stage wings:

> He was the head ... of the German *Reiseburo* in Cairo. And of what else I wondered? I would have taken a bet that he knew the strength and weakness of every British Army Unit stationed in Egypt. He had *Abwehr* stamped all over him .... His smile was condescending – with good reason. Hitler was ascendant; Europe was his for the taking – perhaps more ... though the formal hostilities might be delayed and delayed again there stood between us a mutual, unmistakable declaration of war. We shook hands coolly and he left.[73]

The company had no illusions of winning over committed Nazis like Beckhoff but hoped to steady the nerves of the resident British colony and maintain local allegiance. In an age of militant nationalism and political extremism, Egyptians realised that international bodies like the League of Nations could no longer be relied upon.[74] Britain and France's inability to protect Ethiopia and Libya from Italy's colonial aggression, for instance, were clear indications that weaker nations were living in perilous times. Though there was acceptance amongst the general population that Britain might lose the war, the notion that Nazi ideology had infiltrated Egyptian society itself has subsequently been dismissed. Even so, the presence of 80,000 Italians in Egypt 'nearly all tied to fascism by their purses if not by their hearts' caused the British authorities serious concern.[75]

The famed cosmopolitanism that made Cairo a global success story in times of peace made it a strategic headache in times of war. Part of Britain's response was to make its artistic presence felt within a complex and diverse cultural landscape. The interwar period witnessed a heyday in Egyptian liberal arts, with Cairo offering visitors a degree of personal freedom that associated it with permissive hedonism in the Western imagination. In comparison to the 'polished entertainments' enjoyed by Cairo and Alexandria's francophone upper-class community, the British colony had a reputation for insularity and 'shabby gentility'. As a consequence the Old Vic tour sought to bring some much-needed glamor and cultural esteem to the beleaguered British community, helping to counter the common perception that there wasn't much to British colonial culture beyond 'tennis, polo, horse racing, golf, bowls, croquet, and cricket'.[76]

Guthrie's *Hamlet* was just one of a range of staged Shakespeare interpretations available to Egyptian audiences throughout the era of liberal experimentation. The dominant European influences on Egyptian theatre were not British at all, but primarily French and Italian. Ever since Giuseppe Verdi's *Aida* (1871) was commissioned to inaugurate Khedive Ismail's Italian-style Opera House, opera had publicly represented the 'modernising drives of Egypt's rulers' with Italian and French styles of acting influencing Egypt's star performers such as Shaykh Salama Higazi.[77] Shakespeare had long been absorbed into this Egyptian love for the operatic form, with Higazi commissioning the first translation of *Hamlet* in 1901 which he went on to perform in Cairo's Egyptian Theatre, and then again with his Arabic Theatre Company in 1905.[78] 'Abdu's translation featured so many wild departures from Shakespeare's text that his *Hamlet* is considered an 'icon of infidelity' among translation critics.[79] Irrespective of the fact that 'Abdus gave the tragedy a happy ending it was produced at least seventeen times between 1901 and 1910, second only to Najib al-Haddad's musical adaptation of *Romeo and Juliet* titled *Martyrs of Love* (1895).

Such bold adaptations make perfect sense when we remember that most literary translation in Egypt worked from French, not English. A clear illustration of the considerable cultural ground Britain hoped to recover from its European competitors in Egypt was the fact that by 1930, only fifteen English writers had been translated into Arabic compared to one hundred and fifty French authors.[80] Salama Higazi, George Abyad, and the Italian-trained Youssef Wahbi staged Arabic adaptations of *Hamlet* between 1900 and 1930. Inspired by Sarah Bernhardt's 1908 portrayal of the title role, Fatima Rushdi's performances in 1929–30 attracted the attention of the international press with cosmopolitan magazines reporting on how she practiced fencing daily in the Ezbekiya Gardens, a feat that was in turn succeeded by Amina Rizq's *Hamlet* in 1936. All of the above indicate that amongst the growing professional and middle classes who could afford to attend such performances, Shakespeare was considered a global resource that Egyptian artists had long staked their own powerful claim upon.

Cloistered in a privileged world of Embassy parties, the Old Vic tourists seemed unaware of this rich local tradition of Shakespeare adaptation. The sense that Egyptian voices were marginalised within such settings is palpable in Merula Guinness's observation:

> The Egyptian guests were very shy and difficult to speak to. Casson was doing the missionary and kept interrupting a quite interesting old man who did know something about the country, to try to expound his fantastic, muddled theories of the world brotherhood.[81]

The gilded enclaves of cultural, diplomatic, and sporting events that the company inhabited brought British, Levantine, and Egyptian elites into close social proximity. Theatre belonged to an almost-exclusive world of cosmopolitan socialites united in their mutual segregation from the larger population, a climate of 'social apartheid' overseen by a 'ruling caste' ideology based as much on 'class difference as on race'.[82] Power, wealth, and mutual self-interest aligned the international community with the local ruling class, while the ability to demonstrate an appreciation for European high culture was considered an essential social skill for colonial Egypt's ruling elites.

The islands of prosperous content the actors glided between failed to conceal the grinding poverty experienced by the vast majority of Egypt's citizenry however.[83] An expatriate couple, the Lows

> drove us to their house along mud roads with mud hovels on each side and thick with children and donkeys, sheep, goats ... we just drove straight through them – none were killed. Their house and garden are like a piece of England plonked down in the middle of a country completely different, one felt one was on an island and though it was very nice it was depressing. The tea got through all right – not particularly gay, but not many moments of great strain.[84]

Merula Guinness concluded that the company felt more alienated from the wealthy British expatriates they met in Egypt than they had from their hosts in Italy. She found that colonial living seemed to have had a dissipating effect on the British community, and that it had cultivated a guarded and defensive attitude towards all outsiders including fellow countrymen. Though they were 'all kind and polite' they 'only showed a very carefully polished outside'.[85]

As Shakespearean ambassadors, the company were granted brief access to a privileged world in which they did not entirely belong whilst promoting a cultural product that was not especially valued. The grotesque social inequalities on display throughout Egypt served as a reminder of the economic disparities and commercial philistinism awaiting the company back home. Famous for its earnest social policy, threadbare conditions, and air of genteel impoverishment, the Old Vic's cultural capital could not have been higher.[86] Arnoldian sentiments that a national repertory company performing the classics was essential for the nation's soul, however, had little evident appeal to Cairo's cocktail crowd. The tour's cultural mission required the actors to rub shoulders with the wealthiest of elites, not least to garner financial support for the deserving old theatre back home in South-East London. Bringing the necessary touch of celebrity glamour to dull diplomatic events was a regular duty for the company as a whole, while Guinness was enrolled in further acts of quiet diplomacy such as having lunch with the British Ambassador and the Egyptian Prime Minister. On a personal level, such obligations required the couple to blow their modest Old Vic salaries on the necessary attire to

> face the snobs at the Ambassador's garden party with a brazen front. Alec wore his new shirt ... the party was deathly ... [we] were introduced to some young ladies who were so well bred that their fingers melted in one's hand, one of them was too grand to speak at all .... Left as soon as possible and fell into another big hate.[87]

At smaller gatherings 'Alec did his stuff' raising funds by talking 'about the poverty of the Vic very eloquently' though, in Merula's eyes, 'the place was seething with money and they all looked awful'.[88] Following one such fund-raising event, Chester Beatty, a multi-millionaire who confessed to only ever reading Edgar Wallace novels despite owning a valuable collection of rare Arabic manuscripts, gave Alec a paperback edition of *Twelfth Night* as a parting gift, a careless gesture that struck Merula as cruel and unthinking.[89]

Overall, despite the political differences, the company felt that they had shared a genuine cultural entente with their hosts in Italy; a sign perhaps that cultural diplomacy could help sway decision-making elites. Their experience in Cairo however, suggested that the chief beneficiaries of Empire regarded Shakespeare as little more than a worthy cause, valuable only as a marker of national heritage or for the maintenance of outdated class-cultural distinctions. Worse still, the gilded lives of the British expatriate community in Egypt provided a monstrous colonial allegory of the entrenched class and wealth disparities awaiting the actors themselves upon their return to England.

The Old Vic's Mediterranean tour came to an end in Malta in the spring of 1939, a destination that provided a palpable sense of relief for many in the company. Merula and Alec Guinness warmed to the audience of Royal Navy personnel, writing at the time:

> They all have lovely honest faces and kind twinkly eyes ... they are real people and adore their work and are generous and frank about one another – so different from the Cairo Cocktail crowd.[90]

The experience of touring the Mediterranean region during a period of mounting political tension left many Old Vic actors wary and conflicted. Despite their attempt at improving the international situation by fostering closer cultural relations between nations, the tour's direct appeal to ruling elites seemed to confer cultural kudos upon the very people most responsible for the war's approach in the first place. For this late-bohemian generation of English actors, the belief that art existed above politics was shaken to the core, especially as they had seen Shakespeare effectively recruited to the cause of their adversaries. In turning away from the last vestiges of interwar privilege, however, they would ultimately come to be identified with the 'warm glow' and 'wholesome militarism' of the Second World War.[91] The fight for democracy at home and abroad would transform Britain's theatrical landscape and strengthen its willingness and ability to project Shakespeare overseas through touring practices.

CEMA, ENSA, and the Cairo and Alexandria Drama Festivals

State sponsorship of the arts, including theatre, began in Britain as a direct consequence of the Second World War.[92] The demoralising effects of Britain's cultural blackout in the conflict's early stages, then dubbed the 'phony' or 'bore' war, led to the formation of the Council for the Encouragement of Music and the Arts (CEMA) with its stated aim of providing 'the best' entertainment for 'the most' people.[93] Tyrone Guthrie saw CEMA's arrival as a necessary and long-overdue state intervention in a threadbare arts sector; an epochal change to Britain's cultural landscape that finally materialised once 'Old Britannia suddenly realised that she would need more than a trident and a shield to keep her reputation'.[94] Guthrie understood that the conditions of total war could save Britain's beleaguered classical repertory theatres by transforming them into an indispensable engine for national morale and cultural communion at home, and as a reflection of national prestige overseas:

> for the first time since the Tudors, the British Treasury has made manifest a belief that Art in general, and the art of theatre in particular, is not merely a graceful amenity but a necessity to a great nation which considers itself, and wishes to be considered, civilised.[95]

Although the government's conception of culture was narrow, highbrow, and 'improving', it sought to reach as many as possible by bringing 'arts, hitherto unattainable for the lower strata of British society, to the people'.[96] As West End theatres sent their productions on lengthy national excursions to escape the blitz, a new era of domestic theatre touring ensued. The Old Vic, which became one of the first professional theatre companies to join CEMA, relocated to Burnley and settled into its wartime role of bringing classical repertory theatre of the highest standards to the mining and industrial regions of Wales and Lancashire.[97] Despite its stated aims, CEMA allocated a disproportionate amount of financial support to these displaced 'high' cultural providers from London, often to the neglect of smaller regional clubs and organisations that provided more popular cultural fare.[98]

In Egypt, the pre-war collaboration between the local Government and the British Council was resumed under the aegis of the Entertainment National Services Association (ENSA) in early 1944. Under the directorship of Basil Dean, ENSA tours provided entertainment to hundreds of thousands of people living or serving overseas throughout the conflict, with an estimated four out of five members of Britain's entertainment industry working for the organisation at some point.[99] The global mobilisation of Britain's theatre industry during the conflict meant that Dean was able to organise three annual Drama Festivals in the transit cities of Cairo and Alexandria towards the end of the war. The first in 1944 starred Emlyn Williams in *Blithe Spirit* (1941), *Night Must Fall* (1935), and *Flare Path* (1942); the second in 1945, featured the Donald Wolfit Company's stagings of *Hamlet*, *Twelfth Night*, *Volpone*, and *Much Ado About Nothing*; and the third headlined with the John Gielgud Company's *Hamlet* and *Blithe Spirit* in 1946.[100] Once again the initial idea for the festival originated with Bridges-Adams, the British Council's dramatic advisor who also served on ENSA's Advisory International Council. On the Egyptian side, the Drama Festivals were made possible with the support of the director of the Khedivial Opera House, Soliman Naguib.[101]

The image that Britain projected overseas in the mid-1940s reflected the enormous changes that had taken place in its own cultural landscape. While audiences at home consisted of civilians, school children, and factory workers, in Egypt audiences were mostly made up of British and Commonwealth troops. Towards the end of the war, servicemen who were soon to be voting citizens with expectations of meaningful social change upon demobilisation, were given access to a programme of classical entertainment on top of the usual end-of-the-pier variety acts. In adopting a more populist and inclusive tone, the 1945 festival aimed at portraying Britain as a unified and victorious force for freedom and democracy in the world rather than as an occupying imperial power. The man appointed for this particular diplomatic mission was Donald Wolfit; an actor-manager whose troupe had more than a whiff of late-nineteenth-century stage practice in its approach to classical theatre, thus evoking a bygone era when Shakespeare in performance truly was popular amongst working-class audiences.

The Donald Wolfit Company in Egypt (1945)

The Donald Wolfit Company was invited to play Egypt because of its popularity with the troops while touring France and Belgium in the wake of the German retreat. After attending Wolfit's *Hamlet* in Brussels, General Montgomery climbed on stage to exclaim to the assembled military audience that, having seen Wolfit 'so often at Stratford-upon-Avon', 'this is what I said the men have wanted for a long time'.[102] Although one of the proudest moments in Wolfit's life, Montgomery's statement was pure politics following the realisation that with the war drawing to a close it was deemed unwise to condescend the troops.[103]

Wolfit's initial invitation to the European front arose from the decisive role he played in reinvigorating popular appreciation for Shakespeare during the conflict. Despite the appearance of personal sacrifice in service to public morale, there was a good deal of commercial self-interest behind Wolfit's extensive tours of Britain. The cultural evacuation of London by West End theatres cleared the way for the actor-manager to take his company of latter-day strolling players into the vacated heart of the capital itself. There, Wolfit's defiant performances of *King Lear* during the blitz became the stuff of legend and were later celebrated in Ronald Harwood's stage play *The Dresser* (1980).[104] Wolfit's old-fashioned, turn-of-the-century delivery conjured up the grand rhetorical style of a bygone populist era. As such, it satisfied the needs of the hour by maintaining some fortifying national myths and bringing welcome relief to the beleaguered democratic spirit of the time. By the end of the Second World War, Wolfit's apostolic belief in Shakespeare's relevance to the common man played an important part in dispelling the War Office's reticence to provide Shakespeare for the troops.

Dean described Wolfit as 'the star' of Egypt's second Drama Festival of 1945 and that, with 'his gusto and downright way with Shakespeare', the actor-manager was 'immensely popular, both in the camps at home and overseas'.[105] An illustration of how Wolfit's cultural evangelism was met with popular approval can be seen in his account of travelling from Liverpool to the Mediterranean aboard the *HMS Durban Castle* as part of a troop convoy heading out to the Pacific and Indian theatres of war. Wolfit persuaded the ship's Captain to allow his company to give an impromptu performance of *The Merchant of Venice* to an

> audience of eighteen hundred men squatted close-packed on the deck in their shirt sleeves ... they cheered when Bassanio chose the right casket:

> they cheered again at the elopement and at the confusion of Shylock in the trial scene .... I asked the audience how many of them had ever seen a play before. About one hundred hands went up. To my further question as to how many had seen a play by Shakespeare fewer than twenty hands showed. Thus did we treasure our literary and dramatic heritage in the year of grace nineteen-hundred-and-forty-five![106]

Uplifted by the hopeful spirit of the time, the actors were waved off the ship at Port Said by over a thousand men while the ship's band played 'For He's a Jolly Good Fellow'.[107] On his first morning in Cairo, Wolfit discovered further evidence of the soundness of his cultural campaign when he witnessed:

> a long line of khaki commencing at the box office and stretching right across the front of the theatre ... by eleven o'clock the theatre was sold out for the first week ... in successive weeks each member was booking hundreds of seats for his unit.[108]

Though Wolfit clearly benefitted from playing to captive audiences and entertainment-starved military personnel, his productions brought some welcome relief to servicemen weary of the broad humour and plodding jingoism that so often characterised ENSA's entertainments. As one soldier vividly recalled:

> The opportunity of seeing the Wolfit Company was like a visit to a forgotten world of sanity, and I felt at the time that by his efforts he had given an amount of pleasure to his audiences that is rarely within the power of a performer to offer.[109]

The tour's administrators interpreted such enthusiastic responses as evidence that their endeavours were successfully nurturing the audiences of the future, and thus keeping the perennial dream of an English National Theatre alive. Rather than simply quenching the common man's thirst for 'high' culture, however, Wolfit was popular because the way he went about performing Shakespeare was so gloriously anachronistic. The actor-manager's barnstorming performances evoked the turn-of-the-century style of Beerbohm Tree or Frank Benson. With threadbare sets, costumes that had become 'shabby' from 'constant touring', and a 'definitely poor' supporting cast aimed at making the leading man look better in comparison, Wolfit's no-frills, self-aggrandising approach to Shakespeare was infamous.[110] As one London critic put it, 'in the theatre of my mind's eye I see Donald Wolfit perpetually bestriding the stage in some two-pence coloured Victorian play-print'.[111] Just as his reputation would epitomise the 'blitz spirit' for future generations, Wolfit's productions radiated nostalgia at the moment they first occurred. Ultimately, his success relied upon the wartime era's ability to temporarily undo and suspend an entire history of class-cultural antagonism that shadowed the inflated claims being made by Britain's emerging cultural institutions.

In terms of Anglo-Egyptian relations, Wolfit enjoyed popularity with Royalist sections of the Egyptian ruling class and those segments of Cairene society that constituted Britain's traditional base of support. Having previously met Wolfit at Stratford-upon-Avon in 1937 during the actor's performance in *The Winter's Tale*, King Farouk attended the Command Performance of *Much Ado About Nothing*.[112] Although such cultural-diplomatic events managed to bring Commonwealth and Egyptian audiences together under one roof, traumatic wartime incidents such as the King's near abdication in 1942 under military pressure from the British Ambassador Sir Miles Lampson, were never far from Egyptian minds.[113] Wolfit's autobiography provides a telling account of Farouk's continuing public abasement, and with it a sense of the wider political theatre that framed the festival itself. In commemoration of Shakespeare's Birthday on 23 April, Wolfit organised a 'Revel' following a performance of *Twelfth Night* that featured 'an enormous cake, said to contain no fewer than two-hundred-and-fifty Egyptian eggs, and surmounted by a laurel wreath and the head of the Bard in sugar icing'.[114] When the item was auctioned for the British War Relief Fund,

> the bidding grew hectic, rapidly rose to one hundred pounds, and after some spirited exchanges, was eventually knocked down to a representative from the Abdin Palace who purchased it for King Farouk for one-hundred-and-seventy pounds!'[115]

In demonstrating Egypt's willingness to continue paying Britain's occupying forces for the war effort the commemorative event provided cultural cover for the Palace's public humiliation, all under the watchful eyes of assembled Allied Pact dignitaries and war-weary British and Commonwealth troops.[116]

The ongoing military presence in Egypt wore down long-standing social protocols, however, further fuelling local resentments against British rule. For instance, the Anglo-Egyptian Union's hope of strengthening social relations between Britain and Egypt's professional classes through shared cultural events organised at the Muhammad Ali Club, was severely undermined when the venue became 'a popular port of call for drunken and violent soldiery'. The Anglo-Italian explorer and travel-writer Freya Stark recalled how 'in and out' of this 'official world' of colonial administration and 'Levantine society dripping gems', came crashing groups of 'cheerful troops' demanding drinks from 'shocked fifth-columnist' waiters.[117] Stark once found her chauffeur 'with his head in his hands' after being 'bashed in by a South African annoyed with him for not being a taxi', and throughout the city, drivers fearful of soldiers returning from desert skirmishes in 'holiday mood', went on strike 'for the right to have a friend sitting beside them in the front seat' for protection.[118] Laurence Grafftey-Smith, a member of the British Consular Service, lamented how 'the persuasion of Egyptians to the British way of thinking was not helped' by the antics of such 'untamed toughs' and felt that the 'memories and resentment of those months of daily humiliation' led directly to the demonstrations that later erupted on 'Black Saturday'.[119] By the time John Gielgud's company arrived in Egypt in February 1946 for the third and final Cairo and Alexandria Drama Festival, remaining local support for professionally staged English Shakespeare began to waver in the face of massive public protests against Britain's ongoing occupation.

The John Gielgud Company in Egypt (1946)

The 'Shakespeare Boom' of the early post-war period saw staged productions of the playwright's work enjoy more widespread popularity than at any time since the Napoleonic era.[120] West End theatres were enlisted to disseminate high culture as broadly as possible and in 1944 Gielgud decided to reprise his fifth production of *Hamlet* at London's Haymarket Theatre prior to taking it on an ENSA sponsored tour to India, Southeast Asia, and Egypt. Dean remembered the tour as being one of ENSA's finest though least advertised enterprises.[121] The celebrated actor was no stranger to cultural diplomacy having taken *Hamlet* to Denmark on a previous British Council visit in 1939 where he had been 'treated like an ambassador' and lauded as 'almost a National Theatre in himself'.[122] Gielgud's manager Hugh 'Binkie' Beaumont announced that the star would do his bit for the war effort by joining the Old Vic and playing 'nothing but Shakespeare and the classics for the duration of the war'.[123] In making 'a solemn vow to join ENSA and take their productions anywhere in the world where there were troops awaiting entertainment', Gielgud epitomised the commercial West End's acceptance that the theatrical establishment had a role to play in providing the people with access to high culture. Gielgud originally intended to tour the turn-of-the-century farce *Charley's Aunt* (1892), but was persuaded to go with *Hamlet* instead as 'everyone assures me it is a mistake to play down to the troops'.[124] The choice of touring Shakespeare surprised many West End professionals, with Gielgud's co-star Nancy Nevinson recalling that 'before we left England, people said, "*Hamlet* for the troops, are you mad?"'[125] Gielgud eventually balanced the repertoire by including Noel Coward's *Blithe Spirit*, though his diaries and letters record his continued surprise at finding *Hamlet* the more popular of the two with garrison theatre audiences.[126]

Egypt had undergone dramatic change between the second Cairo Drama festival of 1945 and the third of 1946. Previously King Farouk and the British High Commissioner had spent the war years embroiled in political manoeuvres to either support or undermine a variety of elected national governments.[127] The King's near abdication in 1942, however, had exposed the coercive and controlling nature of Britain's informal rule for all to see. In the view of ordinary Egyptians, despite their country being nominally independent since 1922, the Wafd Party had repeatedly failed to dislodge the intransigent British.[128] After the war it was clear that the coloniser's troops were intent on maintaining their occupation, as indeed they would until 1956. With the removal of the Axis threat to North Africa, the constitutional deadlock could no longer contain the depth of anti-colonial feeling and Egypt's political landscape began to fracture internally. Heated debates as to what type of nation Egypt intended on becoming featured increasingly incommensurate notions. Struggles between Salifists, Liberals, and Nationalists were intensified further by new ideas imported from Soviet Russia and the United States, with the ensuing civil unrest taking on embryonic Cold War characteristics. Between 1945 and 1952, discontent with Egypt's failed interwar liberal experiment led to labour strikes, student protests, mass demonstrations, and anti-establishment press activities organised by groups as diverse as Young Egypt, the Muslim Brotherhood, and the Communist Party.[129] The year 1946 would signal the start of Egypt's final transition towards full independence during an era characterised by political protests, state violence, the assassination of prominent Egyptian politicians including two prime ministers, and the tactical retreat of the British to the canal zone, setting the stage for their final expulsion in 1956.[130]

Despite the volatile political atmosphere, the British Ambassador thought the timing of the third Drama Festival 'most opportune' while the Minister of State, Lord Hankey, promised to lend it 'every support'.[131] Inauspiciously the festival opened on 9 February, a significant date in the history of Egypt's student uprising that saw thousands of secondary school and university students take to the streets resulting in the injury of eighty-nine protesters.[132] Neither the Royal Palace nor the British Embassy were willing to confirm their attendance thereafter, signalling a withdrawal of official protection that prompted ENSA's Public Relations Officer to visit the Young Muslim Men's Association to ask them not to 'sabotage the Festival nor burn down the Opera House'.[133] With such political uncertainty overshadowing the festival's opening, Gielgud attempted to generate some much-needed publicity by announcing that his Cairo performances would be his last in the role of Prince Hamlet. Delivering an opening speech that was simultaneously transmitted throughout the Middle East by the British Forces Broadcasting Service (BFBS), Dean gave 'a complete circus of thanks' to everyone involved before realising that he 'could see no Egyptian faces in the upraised cocktail glasses'. Members of the Egyptian Government were 'meant to be present alongside accredited representatives of the Allied Powers in Cairo', but the only Egyptian official present was the Minister of Finance who had come to see 'how his money was being spent'.[134] Of the thirty-nine scheduled performances, three would be cancelled due to anti-British student protests and, besides school matinees, Egyptian attendance started low and declined steadily.

Dean's account of arriving at the Opera House only to find it locked due to student demonstrations displays a remarkable determination to put on a show in the midst of major historical events and is littered with the kind of brash confidence and casual racism that Britain's Empire fostered in its administrators. Seeing 'no reason' why the mass demonstrations 'should stop our rehearsals', Dean gathered the company of actors onto the theatre foyer's roof overlooking the Opera Square. Violent assaults on protestors earlier that day had led to an escalation in tensions with shops bearing British signs being selected for 'special treatment'. Undeterred, Dean thought nothing of standing in plain view with his entire cast dressed in regulation ENSA Army uniforms watching as the 'downpour of nationalism began':

> shouting crept nearer and nearer. Presently the tingling of falling glass mingled with it, and the banging of sticks against steel shutters ... in the shimmering noon day heat the figures had a marionettish look, giving to the whole performance an air of unreality, like an extreme long shot in a film.[135]

Dean's narrative fails to mention the political demands of the nationalist students, the recent resignation of the prime minister, or the nationwide insistence that the British leave Egypt. As the National Committee of Workers and Students put it, 21 February was

> [a] day that will make it clear to British imperialism and to the world that the Egyptian people has completed its preparation for active combat until

the nightmare of imperialism that has crushed our hearts for sixty-four years has vanished ... proof of the fact the Egyptian people is resolved not to give up, even for a moment, the evacuation of Egypt and the Sudan ... workers and artisans, students, merchants and officials, our whole people standing solidly together to tear off the infamous badge of humiliation and slavery.[136]

Dean's account merely reduces the students to the role of puppets in a larger political game, while the 'unreality' with which he viewed the protestors' approach, 'like an extended long shot in a film', suggests an inability to accept that Egyptians could be revolting against British rule at all. The next morning Dean recalled his continuing frustration with cancellations, especially when discovering Soliman Naguib 'fearful for the safety of his Opera House' begging the company 'in tears to go away'.[137]

The third Cairo and Alexandria Drama Festival resumed once Ismail Sidky became prime minister, though it did so without government endorsement or Royal consent. The withdrawal of official support for such cultural events loosened the social ties that were a cornerstone of Anglo-Egyptian relations. Since 1938 the Anglo-Egyptian Union, for instance, had quietly evolved into becoming 'an official arm of British cultural policy', funded to 'support teaching' and 'other types of cultural performance and dialogue'. Under the direction of Freya Stark, the Union became a hub for spreading allied propaganda through cultural events that targeted Egyptians who had received their education in British Schools.[138] Stark's organisation, 'the Brotherhood of Egypt', launched a 'whispering campaign' that sought to persuade Anglo-Egyptian Union members that in backing the British they were working 'for what they believed', their own future 'liberty'.[139] Once nationalists subverted the organisation's message and co-opted its methods to their own ends, however, it became increasingly 'difficult to control the conversation in the committees'. In theory Stark assumed that by working in tandem with cultural institutions like the British Council, the Brotherhood of Egypt could continue to influence Egyptian public opinion in Britain's favour once the war was over. In reality such covert methods came back to haunt the British as 'the elites, and colonials that stayed on after the war, were left only to contemplate the hollowness of the British 'gospel of peace".[140] In 1945 there were 750 Egyptian and 500 British members enjoying 'teas, films, concerts, and lectures', but by 1949 Egyptian membership had shown 'solidarity with demonstrators' by withdrawing entirely from the Union leading to its closure.[141]

At the time of Gielgud's visit, Britain faced a broad coalition of students and unionists who received unofficial support from the Soviet Union (following the recent scrapping of a wartime ban on Communist political materials), and the United States (who encouraged young nationalist military officers who were both anti-Communist *and* anti-British).[142] Education had clearly become a key ideological battleground in Egypt's struggle for independence, and Britain's ongoing failure to maintain its historical advantages in this crucial field vexed imperial administrators greatly. Dean's frustration was evident when he compared the relative success of exclusive school matinees with the larger political turmoil gripping the country:

> We were still without open support from the palace, although the Queen Mother and one of her daughters attended a student's matinee of *Hamlet* incognito. A strange sight that was: the rows of nodding [students] ... following the play from printed texts held before them like prayer missals, accompanying the exciting moments with sibilant gusts of pleasure, much pleasanter than their fire-eating oratory in the streets.[143]

Dean's vignette elevates the students' passive appreciation of Shakespeare to a pseudo-spiritual level, transforming 'printed texts' into 'prayer missals' while suggesting that the playwright had the power to provide a 'civilising' antidote to the political upheavals convulsing the country. Edward Said, the pre-eminent anti-imperial academic and writer, was a schoolboy in Cairo at the time. Said's first-hand experience of the British educational system in Egypt, and the visiting Shakespeare tours that supported it, led him to the very different conclusion that such institutions sought primarily to 'discipline colonial subjects and produce collaborating elites'.[144]

Edward Said on Gielgud's *Hamlet*

Britain's reliance on successful trade and a strong military presence was exposed as a dated and neglectful form of colonial rule in the early twentieth century.[145] As early as 1919, Lord Allenby requested permission to inaugurate British cultural programmes in order to assuage the demands of the independence uprising only to be informed that, because of the treasury's stranglehold on cultural funding, 'we shall have to rely on successful administration for propaganda in Egypt'.[146] On becoming High Commissioner of Egypt in 1933, Sir Percy Loraine complained:

> The failure of England to make use of the forty years from 1882 to 1922 to create for herself a strong cultural position in Egypt is one of the most extraordinary phenomena of our illogical imperial story.[147]

The issue was particularly pressing in the field of education. Comparing European colonial educational policies across North Africa, Russell Galt of the American University in Cairo concluded:

> In Egypt England had an Army – the French an idea. England had educational control – France, a clear educational philosophy ... the French pen has proved mightier than the English sword.[148]

The British colony in Egypt had long been reliant on French and Italian institutions for schooling and as a result many students were 'brought up with little knowledge of British history or culture'. Once the tacit assumption that colonial subjects would naturally identify with the British Empire was recognised as fundamentally flawed, English Schools began to be established in Egypt from 1926 onwards following pressure from the British Union.[149]

The British Council responded by establishing a Near East Committee overseen by Lord Lloyd prior to his promotion to Chairman in 1935. In Lloyd's words, the initial aim of English schools was 'not to spread British cultural influence, but to consolidate colonial identity and solidarity':

> The establishment of a sound educational system for British subjects in that area should provide a solid foundation [for] the spread of British Culture amongst the non-British peoples.[150]

Such institutions could help maintain Britain's imperial jurisdiction whilst simultaneously providing Egypt's burgeoning middle classes with access to a Western-style education. In James Whidden's assessment, 'Empire depended on the construction of British cultural pillars' and local Egyptian elites 'were happy to support educational institutions and initiatives that replicated cultural standards and models established in England'.[151] Overall, if Britain could be seen as a known and trusted partner offering 'tactful' and 'disinterested' aid and advice to Egypt as it set out to realise its goals for modernisation, it could hope to secure and maintain considerable influence in future.[152]

The most prominent British school in Egypt was Victoria College which, according to its promotional pamphlet, subscribed to the view that 'the training of character is best achieved by means of a British education'.[153] The school's stated purpose was to 'win respect for English ways of thought and life, and provide the most successful means of strengthening friendly and commercial ties between England, Egypt, and the Near East'.[154] Edward Said was a student in Cairo at the time of Gielgud's tour, first at the British Council affiliated Gezira Preparatory School and later at Victoria College. He recalled that the student body at each institution comprised a diverse range of national groups under the British flag, that the schools taught English history and literature primarily to instil identification with an imaginary 'home' and Empire, but that such schooling could engender a powerful sense of dislocation rather than belonging amongst students.[155]

Said's autobiography *Out of Place* provides a detailed and powerful personal account of attending a matinee performance of Gielgud's *Hamlet*, an insightful narrative that attests to the ways in which visiting Shakespeare productions functioned as an extension of British imperial rule that impacted young student audiences profoundly.[156] For the school child, attending a performance of Gielgud's *Hamlet* entailed careful study and preparation:

> Mother's idea was that she and I should gradually read through the play together. For that purpose, a beautiful one-volume complete Shakespeare was brought down ... its handsome red morocco leather binding and delicate onion-skin paper embodying for me all that was luxurious and exciting in a book.[157]

The opulence and drama of Henry Fuseli's illustrations seemed to come to life on the Opera House stage:

> I was jolted out of my seat by Gielgud's declaiming, 'Angels and ministers of grace defend us' ... the trembling resonance of his voice, the darkened windy stage, the distant shining figure of the ghost, all seemed to have brought to life the Fuseli drawing that I had long studied.[158]

The production raised Said's 'sensuous apprehension to a pitch' he did not think he had 'ever again experienced at quite that intensity'. Despite this aesthetic charge, Said's recollection is marred by equally powerful feelings of shame and alienation. Said had recently been prevented from walking to Gezira Preparatory School by a British stranger in the street who assumed, from Said's ethnicity, that he was trespassing in the European part of the city. The shock of this social stigmatisation was a formative experience for the ten-year-old, making him suddenly and painfully aware that the European sections of Cairene society had the power to simply dismiss him as an intruding 'Arab boy' despite being enrolled in one of the most prominent British-administered schools in Cairo.[159] Said felt

> disheartened by the physical incongruencies between myself and the men, whose green and crimson tights set off fully rounded, perfectly shaped legs, which seemed to mock my spindly, shapeless legs, my awkward carriage, my unskilled movements. Everything about Gielgud and the blond man who played Laertes communicated an ease and confidence of being – they were English heroes after all – that reduced me to inferior status, curtailing my capacities for enjoying the play.[160]

When one of Said's American classmates invited him to meet the great actor at his parents' home a few days later, he recalled that 'it was all I could do to manage a feeble, silent handshake. Gielgud was in a grey suit but said nothing; he pressed my small hand with an Olympian half-smile'.[161]

Said's account stands as a powerful and eloquent testimony of how the Shakespearean theatre functioned as an extension of British colonial rule, exerting a tremendous amount of social and psychological pressure upon its youngest audience members. For Said, the task of learning and appreciating Shakespeare appears quasi-religious in its dutiful intensity, substantiating Dean's account of the reverential atmosphere found at school matinees; while the production's staging echoed the authoritative visual para-texts within the available textbook edition, establishing further links between the brilliance of the visiting British theatre company and a much larger cultural tradition attesting to Shakespeare's genius. Overall, the performance invited young colonial subjects to measure themselves against the best that the dominant foreign culture had to offer, and the ultimate effect of such solemn veneration was less identification than the compounding of a deep sense of exclusion and inferiority. As Said admits, his 'capacities for enjoying the play' were 'curtailed' by the voices, bodies, and movements of the English performers themselves. Ultimately, as a culturally interpolated spectator found lacking due to Cairene society's insistence on his racial inferiority, Said was simultaneously attracted to, and excluded by, the visiting English Shakespeare production.

Increased provision of British schooling in Egypt saw the arrival of a sanctioned and authoritative English Shakespeare that aimed to stand above local adaptations. Although *Hamlet* had been performed by both professional and amateur Egyptian groups during the liberal interwar period, British cultural interventions began to change the way Shakespeare was received in the country in the early post-war era.[162] *Al-Thaqafah*, a popular Egyptian cultural magazine, provided a review of the Gielgud production that lacked critical commentary or local reviews on the production's merits and weaknesses and simply provided a plot outline, comments on characterisation, a gloss on the play's themes, and the suggestion that audiences should read the play (either in English or in a more recent translation made directly from English) if they wanted to properly equip themselves to appreciate the Gielgud Company's staging.[163] Evidently Britain's publishing, theatrical, and educational fields were working in tandem in early post-war Egypt, functioning as a whole to establish an authoritative status for imported English language Shakespeare above that of surviving local claims. Such strategies for post-war colonial education in Egypt mirrored those used in Britain itself before the turn of the century, a time when the specialisation of English Literature meant that 'rather than being a writer to be informally discovered, read and cherished', Shakespeare became 'an author who needed to be studied ... in the company of properly professional commentators and interpreters'.[164] In post-war Egypt then, English touring productions supplemented the professionalisation of Shakespeare studies within formal colonial educational settings. Although Wolfit's populism seemed appropriate for the celebratory atmosphere of 1945, by 1946 coordinated attempts were being made to bring England's national poet firmly back onto the side of foreign and controlling elites.

***

On 21 February 1946, student-led mass protests brought Egypt to a complete standstill. That same day Brian Jones, the British Council's Middle East Regional Officer, sought clarifications from London about the sudden and impressive cultural inroads that America was making throughout the region. Jones had recently learnt that the United States had raised a staggering $15,000,000 for investment in the American University of Beirut, the American University in Cairo, and Robert College of Istanbul, and that this was only their latest expenditure following the opening of a brand-new American Cultural Centre in Cairo.[165] Jones commented dryly that 'it seems that the Americans are to do things in a big way' and, to make matters worse, appeared to be doing so on the back of recent British failures.[166] His report included an editorial piece taken from a local newspaper that claimed:

> The good reputation of these [American] colleges is due to the fact that they exist solely for educational purposes and have never been propaganda spearheads for any political or economic purposes.[167]

Despite taking place during the interregnum period of 1945–47, political events in post-war Egypt took on distinctly Cold War characteristics. Ultimately the process of decolonisation would be determined by Soviet and American gamesmanship within the country, as much as by deteriorating Anglo-Egyptian relations.[168]

Given the dramatic reversals it suffered during the Second World War, Britain lacked the political and economic resources it required to dissuade such powerful international actors from influencing Egypt's internal affairs. The loss of national prestige, the rejection of aspirational values associated with receiving a British education, and the social ostracism of the British community in Cairo and Alexandria, signalled a critical turn in colonial relations.[169] In truth, British rule had been unravelling throughout the war years. As Grafftey-Smith recalled, 'everything possible had [been] done to associate the mass of Egyptians with ourselves in a common interest in British victory' but the 'professional thinking of the military authorities ignored the mass of Egyptians altogether'.[170] Useful imperial fictions carrying over from the nineteenth century, that 'modern European colonisation reactivated civilisation', for instance, served Britain well throughout its long informal occupation but ultimately failed to disguise the resource plunder characteristic of colonial-industrial modernisation. As economic divisions, extreme income disparities, and unjust social stratification fuelled mass political unrest, the frustrated Egyptian middle classes began swelling the ranks of protesters agitating for Britain's complete evacuation. Ultimately, the colonisers were 'unable to control the political and social forces' its own technical, economic, and political project had set in motion, and in February 1946, 'rather than a revolutionary mass overthrowing the 'cosmopolitan' elites, the masses *and* the Egyptian elites' united in abandoning the British.[171]

The early experiments in touring Shakespeare that began on the eve of war had become regular practices by the end of it. Anticipating the important role that cultural diplomacy would come to play in the post-war period, Britain's Information Services (BIS) established the Cultural Relations Department (CRD) as early as 1943. The CRD replaced the small Foreign Office information department that had supported British Council work up to that point and began directly managing the 'political and policy aspects' of the burgeoning field of cultural relations. The Cairo and Alexandria Drama Festivals were early examples of a newly politicised cultural strategy aimed at helping Britain maintain control within increasingly contested colonial spaces, and the CRD would continue to give the British Council more 'political direction' in the face of mounting post-war challenges.[172]

On the day that Brian Jones filed his report for London, Dean and Gielgud stood on the roof of the Cairo Opera house foyer watching the demonstrations taking place in the square below:

> after a while he and I fell into keen discussion about the future of the publicly endowed theatre at home. John declaring that all theatre schemes were the outcome of personal initiative and tended to pass with those who originated them. The incongruity of time and place for such discussion did not occur to us.[173]

Far from being inappropriate, the conversation suggests an intuitive awareness that mass politics posed a direct challenge to the traditional authority enjoyed by the English classical theatre itself. In truth however, the cultural establishment to which Gielgud and Dean belonged would thrive within the new post-war cultural consensus, albeit in a more institutionalised and publicly endowed form. As Tyrone Guthrie noted, it was only under the pressures of total war that the British state began to recognise the importance of supporting its own classical theatre, prompting developments that helped salvage many of England's remaining theatre companies. Emerging opportunities to undertake international tours would have a significant impact, especially on prominent theatre companies like the Old Vic and the Shakespeare Memorial Theatre who would welcome the financial opportunities and international prestige that touring provided.

One of the most enduring Shakespearean myths that was cultivated during the conflict was Alfred Harbage's portrayal of the Elizabethan theatre as a proto-democratic site for the recovery of class cohesion and social harmony. This myth would serve both left and right in the early post-war period, promising more cultural inclusivity for the one whilst providing an emblem for the potential recovery of a lost England for the other.[174] As cultural diplomatic touring entered a golden age in the first decade of the post-war era, taking English Shakespeare to the white-settler Dominions provided an ideal opportunity to test the belief that the playwright had once belonged 'to a genuinely national culture, to a community in which it was possible for the theatre to appeal to the cultivated and the populace at the same time'.[175] Australia, especially, seemed promising cultural territory for reviving the lost 'organic community' glimpsed by some in Shakespeare's works.

CHAPTER 2

Recolonisation in Australia (1948, 1953)
Richard III and *Othello*

In 1948 the American film producer Samuel Goldwyn asked Laurence Olivier, 'Why are you, the greatest actor in the world, taking a touring company to Australia of all places?'[1] In prioritising an Old Vic circuit of *Richard III* to Australia and New Zealand, Olivier sacrificed four film contracts including Hollywood adaptations of *Othello* and *Cyrano de Bergerac* (1897), a British comedy with Vivien Leigh, and a personal project to direct and star in a Shakespeare biopic.[2] For Olivier, despite these creative and commercial losses, the Commonwealth Tour was vital for securing the Old Vic's candidacy to become England's National Theatre. To finance this ambition, Olivier Lyttelton, Lord Esher (a member of the Old Vic Governors and Chairman of the British Council's Drama Advisory Committee), and Tyrone Guthrie (then secretary of the Old Vic Governors) set up a joint committee calculating that the spectacle of the Old Vic actively engaged in an ambitious cultural-diplomatic circuit of the Dominions would loosen the government's purse strings. The plan succeeded and during the tour the British Treasury announced that it was prepared to provide £1,000,000 towards the establishment of a National Theatre.

As well as setting up a new theatre school, Olivier envisioned splitting the Old Vic company into three parts with the first playing London, the second touring England, and the last touring overseas:

> we could have a proper little Empire ... I'll get together a company and I'll go to Australia for the best part of a year ... they will be a decent company by the time I get back. It will be respectable and worthy of being called one of the National Theatre companies.[3]

Olivier led 'from the front' alongside his world-famous wife Vivien Leigh. In Australia the glamorous couple were nicknamed 'God and the Angel' and fully committed themselves to their public roles as cultural ambassadors and 'star' actor-managers. Olivier felt that their global celebrity would help 'leaven the sepulchral destiny inevitably associated with such institutions' and stated that he felt he was embarking on a grand twelve-year plan.[4] Overall, the national and political symbolism of the venture could not have been more loaded. As Garry O'Connor, the author of *Darlings of the Gods*, asks 'what could be more directly in the line of duty of a National Theatre after a world war than to be leading a triumphantly successful tour of the Dominions?'[5] However, despite the Oliviers' personal investment, the Old Vic's institutional ambition, and the resurgent Empire-building spirit of this post-war generation, the project was ultimately a failure. Olivier was to return to London fired from his position at the Old Vic, the lift that the tour was meant to provide the Australian theatre scene failed to materialise, and the establishment of an English National theatre was postponed once more.

Following in the wake of the Old Vic venture, the Shakespeare Memorial Theatre (SMT) embarked on two further tours of Australia under the management of its new artistic director, Anthony Quayle. Like Olivier, Quayle understood that establishing his regional theatre as a viable candidate for England's National Theatre meant demonstrating its global use and potential. Learning from Olivier's fate, Quayle sought to keep his endeavour strictly commercial. His 'innate conservatism and distrust of state aid' led him to look for financial opportunities abroad in order to be free from what he saw as the inevitable 'compromises', 'bureaucracy', and 'outside influences' that came with grants.[6] Despite the commercial nature of the enterprise, Quayle embraced the role of Shakespearean cultural ambassador with as much gusto as Olivier had, enthusiastically aligning his company's circuits of Australia and New Zealand with the broader ideology of New Elizabethanism. By 1951 Quayle was publicly declaring that:

> The fruits of Foreign Policy, to date, are two overseas tours. A start was made when the company visited Australia in the autumn and winter of 1949 ... the tour was financially successful ... it was also theatrically successful ... But the real success and fascination of the adventure ... lay in the linking of the Elizabethan age to our own ... Shakespeare must have often seen the ships and talked with the men who were then seeking *Terra Australis*. And here now was Shakespeare's own company of players, acting his plays to their kinsmen in that very *Terra Australis* – that strange, old-new land beneath the globe.[7]

This chapter explores how the Old Vic's 1948 Commonwealth Tour was shaped and determined by a diplomatic context that demanded the strengthening of 'Greater-British' ties. It reveals the Cold War and imperial concerns that lay behind the undertaking; explains how an enormous appetite for British culture enabled the UK's 'recolonisation' of Australia; details the role that touring Shakespeare played in strengthening Anglo-Australian relations; and shows how the desire to establish an English National Theatre was advantageously coupled to the creation of an Australian one.[8] In its second part, the chapter considers the SMT's 1953 Coronation Tour that served as the cultural advance party for the Royal Dominions Tour of 1954. In light of the resurgent British imperialism evident in Quayle's proclamations quoted above, we consider the ways in which touring Shakespeare was used to pull disparate racial, historical, and political notions together; how the SMT tour synchronised with larger displays of British constitutional power; and how it promoted notions of New Elizabethan idealism.

The Post-war Recolonisation of Australia

The arrival of the British Council in Australia was a preliminary step in the post-war consolidation of Greater Britain, the long union of the United Kingdom to its white-settler Dominions. James Belich states that although Greater Britain possessed 'no formal shape, no federal constitution' it was 'an important economic and cultural reality, a creature of re-colonisation'.[9] Although politically separate entities (Australia was federated in 1901 and enjoyed nominal parity with the UK since the Statute of Westminster Commonwealth Acts of 1931 and 1942) this Anglo-world was strongly unified, both culturally and economically up to and beyond the stresses of the Second World War. Following the rhythm of economic cycles, boom periods (such as the creation of Melbourne within a single generation) witnessed 'explosive colonisation', while bust periods (like the sterling crisis that followed the Second World War) were characterised by recolonisation. Typically, this meant the reintegration of peripheral settler economies, including their cultural and social gravitation, back towards the dominant metropolitan centre.[10]

Anglo-Australian economic ties strengthened considerably in the mid-to-late 1940s, with Australia and New Zealand functioning as primary goods producers within Britain's world system. London's ability to mitigate its economic duress through the bulk buying of Australian food produce well below international market prices clearly illustrates the imperial characteristics of the relationship, and its paramount importance to Britain's post-war recovery. Such economic imbalances were mitigated through the strengthening of social and cultural ties. Fortunately for Britain, despite having briefly turned to the United States for military protection and export markets in 1942, many Australians were more than willing to 'turn back the clock' after 1945. The idea of kinship was a key driver, as the sense of belonging to a shared Greater-British identity was arguably more prevalent at the time than the desire to consolidate a more independent Australian one. An opinion poll taken in late 1947, for instance, found that sixty-five per cent of Australians preferred to keep their British nationality. Such views led Robert Menzies, Australia's longest serving Prime Minister during 1939–41 and 1949–66, to declare that 'the boundaries of Great Britain are not on the Kentish coast but at Cape York and Invercargill'.[11] Though Britain was able to exert powerful social, cultural, and economic influence in post-war Australia, the relationship was far from one of domination and subjugation, however. Australia's parity with Britain since the turn of the century saw it instinctively prioritise its own strategic and national interests whilst simultaneously considering itself an integral part of Greater Britain.

The nature of Anglo-Australian relations in the post-war period supports and illustrates J.M. Lee's argument that Britain turned to cultural diplomacy primarily as an antidote to 'the trauma of losing great power status'.[12] In a return to pre-war commercial practices, Clement Atlee's Foreign Office policy directive 'The Projection of Britain' instructed all Information Departments to spread 'British ideas and British standards' abroad, with special emphasis placed on the 'promotion of British exports, and the explanation of British trade policy'.[13] As rationing continued well into the post-war period, Britain relied heavily on its protected sterling area for key imports, especially foodstuffs. In terms of recolonisation, overt attempts to associate the export of Australian food with the reciprocal importation of British culture can be seen in the British Council's earliest press coverage:

> Britain, in her tremendous struggle to defeat the hideous cults and forces that waged war on humanity, sacrificed her material treasure and, with it, much of her strength in the realm of power politics: but that she has not lost a deeper source of power is seen in the work of the British Council, to whom we owe credit for the visit of the Boyd Neel Orchestra.[14]

The Boyd Neel Orchestra was a London-based string orchestra that toured Europe and the UK extensively before the war; and Canada, Australia, Europe, New Zealand, and the United States immediately after it, performing specially commissioned pieces composed by Vaughan Williams and Benjamin Britten.[15] Although it seems unlikely that touring English orchestras and classical theatre companies could achieve a great deal in terms of alleviating Britain's post-war slump, Philip M. Taylor reminds us that even if propaganda ultimately fails to 'disguise weakness or the realities of decline' it can provide real and immediate benefits for a national economy by providing an 'illusion of strength and confidence' convincing enough to 'aid foreign policy objectives in effective short-term ways'.[16]

Like the Boyd Neel Orchestra, the Old Vic tour of *Richard III* helped circulate shared tastes, values, and ideas throughout the Anglo-world.[17] Olivier and Leigh's international fame greatly appealed to the goodwill of individual Australians and was a crucial factor in the success of the cultural diplomatic mission overall. The Australian actor Michael Blakemore captures the celebrity status that the Oliviers' enjoyed at the time, stating that for him they were:

> stars whose two-dimensional image had been among the first to spread across the world like a virus. In that brief period of 'the talkies', before the theatre had lost its prestige with the general public, before television ... this acting elite held sway in both mediums ... they were famous, rich, lacquered in glamour and magically skilled ... Olivier ... had somehow juggled huge celebrity with artistic achievements of the highest order.[18]

The British Food Appeal relied upon the glamorous couple to personalise its plea for assistance. The petition aimed at persuading Australians to donate 1,000 tonnes of livestock to Britain every week through the voluntary surrender of 6,500,000 meat coupons, the equivalent of one coupon per month and roughly a seventh of every Australian's meat ration. The British Food Appeal clearly needed additional celebrity endorsement because only 250,000 coupons had been donated after its first month in May 1947.[19]

Besides trade, the immediate post-war period saw Cold War antagonisms evolve into conventional military confrontations, causing considerable concern about the deteriorating geopolitical situation and attendant anxieties over lax intelligence security throughout the British Empire. Following the independence and partition of India and Pakistan in 1947, Myanmar (formerly Burma) gained independence and departed the Commonwealth in 1948, whilst Sri Lanka (formerly Ceylon) achieved full independence the same year.[20] As the Cold War became increasingly global in scale, Western fears that communist infiltration would inevitably follow Britain's hasty withdrawal from former imperial territories became acute. Momentous events such as the Berlin Airlift of 1948–49, the establishment of the People's Republic of China in 1949, and the

Korean War between 1950 and 1953, foretold an increasingly volatile future in which the strengthening of Anglo-Dominion ties, and the close alignment of their respective anti-communist policies, seemed imperative for the Commonwealth's survival.

US strategic thinking during the early Cold War was shaped by the 'domino theory', a belief that communist influence could spread rapidly throughout the Asia-Pacific region in the wake of decolonisation. Consequently, Britain's intelligence gathering capabilities within countries considered susceptible to Soviet influence ensured US tolerance towards a policy of deferred independence.[21] Although Britain's continuation as a world power alongside the United States rested upon its effectiveness in the anti-communist struggle, the Soviet penetration of Australia posed a significant threat to the successful establishment of an intelligence sharing alliance throughout the anglophone world (known colloquially as the Five Eyes). Following the discovery of ongoing espionage and high-level intelligence leaks dating as far back as 1943, the Australian Security Intelligence Organisation (ASIO) was established under close British guidance in July 1948.[22] A surprising ambition that demonstrates Britain's desire to rebuild relations with both Dominions and Dependent Colonies upon robust cultural and economic lines, was the creation of an 'Interdepartmental Committee to Advise and Assist the British Council on Relations with External Territories of Australia'. This task force considered the ways in which Australia could project Greater-British culture into non-settler British colonies like Malaysia (then Malaya).[23] Due to rubber and tin's dollar-earning potential, Malaysia remained vital to Britain's post-war economic recovery and the resulting Malayan Emergency (1948–60) saw British, Australian, and other Commonwealth forces deployed to 'protect' plantations and counter a rural anti-imperial uprising led by the Communist-inspired Malayan National Liberation Army.[24]

The consolidation of the anglophone news media provides a final instance of the strategic benefits that came with recolonising Australia and aligning it with Britain's post-war ambitions. A committee set up to advise the British Council on Australia's relations with external territories noted the urgent need to strengthen Anglo-Australasian links through news-sharing companies such as Reuters. In a sense this was the latest stage in a trend towards greater consolidation that had started with Empire Service broadcasts back in 1932. Broadcast media was instrumental in the maintenance of the 'imagined community' of Greater Britain, disseminating identity-forming cultural content that maintained social and economic cohesion throughout the global population under the British flag.[25]

In competitive Cold War terms, the consolidation of the anglophone news media shows that the Greater-British project sought to counter America's wartime encroachment into the Commonwealth's white-settler Dominions. Indeed, the Australian Associated Press and New Zealand Press Association had agreed to join in the ownership of the London-based Reuters News Company in March 1947 through no 'ordinary business deal' but one characterised as having 'ideal' motives 'designed to widen the ownership and strengthen the competitive power of the only British-owned world news service'.[26]

Overall, we might think of the Old Vic and SMT Shakespeare tours as being situated at the bright edge of a much broader spectrum of diplomatic initiatives aimed at establishing closer Anglo-Australian ties in response to Britain's pressing post-war concerns. Reflecting the delicacy of such cultural-diplomatic manoeuvres, the British Council sought to avoid any public objections to their arrival in Australia from the outset. Administrators realised that preparation for the Old Vic tour under a blizzard of advanced publicity could provide ideal cover for the establishment of a network of British Council offices in each Australian state. As one internal report put it, it was hoped that the tour would 'appear to justify' the British Council's 'presence and also help to allay any suspicions that ... [we are] there to push any political propaganda under the guise of cultural activity'.[27] Although the stated policy upon arrival in Australia in 1947 was to 'hasten slowly' and find out in what ways the British Council could 'best fit in with the wishes and interests of Australia', from the outset the tour was freighted with a range of specific schemes aimed at exploiting the commercial opportunities that arose from greater UK–Australian integration.[28] Central to these was Britain's intention of persuading Australia to establish a National Theatre of its own. The overt narrative was that tours of the best English productions would provide a 'decisive stimulus' for transforming Australia's moribund theatre scene. They would not only boost attendance and revenue, but also provide 'a turning point in the policy of [Australia's] theatre management' and undermine 'the opinion that good drama cannot be made to pay here'.[29] Though merely advisory, the sustained enthusiasm with which the Old Vic's 1948 Commonwealth Tour promoted the idea of an Australian National Theatre indicates a deliberate and well-coordinated strategy that would continue, despite stiff local resistance and numerous setbacks, up to and beyond the SMT Coronation tour of 1953.

The bold ambition of the Australian National Theatre scheme can be deduced from administrative reports that considered the project a 'problem' that must be tackled federally. The best solution would be for some commonwealth authority to set up an organisation for starting a National Theatre, the Commonwealth Education Office perhaps .... The Australian treasury is not short of funds. It is willing to expend large amounts on the National University in Canberra. What one hopes is that the Australian authorities will come to realise the appalling condition of Australian theatre and the opportunity they have to remedy it. The national 'theatre' should, of course, not be a building but two or three companies who would train and perform more or less on the lines of the Old Vic .... [Olivier's tour] will ... have a stimulating effect on Australian drama. It will show up the deficiencies and low standards of Australian theatre. But this will merely cause frustration and despondency unless their visit is followed up with positive assistance. One thing that is wanted is plain – skilled and experienced producers willing to undertake a pioneering job inviting the certainty of a good deal of heartbreak.[30]

Clearly it was recognised that with the possibility of generous federal funding, a great opportunity lay ahead for 'pioneering' cultural bodies that could exploit the 'raw materials and enthusiasm' of Australia's fledgling professional theatre community along with its potential audiences and revenues. In theory, the best examples of British theatre would stimulate the kind of demand that only Britain's more 'skilled men of the stage' could then go on to fulfil. Such a scheme could potentially provide enormous financial opportunities for the Old Vic Theatre and the SMT and be integral to their individual campaigns to become England's National Theatre. Beyond the incredible receipts that the initial venture would receive, alternative forms of cultural export from the settler economy were established, such as the recruitment of the best grant-funded dominion talent to the Old Vic's new Theatre School back in London.[31]

The Old Vic's *Richard III* in Europe (1945)

The belief that a Shakespeare tour led by Laurence Olivier would be the best choice for promoting British theatrical culture in Australia had its roots in some of the more successful instances of wartime cultural propaganda. The Old Vic's touring production of *Richard III* had previously been deployed to Western Europe during the final stages of the conflict. This was itself preceded by Olivier's greatest achievement in using Shakespeare for British national mobilisation, his film adaptation of *Henry V* (1944).[32] In receiving universal acclaim from audiences and critics, successfully adapting Shakespeare into a new cinematic idiom, and earning the British film industry international recognition, *Henry V* demonstrated

Shakespeare's propaganda value for the British state.[33] The film synthesised many of the diverse claims made upon English Shakespeare in the mid-twentieth century, pressing them collectively into national service. Utilising a medium that had arguably the greatest impact on the nation's cultural life at the time, *Henry V*'s successful adaptation to the big screen brought Shakespeare to a truly mass audience. Olivier's film elevated Shakespeare above entrenched class divisions by suspending the notion that it was merely worthy and improving, and by showing how theatrical and cinematic art forms could be successfully integrated. As Olivier learnt how to import cinematic techniques back into the theatre itself, the film even satisfied some of the modernist tastes that had typified the pre-war theatre scene. Given the role that *Henry V* played in boosting national morale at a decisive stage in the war, it is unsurprising that the film instilled a belief that Shakespeare could play a leading role in British cultural diplomatic endeavours overseas.[34]

Just prior to the end of the Second World War, Olivier and Ralph Richardson were released from active military service on the grounds of their 'indispensability to the rehabilitation of the Old Vic', an assignment that was considered 'a matter of national importance'.[35] Assisted by generous Arts Council funding, Olivier and Richardson were tasked with helping the Old Vic settle into its temporary London residence at the New Theatre with a triumphant 1944 season that included Henrik Ibsen's *Peer Gynt* (1867), George Bernard Shaw's *Arms and the Man* (1898), and Shakespeare's *Richard III*.[36] Although Tyrone Guthrie and Emlyn Williams' 1937 production had failed to bring *Richard III* into fashion, the war years witnessed a marked revival in the play's reception first through a popular production by Donald Wolfit and then by Olivier himself. Wolfit's inimitable style began a trend that moved away from the 'poetry, passion and pathos' of interwar staging and towards more populist melodrama; an effective approach that Olivier built upon and perfected technically.[37] Concerning his 1942 Strand Theatre production, Wolfit recalled that:

> The more I studied [Richard] the greater grew his resemblance to Hitler .... My wig of long red hair with a cowlick over the forehead gave a most curious resemblance, in an impressionistic way, to the Fuhrer.[38]

What may have appeared embarrassingly stagey to interwar audiences became acceptable within the context of Britain's wartime struggle against Nazism, as 'the spectacle of unexplained evil' no longer seemed 'incredible or shocking'.[39] Olivier's *Richard III* retained the melodramatic essence of

Figure 2.1 Laurence Olivier in *Richard III*. Old Vic Theatre Company's 1948–1949 tour of Australia and New Zealand.
Directed by Laurence Olivier. Photo by John Vickers. © ArenaPAL. Used by permission of University of Bristol Theatre Collection.

Wolfit's interpretation, leaving critics such as Harold Hobson and James Agate astonished by the shameless theatricality that he brought to the part:[40]

> Richard is presented as a monstrous fact, a *fait accompli*, the solitary spectacle of it is a wonder, a nightmare, an extraordinary phenomenon, but without context it is unrelated to anything that might make it more than good theatre.[41]

Although Olivier's Richard appeared to have 'no inwardness', the character spoke directly to audiences' own wartime experience.[42] In breaking the fourth wall convention, 'tipping the wink' directly to playgoers, and gleefully revealing his evil intentions in audience asides before then carrying them out, Olivier's portrayal was pitched at popular conceptions of Hitler's mental traits. As Edward Spears, the leading liaison officer between British and French forces during the war, asserted, Hitler had a tendency to 'announce beforehand with amazing audacity what he intended doing – then did it'.[43] Alan Dent's pen portrait of Olivier's Richard stated that his

> range of expression is extraordinary, even for him, his eyes are Machiavellian, his nose is a sinister sonnet of Baudelaire, and his hands in his scarlet gloves are quick and shrewd. He lives the life of Richard with an almost alarming gusto, and he dies the death horribly – like an earthworm cut in two.[44]

Olivier's bold interpretation spoke powerfully to its own historical moment and had an enormous impact on subsequent staging of the play (Figure 2.1).[45]

On 8 May 1945, eleven days after the European conflict had come to an end, the Old Vic Company took the repertoire of their 1944 season on an ENSA sponsored tour to the continent. Starting in Hamburg, the Victory Tour was greeted by scenes of total devastation in the middle of which stood, miraculously intact, the grand Staatliche Schauspielhaus Theatre. Basil Dean confidently asserted that with troops pouring into the theatre from miles around 'never has classical drama been performed to greater enthusiasm'.[46] The actor Peter Copely stated more pragmatically that 'they packed the theatre every night, and we thought, Ah, this is the young audience of the future. But they had absolutely nothing else to do'.[47] The Victory Tour played Bergen-Belsen concentration camp after the head of the Red Cross medical team stationed there requested a visit. Arriving only two months following the camp's liberation, the company discovered five hundred troops overseeing forty thousand survivors and ten thousand unburied corpses. Sybil Thorndike later recalled that the company's performances there were given in 'a haze, a nasty evil-smelling haze'.[48] Following such apocalyptic scenes, the Victory Tour concluded in conventional triumph with a two-week residency at la Comédie-Française, enjoying the prestige of being the first foreign company to perform in France's National Theatre, and doing so during the 14 July celebrations that soon followed the war's conclusion in Europe.[49]

The Old Vic's Commonwealth Tour of Australia (1948)

Arriving in Australia in March 1948, a few months later than originally scheduled due to Olivier's filming of *Hamlet*, the Old Vic company began their tour of *She Stoops to Conquer* (1773), *Skin of Our Teeth* (1942), and *Richard III* (Figure 2.2).[50] Performances often took place in converted cinemas with demanding acoustics and hundred-degree temperatures. The response from audiences largely made up of people who had rarely or never seen a classical play in performance was overwhelmingly positive, with *Richard III*'s opening night drawing an additional crowd of eight thousand people who gathered simply to watch the audience enter the theatre.[51] Though the tour basked in Australia's enormous appetite for celebrity-led British theatre, Olivier often complained that his diplomatic duties bordered on the absurd. To his embarrassment he twice found himself taking the salute at naval march pasts, while:

> For grand balls and any big occasion, a speech was always expected, but even at small gatherings someone would toast the King in a cup of tea and one was on, replying to the toast apparently on behalf of the King.[52]

While adapting to this quasi-ambassadorial role, Olivier underestimated the hostility that many Australians felt towards Britain following the stresses of the Second World War. General enthusiasm for all things British disguised lingering resentment over the fall of Singapore in 1942 and the subsequent invasion scare that had led to calls for Australian troops fighting in Myanmar and the Middle East to return and defend their homeland. Describing the capitulation of Singapore as the 'greatest disaster to British arms in history', Churchill refused to concede the Australian prime minister's demands and even suggested that the country 'turn to America free of any pangs as to our traditional links with the United Kingdom'.[53] In fact, the head of the British Council's Dominions Section, Sir Angus Gillan, initially conceived the Commonwealth Tour of Australia and New Zealand as a cultural measure for dispelling the anti-British sentiments that persisted well after the war.[54]

Figure 2.2 Laurence Olivier and Vivien Leigh arriving at Mascot Airport, Sydney, 1948.
Photo by Fairfax Media. © Getty Images.

Amusement at Britain's diminished global status surfaced in press conferences where Olivier faced questions along the lines of, 'Now that Britain is finished ...'.[55] Taking the bait at an Empire youth rally in Melbourne Town Hall, Olivier delivered an impromptu lecture 'on the twin themes of monarchy and Empire' before proceeding to strain Anglo-Australian relations further by treating audiences at Anzac Day celebrations to a long and impassioned speech asserting that

> Britain is not finished. She is merely doing what she has done throughout history – starting again ... If one of your most loving relations in the Mother Country thought for a moment that any of your kindness was provoked by pity, they would hope that not another food parcel, and not even a thought or a sigh, would come from Australia.[56]

The speech's radio broadcast was cut half way through, with the English visitors experiencing a much cooler reception for weeks thereafter. Olivier's tour diary ended abruptly around this time as the strain of mixing stardom and diplomacy began to take its toll.

Back in London, the National Theatre Joint-Committee's scheme for ensuring Government backing came to fruition. In April, Olivier penned Lord Esher 'a tiny note of warmth and appreciation from the southern hemisphere about the cool million that has miraculously descended on us all from governmental skies'. Esher replied on 9 July with a surprise 'Memorandum on the Future Administration of the Old Vic' that refused to renew John Burrel, Ralph Richardson, and Olivier's contracts, stating that the company:

> could no longer be run by men, however able, who have other calls upon their time and talent ... I cannot close without sending you the appreciation of the Governors for the great work, not only for England but for the reputation of the Old Vic, that you and the Company have accomplished in the Dominions.[57]

Olivier responded:

> In spite of the delightfully charming tone of your letter ... one was apt to picture oneself as a pioneer disowned by his country in the middle of a very distant campaign ... one has become accustomed to thinking of anything for the Old Vic in terms of continuity.[58]

As Olivier considered his time in Australia as 'doing active service in the colonies' on Britain's behalf, he viewed Lord Esher's actions as a betrayal taken opportunistically while he and Richardson were out of the country and unable to organise a collective response.[59] Tyrone Guthrie was unsympathetic to Olivier and Richardson's plight, however, stating that he 'objected' in principle to the Old Vic being 'run by a pair of actor-manager knights'.[60]

The charge against Olivier was that while he was enjoying the life of a globetrotting celebrity, the Old Vic suffered a poor season in London due to his absence. As news of the Australian tour's feverish reception down under fed back to the austerity-era British press, public disapproval played a significant part. In fact, in financial terms at least, gross takings for the Australia tour were an enormous £226,318. Of this sum the British Council received £42,000 after tax, the Oliviers earned £5,000 as their personal share, and the Old Vic's large cut not only wiped out all of its London losses but returned a healthy profit for the 1948–49 season.[61] While the Old Vic tour depended on Olivier and Leigh's celebrity to ensure its popularity with overseas audiences, the 'cool million' towards the establishment of an English National Theatre would be provisionally associated with the Old Vic trust regardless of whether Olivier was at the helm or not.

Following Esher's 'betrayal', Olivier continued to advise Australians on the establishment of their own National Theatre and was involved in auditioning students for the Old Vic's Theatre School. At the same time, he began recruiting Australian talent for Laurence Olivier Productions (LOP), a hundred-pound limited liability company he formed in 1947 on the advice of his agent Cecil Tennant. On luring Peter Finch, one of Australia's finest actors, into his London company Olivier declared that 'practicability is my god' and 'adaptability the most natural of the human ways of this world'.[62] Barely skipping a beat, Olivier went on to persuade Peter Hiley who oversaw the Old Vic tour's social programme to quit the British Council and become LOP's company secretary. In short, Olivier continued in the same entrepreneurial spirit that characterised the national mission he was initially employed to carry out. Irrespective of whether it was on a state or private level, Britain's theatre establishment seemed determined to repatriate the best that Australia had to offer back to the metropolis while establishing new and lucrative markets for itself in the Dominions.

Although the story of the Old Vic's Commonwealth Tour was one of packed houses, 'tumultuous applause', and enthusiastic audiences travelling 'hundreds of miles' to 'see a single performance', its immediate effect on Australia's cultural landscape seemed negligible and the medium-to-long-term impact difficult to measure.[63] Guthrie followed up the Old Vic's visit with a lecture tour that allowed him to meet various representatives of Australia's theatrical institutions to discuss 'the problems around the setting up of some sort of National Theatre'.[64] In 1949, Guthrie's report was handed over to the British Council for printing:

> A copy was sent to the Prime Minister, with whom he had had discussions in Canberra. This report is already bearing fruit. A few weeks ago, the Prime Minister announced that he was willing to put up £30,000 for a National Theatre scheme if the states would do likewise, making a total of £60,000 in all. The Prime Minister stated that his proposals were on the lines suggested by Tyrone Guthrie. These include a sum of money for scholarships for Australian actors and theatre technicians, etc. to study overseas, and a fund to assist in bringing first-rate productions to Australia.[65]

Guthrie's report played heavily on the cultural cringe, Australia's pervasive and ongoing sense of cultural inferiority to Britain that was socially and historically rooted in the settler-colonial experience.[66] This tactic was evident throughout, with the Old Vic tour purposefully setting out to make Australians 'realise the appalling condition of [their] theatre and the opportunity they have to remedy it'. Australian theatre practitioners and their audiences were repeatedly and pointedly informed that their cultural landscape was 'de-professionalised', 'smacked of the amateur in the worst sense', and set 'appallingly low' standards in comparison to Britain.[67] As a solution to such prescribed inadequacies, Guthrie suggested an import–export scheme with the regular 'import of a planned series of theatrical productions of the very first class' from Britain over the next three years, and the export of Australia's finest talent through scholarship schemes funded by the Federal government to newly established English Theatre schools, such as the Old Vic's, back in London. After winning the approval of 'sophisticated' London audiences the best of these repatriated graduates would be deemed fit and ready to return to Australia and set up their own companies, thus completing the cycle.[68] Guthrie's proposal was the formal articulation of practices already set in motion by the Old Vic during its Commonwealth Tour, and a vision for the perpetual cultural exploitation of Australia. The scheme was short lived, however. After drawing protest and disagreement from Australia's strongest regional theatres in Sydney and Melbourne, it fell victim to national politics and was eventually scrapped following Ben Chifley's electoral defeat to Robert Menzies in December 1949.[69]

The Shakespeare Memorial Theatre and New Elizabethanism

The handsome profits generated by the Old Vic venture persuaded the Australian theatre manager J. C. Williamsons to book the Shakespeare Memorial Theatre for a tour of *Macbeth* and *Much Ado About Nothing* the following year.[70] The circuit failed to drum up anywhere near the same levels of popular and commercial success enjoyed by the Old Vic and came to rely heavily upon the support of Australia's anglophile elites. Quayle's company received a lukewarm reception during their opening week in Melbourne, and though bookings gradually picked up in Sydney once 'the excellence of the Company's performances became generally recognised', the final Brisbane and Adelaide seasons also disappointed expectations.[71] The traditional view that classical theatre was the preserve of a privileged minority returned soon after Leigh and Olivier's departure. As one British Council administrator lamented, 'among the discriminating the tour created a tremendous impression, but the general public is still more responsive to well-known screen names than to well-acted Shakespeare'.[72] Nonetheless, the SMT tour's profits provided a financial boost to Quayle's company and the much-needed foreign revenues it accrued were invested back into the reconstruction of the main stage in Stratford-upon-Avon in time for its Festival of Britain season.[73] Unsurprisingly then, at the end of the initial 1949–1950 venture Quayle envisioned another visit to Australia and New Zealand, which finally came about in 1953.[74]

The spate of ambitious overseas tours that the SMT undertook in the late 1940s and early 1950s helped ensure its economic survival. From the very beginning of his tenure as Artistic Director in 1948, Quayle lobbied for the SMT's ambitions to be as much 'foreign as domestic' despite the Governors' fear that it

> might bring disaster to their good old chug-along theatre … with two directors, I argued, we could form two companies. I would take one of them away for a year and try to earn some much-needed money.[75]

By the early 1950s, long-running debates within the UK Arts Council on whether to 'raise or spread' public access to the classical theatre had ultimately been settled by funding limitations. The organisation's Secretary-General W. E. Williams argued that it was 'better to face the realistic fact that the living theatre of good quality cannot be widely accessible and to concentrate our resources upon establishing a few more shrines like Stratford and the Bristol Old Vic'[76] The SMT had long established itself as a shrine to Shakespeare of course, and with Quayle successfully enticing actors, directors, and designers away from London's West End for a season or two, Stratford-upon-Avon soon found itself in a position to challenge the Old Vic's candidacy for English National Theatre.

When touring the Commonwealth's global 'provinces', the regional theatre used its status as Shakespeare's birthplace to exploit a growing nativist trend that sought to locate an 'authentic' national identity somewhere in 'Deep England'. This mid-century myth was based on an 'image of the national heartland' that was, in the words of Robert Hewison:

> constructed as much out of folk memories, poetry, and cultural associations as actuality ... This imagined pastoral landscape served as contrast to, and compensation for, all the destruction and stress of war. Somewhere among its bright fields and bosky shades nestled the nation's soul.[77]

This notion of a de-centred Britishness, one that could be located on both national and global peripheries, linked the Greater-British project with Quayle's ambitions for his provincial theatre.[78] Quayle confirms in his autobiography that from the outset his tenure was as consciously political as it was creative:

> With one big effort, the SMT – a well-thought of, well respected, but always slightly provincial theatre – could be turned into the foremost English theatre. And if it became such a centre, then it would become the theatrical centre for all English-speaking peoples. It would be an artistic achievement, and a political one – it would help bond the nations together.[79]

Quayle's bold vision and fervent pronouncements subscribed to a broader current of political thought called New Elizabethanism, a species of conservative idealism that accompanied Churchill's return to power in October 1951 on an electoral promise to arrest Britain's 'slide into a shoddy and slushy Socialism' and instigate the 'march to the third British Empire' of increased partnership between the UK and its white-settler Dominions.[80] As a reactionary discursive stance set against the Labour Party's Welfare State programme, New Elizabethanism hailed the anticipated Coronation of Elizabeth II as a sign of Britain's continuing ability to weather the crisis of post-war imperial retreat.[81] In identifying the latent resources needed to reawaken Britain's adventurous spirit within the nascent maritime Empire of the early-modern era, New Elizabethanism inevitably turned to Shakespeare to promote its revisionist history and late-imperialist worldview.[82] Quayle frequently made bold New Elizabethan pronouncements, such as asserting that Shakespeare was 'more than the national poet; he is the very voice of England', a voice that was needed more than ever 'at a time when the country's danger has never been so great'.[83] A rhetorical move often employed by New Elizabethan writers was to associate socialism with nebulous internal and external threats, another was to reactivate residual notions of British race patriotism and white supremacy. On tour, Quayle persistently deployed such tropes in his attempts to build cultural bridges between Stratford-upon-Avon and Australia.

The Shakespeare Memorial Theatre's Coronation Tour of Australia (1953)

The Shakespeare Memorial Theatre's Coronation Tour of Australia and New Zealand ran from February to July 1953, performing *Othello*, *As You Like It*, and *Henry IV (Part I)*.[84] Arriving in Sydney in April, Quayle delivered a speech on ABC (Australian Broadcasting Corporation) radio that 'left listeners ears RINGING'. While promoting the upcoming tour, Quayle made a series of bold political pronouncements. 'We are living today' he declared 'in a second Elizabethan age' and 'our aim should be to make it as famous as the age in which Shakespeare lived'. 'Our western civilization' he warned 'is in mortal danger' 'from threats without' and 'from corrosion within', and 'unless we can achieve brotherhood among the nations within the next generation we are likely to be overwhelmed'.[85] Quayle argued that acts of 'practical internationalism' like Shakespeare tours could provide 'global defence' by bringing 'together people with a common heritage' like those of the 'British Commonwealth of Nations and the USA'. He concluded that the visit by his company clearly demonstrated that 'the world is one' and that 'theatre has a great part to play' in an even greater 'adventure of unification'.[86] For Australian listeners left wondering what any of this had to do with touring productions of early-modern drama, the company manager stepped forward to explain that 'Quayle is a burning idealist' but also 'a practical one' who simply believes 'in the value of Shakespeare [for] knitting together the peoples of the English speaking world'.[87]

The Coronation Tour attempted to rekindle the jubilant scenes that had accompanied the Old Vic venture of 1948 by presenting itself as a cultural advance party for the upcoming Royal Commonwealth Visit of 1954. The circuit was promoted as 'a great adventure' undertaken by 'modern Elizabethans' who might as well take back the title of 'The Queen's Men'. Distancing themselves from the immediate post-war period of austerity and social reforms under the Labour government (an age when 'the arts too often suffered from anaemia, emasculation or a sickly perfumed decadence' according to Quayle) the SMT claimed to be 'perpetuating' England's longer historical drama 'with true Elizabethan vitality'.[88] *The Geelong Advertiser* informed Australians that the 'British people might be on the verge of a new-spirited Elizabethan era':

> Cynics and sceptics may easily decry this hope as idealism or unreal sentiment, while men of imagination see in supersonic flight and nuclear physics the evidence that this is not a mere passing fancy ... there are clear-cut signs of new spirits abroad.[89]

Prospective theatregoers were informed that they were 'fortunate to have the opportunity' to see 'a conception of the New Elizabethan vigour brought' to 'their feet' in the form of 'a group of strolling players from Stratford-Upon-Avon'.[90] The tour's leader was said to embody the 'dynamic epitome of this spirit', while the company's 'presentation of Shakespeare' was said to contain 'a stimulus which can bring to the surface the latent elements of the New Elizabethan spirit which Quayle believes is in every one of British stock':

> History has challenged us with the advent of our new Queen. Posing the question: What can we twentieth century Elizabethans do to take control of our destiny? ... The impulse which drove the old Elizabethans to expand was one of intense nationalism; the impulse we New Elizabethans must achieve is of practical internationalism; ours must not only be an outward voyaging but a drawing and binding together of what is already so far flung.[91]

In aligning his touring endeavour with New Elizabethan idealism, Quayle presented Shakespeare as a galvanising cultural figure capable of drawing together a globally dispersed Greater British community, and thus renewing Britain's fading imperial status. Though Shakespeare's birthday provided an ideal opportunity to commemorate a shared cultural-linguistic heritage, in frequently evoking notions of 'stock', 'spirit', and 'kith and kin', Quayle transformed the event into a celebration of a shared white racial identity. Quayle marked the date with a small unassuming 'ceremony' that he hoped would continue to 'grow out of Australian soil' and with it the not-so-modest 'recognition that the stream of Shakespeare's vast humanity and immeasurable art flows on, clear and strong in another corner of the world where the English tongue is spoken'.[92] In expanding Stratford-upon-Avon's regional claim on Shakespeare out to the global hinterlands of the white-settler colonies, Quayle invited Australians into an exclusive inner-circle where culture, whiteness, and a shared linguistic inheritance intersected.[93] The director's statement that although Shakespeare's 'people are universal' his 'words are the music of his native tongue' and thus the rightful heritage of Australian 'kith and kin', pandered to topical political debates on linguistic inclusion and exclusion; echoing official pronouncements at the heart of the 'White Australia Policy' whose infamous 'catch-all' clause was that 'any person who ... fails to write out at dictation ... a passage of fifty words in length in a European language ... is a prohibited migrant'.[94]

The venture's scale and logistics were impressive, with 'Commander' Quayle's stage managers describing 'Operation Theatre' in terms of a military exercise.[95] Transporting 200 cubic tons of props, costumes, lighting, and scenery was considered akin to 'planning the movement of a miniature army'. With 'scouts in front and skirmishers at the rear' the whole operation moved 'from date to date like a Caterpillar'.[96] 'As soon as one play is finished in one centre everything relating to it is moved on by road and rail to the next, the new play goes in, while the third, which is to follow, is travelling up from the previous city'.[97] Maintaining their jet-set image, the acting company made extensive use of Australia's expanding commercial airline industry, setting a new record by collectively flying 150,000 air miles between all inter-state engagements with Trans-Australia Airlines, and inaugurating a new direct route from Launceston to Adelaide.[98]

Theatregoers attending the tour's opening night at Sydney's Tivoli Theatre seemed preoccupied with the past as they looked towards the future. Observers noted that the glamorous social occasion had an 'Old World' feel and 'World War I glitter about it'.[99] On the evening of the Coronation itself, a distinguished crowd turned out to see *Othello*, dressed 'for royalty' in 'top hats, opera cloaks, and ermine'.[100] The spectacle synchronised with countless ritual displays of British constitutional power enacted across the globe that day, with the SMT performing its duty in establishing a sense of 'stability, consensus and confidence' at the dawn of a new Commonwealth era. Shakespeare, like the living symbolism of monarchy itself, assured Australians of the Commonwealth's historical continuity and, after the curtain went down, the distinguished audience were invited onto the stage itself to raise their glasses in a toast to the dawning of the new Elizabethan age.[101]

The Shakespeare Memorial Theatre's *Othello* (1953)

Othello enjoyed a rapturous reception on its opening night in Sydney where 'only six curtain calls and two brief speeches would satisfy' the audience. The cast were lauded for their 'excellent teamwork, timing and precision' while the production's 'grouping and dynamic action' was said to have 'startling power'.[102] Designed by Tanya Moiseiwitsch, the production's fixed set and clever use of lighting provided an 'amazing continuity' that eliminated the need for curtain drops by dissolving 'one scene into another as smoothly' as in 'a film'.[103] Though the staging enabled a 'beautifully controlled unwinding of the tragedy' most critics were disappointed by Quayle's 'gentle' interpretation of the title role, arguing that it lacked the 'touch of fervour' needed to make 'the finale credible'.[104] The feisty spirit that Barbara Jefford's displayed in her opening scenes as Desdemona was quickly dampened to complement Quayle's gentle interpretation and, though there were 'flashes of genuine feeling' between the couple, neither player seemed to carry 'the deep conviction so essential to the growth of the tragedy'.[105] The general consensus was that the production was simply 'not real enough; it does not achieve pathos and move us to pity, and it is not tragedy, therefore'.[106] Quayle's performance followed in the English 'heroic' tradition established by Geoffrey Tearle, and many critics were disappointed at his apparent unwillingness to deliver the passion and bombast they expected from the role. Quayle's inability to portray Othello satisfactorily, a problem shared by many English actors of his generation, was used to promote idealised notions of whiteness.[107] His 'failure' was rationalised with the argument that Othello was 'an emotional curiosity' and so 'temperamentally outside an Englishman's range'. It was noted that 'other than Kean', 'few English actors appear to have made much of a fist of the part' and that both Gielgud and Olivier had avoided the role to date. Clearly more at ease with the soldierly elements of the first half than with 'the frenzied African ritualism of a man caught up in a tempest of torment and purification' in the second, critics reasoned that Quayle was 'too coolly thoughtful, too intellectual ... to bring the simple-minded, hot-blooded Moor fully to life'.[108]

The 'one vivid and memorable performance' in the production that had 'much of the stuff of greatness in it' was Leo McKern's Iago.[109] *The Sun* was quick to frame the returning Australian actor's success in terms of national prestige, assuring its readers that if they were ever 'proud of the accomplishments' of their fellow Australians they would be 'devoted to' McKern's 'brilliant, masterly portrayal of the cunning Iago'. Hailed as a performance that brought one of Shakespeare's most outrageous villains down to earth and fully to life, McKern's performance promised to win local audiences over 'to the exclusion of all else'.[110] The Australian actor's Iago was

> no rapier-witted mastermind, no rival to Milton's Satan or Goethe's Mephistopheles. Here is simply a coarse, quick, and arrogant soldier, a smart Alick as full of regard for his own cleverness as an intriguer as he is full of destructive spite.[111]

In a phrase that would attach itself to later interpretations, McKern's Iago was described as an 'NCO type', 'imaginative only in the mechanics of the villainy he was prepared to work on more sensitive people to further his own ambitions', a figure whose 'soldierly bluffness' made it 'far more credible that his fellows should be taken in by 'honest Iago'.[112]

McKern was an inventive and intuitive actor who used everyday observations and naturalistic techniques to bring his characterisations fully to life. His stated intension with Iago was to make the character 'an acceptable reality. He is every bit as real to me as say, the Moors murderers, who are real enough; of course, he is, like them, a monster, but a real monster and not a cardboard character in a melodrama'.[113] McKern had seen other actors fall into the trap of persuading the audience that Iago 'is a scoundrel':

> It seems plain to me that the man *is* a villain, so obviously from the first scene of the play, one would simply waste time and energy demonstrating it; and as he is a successful villain, it seemed equally plain that this fact is completely hidden from every other character in the play. If it is not, Othello becomes an idiot.[114]

McKern found justification for his interpretation in the ways in which Iago's name is repeatedly qualified with the sobriquets 'good' and 'honest', and used the Stanislavskian technique of defining the character's 'superobjective' in as few words as possible, settling on the formulation 'jealousy in excelsis':[115]

> The play is a study in jealousy, but that of Iago's leaves Othello's standing; the latter's centres on his wife and self-regard, Iago's encompasses everything and everybody. I believe he is half-crazed with its torments at the beginning of the play and supplemented with the ecstasy rising from the power he attains over the giant among men, Othello, it drives him on an unstoppable course of murderous paranoia and destruction.[116]

Performance reviews reveal how, in eschewing the usual 'sneering interpretation of the role', McKern struck

> a more subtle note with a dry cynicism, which was perfectly clear and much more convincing. He reserved the violent gesture for his private explosions of hate ... the clipped, derisive chuckles, the smothered gibes, the dangerous protestations of friendship loaded with the seeds of jealousy, then the sudden switch to hearty, backslapping camaraderie – all were given with the utmost conviction.[117]

McKern's villain was 'a first-rate entertainer', 'so likeable' in fact that Australian audiences found their 'sympathies aligning themselves a little with Iago', with *The Sun* enthusing 'what an asset to Australian politics that bloke Iago would have been'.[118]

Ultimately McKern would pay a high price for his ability to 'distort the audience's sensibilities' so effectively.[119] 'The taste of success of my interpretation, accepted in rehearsal and on the tour, was ... transformed into ashes in the mouth when I was told that the part was to be re-cast because my performance "unbalanced the play"'.[120] Having witnessed the applause and standing ovations that McKern received for his performance night after night on tour, the returning company were 'bewildered' by the actor's sudden replacement. Many felt he had delivered the definitive modern Iago and though never reviewed in England it was long known in acting circles that McKern's ill-fated Iago was possibly 'the best of his generation'.[121]

A possible reason for McKern's sudden replacement was that his rapid promotion to third billing within one of the most prestigious theatre companies in England was prompted by the company's desire to create the right optics for touring. McKern's inclusion provided tangible evidence of a meritocratic Commonwealth theatre industry, living proof that talented Australian actors could strike out for the metropolis confident in the hope of quickly making it into the top ranks. It was only when the tour concluded that McKern was, in the words of his biographer, 'shown his place' and 'taught the realities of the British theatre's hierarchy'.[122] That said, the charge of 'unbalancing the play' cannot be entirely dismissed. Critics often noted marked stylistic differences between the two leads. Whilst Quayle never seemed to 'let go his hold on the iambics, in an endeavour, presumably, to preserve the swell and cadence of the period', 'riding the rhetoric and singing his sentences' as a sort of recital, McKern employed a more contemporary 'ease and freely flowing modulation'.[123] The villain's lines were delivered with 'a natural ruggedness proper to his nature' and yet 'their power and poetry' were never 'obscured'. One Melbourne critic enthused that McKern's 'put money in thy purse' speech was 'a masterpiece that one desires to hear again and again. His tricks of manner, his bits of business have a touch and spontaneity that fascinate not only the eye but also the ear, as when, he whistles'.[124] Such naturalistic touches gave McKern total 'mastery' over his many asides which he skilfully deployed to win audiences over. Though they 'never once' intruded upon the stage action, they were often delivered with devastating effect.[125]

A final explanation could be that Quayle's production exposed the limited appeal of New Elizabethan idealism outside of Britain itself. Quayle's interpretation of the leading role was not the only aspect of the touring production that was heavily indebted to Geoffrey Tearle's romantic *Othello* of 1949. In that production, Quayle played Iago in a staging that brought the 'archaic Edwardian romanticism' of Tearle's lead into sharp contrast with the cynical, war-weary, 'Liverpudlian spiv' of Quayle's villain. According to Philip Kolin, the stylistic tension between the lead actors succeeded in evoking 'two authentic temperaments in an historical confrontation relevant to the condition of the audience at the time'.[126] In evoking 'the last vestiges of the prelapsarian world' collapsing in the face of 'modern expediency' Tearle's Othello moved post-war English audiences deeply, presenting them with 'an archetype of heroic decline' in a show that 'rang the changes' 'for a mythic England'.[127] It is possible, then, that Quayle's touring production tried but failed to transplant similar laments over the decline of the English ruling classes to Australian soil.[128] Off stage, Quayle's New Elizabethan company portrayed themselves as the embodiment of a vital and dynamic spirit keenly embracing the challenges of the post-war era, while on-stage its production of *Othello* betrayed a more romantic and elegiac undercurrent of national loss and decline that found little sympathy with the audiences of the young Republic.

Making Shakespeare Popular

Arriving fresh from England to manage the University of Melbourne's Union Theatre, John Sumner cheerfully informed ABC's listeners that their country had 'wide roads in need of repair' and 'narrow minds that need reform'.[129] The Australian media was surprisingly tolerant towards, and interested in, the uninformed views of prominent English visitors in the early 1950s. *The Daily Telegraph*, for example, enthused that 'although he has been so short a time in Australia', Quayle possessed remarkable 'insights into the Australian scene, and into the Australian character'. In the opening weeks of the tour, the press was more than happy to hear Quayle expound his personal theories 'about the rights and wrongs of the White Australia policy, Australia's economic future, and the vagaries of the Australian psyche'.[130] Quayle's views fed an ongoing public debate about whether Australia and Britain enjoyed a shared heritage that needed defending against America's growing cultural influence. Though he confessed to 'hate the word "cultural"', Quayle could not 'think of another' to capture his vision of how shared investment in the English classical theatre could shape the post-war Anglo-world for the better. The 'ultimate evolution' he explained, was to have an Australian National theatre made up of 'Australians writing Australian plays for Australian audiences'. For the time being, however, the country had to accept its low cultural ranking because the main 'theatrical bloodstream' was '100 per cent American, dealing with American problems'.[131] Overall, Quayle proposed that fostering closer cultural ties with Britain would help the Dominion establish a more authentic national voice, and a more resilient national identity, capable of resisting the influence of America's cultural hegemony.

Like Olivier before him, Quayle aligned the economic interests of his own theatrical venture with his broader promotion of Greater-British ideals, using the manufactured crisis of Australia's floundering cultural scene to launch a series of increasingly provocative appeals. The director stooped to asserting that it was 'pathetic' that Sydney, 'the second white city of the British Commonwealth, should have only three professional theatres', before suggesting that the establishment of a 'national Australian theatre' would provide demonstrable proof that Australia possessed 'the same spirit of artistic adventure that fired the first Elizabethans'.[132] In terms of state funding, Quayle claimed never to be in any doubt that the 'large amount of money' required 'would be available' asking people to focus instead on 'the individual, not the blue-print'. Australian's were reminded that uniquely talented individuals were the 'key to all theatrical success' and that 'in England, the most successful commercial management is also the management with the highest artistic standards'.[133] He was proud that, financially speaking, his endeavour stood on its own two feet and broadly advertised the fact that the SMT had taken the risk of selling stock in order to make the initial investment of £160,000 required to undertake its current touring venture. Though presented as a testament to Quayle's personal belief in Australia's cultural potential, it is worth noting that this was not such an outlandish commercial gamble at the time because successful visiting artists could expect to make 'astronomical sums of money in the large play-houses'.[134]

Despite strenuous efforts, Quayle failed to square the culturally improving variant of Shakespeare he promoted in the press with the popular and highly entertaining version of the playwright needed to secure healthy box-office receipts. In short, the gamble of surviving in the commercial marketplace long enough to secure future state subsidy via the establishment of an Australian National Theatre proved risky. Despite being managed by one of the country's leading impresarios with a lease on several commercial theatres, Quayle's 1953 venture ultimately failed to yield its hoped-for riches. Although the tour managed to dig itself out of the red, the final figure was uncomfortably close thanks to sluggish ticket sales throughout. As the tour progressed and the commercial pressures mounted, Quayle's personal investment in Australia's cultural landscape came across as increasingly messianic and detached from realities on the ground. The actor-manager inadvertently 'drew loud laughter' from a student audience at the University St. Lucia, for instance, when he attempted to rouse their spirits with the encouraging news that 'the Australian theatre was now in the position of the American theatre, 80 years ago'.[135]

The idea of social uplift was part and parcel of the scheme to foster a National Theatre upon Australians; a cornerstone of the paternalistic cultural relationship that the 'mother country' sought to exploit. In a Perth Rotary Club talk entitled 'Listening to Shakespeare in the Theatre' the head of the British Council advised Australians to 'learn' how to better appreciate the cultural gifts being offered to them. Audiences were cautioned that they should 'bring to the theatre a ready sympathy if the actors were to give of their best, and the audience was to receive the richness of their message', and Australians were encouraged to remember the maxim 'Gently to hear, kindly to judge' if they wanted to 'more readily get in touch with one of the greatest and most generous minds of all time'.[136] The sentiment that Shakespeare was too delicate and refined a gift for most Australians to appreciate may have gone down well at the Perth Rotary Club: the wider public that the SMT failed to reach in 1949, however, required more than patronising overtures to entice them into the theatre.

On the surface, things looked good for loyalists who wanted to see the strengthening of Anglo-Australian ties through a shared classical heritage. Shakespeare book sales went up during the tour, with journalists noting that 'not for a long-time' were 'so many Pocket Editions being pursued and studied'.[137] Concerned elites were assured that 'the Bard of Avon can R.I.P. in the knowledge that the warning "Brush up your Shakespeare" is being taken seriously by the citizenry' of Australia. The more popular press added, however, that these encouraging signs had as much to do with the popular appeal of recent Hollywood film adaptations as with the English visitors themselves. Sydney's *Sunday Sun* noted that 'apart from their snob audience appeal' the Stratford Players' success was due primarily to 'the box-office pull' of the film adaptations of *Julius Caesar* and *Macbeth* then playing in cinemas.[138]

The company worked hard to dispel the pervasive sense that the classical theatre was only of interest to the middle classes. One strategy was to hold regular auditions for local talent. Six male actors were needed for the entire length of the tour, as well as two boy actors for each region.[139] In an awkward attempt to align the English theatre industry with the kind of martial masculinity commonly depicted in film representations of Empire at the time, the advertisement stressed that only 'robust, athletic men' were needed for the parts because 'in each scene they have to catch Anthony Quayle as Falstaff as he falls off a table ... Quayle weighs 14 stone – and they would not like it if they dropped him. So long-haired types will not do – not even if they can recite Shakespeare act by act'.[140] Another approach was to hold professional auditions 'free of charge' as a 'service to the community for generating a love of the theatre'.[141] The Quayles' commercial instincts were as astute as Olivier's had been five years previously. While Anthony Quayle opened the festival of Australian plays at the Melbourne Little Theatre, Dorothy Quayle attended 'innumerable performances at little theatres in all cities' 'with an eye' open for 'signs of genuine talent'.[142] Australia's Little Theatre scene mounted plays by modern playwrights 'such as Eliot, Fry, Rattigan, Morgan and Ustinov' and classics 'such as Shaw and Sheridan' in productions that reached standards that were 'very often higher than that in the professional theatre'.[143] Consequently, Dorothy Quayle invited Frank Waters to join the SMT after seeing him in Arthur Miller's *Death of a Salesman* (1949) at the Independent Theatre in North Sydney.[144]

As we saw with McKern, the tour's aim of strengthening cultural links between Britain, Australia, and New Zealand, 'influenced' the 'selection of cast' from the outset.[145] The 'Grand Adventure's' incorporation of dominion talent was hailed as proof that 'on the stage' Shakespeare 'is no antique, no academic study – but exciting twentieth-century stuff'.[146] A great deal was made of the 'returning' Australian and New Zealand talents in the company's midst.[147] Keith Michel (who played Cassio, Orlando, and Hotspur) had been teaching in Adelaide High School when he won one of two scholarships to attend the Old Vic drama school during Olivier's visit in 1948, and was subsequently hailed as 'a living example' for aspiring local actors 'that it pays to follow your heart'.[148] Michel informed the Players and Playgoers Association that the establishment of an Australian National Theatre was a necessary step, and that:

> unless Australia soon begins to cultivate the refinements of a great country, it will become just a place in which to grow wheat and wool, and sleep and eat ... Australia is old enough to start having a few thoughts of its own, and to be listened to by older countries.[149]

Still, the notion that Australians were disqualified from a stage career simply on the grounds of their own national accent was prevalent at the time. One article profiling the dominion talent in the company featured a cartoon that ran with the caption, 'Though all the parts will be played by Australians, there will be English translations for the benefit of home listeners to the BBC'. In the early 1950s, Australian accents were rarely heard on the ABC's airwaves, a suppression of local identity that led the linguist A. G. Mitchell to assert that Australia had become 'the only Anglo-Saxon community which was ashamed of having its own way of pronouncing the English language'.[150] Tackling the thorny issue, the English actor

Raymond Westwell equivocated that although 'the Australian accent is a bit of a handicap – any accent is. The same thing is true of Scots or Irish accents'.[151] Having made his own way to London and worked his way up through the class-bound hierarchy of the English theatre, McKern stated more plainly that 'young artists seeking acting work in England do not stand a chance unless they get rid of their Australian accent'.[152]

An unforeseen problem was that *Othello* would have to rely exclusively on adult audiences, a realisation that came after its first matinee performance in New Zealand sent a hall of schoolchildren into fits of restless agitation. Additional commercial pressure came from having to compete with a touring American production of *South Pacific* (1949). In response to both the tour manager, John Scarlett, attempted to market *Othello* as topical and provocative, asking readers to consider 'What is it as a play?':

> Pure sex. It is a story of sexual jealousy, lust, envy, and evil. If it was a modern Hollywood film it would be double A graded, that is if it ever passed the censor at all. It would certainly be banned in the southern States of the US, in Africa and throughout many of the Middle and Far East countries because of the colour question.[153]

Though such sensationalism was cooked up halfway through the tour in response to poor ticket sales, it chimed with the prominent strain of anti-intellectualism that ran through New Elizabethanism:

> Shakespeare knew what sort of entertainment his audiences like and served it up to them. And audiences today still like their meat strong . . . . In Perth, Shakespeare next week will be in his proper place – the stage . . . not in musty libraries or school textbooks'.[154]

The SMT launched a sustained and coordinated attack on Shakespeare's traditional role in state education in an all-out effort to entice disenchanted adult audiences back into the theatre and potential mature students back into the classroom. Mrs Hersey Caroline Flower, the wife of the Governor of the SMT Sir Fordham Flower, flew out to join the tour in Melbourne where she addressed students at the city's Teaching College with the headline-grabbing message, 'if I had my way I'd ban Shakespeare from schools'.[155] Flower made her argument on the grounds that 'it is such a disaster that someone discovered he is "literature"' and then 'made a special hobby of dividing Shakespeare audiences into two categories', a bookish minority of devoted bores for whom the plays were never intended, and a majority of decent honest folk (for whom he presumably wrote) who had been deceived into thinking him intellectually distant and irrelevant to their lives.[156] As a member of the prominent political family of Balfour, and as a niece of former Prime Minister Lord Balfour, Flower's public addresses were covered in great detail in the Australian press. Strategies aimed at enticing adults into sampling classical theatre for the first time involved reassuring them that 'terrible' 'school methods' such as 'the parsing and analysing' of works were much better suited 'for grown men and women' because 'Shakespeare was extremely uninhibited and his plays are filled with episodes of murder, violence and lust that should not be thrust down the gullets of schoolchildren'.[157]

Despite their high-profile promotional campaign, the company continued to face row upon row of empty seats. What began as a bold declaration of faith in Australia's cultural aspiration ended as a direct plea for public help and support. Once appeals to practical internationalism, British race patriotism, and national-cultural uplift failed to draw the seemingly obstinate Australian public into the classical theatre, the company's press statements soured into accusing the host nation of cultural apathy and backwardness. As the tour lengthened, Quayle's company found itself, like Olivier's before it, caught in a Faustian pact with a bored and capricious press industry that turned happily to gossip, scandal, and sensation once the first night reviews were in. Things began to unravel when the actor Charmaine Eyre informed the Melbourne University Lecture Club that Australian playgoers, unlike those in England, 'go to the theatre to criticise rather than enjoy a performance'.[158] For good measure, Perth's *Daily News* reported another actor stating that audiences 'differed enormously between the different states' and that although 'some Australian audiences were among the most responsive' 'some were quite the "deadest"'.[159]

In truth the tour failed to secure broader public support because of basic commercial errors. No amount of bloviating could entice audiences unaccustomed to attending the Shakespearean theatre to hand over hard-earned cash when ticket prices were over-inflated to compensate for the substantial overheads of touring. Potential theatregoers, put off by high prices for bad seats that were difficult to come by, voiced their frustrations and concerns in a press debate that centred on issues of access and ticket pricing. Regular audiences who were more likely to be invested in British notions of high culture declared themselves 'shocked to see empty seats' and chided their countrymen for failing to attend.[160] They reminded readers that Shakespeare is 'the most superb theatrical entertainer' and that the Stratford Company were not just some 'group of pious homage-mongering players'.[161] As the entire SMT organisation 'was doubled up and an American tour postponed' so they could make it all the way to

Perth, it was very 'hard to understand how the theatre can be booked out for vaudeville or variety and a company of such perfection as this plays to such poor houses'.[162]

Shaming less-wealthy members of the community smacked of classism and unthinking privilege, however, exposing entrenched issues around cultural exclusion that reflected deeper social divisions within Australian society. The press received plenty of letters from indignant would-be theatregoers in response. One simply replied, 'I do not need Shakespeare to be recommended, I just want to go – but how?' Another explained that 'it was almost impossible for a man, working from 8 to 6 for little more than the basic wage' to afford tickets. When Quayle made the headlines with the dismissive comment that Australians were 'too lazy to go to a show until it was recommended', one reader countered that 'I have felt far too lazy to put my hand in my pocket and drag out 21/ for the dress circle or stalls, or 15/ for secondary seats', 'far too lazy to strain my ears from the back or from the upper circle for 8/'.[163] Seats that called 'for so much pillar-dodging and corner craning' became 'thoroughly aggravating', but decent rows were block-booked before ticket offices opened to the general public.[164] As a consequence, curious first-timers found themselves being charged 'top prices for poor seats at the sides of the circle'.[165] Another correspondent who did not 'object to paying the top price', did, however, 'expect a good seat sometimes'.[166] The fact that social inequalities manifested themselves in ways that went way beyond ticket pricing was evident in letters asking fellow Australians to understand that:

> If you have struggled, standing for hours with an aching back and two restless children at your side, it is very bitter to find that someone who knows someone who has influence has been able to get the best seats without lifting a hand. Is it fair?[167]

It was widely known that Britain's theatre scene enabled 'the less wealthy sections of the community' to see top classical theatre, but that Australia's did not. It was very late in the tour when Quayle realised that for most Australian 'to get a seat is like asking for a bar of gold'.[168] Quayle's productions could be seen in Stratford-upon-Avon 'for 2/6 on the gallery and 6/ in the back row of the stalls' but in Perth people were being asked to pay 'six shillings or eight shillings in the gallery' 'for an uncomfortable seat' and 'the probability that part of the stage will be obscured from view'.[169] The tour leader wished it had been possible to charge the same prices for seats in Australia as in Stratford-upon-Avon but explained that 'meeting the additional cost' of touring made it impossible.

The Old Vic was hailed as the exact kind of model that Australia needed in order to attract 'the young impecunious male with female partner, or the mother anxious to send her two or three children, or youth clubs etc., to take advantage of the opportunity of seeing "the best plays in the world"'.[170] Though Quayle agreed, he added that the comparison with the Old Vic was unfair as the SMT 'receives no grant or subsidy of any kind'.[171]

McKern recalled that the tour had been a 'very onerous' one for Quayle.[172] Besides witnessing the standing ovations that McKern's 'smart-Alec' Iago received every night, Quayle's faith in the commercial market and his resistance to government grants and subsidies meant that his bold classical experiment faced insurmountable financial obstacles. Disappointed but unbowed, Quayle left Australia with the parting shot that 'preferential booking by mail was the greatest factor militating against the success of Australia theatre' and stated that he could see 'no good coming' from such an 'appalling and inequitable' system.[173] The *Western Australian* wrapped up Quayle's public grudge that Australian audiences had been 'disappointing in size' and 'disappointingly cool in their response' by recalling that Allan Wilkie had made the exact same complaints when touring Australia back in 1929.[174] The journalist pondered 'why should it be so?':

> Are West Australians temperamentally different from, more cold than, Sydney-siders? Are Queenslanders a more intellectual lot than Victorians or West Australians better at understanding Shakespeare? Was the company not good enough?[175]

***

In the opening chapter, we saw that the earliest British Shakespeare tours failed to have a significant diplomatic impact in fascist Europe or achieve the objective of securing Britain's informal rule in post-war Egypt. This second chapter has shown some of the ways in which Shakespeare tours could serve Britain's diplomatic interests very well indeed. Cultural soft power helped Britain successfully pursue a variety of national policies in post-war Australia with Shakespeare playing an especially important role in strengthening the sense of a Greater-British identity that underpinned increased trade and security links. Of particular importance was the intelligence network that Britain secured throughout the Dominions at this time. Establishing the Five Eyes was instrumental in demonstrating the Commonwealth's use and relevance to America in the early Cold War, a development which persuaded the US to tolerate the continuation of British imperial rule in Southeast Asia and the African continent throughout much of the 1950s.

Touring allowed the UK theatre industry to prolong the Shakespeare boom of the post-war period by projecting it overseas, providing the English classical repertory theatre with a golden opportunity to profit from England's supposed cultural authority within the broader Commonwealth. With the invaluable assistance of 'star' actors, the Old Vic tour achieved a level of mass appeal in Australia that seems remarkable in retrospect and is perhaps best understood as an expression of transnational relief and celebration following the stresses of the Second World War. 'Actor-manager knights' like Laurence Olivier and Anthony Quayle became the centre of an expanding state–private network that fused cultural diplomacy with commercial ambition.[176] Quayle's willingness to align the SMT with the reactionary politics of New Elizabethanism saw English Shakespeare recruited into the promotion of British race patriotism within the white-settler Commonwealth.[177] From a diplomatic perspective, the failure to establish an Australian National Theatre under the guidance of British cultural 'experts' did not matter a great deal because the drive to foster a closer cultural identity that was so integral to the Greater British era was tactical, and would be quietly forgotten once Britain joined the European Economic Community (EEC) in 1973.[178]

The era of recolonisation came to an end with the closure of the British Council's Sydney Office in March 1954, a move that came about when the Secretary of State for the Commonwealth and Chairman of the Committee on Civil Expenditure ran a campaign to reduce government spending on Information Services from £10,200,000 to £9,500,000. During the investigative process that led to the Drogheda Report, Lord Swinton arbitrarily wound down similar British Council operations in New Zealand and Sri Lanka.[179] By this stage, loyalist elements in Australia were more enthusiastic about seeing the continuation of Greater British cultural links than the British were themselves. Amidst this growing concern, an informal consultation of Australian opinion for 'any wish to establish some form of Australian-UK machinery to take the place of direct British Council representation' drew a very negative response. This led the British administration to privately conclude that it could 'neither formalise nor exploit' the 'affection for the mother Country' that 'remains extremely powerful ... almost against reason' in Australian public opinion. 'The Australian is proudly Australian yet equally proudly British and therefore, we at the British Council, have to think of ourselves as UK rather than British'.[180]

There was plenty of local dismay over the British Council's abrupt withdrawal from Australia.[181] Editorial pieces frequently responded to the large volume of readers' letters they received giving voice to a real sense of injury. Once again London appeared indifferent towards the cultural life of its Dominions, returning to what Lloyd had characterised as the Empire's disregard for anything besides sport, trade, and commerce. In the seven years since its arrival, those Australians who had the closest class affinities and identity ties to the British Council's ideals of Britishness felt that the organisation had become 'an inspiration to us all' and compared its sudden departure with the loss 'of an old and valued friend' to whom they had 'continually turned for advice and help'.[182] One 'letter to the editor' mourned that 'the touch of the official hand is all too inclined to wither the buds of creative enterprise' and that 'it is not information we require from Britain – the Press already provides this – but inspiration'.[183]

Ultimately, the English visitors failed to persuade Australia to establish a National Theatre of its own under their 'expert' guidance, though as a 'continuing memorial' to the Royal visit of 1954 they put in place the Australian Elizabethan Theatre Trust Fund (AETTF). Upon arrival in Australia in January 1955, Hugh Hunt (a member of the DAC whose brother Colonel John Hunt accompanied Hillary's ascent of Everest) set about 'forming a truly national company' that competed against Australia's own candidate national companies based in Victoria and New South Wales.[184] Learning from Quayle's hard-won experience, the AETTF attempted to replicate the Old Vic model of enabling 'the less wealthy sections of the community' to access well-produced classical drama by securing a lease on the Majestic Theatre 'in an unfashionable district' that required the 'fervour and passion of an Old Vic audience' to succeed.[185] It didn't, though the project's unwelcome intervention and eventual failure arguably led to the collapse of the Victoria and New South Wales companies. By 1956 the pro-British ardour of the immediate post-war years had cooled considerably, and further opposition to the AETTF came with the realisation that like Hunt himself, the Trust's four leading associates (Elsie Beyer, John Sumner, James Mills, and Robert Quentin) were all English and all previous Old Vic employees.[186]

Thanks in part to the Old Vic and Shakespeare Memorial Theatre tours, there were clear signs of growing interest in Shakespeare when staged by Australians themselves, and especially when performed in local accents. John Alden's Australian Shakespeare Company, for instance, undertook an enormous national tour between 1951 and 1952. Following considerable success in Sydney and Melbourne, the company moved to Perth where it 'broke all records for a Shakespearian season in Western Australia' before going on to perform in Brisbane, Launceston, Hobart, and Canberra.[187] Despite establishing a popular following for Shakespeare, the Australian Shakespeare Company was not viewed with enthusiasm by one British Council representative who made the sniffy observation that Alden

> suffers from some of the faults associated with the old actor-manager touring regimes in the UK some years ago. He is sometimes spoken of as Australia's Donald Wolfit, but he has neither Wolfit's stature as an actor, nor (fortunately) some of the faults attributed to Wolfit himself.[188]

The comparison reveals the British Council's indifference to local claims on Shakespeare in Australia or elsewhere, primarily because such creative endeavours were outside of the organisation's direct interests and control. It serves as a reminder of the British Council's institutional habit of utilising its own networks of expertise to disseminate Shakespeare strategically and in support of broader British interests. Despite the decisive post-war shift towards more democratic notions of mass appeal, the Shakespeare that the British Council promoted remained elitist, metropolitan, and freighted with notions of English cultural exceptionalism.

The 'Independent Committee of Enquiry into the Overseas Information Services' that spent a year and a half investigating the projection of Britain abroad by Embassies, the British Council, and the BBC ultimately condoned the use of cultural-diplomatic practices overseas. The Drogheda Report acknowledged that given the multiple challenges of the era, 'a modern Government has to concern itself with public opinion abroad and be properly equipped to deal with it'. In a neat statement acknowledging the realpolitik underlying what may have appeared to be free-floating cultural initiatives, the report concluded that the goal of the Information Services 'must always be to achieve in the long run some definite political or commercial result' for the British state.[189] Irrespective of this clarification of past and future diplomatic practices, important strategic objectives had already been achieved in Australia at the time of the British Council's withdrawal in the mid-1950s. These outcomes included the stabilisation of the UK economy, the creation of ASIO, and Australia's successful integration into the Anglo-American global dispensation. As the practice of 'positive projection' (i.e., advertising the British way of life for seemingly altruistic or non-specific goals) came to an end, cultural diplomacy entered a more overtly political phase. From the mid-1950s onwards it would be part of a range of active measures aimed at countering communist influence at home and abroad following the death of Stalin.[190]

CHAPTER 3

The Cultural Cold War in Eastern Europe (1955, 1957)
Titus Andronicus

By the mid-1950s, the British Council's campaign to promote the UK through theatrical manifestations overseas had fallen well behind those of its international competitors. Despite growing demand, inadequate funding curtailed the organisation's ability to compete within a crowded international field. The DAC's 'Paper on Theatre Export' from February 1956 is worth quoting at length as it provides detailed insights into Britain's struggle to compete within the highly politicised international touring scene that evolved during the early Cold War period:

> since the war more and more countries have ... use[d] their Art of the Theatre ... as a means of cultural propaganda [and] increase[d] their national subsidies for these manifestations. In the same period Britain has reduced her allowance from £40,000 in 1946 to £3,250 in the financial year 1953/54 at which figure it remains for 1956/57. This ... only enables the Council to provide small guarantees against loss ... in easily accessible countries which can contribute substantially to the financing ... Such important areas as Finland, South-East Europe and Turkey, India, the Far East and Latin America are closed to us as are many of the most notable International Festivals ... At the Paris International Festival of Drama, 1955 ... Sweden, Belgium, Germany East, Italy, Norway, Holland, Germany West, Yugoslavia, Finland, Switzerland, Poland, Austria, USA, Canada, China, Ireland, Portugal, Spain, Greece [were represented by companies subsidised by their respective governments] ... And Britain by a small unsubsidised company, Theatre Workshop which got into some financial difficulty from which they were extracted by the French ... the Comédie-Française, Jean Vilar's Théâtre National Populaire, and lesser French companies have visited almost all European countries and Turkey. Yugoslav companies have toured extensively in Europe and as far afield as Malaya. Russia has sent, and is sending, companies to the Far East and India. The Chinese State Opera and Ballet has been touring continuously since ... 1955. The Burg Theatre in Vienna is planning a number of exchanges with Russian and German Companies and the Vienna State

> Opera ... The Moscow Arts Theatre is to tour Yugoslavia and the other Balkan countries this year and the American production of 'Porgy and Bess', having completed a long Latin American engagement and tours in Russia and Poland, is also proceeding to the Balkans.[1]

By the DAC's estimates, Belgium subsidised its theatre annually to the sum of £755,000, France: £1,495,000, Italy: £3,400,000, while Yugoslavia was contributing as much as £59,000 as grants-in-aid. Although the United States gave no direct federal subsidies, the State Department donated $2,500,000 for the promotion of international touring:

> H. M. Ambassadors and the Council's Representatives in half the civilised countries of the world write with increasing frequency, emphasising the importance for British prestige of 'major theatrical manifestations' ... letters refer to the extensive use made ... by other countries in conducting their cultural campaigns and deplore our inability to compete ... Engagements to which particular importance is attached ... include ... a Shakespeare Company for South-East Europe and Turkey.[2]

Britain was not only in danger of failing to deploy anywhere near the number of productions required to compete effectively within this crowded international field but was finding itself the target of other nations' cultural propaganda, especially from America and the Soviet Union.[3] High-profile visits by the Bolshoi Ballet and Bertolt Brecht's Berliner Ensemble in 1956, for instance, were seen as clear evidence of communist cultural advances into Britain itself.

Despite the prohibitive cost of taking a theatre company to Southeast Europe, the British Council managed to sponsor significant tours in the mid-1950s, not only to countries that were expensive to reach such as Yugoslavia but to other politically sensitive destinations behind the Iron Curtain like Poland. This was due in no small part to the DAC's alignment with the Soviet Relations Committee (SRC), a newly established anti-communist unit that by September 1955 was submitting 'a long list of proposals for the exchange of delegations, cultural manifestations etc.', including 'the Stratford Company or Old Vic for three weeks early in 1956'.[4] The stringent cuts made to the British Council's budget in the mid-1950s led to a marked reduction in positive propaganda efforts (the more diffuse projection of 'British values' or 'ways of life'), with the scant resources that remained allocated to theatre tours that countered communism more directly.[5]

This chapter considers the role that touring Shakespeare played in the cultural Cold War by tracing the interrelated political, institutional, and creative elements that constitute the performance history of the Shakespeare Memorial Theatre's 1957 tour of *Titus Andronicus* to

Eastern Europe. Peter Brook's SMT production provides a pertinent case study as it was a successful product of the British Council/SRC programme that took British theatre behind the Iron Curtain. Originally staged in Stratford-upon-Avon in 1955, *Titus Andronicus* toured as a result of a thaw in cultural relations between the Soviet Union and the West.[6] Although the original show belonged to the SMT, by the time *Titus Andronicus* toured Europe, it constituted a joint venture between them, the British Council, and Laurence Olivier Productions (LOP).[7] Revived for touring purposes in 1957 when the opportunity arose, its itinerary included the Théâtre des Nations in Paris for ten performances from 15 to 25 May; La Fenice in Venice for three performances between 28 and 30 May; the National Theatre in Belgrade for three shows from 2 to 4 June; two performances at the National Theatre in Zagreb on 7 and 8 June; four at the Burgtheater in Vienna between 12 and 15 June; and concluded with a short residence at the National Theatre in Warsaw with four performances between 18 and 21 June. Given the extensive touring circuit outlined above, and the highly political slant that Brook's stage adaptation brought to *Titus Andronicus*, this chapter explores how the tour deliberately traversed a fault-line in Soviet hegemony during a critical period in the Cold War.

The Cultural Cold War had far-reaching implications for the artists and institutions enlisted, knowingly or not, into its service.[8] On the company's return flight, a 'weary' Sir Lawrence Olivier congratulated his fellow actors over the public address system with some apposite lines from *Henry V*, 'Where ne'er from France returned more happier men'.[9] Given the speech's association with martial contexts it seems that the acting troupe saw themselves as Cold War warriors returning in triumph. That said, the peculiar effects of lengthy touring were evident during *Titus Andronicus*'s opening night at London's Stoll Theatre, with Olivier delivering 'a weird curtain speech' full of 'flowery phrases and uncomfortable jokes' that gave the impression he was 'apologising for the evening'.[10] The theatre critic J. C. Trewin noted that 'after addressing us as Ladies and Gentlemen in seven languages, Olivier said in his speech of thanks that Titus, once so obscure, was now so popular that it might be filmed, set to music, or skated'.[11] In emphasising the infinite potential for adaptation provided by such an obscure play, one that had long been considered an almost extra-canonical Shakespeare text, Olivier underlined the extreme lengths that were taken in bringing the play up to date and making it speak to contemporary concerns. Olivier's speech begs the question as to why *Titus Andronicus* was chosen to tour Eastern Europe in the first place? In channelling the tragi-comic music hall spirit of Archie Rice (the lead character of John Osborne's *The Entertainer* (1957) and another part that the actor was receiving critical acclaim for that year), Olivier's curtain speech appeared to convey the fundamental insincerity of his most recent cultural-diplomatic mission.

The most enduring legacy of the tour came from the fateful meeting of the production's director Peter Brook and the Polish academic Jan Kott following *Titus Andronicus*'s final performance in Warsaw.[12] At an award ceremony celebrating the twenty-fifth anniversary of the first publication of *Shakespeare Our Contemporary*, the influential Polish émigré stated that

> it was the most important day of my life to see *Titus Andronicus* ... and the beginning ... of my book was with that production perhaps! After that my life changed. I was invited by Peter to come to London, which then was a long, long way.[13]

Kott's acknowledgement that Brook's touring production played a pivotal role in shaping the direction of his life is usually obscured behind the well-established narrative that it was Kott's critical writing that influenced Brook's *King Lear* and had an enormous subsequent impact on the staging of Shakespeare throughout the 1960s.[14] Reviewing *Titus Andronicus* and meeting Brook not only influenced Kott's thinking towards Shakespeare, it provided him with a passport to the West, the realisation of his ambition to become a dramatic and academic advisor on a number of theatrical productions, and even determined the development and writing of *Shakespeare Our Contemporary* itself. Brook would be instrumental in getting *Shakespeare Our Contemporary* translated for the English-speaking market, and this seminal text would play a decisive role in helping the English Shakespeare establishment present itself as politically engaged during the counter-cultural decades of the 1960s and 1970s. Such far-reaching consequences beg the question of how Brook and the wider British cultural establishment benefitted from having such a close relationship with the dissident academic. What was Kott's political and intellectual biography when *Titus Andronicus* arrived in Warsaw in the summer of 1957? How was it that a prominent member of the Polish Communist Party's cultural apparatus became instrumental in validating British assertions that Shakespeare could provide unique insights into the iniquities of Soviet Communism?[15]

Military Stalemate and the Rise of Culture

The *Titus Andronicus* tour 'Behind the Iron Curtain' is an example of how cultural diplomacy rose in response to military stalemate during a decisive period in the Cold War. The Soviet Union's formation of the Warsaw Pact in May 1955 (a direct response to the West's expansion of the North Atlantic Treaty Organization (NATO) to include the Federal Republic of Germany), illustrated the hardening of divisions across Europe at the time. Despite Stalin's death in March 1953, there had been little success in de-escalating tensions on the continent, especially with America maintaining the binary view that the Cold War remained an 'irreconcilable conflict'.[16]

In 1955 Austria became a sovereign neutral state following the retreat of both Soviet and Allied military forces from its territory. Soon after, Khrushchev's 'secret' speech at the Twentieth Party Congress in February 1956 denounced Stalin's crimes and conceded the possibility of different paths to Communist Socialism, a point of significant importance to Eastern Bloc states, emerging postcolonial nations, and non-aligned communist countries such as Yugoslavia.[17] Although many Third World resistance movements had long been attracted to the Marxist–Leninist revolutionary model, Stalin's intolerance towards any autonomous or non-Soviet socialist movements had proven a hindrance to the anti-imperial struggle.[18] Khrushchev's decisive shift away from Stalinist orthodoxy led to a massive increase in the amount of Soviet material support going to decolonising nations throughout Asia and Africa, increasing Moscow's global influence and setting the scene for numerous armed anti-colonial struggles and proxy wars over the coming decades.[19]

Encouraged by Khrushchev's declarations, Poland and Hungary tested the limits of the new Soviet stance by attempting to establish a more independent and national form of communism for themselves. Poland's summer uprising of 1956, which was subsequently quelled by the Red Army, led to an apparent compromise with the instalment of Wladyslaw Gomulka as Party Chairman. Though Hungary attempted to go further by declaring itself a fully neutral nation via Radio Free Europe, Khrushchev used the Anglo-French-Israeli invasion of Egypt as an opportunity to deploy a two-million-strong military force against the uprising. As the Red Army advanced upon Budapest, the appeals of the Hungarian resistance for intervention from the 'free world' and the United Nations went in vain.[20]

Ultimately, the crushing of the Hungarian uprising exposed the West's unwillingness to confront Russia militarily within its established sphere of influence on the European continent. The fact that the Suez crisis occurred simultaneously reinforced the notion that, from the viewpoint of weaker nations, Western and Soviet modes of domination were practically equivalent. The Suez crisis was a stark reminder of the ways in which the legacy of European imperialism complicated American Cold War policy.[21] The debacle earned Britain the unique experience of being lambasted from all international corners, eliciting both a Soviet threat of retaliation and America's forceful condemnation. After the events of 1956 in Hungary and Egypt, the 'existing *status quo* in Europe' was recognised as something that neither side 'would risk war to overturn', while the Third World was identified as a significant site of Cold War contestation, a development that, as we will see in the following chapter, would prompt the projection of Shakespeare tours to West Africa following independence.[22]

The military stalemate in Europe led to a tentative 'thaw' in East–West cultural relations, with the arts becoming a prominent battleground in a war of ideas, ideology, and propaganda. *Titus Andronicus*'s itinerary from Paris to Venice, Belgrade, Zagreb, Vienna, and Warsaw illustrates how the tour sought to encroach upon the Soviet Union's sphere of influence by playing nations that strove towards greater autonomy, neutrality, and independence; countries where Britain stood to gain a great deal by forging or restrengthening cultural ties. France, for instance, had long been considered a hotbed of communist sympathisers and fellow travellers, prompting the CIA-funded Congress for Cultural Freedom (CCF) to relocate to Paris from Berlin in order to be more effective in its aim of converting neutralists and the moderate left to the anti-communist cause.[23] Following the Hungarian uprising, prominent French communist intellectuals such as Jean-Paul Sartre turned publicly against the new Soviet leadership labelling them 'a group which today surpasses Stalinism after having denounced it'.[24] At the same time Austria found itself receiving thousands of Hungarian refugees fleeing the Soviet reprisals after the failed October revolution, while Poland tested the cultural thaw by permitting new levels of artistic freedom that reflected aspirations for a more independent form of national communism.[25] Polish theatre artists that sought to test the limits of official tolerance often turned to Shakespeare, with Krystyna Skuszanka's 1956 *Measure for Measure*, for example, exploring the predicament of individuals living under totalitarian rule; a subversive political gesture that the state was temporarily willing to tolerate within the more permissive political climate.[26]

Yugoslavia held a dual interest for Britain, both as a chink in the armour of Soviet hegemony and as a new and formidable adversary to British imperial interests throughout the world.[27] In 1957 Josip Broz Tito was in the process of making Yugoslavia the leading European champion of global non-alignment; a coalition of small, independent, and decolonising nation-states that saw their mutual survival predicated upon extraction from the binary logic of the Cold War. Despite breaking from the Soviet

Union in 1948, Tito's ability to maintain commitment to socialist principles while also accepting US aid provided post-colonial governments with 'an attractive model'.[28] Yugoslavia's staunch support for anti-colonial causes won it 'friends around the globe', especially as non-alignment came to be accepted as an 'eminently sensible' response to the irreconcilable Cold War differences that threatened 'to submerge the independence of weak states within a broad geopolitical agenda'.[29] Overall, as the Cold War's global dimensions appeared to grow in proportion to Britain's diminishing military power, increased investment in cultural diplomatic initiatives made a great deal of sense. This was especially so in Eastern Europe where age-old cultural ties, subsumed national identities, and shared Enlightenment values predated current Cold War antagonisms.

The Soviet Relations Committee

The Soviet Relations Committee (SRC) was an anti-communist board placed within the nominally non-political and non-governmental body of the British Council with the aim of regaining control of cultural exchanges between Britain and the Soviet Union.[30] Formed in 1955 for the promotion of closer relations between Britain and the USSR, the SRC sought to undermine communist-friendly domestic groups such as the British-Soviet Friendship Society, and the Society for Cultural Relations with the USSR. At the time such organisations received legitimacy and support from Moscow by arranging bilateral cultural exchanges that circumnavigated the UK's artistic establishment and more entrenched cultural institutions; effectively operating in an arena of unregulated cultural exchange that escaped UK government oversight and control.[31]

Given the Soviet Union's stringent efforts to filter out all forms of Western propaganda, Shakespeare was one of the few British cultural exports that stood a reasonable chance of being invited to Russia and its satellite states, primarily because the playwright had been designated orthodox status throughout the Communist world since the dawn of the Russian Revolution.[32] The Soviet embrace of Shakespeare was initially based on fostering 'political ideology, to educate the proletariat, and to establish Western roots in the previous great rebellion, the European Renaissance'.[33] Karl Marx regarded Shakespeare a writer of genius whose own historical moment held the potential for the creation of a classless society which had been thwarted by the rise of a new merchant class.[34] Hailed as a shining example of cultural humanism, Shakespeare was included in the canon of Socialist Realism with five million copies of the playwright's works published in the twenty-eight languages of the Soviet Union between 1917 and 1939.[35]

Though there were more productions of Shakespeare being staged in the Soviet Union than in Britain and America combined prior to the Second World War, the playwright came under increased scrutiny and control during Stalin's rule. The dictator recognised that Shakespeare constituted a protean and ungovernable site capable of voicing internal political dissent, and that stage adaptations had the potential to host slippery anti-doctrinal elements that state-censors could struggle to decode or detect fully. Revealing the strength of Stalin's personal antagonism towards Shakespeare, Dmitri Shostakovich wrote:

> *Hamlet* and *Macbeth*. Stalin could stand neither of those plays ... Shakespeare was a seer – man stalks power, walking knee-deep in blood. And he was so naïve, Shakespeare. Pangs of conscience and guilt and all that. *What* guilty conscience? ... our best Lear was Mikhoels in the Jewish Theatre and everyone knows his fate. A terrible fate. And what about the fate of our best translator of Shakespeare – Pasternak? ... no it is better not to become involved with Shakespeare ... That Shakespeare is highly explosive.[36]

Between 1954 and 1960, Khrushchev's cultural 'thaw' saw the reinvigoration of Soviet Shakespeare with the publication of a major new edition of the complete works with commentary by Alexandr Smirnov and Alexandr Anikst. The playwright's gradual return to the stages of the Soviet Union and Eastern Europe provided regional directors with a vehicle for critiquing aspects of Soviet rule, thus making it an effective agent for Britain's own cultural offensive behind the Iron Curtain. Shakespeare not only evoked a rich intellectual heritage that was shared between Britain and Eastern Europe prior to the schisms of the Cold War but had the potential to foster and encourage anti-communist sentiment.

Chairing the Soviet Relations Committee and thus giving political direction to the British Council's cultural deployments at the time, was Christopher Mayhew. Mayhew had been Junior Foreign Minister under Aneurin Bevan and was the founder of the Information Research Department (IRD), Britain's principal anti-communist intelligence unit that fed authoritative and facts-based anti-Soviet propaganda to global news networks via embassies, publishers, and press syndicates during the earliest stages of the Cold War.[37] Mayhew felt that the best way to 'dispel the illusion' that Russia could use its 'friendship societies' to bypass and ignore the British cultural establishment was to 'chok[e] off Soviet contacts with the left wing'.[38] The strategy was highly effective and within a short time Mayhew was meeting with the Soviet Minister of Culture:

> on behalf of a dazzling array of leading cultural and educational establishments ... [it] marked the beginning of a bizarre cultural cold war. Both sides wanted to increase contacts, but both disagreed sharply about their nature and purpose ... our aims were political. We wanted to break down the isolation of the Soviet people from the West and to disrupt their ties with British communists and 'fellow travellers'.[39]

Between 1955 and 1959, the SRC managed to increase the number of British artists, scientists, and students visiting the USSR significantly. Although the British Council oversaw the detailed handling of professional visitors to the UK it was the SRC, a group 'laced with political intent', that vetted and instigated such exchanges in the first place.[40] Aiko Watanabe summarises the nature of the relationship succinctly:

> Whilst resisting Soviet advances to create a formalised agreement, the SRC acted as a stent, keeping open a channel of communication with the Soviet authorities, and implanting – in Soviet eyes – the corruptive seeds of democracy ... Britain's cultural diplomacy in this period was a raft of unique and subtle strategies, which ... attempted to challenge the Communist cultural hegemony.[41]

As it took the machinations of state–private networks to wrong-foot Soviet censorship, there is a strong possibility that some domestic theatrical productions were conceived and produced with the prior hope and intention of touring the Eastern bloc. The 1955 Shakespeare Memorial Theatre production of *Titus Andronicus* is a strong candidate for such a role as it had some intriguing characteristics. On a practical level, 'when the contract for the 1955 Stratford Season was made' all actors had 'agreed' that they would be available for foreign touring though the intended destination was never specified.[42] The production itself displayed a sharp antagonism towards Soviet notions of history, a key tenet of communist ideology. Performance documents indicate that Brook's adaptation countered the notion that a rational understanding of history could provide the basis for the better organisation of society or lead towards the kind of utopian world that Soviet propaganda claimed itself to have achieved. *Titus Andronicus* replaced such a teleological view with an early iteration of what Kott would later call 'the Grand Mechanism', a pessimistic vision of history as the inexorable repetition of violent power struggles brought about by the mysterious inner compulsions of an innately destructive human nature. Given the public airing of Stalin's crimes and the recent suppression of the Hungarian uprising, Brook's adaptation promoted the idea that communist ideology was deluded and fundamentally flawed, and that Khrushchev was destined to follow the same blood-stained path as his predecessor.

Though severely underfunded, with the SRC's political guidance behind it, the British Council became adept at responding flexibly to rapidly changing circumstances. In 1955, the DAC considered a sudden Russian request for a winter Shakespeare tour that was secured by the SRC:

> As neither the Shakespeare Memorial Theatre Company of Stratford nor the Old Vic would be available to visit Moscow during the Winter of 1955 the Committee was asked to consider a suggestion that the Russians should invite Tennant Productions Ltd. to present Peter Brook's production of *Hamlet*. This company could visit Russia for 2 weeks from 20th November.[43]

Moscow's last-minute request for a winter visit was impossible for the Memorial Theatre to fulfil as it only ran a short summer season. Once this golden opportunity to take *Titus Andronicus* to the Soviet Union was missed, however, LOP took the unusual step of purchasing the entire show and placing it in storage while awaiting a further invitation to tour the Communist world, an offer which finally materialised in 1957.

Competing *Hamlet*s in Moscow (1955)

The challenge of getting to Russia quickly enough to avoid censorship was considerable and required a creative and flexible approach. Indeed, when *Titus Andronicus*'s Russian-speaking director, Peter Brook, accepted Moscow's invitation, he had only three weeks to put a new production together. Brook's strategy was to turn such an impractical challenge into a propaganda victory by devising a sparse, minimalist production of *Hamlet* with a young cast and fluid staging which allowed the action to move 'like the wind'.[44] The choice of play was deliberately provocative, as everything 'lauded in Brook's *mise-en-scène*' stood in direct opposition to Moscow's first major Shakespeare production since the end of the Second World War, Nikolay Okhlupov's gargantuan staging of *Hamlet*. The result of over a year's rehearsal, Okhlupov's 'monumental' and 'visually complex' production featured a company of seventy and an orchestra of thirty. Brook's staging on the other hand, was 'dark', 'plain', and 'spartan' with thirty players and no music whatsoever. Okhlopkov's Prince Hamlet, Yevgeny Samoylov, was forty-four years old and 'came across as a *danseur noble*' whilst Paul Schofield, ten years his younger, 'diffused a sense of moral goodness from within' (Figure 3.1).[45]

Figure 3.1 Ernest Thesiger, Mary Ure, Paul Schofield, Diana Wynyard, and Alec Clunes (The Peter Brook Company) in Moscow, 1955. Photo by Reg Burkett.
© Getty Images/Hulton Archive.

The central motif of Okhlopkov's production, that 'Denmark is a Prison', governed the production's visual conceptualisation. Vadim Rydin's set consisted of a wall of bronze gates that opened into twelve separate cell-like platforms:

> This metallic superstructure was always present as the overriding metaphor of incarceration and repression, the 'confines, wards and dungeons' that hem the human spirit ... the gates suggested the mechanical maw of an ominous state, half living, half automation.[46]

The Russian Shakespeare scholar Aleksandr Anikst states that Moscow audiences clearly understood the director's initial intention, but that once the Ministry of Culture's Committee for Artistic Affairs' forced colour and painted realist backdrops upon the set, Okhlopkov's staging:

> emerged not as a tragedy, but as a joyous, festive production expressing his gratification that Denmark the prison is no more, that he – the artist – has been unfettered, that he has freedom to create.[47]

These Socialist Realist touches resulted in a kind of 'totalitarian baroque' that contradicted the production's veiled critique of life lived within Soviet society. Kenneth Tynan captured the official view, that in the USSR tragedy existed only in the past, in his review of Brook's Moscow tour for *The Observer*:

> Mr Zubov, the director of the Maly Theatre, put it to me very clearly ... social tragedy was unthinkable. In Soviet society a man could never be trapped. I mentioned *Hamlet*. 'Ah' he said ... 'it is a golden page of the past.' And he added that the circumstances which created the anguish of Lear and Macbeth simply did not exist. 'In our society,' he concluded, 'there may be collisions but there are no defeats'.[48]

Brook elaborated further on the tensions and contradictions of the post-war Soviet theatre, stating:

> The Russian has fallen into a subtle trap. He wanted to both win his war and yet preserve all that he treasured. The Russian revolutionary (to his undying credit, it must be said), having recognised the value of his opera and ballet and his dramatic theatre, preserved these institutions completely with their traditional way of work ... splendour is coupled with reverence, lavishness and mastery of execution ... the theatre of an actively militant nation became deeply traditional: slow in method, mature in result, romantic in quality, escapist in effect.[49]

Even so, there were some notable inconsistencies in receptions to Brook's *Hamlet*. While Muscovites greeted the English production with immense enthusiasm (as much as to acknowledge 'a new East–West entente' as to welcome 'a fresh approach to Shakespeare'), the production's reviews upon its return to Britain were subdued.[50] The fact that most London critics considered Brook's *Hamlet* to be a tepid, uninspiring, and pedestrian production reveals a striking inconsistency in the reception of shows that were produced in Britain but intended primarily for audiences overseas. A similar discrepancy can be found in *Titus Andronicus*'s initial reception in Stratford-upon-Avon in 1955, two years prior to touring the Communist world itself.

The Canonisation of *Titus Andronicus* for Cold War Audiences

Peter Brook's *Titus Andronicus* was a landmark production in the play's performance history.[51] Though subsequently performed with regularity on the British stage, the consensus view prior to 1955 was that the play's violence made it unpalatable for most audience's sensibilities. This in turn corresponded with doubt over Shakespeare's authorship, a view stretching back over 350 years. Before considering how and why Brook overcame such an unpromising performance history, it is worth briefly establishing the nature of the play's reception up to that point.

The preface to Edward Ravenscroft's 1687 adaptation provides the first textual evidence suggesting that the piece was co-authored, a view continued by subsequent critics who voiced a general disbelief that Shakespeare could have written such a 'barbarous' text.[52] According to Brian Vickers, these early doubts 'expressed an aesthetic-ethical dislike' for the play's numerous scenes of brutality rather than being based on scholarly evidence. Victorian-era critics simply rationalised their 'distaste for the play's offences against 'taste and decorum' by 'denying its authenticity'.[53] The twentieth century saw the emergence of scholarly tests that began to support the idea of co-authorship. Building upon the accumulated history of textual studies that focus on the play's rhetorical characteristics, Vickers determines that 'qualitative differences clearly distinguish two different hands at work', concluding that George Peele wrote Act I and quite possibly II.1, II.2, and IV.1.[54]

Brook deliberately set himself against this unpromising reception history when choosing to stage *Titus Andronicus* over *Macbeth* for the 1955 season. At the time *Titus Andronicus* was the only remaining play in the First Folio that had never been performed at the Shakespeare Memorial Theatre, and Brook set out to reclaim the vexatious text for the Shakespearean canon through performance. The decision was determined by the director's conviction that the play's notorious violence was timely and had something important to say to Cold War audiences. As Alan Dessen notes, Brook felt that British audiences 'only ten years removed from the horrors of the Second World War' would be more receptive to the play's gruesomeness.[55]

In truth, reviews of the original 1955 staging suggest that English audiences had trouble viewing the play as a tragedy and resisted the notion that it was somehow topical. Critics noted that laughter was the most common response to the production's highly stylised treatment of violence and to its numerous scenes of spectacular cruelty. Almost all the British press followed the *Daily Telegraph*'s headline interpretation 'Stratford does Shakespeare's Horror Comic'.[56] David Lewin wrote, 'Horror? At one point the audience was laughing'.[57] John Coe reviewing for the *Bristol Evening Post* under the caption 'Impressive – but Still Revolting', argued that

> Peter Brook is entitled to his opinion, but whether many of last night's capacity audience were in agreement must be doubtful ... a modern audience's reaction to the four deaths in 20 lines with which the action culminated? Laughter, can be a pointed commentator.[58]

The Canonisation of Titus Andronicus for Cold War Audiences 99

Brook maintained the claim that *Titus Andronicus* spoke to the horrors of totalitarianism by ignoring these initially hostile British reactions and pointing instead towards later European audience responses. He stated that the production's expression of 'the most modern emotions – about violence, hatred, cruelty, pain' were more openly accepted during the 1957 Iron Curtain tour.[59] This assertion is questionable. Not only is it difficult to corroborate given the ideal conditions that touring creates for partial reporting (many of the translated reviews included below contradict Brook's claim), but it seems self-serving when used to describe a production that was a deliberate cultural intervention in the Cold War itself.

Brook's successful reclamation of *Titus Andronicus* for the Shakespeare canon centred on demonstrating how the problematic text could be made to work in performance. Its status as an obscure play gave the director a free hand in editing the verse and creating a successful piece of producer's theatre. Though the play's conceptual staging was presented as the result of a long process of painstaking textual analysis, Brook's relentless editing and elision was an early example of what Alan Sinfield later identified as the Royal Shakespeare Company's (RSC) practice of claiming to respect 'scholarship' to 'authenticate the process' of reaching preconceived theatrical and political interpretations. The argument that beneath a veneer of 'radicalism' and experimental aesthetics 'political' Shakespeare adaptations of the early 1960s expounded a deeply conservative worldview is certainly applicable to Brooks' production.[60] J. C. Trewin's early biography of Brook did much to establish *Titus Andronicus*'s subsequent reception history, stating that 'its neo-Senecan horrors absorbed him as work for a theatre theatrical'.[61] Brook had long contemplated various 'experimental' ways of approaching the play, once with an all-Black cast and once again with modernist sets designed by Jacob Epstein. His final approach confronted Stalinist cultural practice head on by consciously building upon the kind of avant-garde work instigated by dissident Russian practitioners from the 1920s and 1930s:[62]

> Descend[ing] in an unbroken line from the work of Komisarjevsky. I had leading actors such as he had never had, but it was the totality – the sound, the visual interpretation, everything interlocking, that made it happen.[63]

Brook strove to control his 'interlocking' spectacle on every level. As the original programme stated, the production was not only 'Directed by Peter Brook' but was also 'Designed by Peter Brook' and featured 'Music by Peter Brook'.[64] Despite this highly regulated approach, Brook claimed he was uncovering previously hidden 'truths' buried beneath the surface of the problematic play-text.[65] The director stated that the play 'began to yield its secrets' once he bypassed its 'gratuitous strokes of melodrama' and looked for its 'completeness'. That, in identifying a 'dark, flowing current' that 'rhythmically and logically related' the play's horrors, he had unearthed a 'powerful' and 'barbaric ritual' resting beneath the surface.[66] Explaining the marionette quality sometimes adopted by the performers, Brook said that stylistically he was aiming at creating a series of expressionist archetypes that presented the horrors of the play in 'a form that became unrealistic', 'transcended the anecdote', and was 'quite abstract and thus totally real'.[67] This modernist pursuit of a kind of universalism through expressionist abstraction extended to the production's movement and staging, much of which flowed through and around the centrepiece of a giant and unfolding metallic cylinder. Brook's production aligned the aesthetics of modern mechanistic slaughter with vague notions of an ancient and inexplicable ritual, suggesting that the barbarity spiralling through Shakespeare's bloodiest play emanated from inescapable transhistorical forces that plunged human societies into cycles of political violence that recurred again and again. In short, history in Brook's production was an anticipation of what Jan Kott would later come to theorise as the Grand Mechanism.

The director's presentation of *Titus Andronicus* as a weighty tragedy was greeted with scepticism by many reviewers:

> How has Mr Brook come to this view? Simply, I maintain, by forcing the play, Procrustes-wise, to fit his opinion. For Mr. Brook has committed upon the text a butchery scarcely less severe than that suffered by most of the people in the play.[68]

Another critic detected a false note in Brook's depiction of violence as ubiquitous rather than emerging through the agency of individual characters, suspecting that Aaron:

> instigator of all the bloodshed, revels in his vileness, too nauseatingly for Mr Brook's conception, and certain of his speeches have been cut. These cuts are small, but they obscure to some extent the fact that it is Aaron alone who sets the wheels of vengeance in motion.[69]

In 1955, the British public struggled to regard the play in the serious tragic mode that Brook so strenuously insisted upon and were more inclined to consider its violence preposterous and its horrors absurd. Such disdain vexed the director greatly and he had to cut the text drastically to ensure that 'his actors could let fly' without 'dread of mocking laughter'.[70]

In scenes where the problematic text could not be tamed fully, Brook employed the 'protective atmospherics' of *musique concrète* to ensure the desired continuity of tone.[71] The production's soundscape was so sensational, Ian Holm recollected that

> to be on his stage was to be in one of Hell's circles ... the music, all plucked strings, single drumbeats, and eerie throbbing sounds. Just being on stage, even for a few minutes, was a strange, almost frightening experience, during which my senses were shockingly assaulted.[72]

Musique concrète, later termed radio-phonics in much British commentary, would become a signature sound of the late 1950s and 1960s with Britain's most famous manifestation being the collective output of the BBC's Radiophonic Workshop. Its basic technique was the recording and manipulation of found sounds to create evocative and conceptually challenging audio landscapes. As recorded sounds can be sped up or slowed down to alter their pitch, it is possible to create distinct notes and thus compose conventional music from unconventional sources.[73] Assailing audiences with its disconcerting soundscape, *Titus Andronicus* provided an entirely unique acoustic experience that was instrumental in staging the play as tragedy. Under the headline 'Mr Brook Decided to Make His Own Primitive Roman Music' the director stated he 'could not think how to get from any composer I know, music' that was 'barbaric' enough for his purposes.[74] Although such sounds began establishing their own conventions in Science Fiction films from the mid-1950s onwards, these popular associations had yet to be fixed at the time of Brook's *Titus Andronicus*.[75] As a consequence, many commentators struggled to place the sounds they were hearing within any meaningful frames of reference, with one describing the production's soundscape as 'an alarming mixture of an immense organ and a gigantic double-bass in a primitive blood-lust rhythm'. Another found it 'a barbaric collage' sounding 'rather as if it were scored for Malayan nose-flute, deep sea tuba, and the Gorgon's eyeball'.[76] Overall, Brook's reliance on *musique concrète* evidences how far he needed to push the production's performance effects in order to drown out distracting audience laughter, ensure that the 'truth' of his interpretation was 'discovered', and be certain that the 'latent absurdities of the play were skirted'.[77]

In contrast to most other reviewers, J. C. Trewin later claimed that 'one heard people, normally decorous, shouting at the pitch of their voices, hardly knowing that they did so, and denying it afterwards; a critic said it could have been the scene of a cup final'.[78] Such sensational claims helped endorse Brook's later assertion that the staging elicited 'uncomplicated emotions' of 'violence, hatred, cruelty, [and] fear' from English audiences.[79] In fact, the only British reviewer to associate the production with the atrocities of totalitarianism in 1955 was Harold Hobson, whose piece in the *Sunday Times* chastened fellow critics for entirely failing to note the production's political relevance. Hobson stated that:

> for post-Buchenwald generations the play's profligate brutalities no longer seemed comfortably remote, or ridiculous ... The horrors in *Titus* ... will not be wasted if they wake up the British stage to a sense of reality. Fifty or a hundred years ago the incidents in this play might well have seemed exaggerated. But now ... there is absolutely nothing in the bleeding barbarity of Titus which would have astonished anyone at Buchenwald ... Titus parallels exactly our own age ... The audience which thinks that its sensationalism makes Titus unreal and absurd is probably weak in the stomach; it is undoubtedly weak in the head.[80]

The Cold War concern driving Brook's production is clearly spelled out by Hobson's well-informed corrective. With such an influential critic berating British audiences for not taking the threat of Soviet totalitarianism seriously, and for not taking such concerns with them into the Shakespearean theatre, Hobson's review was instrumental in putting the production's reception back on track prior to touring the Eastern bloc.

Reaching Eastern Europe through State–Private Networks

The Cultural Cold War was driven by the global dissemination of film, books, music, theatre, radio, magazines, television, and art exhibitions.[81] Both covert and overt methods were used to project competing ideological worldviews throughout the globe, practices that led to a collapse in state–civil boundaries and the creation of what Scott Lucas terms 'state–private networks'.[82] Such networks of covert sponsorship and informal collaboration in service to anti-communism inevitably compromised the cultural institutions and individual artists that operated, wittingly or not, within its paradigms.[83] State-private networks played a decisive role in getting English Shakespeare productions overseas in service to British cultural diplomacy. The struggle to get *Titus Andronicus* behind the Iron Curtain evinces how private individuals, government departments, theatrical institutions, and arms-length governmental bodies worked in unison in the fight against Communism in the mid-1950s. The fact that *Titus Andronicus* did not tour until 1957 is not so surprising when we consider that the SRC often had to improvise to wrong-foot Soviet censorship, especially with Russia's Ministry of Culture carefully vetting each and every manifestation that Britain proposed sending. Yugoslavia provides an illustrative example of the determining role that state–private networks played in bringing together the artistic, financial, and diplomatic elements needed to project English Shakespeare productions behind the Iron Curtain.

Britain prioritised Yugoslavia for cultural-diplomatic exchanges following Tito's break with Stalin in 1948. Anthony Quayle offered 'the services of the Shakespeare Memorial Theatre' for 'a short (five week) European tour' to follow their 1951 season, a venture which eventually became impossible to undertake for financial reasons, causing 'considerable disappointment abroad, especially in Yugoslavia'.[84] In January 1952, the Foreign Office made a direct request 'for the Shakespeare Memorial Theatre to visit Yugoslavia for one week', though the estimated cost of '£7000 for two weeks – one playing and one travelling' was deemed prohibitive. A proposed solution for overcoming the recurring financial setbacks was to make Yugoslavia 'part of a larger tour' including 'visits to Italy, Austria, and Holland' and thus ensuring that 'the costs would be reduced proportionately i.e., from £1,733 per performance for one playing week to £336 for the longer period'.[85] In February 1955, the DAC's secretary Stephen Thomas reviewed the situation, concluding that touring Yugoslavia

> had been considered and investigated on many occasions and was, indeed, constantly under review, but ... the funds available were hopelessly inadequate because the Yugoslavs were ... only able to contribute a very small proportion of the cost.[86]

By the mid-1950s, much of the British Council's work in key European countries like West Germany had been taken over by the Foreign Office's CRD.[87] Thanks to the SRC's success in steering Anglo-Soviet cultural relations away from communist-friendly groups in the UK, Russia and Poland approached the SMT in July 1956 inviting them to visit at the end of the season. With this breakthrough, the DAC finally saw an opportunity for a tour that 'could be extended to Yugoslavia with little cost to the Council and would fulfil a longstanding project'.[88] By October 1956, the DAC was discussing the upcoming opening of the Théâtre des Nations in Paris, the actualisation of a scheme established by UNESCO's International Theatre Institute in 1946. As the intended date coincided with a visit to Paris by Queen Elizabeth II, the organisers 'approached Sir Laurence Olivier' 'through the British Ambassador in Paris and French Ambassador in London' in the hope that an 'English company would open the season' (Figure 3.2).[89] It was at this point that Brook's *Titus Andronicus* came up in discussions.[90]

Figure 3.2   Laurence Olivier as Titus Andronicus, backstage at the Théâtre Sarah-Bernhardt, Paris, 1957. Photo by Gamma-Keystone.
© Getty Images.

The need to reach Eastern Europe with a Shakespeare tour was politically urgent because, according to Watanabe:

> A closed document produced by the British Embassy dated October 1956, indicates just how encouraged they were by news of the 'extent to which the discussion on the arts in the satellite countries has run ahead of that in the Soviet Union', and a Soviet literary critic revealed overall 'Soviet anxiety' concerning this new climate. He describes, for example, that Soviet Socialist Realism, originally established in the 1930s, was rejected by Polish and Yugoslav writers in the 1950s regarding it respectively as 'a weapon for destroying art' or as being 'antiquated', and internal forces in the USSR

were in part responsible for revising it with a sense of 'full horror of Satellite deviation'.[91]

By January 1957, Olivier's tour was proposed 'in the first instance for Eastern Europe, and the Council had approached the Foreign Office for an extra grant', which was forthcoming.[92] Financially speaking, Paris, Vienna, and Venice were essential for mitigating the prohibitive costs of touring Eastern Europe, though Poland and Yugoslavia had long been primary political targets for cultural outreach. In the final analysis, it seems that it was only with the help of extensive state–private networks that the cash-starved British Council was able to put together tours to the Communist world.

Titus Andronicus 'Behind the Iron Curtain' (1957)

Actors' accounts of the *Titus Andronicus* tour are loaded with the popular Cold War tropes that were in circulation at the time. Themes of espionage were very much in evidence, especially as the actors considered themselves to be embarking upon a special diplomatic mission as the first English-speaking company to have 'ever penetrated inside the Iron Curtain'.[93] Prior to departure, the troupe were advised to be mindful of their conduct in all communist countries, to remember that 'Tito was above criticism' in Yugoslavia, and to never discuss politics at a restaurant table in Poland just in case the waiter happened to be a party agent.[94] In Belgrade the actors were constantly escorted by John Julius Norwich, the third-secretary to the British Embassy and son of the wartime Minister of Information Duff Cooper, whilst in Zagreb 'a terrible man' was specifically tasked to keep a close eye on the tour's capricious leading lady, Vivien Leigh:

> We called him 'Otto the agent'. He worked for the British Council. He was a kind of Hollywood gunman. He did not have a revolver, but he looked as if he did. After four days he was always saying 'Vivien, I love you'. He fell madly in love with her. But she wrangled the man so much. He must have lost two stone. He was a gibbering wreck. He came out with us every night and it was serious.[95]

Ian Holm's autobiography confirms how the 'expedition' had a 'whiff of unreality about it' that often veered towards the surreal.[96] Humour helped lighten any tensions that the actors' own presence created. Crossing the frontier into Yugoslavia aboard the Simplon-Orient Express, Frank Thring leaned out of the carriage window yelling 'the Shakespeare Memorial Theatre! By land, sea and yak!' Language problems led to comic incidents, such as when the company were mistaken for a delegation of post-office workers. Holm felt that the stress involved in undertaking such a highly sensitive cultural mission was alleviated by being:

> glimpsed through a peculiarly English lens, grim fact eased by the burlesque of our expedition, the flying Oliviers and their performing troupe, Terence Greenridge and his Bananas, and of course the certain knowledge that we would soon turn round and return home. We were sedated against experience of the full-blown austerity by circumstances and temperament, moments of starkness being counterbalanced by instants of humour or flashes of the absurd, many of these deliberately sought in a very English way. Despite all the eye-opening and the affecting scenes of hardship, I was keen to travel back to Stratford.[97]

Though Holm's autobiography recorded several moving encounters (such as seeing 'elderly, dignified Polish man being overwhelmed at the apparent luxury of a sticky bun', or travelling through 'reverberating underground tunnels which had hosted shooting matches and executions only a few years before'), he readily admitted to possessing limited touristic insights into the countries he visited.[98] Michael Blakemore's memoire on the other hand followed in the tradition of anti-conquest modes of travel writing, going out of his way to establish knowledge and understanding of the people and societies through which he passed in order to help or assist them in some way.[99] Blakemore found life behind the Iron Curtain very different to what he had been led to believe:

> the propaganda of the Cold War almost led one to believe that Technicolor would give way to black and white as you crossed the border ... it was interesting to see people enjoying their lives in bars, restaurants, and modest night spots despite having their acquisitive instincts tempered. Whatever was wrong with it, Tito's Yugoslavia was not Communist Russia.[100]

Ultimately the performers took refuge in their work, even to the extent of gauging the politics of the countries visited through the lens of *Titus Andronicus* itself:

> Nowhere did the grim events of the play seem more plausible than they did in Poland. Every person one met had some extraordinary and horrific tale to tell ... These were commonplace experiences. In a tentative, almost apologetic way our Polish hosts wanted us to know a little of what they had been through.[101]

Though receiving the highest accolades in Paris, the actors could feel the 'apathy' of the Vienna audience 'from the moment the curtain rose'.[102] A welcome return to critical acclaim in Belgrade prompted some to conclude that the intensity of goodwill was a coded but unmistakable message: we are your friends, and only the politicians and the military shake their fists at one another ... it was very moving, one of those occasions when what people are permitted to express is fed and intensified by what they are not. You felt this event would resonate far beyond the walls of the theatre.[103]

These shifts from Western apathy to Eastern enthusiasm were interpreted as a barometer of the production's political relevance to Eastern European audiences and hailed as evidence of its supposed insights into the iniquities of Communist totalitarianism.

Though Viennese reviewers responded positively to the principal actors and the production's technical aspects they questioned the choice of play for advertising British theatrical culture overseas. As the theatre critic Hans Weigel put it, the production was 'an example of an ideal Shakespeare interpretation applied to an unsuitable object', adding that the audience only 'tolerated the play as a pretext for meeting Shakespeare performed by Olivier and his English company'.[104] Austrian reviewers were quick to identify and dismiss the production's ideological aspects; both its assertion of humanity's innate savagery, and the political motivation behind Britain's decision to tour such a vision in the first place. The opening lines of Friedrich Heer's review 'A Moment in History in the Theatre' could not have been closer to Brook's intentions:

Hatred, wickedness, grief, revenge, and horror, brought down to their primary form, rule the stage. A passionate, barbaric, and archaic spirit rules it ... The action rolls off as if it were following some sinister and solemn ritual full of pathos surging from mystical depths ... accompanied by the sinister deep echoes of a remote human past ... that this play is able to move us is greatly due to the fascination of its scenery and accompanying sounds.[105]

Moving on, however, Heer pins Brook's assertion of humanity's innate, ahistorical, and universal savagery back onto the particularity of the British themselves, and knowingly in terms of their imperial history:

[in] this consonance of the ancient and the most modern ... Shakespeare is recreated with the archaic elements present to his day and to his mind (what cruelty, barbarity, calmness, and grandeur there are in this mentality of the British: the development from the Battle of Hastings to Cecil Rhodes).[106]

Heer's devastating conclusion was that 'the British Council to which we owe the Vienna visit ... could not have found a more effective and fascinating propaganda for modern British world power'.[107] Austrian critics were clearly intent on exposing the ideological intentions behind the latest English Shakespeare production to visit their country:

> According to their own statement the English company is touring ... because the play is seldom performed and practically unknown abroad ... all this was admirably bridged over by the producer. But it could not make us get over the horror which such atrocities, fundamentally bare of any human feeling, create in us. Art triumphed, but England lost a battle by this performance. The frenetic, unparalleled, and more than well-deserved applause could not make us overlook the fact that the question as to what had been played here, had to be put ... It testifies to an incredible cruelty which somehow falls back upon the English who not only consider a drama like this part of their national treasure, but who so much approve of it that they even go touring with it.[108]

The Foreign Office style of cultural diplomacy that prioritised local decision-making elites was still exercised in the mid-1950s. British Embassy staff and British Council Regional Representatives were prone to judge a touring production's success by gauging the reactions of the social elites they moved amongst. 'Popular enthusiasm', for example, 'was assumed to be equalled by that of the Yugoslav Government, many important members of which were seen at the theatre on two or three successive evenings'.[109] Social events were such an integral part of the tour's diplomatic mission that Olivier persuaded the entire male cast to purchase dinner jackets prior to leaving the UK, reassuring everyone that they would be getting good use out of them.[110] In Belgrade, Marshall Tito 'and three of the four vice-presidents and their wives' invited 'the four principals together with Mr and Mrs Peter Brook to his box in the interval to offer his congratulations'.[111] Embassy staff were buoyed by the success of closing night where

> about five-hundred people were offered a lavish supper, with dancing to follow on a scale that has, I think, seldom been known at any government function below the White Palace level.[112]

The British Embassy noted that although anticipation had been 'steadily rising', 'ridiculously few' tickets were available to the wider public once 'the demands of the Yugoslav Government and Party officials, members of the local theatres, opera and ballet, and representatives of the press as well as the Diplomatic Corps' had all been met:

> By the last days of May, the black-market price of a thousand-dinar ticket had risen to eight or nine thousand dinars. Advance publicity presented no problems; all sections of the press were avid for information and photographs.[113]

The tour's appeal to all sections of society chipped away at the Communist state's veneer of equality with 'classified advertisements offering high prices for tickets' appearing for the first time ever 'in the history of the Yugoslav press'.[114] As compensation for the lack of available tickets the company made an altruistic visit to the University of Belgrade, with Leigh and Olivier giving readings in the great hall 'for students only'. Although the couple's performance took on an 'impromptu nature' that reflected 'a noticeable lack of polish' it was felt that this:

> served only to emphasise their anxiety not to disappoint the students who appreciated their kindness all the more. The programme itself was, to say the least, representative. It consisted of some of the most famous speeches of Shakespeare, an extract from *A Streetcar Named Desire* and, as a *tour de force*, a song-and-dance routine by Sir Laurence from his recent London performance in *The Entertainer*.[115]

This successful visit became a diplomatic staple, with subsequent tours by the Old Vic *Hamlet* in 1958 and Franco Zeffirelli's *Romeo and Juliet* in 1960 providing similar 'impromptu' performances for university students lacking the money, status, or social connections needed to secure theatre tickets.[116]

The leading couple's visit to the Film Workers of Yugoslavia paved the way for new commercial partnerships that would later prove invaluable to Britain's entertainment industry. Leigh's celebrity status carried considerable weight throughout Eastern Europe. Though few people in Poland and Yugoslavia had heard of Olivier, Leigh was instantly recognisable for her role in *Gone with the Wind* (1939), a film that moviegoers throughout the world associated with their own struggles during the Second World War.[117] Despite playing the slight supporting role of Lavinia, Leigh received top billing in all promotional materials. As crowds gathered outside theatres in Eastern Europe and 'shouted for Scarlett' in scenes reminiscent of the Australia tour of 1948, Leigh's international stardom continued to draw audiences who were largely indifferent to Shakespeare.[118]

The Yugoslavian film industry was undergoing enormous growth at the time and was on course to become one of the strongest in Europe.[119] Due to the country's experiment of allowing socialist market mechanisms within its centralised economy, the period witnessed soaring growth in both the production and consumption of cinema. In decisive Cold War terms this signalled a significant loss of cultural influence for the Soviet Union as Yugoslavia became more successful and Western oriented. Between 1945 and 1950, 220 films were imported to Yugoslavia from the USSR with only 30 coming from the United States. From 1951 to

1960, US film imports rose to 579 while the USSR's fell to 97. The yearly production of Yugoslav films between 1955 and 1960 more than doubled, while the country went into 'coequal financial and artistic feature film production' with many foreign and Western European studios from 1954 onwards. Between 1951 and 1960 cinema admissions rose from 5,656,000 to 17,133,000 for domestically produced films, and from 57,875,000 to 112,991,000 for foreign films.[120] In sum, this revolution in the Yugoslav film industry evidenced a wider rupture in the Soviet cultural sphere at the time, as many Communist-Socialist states struggled to free their creative industries from the dead hand of Socialist Realism. Besides cinema, Shakespeare came to play an important role in the creative defiance against Moscow-dictated cultural policy gathering pace across the Eastern Bloc during Khrushchev's thaw, especially in Poland.[121]

Making Shakespeare Contemporary: Jan Kott and the *Titus Andronicus* Tour

In his preface to the first English language edition of *Shakespeare Our Contemporary*, Peter Brook recounted the dramatic circumstances in which he first met Jan Kott at a party following the final performance of the *Titus Andronicus* tour. The pair became embroiled with the local police over the arrest of a young Polish actress and ended the evening sharing a cell together. For Brook, the incident illustrated the following:

> Here we have a man writing about Shakespeare's attitude to life from direct experience. Kott is undoubtedly the only writer on Elizabethan matters who assumes without question that every one of his readers will at some point or other have been woken by the police in the middle of the night.[122]

For British readers encountering Kott for the first time, the anecdote presented the Polish academic as an ideal native informant, uniquely qualified to disclose how Shakespeare's works provided important insights into tyranny, totalitarianism, and oppressive state rule. Brook went so far as claiming that 'Kott is an Elizabethan' because Poland

> has come closest to the tumult, the danger, the intensity, the imaginativeness, and the daily involvement with the social process that made life so horrible, subtle, and ecstatic to an Elizabethan. So it is quite naturally up to a Pole to point us the way.[123]

In an accompanying introduction, Martin Esslin concurred that, after the 'astonishing liberation movement of October 1956', Poland offered 'the urgency, the burning topicality, and the overwhelming emotional intensity' of a 'communion with kindred spirits who have faced similarly extreme situations'.[124]

Such tributes presented Kott as an authentic 'other' whose noble suffering could be gazed at and appropriated by Western readers, academics, and practitioners. The chance encounter would prove to be fortuitous for Kott and Brook themselves, and highly significant for the development of the English Shakespearean theatre. For Kott, the *Titus Andronicus* tour shaped and nurtured his central ideas while bringing him into contact with influential Westerners willing and able to bring him to the UK and the US. For Brook, Kott's work provided 'evidence' of Shakespeare's extraordinary relevance and universal insight into the iniquities of communist rule. Kott's publication provided independent academic validation for the producer's programme of mining Shakespearian texts for the 'discovery' of hidden 'truths' buried beneath the surface. The initial indifference and hostility of British critics and audiences to the Cold War appositeness of productions like *Titus Andronicus*, would eventually be assailed, undermined, and replaced by such an influential academic text, not to mention the accumulated weight of subsequent RSC productions inspired by Kott's writing throughout the 1960s. Over the coming decades, Kott's ideas would furnish the English-speaking Shakespeare industry with a powerful claim to political insight, concern, and engagement.

The precise nature of the relationship between Kott and Brook has been obscured by the prevalent notion that Kott's writing shaped Brook's landmark production of *King Lear*, not to mention the mythology built around Kott's émigré status as a Cold War warrior from the outset. There are, however, striking similarities between Brook's production of *Titus Andronicus* and Kott's later theories. Esslin's account of Kott's central notion of the Grand Mechanism is especially applicable to the debate on history that lay at the heart of Brook's touring production:

> Marxists in contemporary Eastern Europe are trained to look at the world as a manifestation of the historical process working itself out towards a preordained goal. In the last twenty years they have learned the violence and mutability of history, but they have also learned to view the attainment of preordained goals with healthy scepticism. In Shakespeare they can find the historical process itself, stark, violent, and relentless, but totally free of any vulgar teleological conception, a great wheel of power, endlessly revolving.[125]

By the time Brook went on to direct his acclaimed production of *King Lear* in 1962, Kott would be starting his new life as an exiled writer living in Brook's London apartment from where he lent assistance. Given Brook and Esslin's portrayal of Kott as a modern-day Elizabethan embroiled in life-or-death dramas playing out behind the Iron Curtain, we should revisit Kott's intellectual and political biography in the light of the visiting *Titus Andronicus* production.

Jan Kott discovered Shakespeare's works while serving in the Polish resistance during the Second World War, later recalling that he was 'fascinated by the idea of great turning points in history' during the war because 'they alone offered hope'.[126] Kott felt that 'in times of terror, human dramas – even the most common and universal – somehow became final and are purified of anything accidental'.[127] As these notions of 'typicality' suggest, Kott was reading Georg Lukács at the time and 'from then on' for 'more than ten years' he 'remained under his spell, for better and for worse'.[128] Lukács's conception of 'typical characters under typical circumstances' seemed to constitute 'a magical formula':

> Lukács is dry but makes history transparent in texts. The drama of the protagonists is the drama of history – sometimes even the tragedy of history. That is what I learned from Lukács. I [then] showed the workings of the Grand Mechanism in Shakespeare's history plays.[129]

As Fredric Jameson summarises it, Lukács's general notion of realism is 'dependent on the possibility of access to the forces of change in a given moment of history', a formulation that is quite distant from Kott's later theory.[130] Apart from the important distinction that Lukács is primarily concerned with the nineteenth-century novel whereas Kott is interested in Elizabethan and Jacobean theatre, Kott's more modernist approach diminished the historical particularity of the people and events portrayed in Shakespeare's plays, reducing them to archetypes and the kind of modernist allegorical figures that Brook sought to portray in his production of *Titus Andronicus*.[131]

Although Kott's schooling in Marxist thinking provided him with the basis for a materialist reading of Shakespeare, the experience of living under Stalinist rule had a profound influence on the development of his ideas. In communist Poland following the war, as well as becoming co-founder of the Institute of Literary Research and holding three professorships, Kott became co-editor of *Forge* magazine and was tasked with implementing the new edicts of Socialist Realist literature coming from Moscow.[132] As one of Poland's leading literary tsars, Kott earned a reputation for being a strict and orthodox member of the Party's cultural apparatus. Many Poles never forgave him for his actions at the time, deeds such as proscribing Joseph Conrad's writing and publicly attacking

Czeslaw Milosz's anti-communist polemic *The Captive Mind* (1953). Looking back over this period of zealous party loyalty, Kott admitted that he had

> great difficulty recognising myself in those first two years after the war. And still more trouble judging myself ... We were sure we would change history by what we wrote. We were sure of history as though it belonged to us. It was the same old 'Hegelian sting' but we did not yet know that term and it was rather we who were biting history than the other way around.[133]

Concerning the staff at *Forge* magazine, he felt they were all 'quite well aware' that

> socialist realism and Zhdanovism meant the death of all creativity. The problem was how to open the way to socialist realism – for after all, that was what we were doing – and yet at the same time somehow get free of it. In other words, how to put one's neck in a noose and convince others to do so – but prevent the noose from tightening.[134]

Kott began to consciously drift away from the Communist Party around January 1953 due to the realisation that most of his wartime comrades had disappeared in the latest round of purges and that his own life was in jeopardy during the 'doctor's plot' prior to Stalin's death.[135] In terms of literary culture, the arrival of the first Socialist Realist production novels 'of the worst, most schematic variety ... portraying Stakhanovite heroes surpassing work quotas many times over without knowing any temptation of body and soul' was more than Kott could stomach.[136] As one obituary writer put it, Kott 'fought for socialist realism in literature right up to the point when the first socialist-realist books appeared'.[137]

In 1956, at Jean-Paul Sartre's invitation, Kott put together an anthology of essays about the changes taking place in Polish Socialism for *Les temps modernes*. Although de-Stalinisation began after the Soviet Communist Party's Twentieth Congress in February 1956, Kott formally resigned from the Polish Communist Party in November 1957 due to its refusal to allow the publication of a new literary monthly to be titled *Europa*.[138] Prior to leaving, Kott had already taken preliminary steps in betraying Poland's ruling party. On frequent visits to Paris and once in Munich, Kott met up with Jan Nowak of Radio Free Europe to tell him 'in as much detail' as he could 'what was going on in the party':[139]

> Even now I am unable to explain exactly why I did that ... Nowak and I were separated by our political past and our outlook on the future. I was on the other side and would remain so for quite some time yet. But even then I could clearly see that ... Radio Free Europe was an ally and a support.[140]

Kott presents his reasons for abandoning the Polish Communist Party as a mystery even to himself, though it is implied as being a patriotic, pro-European, and anti-Soviet decision founded on the hope of increased Polish independence within the Communist bloc. Given Kott's subsequent émigré status in the UK and then the US it should be noted that, in its support of Radio Free Europe, Britain was instrumental in helping to organise the transfer of Soviet and Eastern-European defectors to the West at that time.[141]

In September 1956, Roman Zawistowski's production of *Hamlet* (then dubbed the '*Hamlet* of the Polish October') made a tremendous impression on Kott, as can be seen in his review '*Hamlet* after the Twentieth Party Convention'. Kott considered the production a 'thoroughly political drama' that subversively reflected the events and attitudes of the time.[142] Similarly to Okhlopkov's 1955 production in Moscow, the fundamental conceit that 'Denmark is a prison' enabled a veiled critique of Soviet rule. By the time Brook's touring production of *Titus Andronicus* played Warsaw from 18 to 21 June 1957, Kott had two volumes of his theatre reviews published. 'The Kings', the essay that sets out Kott's key notion of the Grand Mechanism in *Shakespeare Our Contemporary* was published in Polish in November 1957, a couple of months following his review of *Titus Andronicus* and his initial meeting with Brook.

Kott's original piece on *Titus Andronicus* appeared in *Cultural Review* under the title 'Shakespeare Cruel and True'. The review was careful not to draw attention to the ways in which the visiting production criticised Communist ideology, focusing instead on the strengths of its formal qualities, and especially the influence of film upon its staging. With the movie adaptation of *Henry V* and *Richard III* in mind, Kott claimed that Olivier was the first 'to show the true Shakespeare convincingly' because 'the living Shakespeare of our time has been presented, first and foremost in film ... it is the return to the true Shakespeare in the theatre through the experience of film that amazes us most'.[143] The article's rapturous language employs hagiographic phrases reminiscent of Brook's own sweeping claims, suggesting a kind of conversion narrative. Kott states, for instance, that 'Shakespeare is truer than life' and that Olivier's films have achieved some 'super-truth more than any theatre has'.[144] Proof that Shakespeare correlates with contemporary concerns is drawn from the broadest of assertions, that 'he is violent, cruel and brutal, earthly and hellish' and that his work 'evokes terror as well as dreams and poetry'. The review concludes giddily, with the claim that Shakespeare 'is most true and improbable, dramatic and passionate, rational and mad'.[145]

Enthusiasm for the archetypal and trans-historical aspects of modernism is evident in 'Shakespeare Cruel and True', while the historical particularity of the Shakespearean text is discarded. Kott's celebration of the impact of modernist techniques upon stage practice hints at the influence of Brecht, demonstrating some affinity perhaps with the German dramatist's long defence of using modernist experimentation within Marxist aesthetics. This was a perennial debate going back to the 1930s and, in an essay not published until 1954, Brecht wrote:

> Tying a great conception like Realism to a few names is dangerous, however famous they may be, and so is the bundling together of a few forms to make a universal-applicable creative method, even if those forms are useful in themselves. Literary forms have to be checked against reality, not against aesthetics – even realist aesthetics. There are many ways of suppressing truth and many ways of stating it.[146]

Careful not to identify his adversary explicitly, Brecht's polemic was a response to Lukács's influential ideas on Realism; motivated in part by Brecht's understanding of the threat posed by state-legislated Social Realism, and in part by his desire to avoid the emergence of the kind of centralised cultural programme that Kott himself helped implement before subsequently renouncing it.[147] Positioning Kott somewhere between Brecht and Brook is problematic, however, because, in terms of political character and political intent, the two could not have been further apart. Brecht's use of modernist and expressionist techniques was selective, experimental, and driven by a desire to accentuate existing historical social conflicts to galvanise his audience into action outside of the theatre, whereas Brook's modernism merely mystified and validated the unveiling of his own preconceived conservative beliefs.[148]

A number of objections have been raised against Kott's work, especially his theory of the Grand Mechanism and assertion that Shakespeare is contemporary.[149] Jonathan Dollimore and Alan Sinfield have argued convincingly that Kott's work enabled the fledgling RSC of the early 1960s to maintain a 'mystifying confirmation of the *status quo*' through the very imprecision of its supposedly radical gestures.[150] As an integral part of what they termed the 'Brook-Hall convergence', Kott's 'implacable roller of history' that 'crushes everybody and everything' enabled the institutional entrenchment of a 'pessimistic revision of the Marxist emphasis on history'.[151] Sinfield argued that in Cold War Britain, Kott's theory supported a despairing worldview that diverted left-wing political energy away from action and towards quietism and surrender. More recent commentators such as Zofia Sawicka claim that *Titus Andronicus* had a profound impact on the Polish academic because it was

> the first time since the war [that] Kott saw a Shakespearean play not contaminated by any ideology, not burdened with Stalinist experience, produced far away from the political reality known to him. And at the same time alive and moving, unexpectedly brutal and first of all – contemporary.[152]

Sawicka interprets the *Titus Andronicus* tour as 'a catalyst' which helped take Kott out of the habit of seeing Shakespeare's plays 'exclusively through the prism of totalitarian experiences'.[153] Though the notion of a natural alignment between Brook and Kott's ideas is conventional, it is extremely doubtful that Kott, a previously senior member of the Polish Communist Party's cultural apparatus who went on to provide intelligence to the West, would have viewed the British touring production as being free of ideological intent.

Ultimately, it is better to regard Kott's ideas as emerging from a compromised response to the profound cultural changes and revisions taking place within Poland following the death of Stalin. Highly allegorical interpretations of Shakespeare that provided oblique criticism of state abuse within the Soviet sphere were a common feature of the time.[154] The early Khrushchev era gave licence to this type of unorthodoxy, one that Stalin would never have tolerated, and that Britain's information services were only too happy to exploit. Arguably the dissenting political Shakespeare that Kott saw on the stage in 1950s Poland represented 'radical' gestures that were unthreatening enough to be permitted by the apprehensive rulers in power at the time. Krystyna Skuszanka's 1956 production of *Measure for Measure*, for example, evinces how Shakespeare became an acceptable vehicle for expressing a limited degree of dissent.[155] Though her interpretation drew public attention to the dilemma of recognisable individuals caught within a political system that abjured personal rights, she later recalled that many Communist Party officials came to see the production in order to display 'their identification' with its 'ideological subversion within the unquestionable Polish Communist Party status quo'. Following significant political upheavals like the brutal confrontation between the Poznan workers and the army, such temporary and limited acts of cultural dissent simply 'assisted in entrenching' the Communist regime into the new political settlement prior to re-establishing a more oppressive cultural orthodoxy in due course.[156]

***

Brook's stage adaptation of *Titus Andronicus* was facilitated by the unfamiliarity and unevenness of the text itself. The play's uncertain status justified an extreme level of directorial intervention which in turn supported a grand claim of not only discovering the 'real' Shakespeare, but one that provided timely insights into the nature of totalitarianism. Brook's interpretation was granted authority and political weight because it claimed not to be coming from him, but from 'Shakespeare' itself, and was validated further by being brought to light by England's preeminent Shakespeare company. As Alan Sinfield has asserted, Shakespeare 'is the cultural token which gives significance to the interpretations which are derived from him'.[157] Touring such a politicised Shakespeare production to the Eastern bloc was advantageous for Britain because, rather than being seen as planting the seed of Western cultural influence from without, English productions supported anti-Communist Shakespeare productions coming from within. Thanks to a shared European cultural heritage, Shakespeare played an actual historical role in allowing the British visitors to gesture towards texts and ideas that predated Sovietisation.

Lukács read *Shakespeare Our Contemporary* following its translation into German and, in a private letter to Kott, pointed out that not only had he 'failed to recognise in Shakespeare the characteristic Renaissance belief in a better world' but that his theory of the Grand Mechanism was 'a generalisation based on the limited historical evidence of Stalinism' itself.[158] Kott conceded that 'undoubtedly Lukács was right to a large degree' but qualified his admission with the comment that 'that was precisely what made Shakespeare our contemporary'.[159] This slippery response seems emblematic of the circular logic and contradictory claims being made on both Shakespeare and history within Kott's work and legacy. Within the context of the cultural Cold War of the mid-1950s at least, it was the playwright's instrumental value to the British state while touring behind the Iron Curtain that helped make Shakespeare contemporary.

CHAPTER 4

Decolonisation in Nigeria (1963)
Macbeth

On 11 July 1962 the British Council's Drama Advisory Committee held its second quarterly meeting of the year. Following a discussion on the forthcoming Bristol Old Vic tour of Pakistan, India, and Sri Lanka, the committee considered what plays might be suitable for an upcoming tour 'of West Africa by Nottingham Playhouse Company'.[1] By that stage the Nottingham Playhouse Trust had already approved the tour in principle, envisaging a run of ten weeks:

> giving approximately 23 performances at six towns in Nigeria, 11 performances at four towns in Ghana and 9 performances at two towns in Sierra Leone ... the Company will take three plays, one of which will certainly be *Macbeth* since it is a set book, but the other two are still under discussion [...] the Company would be led by John Neville, who is very anxious to undertake this tour, and he will also be responsible for one or two of the productions ... The sum of £15,000 has been provisionally set aside for this tour and rough budgets are now being prepared.[2]

The minutes reveal that some of the meeting's participants had difficulty imagining Shakespeare playing in West Africa at all. As paternalistic colonial attitudes were still prevalent at the time, the venture was considered ground-breaking and even overly ambitious. One committee member opined, for instance, that 'audiences in West Africa' were likely to be 'less sophisticated than those in the Indian Subcontinent' and suggested sending 'just one Shakespeare play and two other plays of high quality suited to the audience'.[3]

In its final formation, the Nottingham Playhouse tour of West Africa ran from 6 January to 15 March 1963 performing Shakespeare's *Twelfth Night* and *Macbeth*, as well as George Bernard Shaw's *Arms and the Man*. Officially the circuit involved forty-eight performances in thirteen towns and cities across the three nation-states of Nigeria (which gained independence from Britain in 1960), Ghana (which became independent in 1957), and Sierra Leone (which achieved its independence in 1961). Anecdotally the tour gave something closer to seventy performances in venues ranging from school halls, sports stadiums, open-air cinemas, missionary outposts, and even President Nkrumah's Palace.[4] The tour was supported by Alfred Farell as manager, Simon Carter as stage manager, Anthony Church as sound and lighting technician, and Doris Nicholas in wardrobe. The Playhouse's acting company was led by John Neville and consisted of fifteen actors including Terence Knapp, James Cairncross, Paul Daneman, and Judi Dench.[5]

The leading figure behind the tour's organisation was Valery West. Reviewing her twenty-seven years working with the British Council's Dance and Drama Department, West described her role as:

> planning and organising groups of theatre companies, touring abroad. Promoting Britain, really ... the largest part of the British Council's work is English language teaching and the cultural part of it, cultural exchange, was in support of that, more or less. And we were supported by the Foreign and Commonwealth Office.[6]

West recalled that previously 'companies would come to us saying "we have been invited to Japan ... and we need some money"' and that her department was simply 'doling [it] out', but that by the early 1960s the British Council was becoming more directly involved in 'commissioning tours'. So 'if you wanted to tour to Africa' and you wanted 'a company ... able to put up with the sort of conditions that they would get there' the British Council would help arrange it. In the case of the Nottingham Playhouse tour,[7]

> they wanted something in West Africa ... And the Foreign Office people, the High Commission, consulted all the business people who were exporting to West Africa, and said, 'what sort of show do you think would go down well? Would you like variety shows?' And they said, 'no, we want Shakespeare'. And so Shakespeare's what they got.[8]

The fact that the Foreign Office sought the advice and guidance of British businesses operating in West Africa, thus giving them a guiding hand in the tour's formation from the outset, serves as a reminder that the British Council was built in the final days of the 1930s liberal economic era and that its original remit was to garner private funds for pro-British cultural exchanges. Supporting the commercial interests of prominent British companies overseas still fell within the British Council's remit in the early 1960s because, as findings of the Drogheda Report clarified, British cultural exchange could be undertaken in service to commercial, as well as diplomatic, aims.[9]

Though the idea that there was any corporate advantage in deploying Shakespeare throughout West Africa in the early 1960s might seem surprising, the book publishing industry provides an illustrative example of the commercial links that existed between West's 'people who were exporting' to Nigeria and the Nottingham Players' tour. With *Macbeth* assigned as a set text on the secondary school English Literature curriculum at the time, UK publishers stood to make substantial profits by maintaining their hold on the burgeoning educational book market that encompassed much of the Commonwealth.[10] Following independence, a great deal of state-funded investment was directed towards rapid modernisation, with education and skills-training identified as the surest way to turbo-charge Nigeria's national development. The conventional post-independence economic practice was a rush to invest in the hope of catching up with the more mature economies of America and Western Europe. A commission on Nigerian education headed by the British educationalist Sir Eric Ashby, for example, recommended the country invest £75,000,000 over ten years to combat an illiteracy rate of 85 per cent.[11] Given Britain's compulsion to persuade fledgling nation-states to borrow and spend exorbitant amounts in order to mitigate the debilitating legacy of its own colonial rule, it is reasonable to state that the UK sponsored Nottingham Playhouse tour operated within broader patterns of neo-colonial control and intervention.

On a diplomatic level, the tour 'was the result of a very urgent request from Lord Head' (the British High Commissioner for Nigeria) 'for a company to counterbalance the success of companies mounted by the Russians and the Americans'.[12] As decolonisation brought the cultural Cold War to the African continent, theatrical manifestations were called upon to counter the cultural advances that Russia, France, and the United States were making into Britain's traditional sphere of influence. The Soviet Union, for instance, began touring circuses and musical events throughout the region with the University of Ibadan's Arts Theatre hosting Russian theatrical companies as early as 1961.[13] In terms of European rivalry, the Nottingham players hoped to enjoy the symbolic prestige of being 'the first visit to West Africa by any professional theatre company' once a French tour planned for that year 'had to be cancelled' following the region's outrage over 'French nuclear tests in the Sahara'.[14] Meanwhile, the Northern Nigeria Regional Representative's report of 1962/1963 evinces a growing sense of competition between the British Council and the United States' Information Services (USIS):

> During the year ... [the Americans] have increased their activities, and have formed American-Nigerian Cultural Clubs, rather in the style of what the Council used to do in the old days ... one of their major manifestations was staging Cozy Cole and his Jazz Band.[15]

Christened 'Kwesi' Cole in the local press, Cole's band toured Ghana in early 1963 and enjoyed a great deal of local support for its West African high-life-inspired jazz project.[16] Throughout the 1950s and 1960s many African American musicians were conscripted into the service of the United States' cultural Cold War, in part because America's history of slavery, segregation, and Jim Crow severely tarnished its global reputation and threatened to undermine its foreign policy aims across Africa.[17] In the face of mounting international competition, and as the ex-colonial power in the region, it was felt that Britain needed to act quickly if it wanted to regain lost cultural ground and improve Anglo-Nigerian relations following independence:

> While on the one hand the [Nigerian] Ministries ask us for a great variety of obligements, on the other hand they are ready, particularly on a special occasion such as the visit by Nottingham Playhouse, to help us in any way they can. Personal contacts help to sustain this happy relationship of mutual respect but it is founded on fifteen years of honest endeavour by the Council in this region. The useful things done in colonial days are still in demand today.[18]

The sense of post-imperial continuity evident in such administrative reports belies the fact that, in the realpolitik of the global standoff between the Soviet and American superpowers, Britain simply did not enjoy the degree of international stature that Lord Head's comments suggest. Though the potential spread of Communism throughout the decolonising world was a major concern for the ex-imperial powers, it was not considered an immediate threat in Nigeria at the time. In truth, Britain's overarching aim following independence was to work closely with the United States to tie decolonising African nations to 'the West' culturally, linguistically, and economically at the very moment that they separated politically.

American Philanthropy, The British Council, and English Language Teaching

The Cold War provided ideological cover for predatory neo-colonial manoeuvres aimed at easing European nations' transition from exercising formal power to informal influence in West Africa.[19] Awareness of such Cold War tactics within the context of decolonisation is key to understanding the formation and reception of the Nottingham Playhouse tour. In Nigeria, Britain and America worked both separately and in tandem across several fields in which Shakespeare played a significant role. These areas included investment in educational infrastructure, the establishment of seemingly non-political cultural bodies, and the promotion of English as a global language through the birth of English Language Teaching (ELT).

America's charitable investments in the foundation of Nigerian educational institutions is one context in which Shakespeare tours can be understood as part of wide-ranging Anglo-American neo-colonial policies. As Edward H. Berman summarises it, the Ford, Carnegie, and Rockefeller Foundations bound 'the newly independent African nations' to the West by 'devising programmes linking the educational systems of the new African nations to the values, *modi operandi*, and institutions of the United States'.[20] A typical characteristic of America's post-war economic diplomacy was to present financial aid as non-political and solely technocratic in nature, as much-needed investment aimed squarely at fostering development by providing access to the instruments of rapid modernisation.[21] Given Nigeria's mineral resources, huge population base, and geopolitical mass and importance, the Ford Foundation saw fit to invest $25,000,000 between 1958 and 1969. $8,000,000 of this investment underwrote university development with $5,000,000 going to the University of Ibadan. Including university-centred investment programmes in planning, public administration, and economic development, $15,000,000 was spent on higher education in Nigeria by this one foundation alone.[22]

Such largesse earned America considerable influence in independent Nigeria.[23] In Cold War terms, Britain and America justified their interference in the developmental goals of West African nations as a necessary measure aimed at countering potential Soviet infiltration. As for economic advantages, financial investments ensured continued access to raw materials, the provision of lucrative investment opportunities, and unfettered access to growing African markets. As one foundation asserted at the time, dollar diplomacy would help the US 'exert an extraordinary leverage' following the formal dissolution of European Empires across the African continent.[24]

In 1963, the British Council was in a unique position to influence the direction and evolution of Western-style culture and education in Nigeria, chiefly because it enjoyed a reputation for being non-political. Its earliest activities in West Africa began with the establishment of Representatives in

Ghana, Nigeria, and Sierra Leone immediately following the Second World War. Even at this initial stage, the Colonial Office's long-term educational and cultural aims were framed in Cold War terms:

> In the long term we want to strengthen the links between Britain and the colonial peoples so that the latter, as they obtain greater control over their own affairs, will still value the British connection ... We feel that the Council can do valuable positive work in countering Communist propaganda by showing that Britain and the Western tradition for which Britain stands has something better to offer than the Communist way of life.[25]

Despite its long affiliation to the Foreign Office in Europe and elsewhere, the British Council's work in Africa was transferred to a Colonial Office vote from 1945 onwards, thus making the Secretary of State for Colonies answerable to Parliament for educational and cultural advancement across Britain's African Dependencies.[26] It is telling, therefore, how British Council activities grew in proportion to the retreat of Colonial Office administrations in Asia and Africa between 1945 and 1963.[27] Though decolonisation presented significant political challenges, it also brought the organisation considerable commercial opportunities. Indeed, the end of Empire constituted a pivotal moment that saw the British Council extend its activities into the new and lucrative fields of English language teaching and educational development. Perversely, such opportunities arose from a pressing need to mitigate the effects of the underfunded and unbalanced education system that Britain itself had bequeathed Nigeria during its imperial rule.[28] Although Independent Nigeria was reticent to accept 'aid' from Harold Macmillan's Department of Technical Cooperation, the British Council's apparent independence and autonomy helped allay such fears.[29] As the organisation presented itself as working globally across a diverse range of foreign, developing, and Commonwealth countries, any lingering sense of post-imperial patronage was mitigated.[30]

In terms of Anglo-American cooperation, a senior British Council representative reported in 1960 that 'the Americans were planning a 'great offensive' to make English a world language' with Britain committed to working alongside them in implementing an 'English language campaign on an unprecedented global scale'.[31] British and American academies formed a close working relationship around the global provision of English Language Teaching and from 1954

> Cabinet approval for [the Drogheda Report findings] ... ensured financial support for the massive expansion of the ELT field. The creation of university departments for teaching and research, the provision of ELT

training in Britain and more attractive conditions of employment abroad for British teachers of English (as well as other subjects), training in Britain for key ELT people from abroad, co-ordination with British publishers, support for British books overseas – all these were to be promoted in order to provide professional and logistic backing for the effort to make English a world language, an undisputed 'universal second language'.[32]

A landmark event in the history of ELT in Africa was the 'Conference on the Teaching of English as a Second Language' that took place at Makerere University, Uganda, in January 1961.[33] The conference articulated demands for better training for teachers, the publication and dissemination of professional textbooks, and the creation of new educational institutions and curriculums on a vast and coordinated scale. On a commercial level, the conference provided enormous business opportunities for UK publishers such as Oxford University Press and Longmans while promoting an important stream of revenue for the British Council itself.[34] Though officially supplanted by indigenous languages in most instances, English was still considered the *lingua franca* of many multilingual ex-colonial nation states. The English language retained its historical dominance as a common argot for the professional classes, while America's economic diplomacy strengthened the association of English with international commerce and industry. In West Africa, knowledge and use of the English language became synonymous with an international standard of education, signifying both personal and national advancement in an increasingly competitive and globalised world.

Geoffrey Axworthy's *The Taming of the Shrew* (1962)

Judi Dench joined the Nottingham Playhouse Company tour at the end of her first season with the RSC. In her autobiography *And Furthermore* (2012), Dench states that 'such a tour had never been done before' and that 'we went out there long before Peter Brook, who claimed to be the first some years later'.[35] Though challenging Brook's remarkable assertion that he had inaugurated the arrival of 'western' theatre to the continent, both comments evidenced how badly informed British visitors could be about African theatre. At the time of the Nottingham Playhouse visit, for instance, the future Nobel Prize-winning dramatist Wole Soyinka was actively researching indigenous Nigerian theatre and adapting it to create new forms of West African drama that were performed to critical acclaim both in the UK and in his native country. The young playwright was one of many emerging dramatists working within the independence-era's lively cultural renaissance, with his play *A Dance in the Forests* (1960) celebrating Nigerian sovereignty three years prior to the Nottingham company's visit.[36] That said, Dench's view that 'in West Africa they had never seen a theatre company before and had no idea what to expect' is representative of British attitudes towards the touring venture at the time.[37]

The Nottingham Players' visit was not the one-off Shakespeare touring event it portrayed itself as, but followed in the immediate wake of numerous Shakespeare tours undertaken by the University of Ibadan's Travelling Theatre.[38] The appointment of the British academic Geoffrey Axworthy as the head of Ibadan's new Drama Department in 1961 instigated thriving research into the practices and traditions of Yoruba travelling theatre. Yoruba had long been associated with Nigerian nationalism, with postwar protest plays like Hubert Ogunde's *Africa and God* (1944), *Strike and Hunger* (1945), and *Worse than Crime* (1945) subjecting various aspects of British colonial rule to public scrutiny.[39] The University's research into Yoruba theatre resulted in the successful fusion of Western drama and indigenous performance practices. Under Axworthy's guidance, somewhat derivative student productions of European dramatists like Pinter, Beckett, and Anouilh evolved into creative adaptations performed in a more local idiom with highly successful productions of Moliere and Shakespeare selected to tour throughout Nigeria.[40] The residency of the Yoruba theatre practitioner Kola Ogunmola at the University of Ibadan's Drama Department was especially consequential, culminating in a powerful stage adaptation of Amos Tutuola's Onitsha market literature novel *The Palm-Wine Drinkard* (1952), a creative and popular success that signalled the arrival of a new mode of Nigerian theatrical expression for the independence era.[41] It is important to emphasise, however, that these endeavours to create syncretic forms of popular national drama aimed at drawing in new audience constituencies had their origins in Nigeria's first University campus at Ibadan; an elite institution steeped in Western academic traditions and mostly staffed in its initial stages by European and American scholars.[42]

Geoffrey Axworthy's University Travelling Theatre production of *The Taming of the Shrew* (1962) is a vivid example of the successful Nigerian claims being made on Shakespeare prior to the Nottingham Players' visit. Axworthy felt that his academic department had 'a tremendous amount to learn' from Kola Ogunmola about 'rapport with the audience', while the Yoruba practitioner 'could learn something from us about the technical side of theatre'.[43] Typical Yoruba Travelling Theatre productions featured chants, songs, improvised dialogue, and robust audience participation. They also provided up-to-the-minute socio-political commentary, opening 'a window into popular consciousness' through the airing of pertinent issues of the day in an open public forum.[44] *The Taming of the Shrew* employed several Yoruba theatrical techniques to great effect. The adaptive use of pidgin English for 'low' comic characters, for instance, had its roots in Onitsha Market Literature and had originally been devised in the recent stage adaptation of *The Palm-Wine Drinkard*.[45] Understanding the degree to which Nigerian audiences expected to play an active role in performances, Axworthy's students set out to engage spectators as fully as possible.

Describing the production, Axworthy recounted that audiences were kept waiting before the spectacle of an empty stage on which an old high-life phonograph record played, before the stage manager appeared and apologised that the company had been held up and that the show, unfortunately, was cancelled. Actors 'already sprinkled through the audience ... charged the stage, heckling the manager, and demanded he provide props and costumes for an impromptu performance by the audience itself'.[46] The show began haltingly with scripts in hands but 'gradually the pretence was dropped' once the audience realised what was happening. The director described the climax of the spoof:

> A whisper passes around the hall, growing into an overwhelming wave of laughter, which stops the play. Such audiences love a practical joke and by this time are truly hooked. They even carry on the pretence. When Katherina, in the closing scene, drops back into her original character of an emancipated Nigerian girl ... and refuses to do the submission speech, the actors, and then perhaps the whole audience, may beg her to carry on, for the sake of the show. She agrees, it being understood that no self-respecting Nigerian woman would behave like this nowadays.[47]

Such 'total theatre' devices acknowledged the central role that audiences played in determining the success of the students' production, by inviting them to interrogate the problematic sexual politics of Shakespeare's play. The approach undermined any notion of the English playwright's universality by allowing for a variety of audience responses across Nigeria's vast geographical and cultural landscape. In stepping out of character, the actress playing Kate prompted 'an interesting interaction of the audience with the play'.[48] In Onitsha 'the proscenium wall was literally broken as female members of the audience were cheering for Katherina' though, according to Axworthy, 'it took some courage' for her 'to make this point before an all-male Muslim audience in Northern Nigeria'.[49] Evidently, Nigerian audiences enjoyed interacting with the performers and openly voiced their concerns about the play during performances. In this sense, both actors and audiences put the Shakespeare play-text under scrutiny within the context of their own cultural time and place. Yoruba performance techniques enabled both renewed engagement with, and ongoing irreverence towards, the ex-colonial power's most canonical writer. It seems probable that, in seeing a global cultural figure like Shakespeare adapted so successfully to one of Nigeria's most prominent forms of theatrical expression, the University Travelling Theatre production garnered a sense of national pride following independence.

Book Publishing and Mbari Centres

Book publishing and Mbari centres are two further instances where Shakespeare tours supported broader British and American efforts to shape and influence Nigeria's cultural landscape following independence. Decolonisation provided British publishers with a tremendous opportunity to maintain their monopoly on the supply of school textbooks throughout West Africa's most populous regions at a time of rapid expansion and massive investment. Publishers enjoyed the advantage of having their set-texts such as the school edition of *Macbeth* prescribed for school and university exams through the 'retention of a British-style education system' and the 'continuation of British-staffed education boards'.[50] According to Caroline Davis, British publishers continued to 'operate under colonial modes of publishing' well into the independence era, retaining an advantageous commercial position in West Africa that had broader implications for English language educational publishing across the entire Commonwealth.[51]

Furthermore, British publishers' support for the burgeoning field of Nigerian literature following independence influenced public perceptions over the continuing presence of foreign monopolies. Oxford University Press, for instance, acquired a comprehensive catalogue of the latest works by emerging Nigerian authors who would go on to constitute a large part of Africa's Anglophone literary canon. The outlay involved in supporting unknown local writers made economic sense because, even when such ventures ran at a financial loss, British publishers accrued valuable cultural capital by being seen to support Nigerian literature.[52] Meanwhile, the publication of vast numbers of school textbooks provided 'unprecedented profits' for the London businesses.[53]

In addition, cultural centres known as Mbari clubs were set up in support of Nigeria's renaissance in arts, music, theatre, and literature.[54] The original Mbari centre in Ibadan, established by Ulli Beier in 1957, hosted the first generation of literary dramatists including Wole Soyinka and J. P. Clark.[55] By 1963, a growing network of cultural sites encouraged theatrical developments on a national scale. John Ekwere's Ogui Players, later known as the Eastern Nigerian Theatre Group, found a home when the British Council opened two Mbari clubs, one at its Port Harcourt centre and another in a purpose-built extension to its building in Enugu.[56] The Regional Representative reported to London:

> The Ogui Players and their leader John Ekwere are in the forefront of Mbari and the British Council in Enugu is still their home. With the new extension, open air theatre is now possible and among the performances put on by this group during the year, two have been outstanding, *The Song of The Goat* and *Brother Jero*, both completely Nigerian in origin and feeling.[57]

The investment provided a new Eastern venue for touring companies, with the Enugu site hosting a total of six groups in 1963 including the Ibadan University Travelling Theatre's production of *The Comedy of Errors*. Following the visit of the Nottingham Players, the local Representative enthused:

> There is no doubt that one of the important by-products of the visit ... was the 'shot in the arm' which it gave to local amateur groups ... The British Council, which has been referred to in the local press as 'our old friend in the arts' has a duty to perform in the encouragement of this serious amateur drama – out of which the professional must come in this part of the world.[58]

The Nottingham Playhouse *Macbeth* (1963)

Nottingham Evening News was tremendously proud that the British Council had 'invited the Nottingham Playhouse to make the first-ever visit of a British theatre company to West Africa':[59]

> Nottingham Playhouse has become, in theatrical circles, as famous as the Old Vic. Our company – not theirs – has been chosen to be the first to visit West Africa under the auspices of the British Council ... it is a wonderful tribute to the worth of our own repertory company that we should be invited.[60]

By the early 1960s, the Nottingham Playhouse had built a strong local following while achieving national acclaim for productions that were hailed as a triumph of creativity over cramped conditions.[61] Overseas touring opportunities arose from 1961 onwards following the appointment of Frank Dunlop as Artistic Director. Dunlop brought with him an initial invitation from the British Council to take a Nottingham production of

Macbeth to schools in Malta. The ensuing tour was led by Eric Thompson (a previous member of the Oxford Playhouse Company with experience of touring India, Pakistan, and Sri Lanka in the late 1950s) and continued its run as a regional school tour for theatre-less towns outside Nottingham upon its return.[62] The local press reported that the invitation to tour West Africa was 'a direct result of the success of the Malta venture at the end of 1961' which had served as a trial run.[63]

Dunlop understood the long-term advantages of accepting what was broadly considered to be a risky proposition, persuading the theatre's board of directors that it would add 'considerable prestige advantage' and consequently help 'attract artists of the right calibre to the company'.[64] The fact that the Trust was willing to 'neither make a profit nor suffer any loss' over the venture indicates how greatly the opportunity to foster important state and industry contacts was valued.[65] Indeed, the cultural cachet that came with undertaking the high-profile foreign tour helped the Nottingham Playhouse attract up-and-coming talent like Judi Dench from the RSC and Paul Daneman from the Old Vic, with both actors staying on to complete a season at the regional theatre following the tour.

Although John Neville had recently played Macbeth in Peter Dew's production for Malta, it was decided that the West Africa tour would feature a new and specially adapted staging directed by Frank Dunlop and designed by Rosemary Vercoe.[66] Prior to setting off, the company presented their revised version of *Macbeth* 'with an oriental twist' for a week's preview before local audiences.[67] The regional press were presented with actors clothed in 'light, cotton costumes' aimed at giving them 'an airier and more barbaric look ... suitable for the equatorial climes' they would soon be finding themselves in.[68] This attire was the most immediate and visible manifestation of an over-determined production plagued with deeply misguided notions regarding the style of Shakespearean adaptation that might 'appeal' to West African audiences.[69] The captions that ran alongside the production photos issued by the British Information Services explained that the production had been given 'a Japanese look to emphasise the barbaric nature of the play'.[70] Inviting West African audiences to associate Japanese culture with 'barbarism' was an unwelcome return to the reductive and essentialising view of 'culture' that had recently supported British colonial rule in West Africa itself. The deliberate reactivation of racial hierarchies dating from the colonial era suggests that, despite the end of indirect rule, British officialdom was still trapped in colonial habits of thinking that intuitively promoted white racial superiority.

The invited Nottingham press were evidently baffled by the spectacle and struggled to understand the thinking behind the production. As one reporter confessed:

> The logic of presenting *Macbeth*, which is about a Scottish tyrant, in Japanese costumes before audiences in Nigeria, Ghana and Sierra Leone, escapes me for the moment. Maybe the West Africans will appreciate the kimono-type robes and samurai swords without the occasional irreverent association with 'The Mikado' that crept into me ... there was a certain unease about Frank Dunlop's production.[71]

Though never formally acknowledged, the idea of staging *Macbeth* in a Japanese idiom almost certainly came from Akira Kurosawa's *Throne of Blood* (1957) (Figure 4.1).[72] Dunlop may have identified in Kurosawa's adaptation of *Macbeth* a template for mounting a cross-cultural production of his own, one that he perhaps hoped would leap across social, cultural, and linguistic barriers as successfully as Kurosawa's had. Needless to say, appropriating random elements of Japanese and 'African' iconography was a highly reductive approach, providing an inept and inadequate solution to the difficult question the British Council and the Nottingham Playhouse had set themselves: that is, how to stage a cross-cultural production of Shakespeare for West African audiences it paternalistically assumed had never seen a theatre production before; and how to stage *Macbeth* effectively for secondary school children approaching the play as a set-text on the English Literature curriculum?

In attempting to answer such questions the production made some eccentric decisions, especially in terms of the acting style adopted by its performers. In contrast to Neville's nuanced portrayal of Macbeth in Malta, 'the lines were shouted – sometimes roared – but there was little feeling beyond rant and melodramatic gesture behind them'.[73] By way of explanation, Nottingham reviewers received a note before performances reminding them to consider it 'a unique experience because this version is not really meant for us'.[74] Though the producers aimed to place

> emphasis on [the] spoken word rather than atmospheric spectacle. One would imagine that the people of Nigeria, Ghana, and Sierra Leone would have wanted it the other way around ... With such an international array, it is difficult for home audiences to appreciate this business of the spoken word, particularly as the weird sisters wear African type witch doctor masks: the throne has a leopard skin on it, and the heads come out of the cauldron like ventriloquist dummies with chubby faces.[75]

The *Nottingham Evening Post* found that, with its 'exaggeration of gesture and voice', 'the deeper subtleties of the tragedy were not plumbed'

Figure 4.1 James Cairncross as Banquo in the Nottingham Playhouse *Macbeth*, 1963. Directed by Frank Dunlop. Photo by Allan Hurst. Image held by Nottinghamshire Archives, DD/NP/2/2/10/3. Used by permission of Nottingham Playhouse and Nottinghamshire Archives.

and that the production constituted 'a melodrama that occasionally dipped even lower'.[76] Whatever the underlying 'intention', the overall effect seemed to be an emphasis on 'simplicity and stark essentials'.[77] Despite devising such an eccentric production, the British Information Services' advance publicity in West Africa promoted the Nottingham Playhouse as exemplary. The *Nigeria Morning Post* duly reported that the visiting company's 'close connection to such famous Shakespearean actors like Sir Laurence Olivier, and Lady Olivier – who was herself a former member of the Nottingham Playhouse company – must be a pointer to the success people expect'.[78] In more modest terms (though still under the portentous headline 'The Formidable Force from Nottingham') the company promised to 'bring to West Africa the strongest Nottingham Company on record'. In response, one Nigerian journalist predicted that the visitors' specialism in verse speaking was something that 'should commend them to Nigerian audiences' who could 'be trusted to know the Shakespearean text'.[79]

Opening Night in Lagos

The Nigerian leg of the tour began with six shows in Lagos between 6 and 15 January. The company's first performance inaugurated the opening of the New Glover Hall Theatre, a refurbishment of the old Memorial Hall that was built in 1899 by European settlers and local elites. Originally hosting the kinds of concert parties that were the main manifestation of colonial-era theatre, the venue had long associations with British imperial rule. Following independence, the New Glover Hall aimed at being 'one of the most modern' theatres in West Africa despite 'not actually [being] designed as a drama stage' at all.[80] Dench recalled that the venue provided 'the only real theatre we played in on the tour' and that elsewhere the company performed 'in the open air'.[81]

The reviews of *Macbeth*'s debut indicate that the British visitors had seriously underestimated the sophistication of their Nigerian hosts. Given the symbolism of the event, the high expectations built up in the local press, and the atmosphere of national celebration that surrounded the New Glover Hall's refurbishment, Lagos audiences were vocal in their disappointment with the Nottingham Players' *Macbeth*. Local playwright Samy Imayu pulled few punches when he stated that 'in view of the fact that they are a professional group' the show 'fell below expectation', seemed 'more like a farce or a comedy', and failed to 'convince the audience that it was a tragic play' at all.[82] Another reporter felt that the spectacle 'failed to justify' the Nottingham Players' 'leadership of the British theatre industry', and that the company indulged in both 'over-acting and under-acting at various stages of the performance'.[83] Reviewers were perplexed by the didactic style of acting that the performers adopted throughout, with one commentator complaining that the lead

> should have given a greater solemnity and action to his soliloquy instead of making one feel he was doing a formal recitation. This I did not expect from a professional actor. Nevertheless, this flaw was excellently made up for by John who, while on the stage, pulled a muscle. His resultant limping was so grandly done, that spectators must have taken him to be depicting a limping Macbeth.[84]

The awkwardness of the production, and especially the eccentric vocal delivery adopted by its performers, astonished Nigerian audiences to the point where derisive laughter seemed the only apt response.

A review written under the moniker Peter Pan illustrates the complex post-imperial world that the British tourists had stumbled into and hence the range of disparaging responses that greeted their production on its opening night. In initially appearing to defend the English visitors by taking the unruly Lagos audience to task, Pan delivers a biting satire on the residual colonial attitudes evident in the Nottingham Players' visit. The article begins with a recollection of schooling during the colonial era, one presumably familiar to many theatregoers:

> A muddleheaded classmate of mine, by a curious stroke of sheer luck, once had an envied part in an end-of-term production of a Shakespeare play. It was the 'Merchant of Venice'. The fellow tried to make good his chance. His eloquence was brilliant. His oratory, unrivalled. Until he came to this Freudian thunder-clap ... "If I PRICK you", he thundered, "do you not laugh? If I TICKLE you, do you not bleed?" Our English teacher, a hulking true-blood Yorkshire man, went about his business the rest of the term with a dazed, tortured look on his face. Even in those colonial days, he won our sympathy. [85]

Pan's anecdote is a reminder of the ways in which many Nigerians viewed Shakespeare through a dual lens of colonial-era schooling and irreverent local counter-claims.[86] Though ubiquitous, Shakespeare was treated with deliberate impertinence and discourtesy in Nigerian popular culture and, as the preeminent cultural symbol of the former colonial power, was a natural target for parody and lampooning.[87] Writers of Onitsha market literature would often call upon Shakespeare in moments of heightened drama and emotional intensity, only to then deliberately invert its metaphors and image-laden language for ironic and comic effect. For Nigerians, Shakespeare was rich territory for puns, rhymes, and wordplay, as the journalist's classmate's 'Freudian-thunder-clap' ably demonstrates.[88] Due to a mixture of linguistic habits, love of proverbs, and an ambivalent attitude to the notion of Shakespeare as worthy or 'improving', Nigerians had a complex and uneasy relationship with the English playwright. In a long-standing tradition of rebelling against colonial schooling (richly manifested in popular and widely consumed 'pulp' literatures), quoting and misquoting Shakespeare was 'a persistent and instinctive linguistic reality' in Nigeria.[89]

Peter Pan articulated this indivisible link between Shakespeare and British colonial rule and shared it with a knowing readership:

> William Shakespeare among the English is an institution. The Englishman takes Shakespeare as seriously as the worship of his religion. When ... the poor Yorkshire man ... requested to be invalided from service and had sworn never again to return to the African continent, we were not at all surprised.[90]

Having coupled Shakespeare with colonial-era education, Pan went on to lament the sudden return of both in the form of the Nottingham Players' *Macbeth*. The performance prompted an unwanted return to a best forgotten era, as the writer 'never thought the day would come again when I would watch Shakespeare held to ransom. But there it was again last week ... The classic contradiction, the weird mix-up'.[91] The fruitless cultural exchange meant that

> the Nottingham Playhouse Repertory ... might easily think that we are a lousy blood-thirsty lot ... Shakespeare meant 'Macbeth' as a tragedy and wrote it as such. And the Nottingham Players, in spite of overwhelming opposition by the Lagos audience, did their damnedest to interpret it that way. But the audience was determined to have a roaring time and no tragedy, Macbeth and all, was going to stop them.[92]

Given the diplomatic significance of the event, some reviewers felt compelled to explain the audience's seemingly inappropriate response, pointing out that the visitors' weak production became hostage to a crowd that had

> gone out for enjoyment. That is why it is not surprising that 'Macbeth' – a tragedy, tended towards comedy ... I managed to ask the person sitting near me why he was laughing. He told me it was because Lady Macbeth acted more boldly than Macbeth ... another person told me it was because Macbeth did not behave like a murderer ... I'm sure none would have told me he laughed because he delights in seeing blood.[93]

Most newspapers picked up on the audience's reaction to Act II. 2. immediately following the murder of Duncan:

Macbeth emerges from the room of crime and shows his blood-stained hands to his wife. He is incensed at the damnable murder. To my alarm a large section of the audience inspired by this gruesome scene, were suddenly gripped by spasms of giggles and laughs! My blood ran cold ... Each determined effort to retrieve the mood of pathos was resolutely defied by an audience half berserk with absurd levity.[94]

Recalling how Nigerian audiences would laugh or call out at seemingly inappropriate moments during performances, Dench stated:

> Every time I said, 'The Thane of Fife had a wife,' it used to bring the house down; everything that rhymed they found hysterically funny, and would call out, 'Say that again, say that again,' and then fall about. Anytime we touched each other they absolutely howled with laughter, and they found the witches equally funny.[95]

Dench, who received some of the best reviews along with Daneman, considered the tour an important learning experience as an actor, concluding that 'nothing will ever throw you again when you have played to those audiences' (Figure 4.2).[96]

Figure 4.2   John Neville and Judi Dench as Macbeth and Lady Macbeth in the Nottingham Playhouse *Macbeth*, 1963.
Directed by Frank Dunlop. Photo by Allan Hurst. Image held by Nottinghamshire Archives, DD/NP/2/2/10/2. Used by permission of Nottingham Playhouse and Nottinghamshire Archives.

Kole Omotoso, an academic who has written extensively on African theatre, was assisting the company at the time as a final-year A-Level English Literature student at King's College Lagos. Omotoso recalled:

> At the point where Macbeth puts out his hand and talks about how 'this my hand will the multitudinous seas incarnadine, making the green one red' the Lagos audience would burst into laughter. The actors and actresses wanted us to explain that peculiar reaction. All we could say was that as far as the audience was concerned, the person playing Macbeth was taking the whole thing too seriously. After all it's only a play![97]

Another reason for the infectious laughter that gripped the audience during *Macbeth*'s opening night may have been the actors' resemblance to the bombast characters then prevalent in popular market literature. Bombast characters were created by pamphlet authors to lampoon pretension and verbosity, with poetry, medical jargon, technical discourse, and political rhetoric all becoming grist to their satiric mill. Though Shakespeare was a source of interest and fascination in Nigeria, many would instinctively shy away from the playwright's more sonorous lines, finding them indicative of arrogance and pomposity.

The British Council sought to rationalise this disastrous opening night by stressing the audience's unfamiliarity with Shakespeare. Their Annual Report framed the event as

> a sure sign that the convention of Shakespearian tragedy is unfamiliar to many; as indeed it was in Paris when *Macbeth* was first performed there centuries ago. In Lagos, as in Paris, some uncomprehending laughter was heard.[98]

Pan's review not only anticipated such official protestations but caricatured them with some excellent bombast of his own, concluding with a mock lament that the 'base and crass ignorance displayed with such riotous venom on Friday was disgraceful evidence that we were not – with it!':

> Since when did premeditated murder become an affair for kicks and laughs? Or is it simply that the genius of Shakespeare is beyond the native wit of Nigerians? Zounds! I hope it is the last time we torment the memory of the Legend of Stratford.[99]

Twelfth Night and *Arms and the Man* enjoyed a much better reception because they had not been adapted to the stage for touring purposes alone.[100] The 'general feeling amongst all levels of opinion' was that *Twelfth Night* was 'a colourful, vivid and highly entertaining production' that was performed 'with skill and exuberance'.[101] West fondly recalled the production's opening performance before a school audience:

The first place – we opened in Lagos ... was a biggish hall. And we'd started with *Twelfth Night*. And we did not know what it was going – you know, what the reaction was going to be. It was a school audience. And when the two twins came on [at] the end, the whole audience threw their programmes in the air with delight, and it was absolutely lovely.[102]

Arms and the Man was another production not specifically tailored for touring:

It had generally been predicted before the company arrived in Africa that only the two Shakespeare plays in its repertoire would be well known and therefore well received: the Shaw, it was prophesied, would be too sophisticated, the situations too strange, the comment too subtle.

The show in fact proved 'to be a great and delightful hit" with Nigerian audiences:

The blandness of Bluntschli, the bumbling of Petkoff, the apparent innocence of Raina, the snobbish realism of Nicola, the absurdity of Sergius, the sexiness of Louka and the satire at the expense of them all were appreciated readily and relished vociferously ... in Kano the audience stood up and cheered.[103]

Secular Missionaries: British Accounts of the West Africa Tour

Despite its decidedly mixed reception in Lagos, the UK press would go on to claim that the Nottingham Playhouse tour was a resounding success overall. British journalists tended to focus on the volume of tickets sold, highlighting for instance how local demand created a black market in which *Macbeth* sold at '£2 10s more than face value'. This was an effective strategy to adopt because it avoided any discussion on the production's critical reception and was, objectively speaking, true.[104] The Eastern Regional Representative Report confirms that productions drew large audiences. Open air venues in Nsukka accommodated 1,400 per night, while Port Harcourt Town Hall seated audiences of 500 at each performance, indicating that 7,100 tickets were sold in the Eastern Region in one week alone.[105] The impressive volume of ticket sold meant that the tour was able to make a profit as 'the total receipts amounted to £1,782 (Enugu and Nsukka £1,243, Port Harcourt £539)' whilst the 'estimated local expenditure, including board and lodging' was '£1,203 (Enugu and Nsukka £800, Port Harcourt £403)'.[106]

British newspaper articles that acknowledged local responses were often selective in their reporting, and so quite misleading. A laudatory piece that appeared in *The Stage and Television Today* under the grandiose title

'Shakespeare and Shaw in the Sun: Nottingham Conquers Africa' mixed the most positive aspects of separate school and public performances to present the touring company as modern-day cultural missionaries:[107]

> All along the line audiences were far more demonstrative than at home. At times they were so enthusiastic that they recited the chief speeches with the actors ... it was often a case of reliving the atmosphere of the original Shakespeare performance of the Globe. Heroines were clapped, the villains roundly hissed and booed ... With such a stream of uninhibited playgoers – ready to travel hundreds of miles in some cases – and with such an enthusiastic atmosphere surrounding the entire performance, the tour reached exhilarating heights.[108]

In projecting historical fantasies of Elizabethan England's organic community onto West African audiences, such pieces framed Shakespeare as a universally relevant writer speaking directly to Nigeria's 'proto-democratic' aspirations.

English actors undertaking tours in the post-imperial decade of the 1960s displayed a more irreverent attitude towards cultural diplomacy than previous generations. Terence Knapp viewed Nottingham Playhouse's mission with a mixture of humour and knowing cynicism:

> Neville had been invited to form a Company by the British Council whose function it is to spread the good British news throughout the world when it can afford to do so. Of course I wanted to toddle off to the depths of darkest Africa to play Shakespeare with ... Neville, Judi Dench, old Uncle Tom Cobbley and all. It was the first such expedition to that part of the former Empire although there had been many such tours to South East Asia, the Americas, and often to India where the cognoscenti seemed most fond of the Bard in the Queen's English.[109]

Knapp's self-depreciating style was typical of the British travel writing of the period. As Patrick Holland and Graham Huggan put it, 'the gentleman abroad in a post-imperial context, might well appear ridiculous; but ridicule, precisely, becomes his licence to perform'.[110] Knapp's account admits a pained awareness of the bizarre and anachronistic nature of the cultural mission his company is embarked upon. He takes shelter, however, by recounting the experience askance, as if through a lens of clichés, and saves face by maintaining a stance of amused and ironic detachment.

Irony provided Knapp with a licence to rehash a wide range of colonial-era stereotypes, from black magic and frightening animal encounters to other literary tropes stemming from the nineteenth-century colonial fiction of H. Ridder Haggard. Clichés of 'darkest Africa' – conceits that Patrick Brantlinger labels 'imperial gothic' – haunt the collective memory of the venture and can be found across a wide range of touring ephemera, from actors' biographies and press reviews to programme notes and actors' obituaries.[111] In her introduction to Gareth Armstrong's *A Case for Shylock: Around the World with Shakespeare's Jew* (2004) (an account of another Valerie West tour that, with their typically reduced cast of two by the 1970s and 1980s, were dubbed 'Val's Duos'), Dench reveals how gallows humour helped the company cope with the stresses of touring:

> Recalling Valerie West ... reminded me of a journey from Kano to Kadina when James Cairncross suggested the first line of a limerick: 'One Christmas Miss Valerie West ...'. After hours on a dusty road, I came up with:
>
> > 'One Christmas Miss Valerie West,
> > Laid the Nottingham Playhouse to rest.
> > Over the thirty sad graves,
> > Of these thespian braves,
> > Cried 'I was only doing my best'.[112]

Although the imperial gothic motifs are tongue-in-cheek, they still evoke a kind of Conradian atavism where the dangerous route of journeying deeper into colonial space takes the European traveller backwards in time and towards potential death and destruction. Likewise, such anecdotes present the tour as an anti-conquest with the actors playing the part of cultural missionaries risking life and limb to bring Shakespeare to new territories and grateful audiences.[113]

Imperial gothic motifs colour many of the light-hearted anecdotes of the Shakespeare productions themselves. Vultures would occasionally perch on a screen at the back of the stage during open-air performances of *Macbeth*, and while Frank Dunlop thought 'that could not be more wonderful', Dench liked to tease her fellow actors by advising them to 'twitch' 'For goodness' sake ... when you are killed, they are waiting to pick your bones'.[114] Knapp's account of the first performance of *Twelfth Night* in Kano reads

> we performed in Northern Nigeria in a vast sports stadium that had been built for the Pan-African games. We performed mid-centre stadium, surrounded by several thousand turbaned natives from the area. The desert night was cool ... and the acoustics were fabulous. I was playing Feste in *Twelfth Night* ... I played Feste as a white-faced clown with tear-drop eyes. When I made my first appearance there was an odd response from the audience. In the rowdy scene that disturbs Malvolio's sleep ... there was hardly any laughter in spite of much comic by-play. We came offstage disturbed and troubled. The Nigerian house manager was waiting for us in the wings. He spoke solemnly to John Neville, who played Malvolio, all the while giving me side-glances. John turned to me and said, 'You'll have to take off that make-up. A white face here signifies

a zombie, a ghost, which is what they think you are.' The house manager had told John the audience were literally scared by my appearance. Hurriedly I wiped off the make-up and reappeared clean faced. The audience relaxed. Feste got his laughs and all was well from then on.[115]

Here, attempts to blend colonial-era tropes with the typical self-deprecating humour of post-war British travel writing serves only to expose the tensions underlying the visitors' mission. Though the incident provides a clear example of the cultural misunderstanding that often arose between the bumbling though well-intentioned British visitors and their ever-tolerant Nigerian hosts, it also reveals how Shakespeare in performance could be an unstable and unreliable commodity for British cultural diplomats operating within a post-colonial context. Mirroring *Macbeth*'s unintended reception as comedy in Lagos, audiences in Kano found *Twelfth Night*'s jester (a telling representative of the strolling British players themselves) uncanny and frightening. Overall, though irony and self-deprecating humour helped English actors mediate the anxiety and uncertainty they felt in playing the role of Shakespearean cultural missionaries, it provided them with only a limited license to perform within a postcolonial setting.[116]

***

The British Council was happy to conclude that the Nottingham Playhouse tour had a significant cultural impact in Nigeria, with thousands of 'column inches' and 'extensive coverage on the radio and television services' 'dedicated to it' throughout the region.[117] In diplomatic circles it was hailed as 'very much more successful than any previous foreign tour' to the region that had been put on by either the Soviets or the Americans. Lord Head sent 'a most enthusiastic telegram of congratulations to the Company' while other in-house commentators felt that the achievement had given British culture a much-needed boost in West Africa:[118]

> The image of Shakespeare received a brilliant shine. The tour was most valuable to the Council's work in this region; it did much for our prestige, and more importantly, Anglo-Nigerian relations. It was simply bigger, better, better organised and of more value to Nigerians than the Russian show of 61 and the American show of '62.[119]

Major General W. H. A. Bishop, the High Commissioner of the Commonwealth Relations Office in London, enthused:

> We continue to be extremely satisfied with the co-operation between the British Council and this High Commission. The regular series of meetings

which we hold draw together the threads of innumerable day-to-day consultations which take place between their staff and ours; and the British Council are working admirably as our eyes and ears in the educational and connected fields.[120]

The calm and measured language of official reports gave way to occasional outbursts of self-congratulation, revealing the truly interventionist and neo-colonial nature of the cultural-diplomatic venture:

with over 7000 Nigerians, from the Governor-General downwards, literally clamouring to see Shakespeare ... [the tour] brought home, as no other project could have, just how starved a developing country can become, and just how grateful it can be for what it receives ... The Provisional Commissioner of Port Harcourt summed it up in the presence of the Representative, Nigeria, when he said: 'Shakespeare, Libraries and the English Language – those are the outstanding British Council contributions to eastern Nigeria'.[121]

The tour bequeathed a legacy of its own when the British Council provided Geoffrey Axworthy with a £1000 fund to undertake a nationwide tour of Nigeria to commemorate the Shakespeare quatercentenary of 1964.[122] Continuing to adapt local performance traditions to western technical know-how, Axworthy's University Travelling Theatre equipped one of Ogunmola's 'gaily painted' Yoruba mammy wagons 'with a generator, control board, lights, [and] props', thus converting it into a 'Theatre on Wheels'.[123] The DAC's report on this 'Grand Shakespeare Festival' is worth quoting at length:

a replica of an Elizabethan stage ... built onto a large trailer in such a way that it could very quickly be erected or collapsed for transportation as required. An entertainment entitled 'A Shakespeare Festival' consisting of extracts from seven plays, linked by a tape-recorded narration, was compiled by Geoffrey Axworthy and the Travelling Theatre went on the road in March 1964 ... There is no doubt that artistically the tour was a major success ... Audience response, which at times reached the point of participation, was, as we have come to expect, most rewarding: every argument and every piece of comic business being greeted with spontaneous applause. The performances were enchanting. The calibre of the acting was high, in some extracts very high indeed. The youth and freshness of the cast gave well-worn scenes a new vigour and bloom ... Axworthy estimated that the show had an aggregate audience of 60,000. This figure speaks for itself, and for the future.[124]

While reaping the fruits of performance-based research undertaken by the University of Ibadan's Drama Department, the British Council portrayed Axworthy as a cultural missionary taking Shakespeare 'to overwhelmingly enthusiastic and sometimes riotous audiences in places beyond the reach of a normal touring company'.[125] This wholesale appropriation reached its zenith with proposals for a second Nottingham Playhouse visit to West Africa in 1966. As Knapp recalled, an 'offer from Shell Oil' had been secured 'to provide a travelling theatre, a custom-made pantechnicon' that would afford the possibility of 'long distance freedom' for the British Council's very own company of 'latter-day strolling players':[126]

> Designed as a gigantic truck, it would have its own dynamo for electricity ... A long side would be let down to make a thrust stage. It would allow us to be self-sufficient, eliminating the transportation and performance problems we had encountered before ... All we would need were hampers of costumes, properties, and some basic furniture. Completely self-contained, the vehicle would enable us to travel to far out parts of West Africa where audiences, whether two dozen or two hundred or two thousand would make themselves at ease on the ground around us to view the productions.[127]

This Yoruba Travelling Theatre-style 'Pantechnicon Tour' intended to take Shakespeare further afield, to the far North Western Nigerian city of Sokoto and the small neighbouring nation of Benin.[128] On 15 January 1966, however, ten days before the company was due to set off, the tour was abruptly cancelled when the coup d'état that was a prelude to the Biafran Civil War left the principal date in the North in rebel hands, and Ibadan sealed off with street fighting.[129] Despite this setback, the British Council were able to ship the Nottingham players off to Southeast Asia where they undertook an impromptu two-month tour of Malaysia, Brunei, Singapore, and the Philippines.[130]

The English tours that ventured further and further overseas in the early-to-mid 1960s differed greatly from the celebrity-garlanded affairs previously undertaken by prominent figures like John Gielgud, Laurence Olivier, and Vivienne Leigh. Less prestigious companies embarked on lengthy and increasingly ambitious circuits that young cast members viewed as an unusually adventurous professional opportunity. At the dawn of the postcolonial era, Britain's cultural administrators would go to great lengths to ensure that the Shakespeare quatercentenary of 1964 would be celebrated on a truly global scale. Long established independent nation-states across South and Southeast Asia, however, would see the 400-year anniversary as an opportunity to reassert their own claims on Shakespeare and exercise their right to critique the uneven and threadbare English productions that washed up on their shores.

CHAPTER 5

Globalisation in South and Southeast Asia (1964–1965)
The Tempest, Richard II, and The Taming of the Shrew

To celebrate the Shakespeare quatercentenary of 1964, the British Council set itself the task of 'exporting' Shakespeare to over 80 countries: sending 16 lecturers to 40 countries, 350 sets of photographic exhibitions to 84 countries, book exhibitions to 50 countries, feature films to 59 countries, and touring Shakespeare companies to 40 countries. At home this 'massive export effort' was hailed as 'the biggest' undertaking 'of its kind in the history of the British theatre', while overseas commentators marvelled at the efforts the British were making to ensure that the 400th anniversary of Shakespeare's birth would be celebrated on a truly global scale.[1] Anticipating the arrival of the New Shakespeare Company (NSC) in Pakistan, one journalist mused that though 'cynics might say' that 'when the English start taking interest in something they literally kill it' (just 'look at the fate of their cooking, their railways, their Empire') but that the 'one big exception' to this rule is 'Shakespeare. Not only does their interest never abate in this great institution but ... they are perpetually involved in exploring and giving him new meanings and new interpretations'. Wondering why Britain had placed 'so much emphasis on Shakespeare', the journalist concluded that he 'stands as much for England, its history and traditions, as does the House of Commons', after all 'England never produced a prophet or a saint'.[2] Overall, while the Shakespeare quatercentenary provided Britain with an opportunity to assert its cultural exceptionalism in an increasingly globalised world, nations that had recently laboured under British colonial rule viewed it as an invitation to assert their own claims on the playwright whilst resetting diplomatic relations on more equitable terms. As one Indian journalist put it, the citizens of Bangalore were happy to 'bow to the memory of the immortal Poet who', as the English actor-director David William said, 'is as much our Poet as theirs'.[3]

The NSC tour's reception throughout South and Southeast Asia reflected the interests and concerns of a new historical era that the historian A.G. Hopkins terms 'postcolonial globalisation'.[4] In Hopkin's formulation, it was only following the post-war period of widespread decolonisation that liberatory ideals like 'self-determination' and 'human rights' finally came to be 'applied globally', especially when guaranteed and translated 'into policy' by 'leading international organisation[s]' like 'the United Nations' (UN).[56] The end of Empire saw membership to the UN double from 51 to 117 between 1945 and 1965, with newly independent nation-states encouraged to participate in a thriving network of transnational theatrical-cultural exchanges established by UNESCO-affiliated organisations like the International Theatre Institute and the Théâtre des Nations.[7] For emerging postcolonial nations, development was 'the talisman of the time' with rapid and widespread modernisation across all industries (including theatre) coming to symbolise a 'route to full independence and the good life that colonial rule had advertised but failed to deliver'.[8]

Consequently, host nations viewed the British visit in terms of developmentalism as much as an opportunity to renew or maintain friendly diplomatic relations with the ex-colonial power in the region. The visiting productions of *The Tempest, Richard II*, and *The Taming of the Shrew* were assumed to be representative of the current state of play in English Shakespeare, providing host nations with a rare opportunity to assess the latest technical advances and stimulate local ambitions for more Western-style national theatre industries of their own.[9] Though most previous British Council visits to the region had been limited to the performance of select scenes to university students, the quatercentenary tour would provide school and public audiences with the novel experience of attending full and professionally staged English language productions. Consequently, the tour prompted lively debates on what constituted 'Shakespeare' itself, pitting the textual tradition that held sway in elite educational setting during the colonial era, against more emergent ideas of how Shakespeare-in-performance could be marshalled to support local and national theatrical developments.

Although the British Council framed the visit as 'pioneering work' introducing authoritative and professionally staged Shakespeare to 'new territories' overseas, the English tourists were in fact passing through a series of distinct local claims on the playwright that had evolved out of a shared and complex history shaped, in part, by British colonial rule.[10] Commemorative events in Sri Lanka, for instance, were so extensive that the NSC visit seemed a modest and even minor contribution in a crowded field of local productions and adaptations. *The Sun* could confidently boast that 'the Bard has been remembered all too well in this fair isle of ours' and was no longer considered 'a foreigner'. There had been 'a spate of public lectures', productions 'in both English and Swabhasha', 'musical renderings', 'excerpts', and 'full length plays'. 'Whatever their quality be, one fact remains – there has been a surfeit of Shakespeare.' Although Karl Goonasena's ambitious production of *Macbeth* 'failed', it was considered 'an ambitious venture well worth the attempt'. There was a series of talks on '*Hamlet* in Film' by local critics Reggie Siriwardena, Marvyn de Silva, A.J. Gunawardena, and A.M.G. Sirimanne. For those 'who wanted Shakespeare light and in modern garb' an American 'Broadway producer' was staging a breezy production of KISS ME KATE with an all-Sri Lankan cast.[11] There was rumour that 'a film is being made in Tamil of *Hamlet*'.[12] Meanwhile, the Department of Education held 'oratorical contests' and dedicated 'the School Essay Competition' to the playwright, while the Arts Council published 'a symposium of essays' on Shakespeare and new translations of Shakespeare's plays into Sinhala and Tamil. All in all, with further plans to stage *Portia Nadagama* (1884), a local adaptation of *The Merchant of Venice* and *Romeo and Juliet* attributed to D.B. Wanigasuriya, Sri Lankans could be confident that 'the Bard lives fresh with us as with all literate peoples of the world, and time does not stale a literary genius. We in Ceylon have dutifully paid our share of obeisance. And quite rightly, too'.[13]

Sri Lanka's 'surfeit of Shakespeare' was inflected by residual anti-imperial sentiments, however. The loaded word 'obeisance' acts as a pointed reminder of the validating role that Shakespeare played in supporting Britain's 'civilizing mission' during colonial rule, and Ravi concluded his survey by reminding readers that in the years since 1948, when Sri Lanka won its independence from Britain, the 'theatre-going public in Ceylon' had had 'a taste' of professional English theatre 'from time to time' and now knew how 'to judge the fare offered'. This was no longer the colonial or early-independence era, and long 'gone are the days when everything foreign was lapped up by them like hungry kittens'. Sri Lankans no longer suffered from 'complexes' and now felt themselves to be 'in a position to recognise any patronising attitudes' from the ex-colonial power. No longer the 'savage judge', the ex-imperial subject 'takes his theatre well and recognises the good from the bad'. 'It was in this spirit that the NSC were viewed' and 'if there were instances' where local reactions seemed 'hypercritical', it 'only goes to prove that healthy criticism prevails in Ceylon and sycophancy is never allowed to take precedence'.[14]

The spirit of self-determination that fuelled Sri Lanka's cultural renaissance following independence, and thus its enthusiastic embrace of Shakespeare during the 1964 quatercentenary, ensured that local critics felt free and duty-bound to air their thoughts on the visiting English productions.

The New Shakespeare Company

The year 1964 was a 'successful' if 'alarmingly active year' for Regent's Park's Open-Air Theatre. 'The Park', as it was known colloquially, was under new administration with David Conville as Company Manager and David William as Artistic Director. The 1,600-seat outdoor venue enjoyed an unusually long spell of fine weather that year, helping it drum up 'splendid business' for its stridently patriotic adaptation of *Henry V* and farce-like production of *The Taming of the Shrew*.[15] In the midst of extensive Shakespeare celebrations in the UK it was announced that the Park's NSC would undertake a 'great' adventure and become 'Shakespeare Wallahs' for a British Council sponsored tour of Pakistan, India, Bangladesh, Sri Lanka (then Independent Ceylon), Hong Kong, the Philippines, Singapore, and Malaysia (then Malaya). Conville recalled that, immediately after their London season closed in late September,

> our company of 33 arrived in Karachi, where our sets had been pre-built, bringing with us our properties, electrical and sound equipment, plus a heavy load of 120 costumes ... We proceeded on a 23-week journey, travelling to eight countries, playing in 19 towns or cities. Many theatres were fine, others often of a poor standard ... There were problems of course: an over-heavy schedule, illness, exhaustion (stage management particularly), stifling costumes (our fault), shared bathrooms, homesickness. But there were wonderful compensations: the enthusiasm of the audiences, kindnesses of our hosts, some unforgettable sightseeing on our short times off.[16]

'Wading through the mass of information to hand that relates to Shakespeare festivities still to come (oh yes!)', *The Lady* magazine noted how, under Conville and William's stewardship, the Park appeared to be 'on the cusp of something' and wished the ambitious outdoor theatre company 'a spell of good luck' and decent weather.[17] In a piece that went on to appear in translation in several foreign language newspapers, J.C. Trewin situated the NSC within a long tradition of touring English classical theatre companies. Four decades previously, 'Britain had several provincial touring companies' like Sir Frank Benson, Henry Baynton, and Charles Doran that nurtured the 'young players' of the day, including 'Ralph Richardson, Donald Wolfit, Eric Portman, and Robert Donald'.[18]

The NSC now appeared to be satisfying an 'obvious need for another classical company, one that, if without the resources' of the National Theatre and the Royal Shakespeare Company, could still 'stage Shakespeare with imagination and technical skill, and with a fully-trained cast accustomed to working in unison'.[19] The British Council was keen to work with the NSC for the same reasons that had attracted it to the Nottingham Playhouse the year previously. As a young, highly motivated, and up-and-coming company, the NSC were an ideal troupe for projecting a full repertoire of theatrical productions overseas. For 'the Park', the prosperct of working 'as a unit for ten consecutive months' provided a rare opportunity to shape themselves into 'something approaching' a permanent repertory company.[20]

Conville and William's outstanding early productions of *Love's Labour's Lost* (1962), *A Midsummer Night's Dream* (1962), and *Twelfth Night* (1963) lived down the Park's reputation as an open-air charity, creating the basis for a commercially viable classical repertory company (Figure 5.1). The actor Michael Blakemore felt that, with 'luck and a subsidy', the NSC could emerge as 'a third force' in British theatre between the RSC and the Old Vic, but that if 'the company confined its work to the Park its hopes of being taken seriously would always be compromised' by the short season.[21] Furthermore, Blakemore knew from personal experience that no amount of talent and hard work could protect a production from the typically inclement weather of an English summer. Actors were often left wondering whether a play would go on from one week to the next, looking on as the 'large and enthusiastic crowds' of a season's brilliant opening dwindled 'to a handful of stoic supporters swathed in blankets' peering out at rain-sodden performers 'shiver[ing] beneath the dripping trees'. Conville and William often struggled to capitalise on their early successes as a consequence, a fact that was painfully demonstrated when the Park's 'exquisite production' of *Love's Labour's Lost* went from being a popular and critical hit to resembling 'an abandoned toy, left out in the rain'.[22] Despite the challenges and setbacks, however, playing Shakespeare at the Park evoked the peculiar energy and romance of touring:

> Waiting to make an entrance through a tunnel of leaves, smelling the humid vegetation underfoot, and sensing what one never does indoors, night stealing across the length of Britain and releasing its provocative energies. The last hour of a good production in the open air can have a power all of its own, as, against the odds, the idea of theatre slyly raises its banner.[23]

Figure 5.1 Mary Steele rehearsing *Love's Labour's Lost*. Directed by David William. Regent's Park Open Air Theatre, 1962. Photo by Kent Gavin. © Getty Images/Corbis Historical.

For Blakemore, the venue epitomised 'what is always true about theatrical enterprise – its riskiness and the quixotic gallantry that is sometimes needed to sustain it'.[24] Despite the practical challenges involved, the NSC 'was able to attract young performers considered to have promise' and who hoped to be spotted by the leading London critics of the day.[25]

The thumbnail biographies provided in the Quatercentenary Tour programmes show that the individual actors that made up the New Shakespeare Company had extensive experience of touring overseas. Conville joined the Shakespeare Memorial Theatre and travelled to Europe with John Gielgud and Peggy Ashcroft in 1955, and again with Laurence Olivier in 1957. Edward Atienza had performed in fifteen different countries; David King had been on an Old Vic tour to Moscow and Leningrad; Dinsdale Landen was part of the Old Vic's

1955 tour of Australia; Wolf Morris had also toured with the Old Vic Company across Europe; and Christopher Burgess had done two tours of Australia with the same company before joining the Bristol Old Vic's circuit of India, Pakistan, and Sri Lanka in 1963. Burgess's obituary in *The Stage* stated that 'fuelled by a love of travelling', the actor 'liked nothing better than joining an overseas tour, funded by the British Council, and then making his way back to Britain visiting as many countries as he could'.[26] John Wyse, the Company's elder statesman, had helped set up the first army theatre unit of soldier actors during the war. His experiences with ENSA led to one of the first British Council tours of India and Pakistan in 1951, where he performed Shakespeare extracts to university audiences alongside the DAC chairman Norman Marshall. David William toured with the Old Vic in 1953 and had just directed Ralph Richardson in a production of *The Merchant of Venice* that was touring South America as part of the quatercentenary celebrations throughout 1964. The programme was happy to assure its readers that William possessed valuable 'first-hand experience' of mounting productions successfully 'onto the stages of rarely used theatres, whose equipment was sadly out of date'.[27] A notable exception was the Polish director of *The Taming of the Shrew*, Vladek Sheybal. Before coming to Britain in 1957, Sheybal had been a leading director with the Polish National Theatre in Warsaw and was the star of *Kanal* (1956), an award-winning film about the Warsaw uprising. Sheybal was in exile, working in an Oxford restaurant, when he was recognised by members of the university's Dramatic Society and was subsequently recruited as an informal acting coach. Sheybal's absence during the tour was noted by several overseas commentators, especially as he had recently achieved global celebrity as the sad-eyed chess player in *From Russia with Love* (1963).

Richard II in India and Sri Lanka

A 1944 report on the prospect of establishing British Council offices in India spelt out the prominent role that cultural diplomacy would come to play following independence:

> Indians still look instinctively to England: the extent to which we have Anglicized the Indian public mind is often underrated and is one of the most extraordinary achievements of the British connection. But India is looking to other countries, notably America, and unless steps are taken in a systematic way to maintain the intellectual communion of the past, our best asset may be lost or cheapened.[28]

The British Council established a presence in India and Pakistan following partition, with regular theatre visits beginning with the Eric Elliott Company's short 'reconnaissance tour' performing Shakespeare scenes, followed by the Norman Marshall Dramatic Recital Company's twenty-week circuit in 1950.[29] Marshall was a regular member of the Drama Advisory Committee and went on to become its chairman from 1961 to 1968.

British officialdom viewed Shakespeare tours to university cities as an effective way to 'maintain intellectual communion' with the more 'Anglicised' sections of the 'Indian public mind' following independence. John Wyse played the role of elder statesman, assuring the press that 'in India it is the great love and knowledge of Shakespeare which helps build an instantaneous rapport' between English actors and local audiences.[30] For certain sections of the Indian press, the tour exuded an aura of Empire nostalgia. *The Hindustan Times* reflected that 'to many of us who came of age before independence, a glimpse of English history at once revives the strange spiritual bond that has grown up between the people of India and Britain'. When 'this glimpse happens to be in a play by the bard, things are doubly absorbing'.[31]

Shakespeare was seen as fertile ground for cultivating a post-imperial entente based on close commercial, economic, and cultural ties. Counting themselves 'a loyal, if distant, outpost in the empire of Shakespearean devotees', prominent Indian reviewers 'freely and joyously' acknowledged Shakespeare's 'sovereignty' whilst aligning it with the genius of India's own national poet, Rabindranath Tagore.[32] The NSC's souvenir programme included 'a splendid tribute to England's poetic mastery' by the world-famous Bengali poet who, in 1913, became the first non-European recipient of the Nobel Prize for Literature:

> When in the far-away sea your fiery disk appeared from behind the unseen, o poet, o sun, England's horizon set you near her breast, and took you to be her own.[33]

The *Amrita Bazar* reminded readers that 'Tagore, like many Bengalis saw Shakespeare as the great master – OF LIFE, in any language, and a superb poet, of matchless imagery, of measureless character portrayal'.[34] Tagore's homage to Shakespeare provided fertile ground for celebrating both British and Indian cultural exceptionality, and Anglo-Indian cultural ties were strengthened further when the Calcutta Arts Society presented an ivory tablet of Tagore's poem to the newly opened Shakespeare Birthplace Trust as part of the quatercentenary celebrations that year.[35]

Richard II *in India and Sri Lanka* 151

As Shakespeare came to prominence in India via the colonial education system, associating the Quatercentenary Tour with elite schooling was a reliable and effective way of cementing cultural relations further. As a product of the prominent Cambridge school of Shakespeare practitioners that extolled the virtues of applying 'scholarly' methods to Shakespearean acting and directing, David William assured interviewers that he 'reads and reads and reads the text', that the 'mine is never exhausted despite incessant digging', and that he would never let actors show 'disrespect for the author' by putting 'Shakespeare into their own words' in rehearsals.[36] True to the beliefs and values of what Christopher J. McCullough terms 'the Cambridge connection', William claimed that his academically informed close reading of the Shakespearean text validated the choices he made both as an actor and as a director.[37] Stressing a shared investment in scholarship and textual fidelity in order to flatter his Indian readers, William complained that British theatregoers did not turn to Shakespeare's texts 'as much as they should' and that 'Indian audiences were better than audiences at home' because 'their knowledge of the text was greater and therefore their reactions were more immediate and purer than those of audiences in England who were apt to take Shakespeare for granted'.[38]

In interviews, William celebrated the shared love of Shakespeare that existed within elite educational settings in Britain and India, only to then bemoan cultural regression within broader British society itself.[39] In complaining that 'the tragic hero had become unfashionable' due to 'the love of the cult of the mass as against the individual',[40] William sought to recruit Indian readers into his campaign against the recent work of the RSC, an institution he felt had fallen under the corrupting influence of more socially and politically concerned practitioners like Kott, Brecht, and Littlewood. Early RSC productions achieved an aura of ostensible political engagement by fusing tried and tested aspects of continental practices (elements such as continuous actor training, lengthy and exploratory rehearsal periods, and the maintenance of large ensemble companies), to the more conservative post-war Cambridge tradition that insisted upon the sanctity of textual approaches authoritatively delivered in cut-glass English accents. William dismissed Brecht as 'practical, cool, anti-emotional, antiseptic and intellectual', and claimed Shakespeare as a natural ally against such 'unemotional' and 'de-humanising' approaches.[41] He expressed dissatisfaction that the growing emphasis in Shakespearean productions tended to be visual, claiming that *Richard II*'s 'great virtue was in diction, that is, the value given to the words and meaning of the play'.[42] The actor-director warned that 'the great danger' of the 'modern style' of staging was 'that it reduces Shakespeare to a twentieth century instead of a universal figure', and lamented the fact that British theatre had become 'most violent in outlook and materialistic in the sense of values' with 'nearly all modern writers' questioning 'the way life is lived and [their] beliefs' whilst offering little 'to put in [its] place'.[43] In a parting shot against international socialism William warned that 'the prime responsibility of the artist to resist the power of the big lie, the untruth, which is so prevalent, dominating and dangerous to the world'.[44] When one Bombay journalist asked him 'what is the future of Shakespeare?', William unhesitatingly replied that 'the future of Shakespeare is the future of civilization' itself.[45]

Though there may have been much sympathy for William's sentiments in India, a well-informed review in Sri Lanka written under the moniker 'Iago' attacked it on several fronts. To begin with, Iago dispelled the notion that the NSC were especially faithful to the Shakespearean text, and questioned the associated claim that textual fidelity guaranteed political neutrality.[46] 'There is in England at the moment a religious devotion to the text' which 'by a change of emphasis and a little "business"' leads to a 'reinterpretation of Shakespeare to suit the present mood of the English audience'.[47] One such 'mood' was the nationalism unleashed by the Shakespeare quatercentenary itself. The reviewer informed readers that if they were able to 'witness the New Shakespeare Company's production of *Henry V* at home' they would discover that 'the very first scene has disappeared without a trace, because it is dangerous and subversive'.[48] Iago's well-informed critique voiced concerns that were circulating within the UK theatre industry itself at the time. Michael Blakemore turned down a part in *Henry V* due to its blatant jingoism, complaining that 'despite the text, much "business" [was] imported to vilify the soldiers who, before the battle, challenge and outwit the king'.[49]

Richard II was a last-minute addition to the NSC tour programme and was not in fact a Regent's Park production at all. Conville's original idea was to tour productions that had been staged just prior to departure like *The Taming of the Shrew* or were scheduled to enter the Park's repertoire the following season, as in *Two Gentlemen of Verona*. The British Council's DAC summarily dismissed the latter when its Representatives overseas became 'worried about' promoting a play 'which is scarcely known in India' and 'would not have anything like the same appeal' as '*Macbeth* or *King Lear*'.[50] The preference for canonical Shakespeare displayed fundamentally misguided concerns over local tastes, and little appreciation for the practical difficulties involved in mounting a viable touring production. The Park would enjoy considerable success staging *Two Gentlemen of*

Verona the following year and several Indian critics went on to express disappointment that the less well-known play had not made it into the tour's repertoire. Conville suggested *Richard II* as a suitable last-minute replacement as the play was 'well known', was 'ideally suited to a young cast', and could pass as tragedy when interpreted as a star-vehicle.[51] On a more practical level, William's production had already played the Ludlow Festival and had been part of the BBC's televised serial adaptation of the history plays *An Age of Kings* (1960), and so could be swiftly reprised for touring purposes.

William's performance in the title role was promoted heavily in advance, with *The Pakistan Times* anticipating the 'rich experience' of seeing a lead performance 'acclaimed by London theatre critics as the best since John Gielgud in 1936'.[52] Though the flattering comparison was primarily aimed at drawing audiences into the theatre, it was true to say that William consciously followed in Gielgud's footsteps.[53] Going so far as adopting the 'poetic modulation' of Gielgud's famous spoken delivery, William's production stayed firmly within the 'cult of personality' tradition established by Frank Benson. In terms of characterisation, William followed Gielgud's lead in emphasising the theatrical nature of kingship itself, and the high personal cost of maintaining this public role for Richard the man.[54] Reviewers frequently commented on William's effective portrayal of the King's mercurial character. From being 'a foppish, Midas-touched ruler' at the beginning, to displaying 'the craft and grasping nature of the king' in the central acts, and finally revealing 'the mortal man he was' at the moment of his downfall; William's performance captured 'a pathos which springs from his sensitivity – his ability, when broken and lonely to see the source of the sickness which afflicts him and his kingdom'.[55] The Bangalore critic B. Chandrasekhara lauded the innate theatricality of William's 'splendid, imaginative acting' claiming it was

> what Shakespeare's Richard was – shadow without substance, a shadow seeing his own exaggerated, blown image in the mirror of his fancy, and becoming, in his futile attempts to make the image of the shadow appear the substance, theatrical.[56]

William's 'effeminate' Richard, with his 'delicately handsome, foppish, prancing' seemed

> a mirror of the man's vanity and his weakness. He darts quickly from insolence to self-directed mockery from downright malevolence to a luxuriant savouring of his own martyrdom ... [from] aloof objectivity to hysterical outpourings, for this is a sensitive, fastidious, if weak man.[57]

Figure 5.2　David William rehearsing as Richard II for the BBC Television Drama *The Age of Kings*, 1960.
© Keystone/Hulton Archive/Getty Images.

Indian critics who had primarily encountered Shakespeare in the lecture theatre praised William for bringing *Richard II* from the page to the stage (Figure 5.2). 'Since I studied it for my Intermediate examination' one journalist wrote, 'I have always wondered' at the 'coldness of critics who do not estimate' *Richard II*. The NSC production confirmed that 'it is best understood only on the stage' where it comes across as

> a sheer sustained lyrical elegy. To hear the golden lines, not from the mouth of a professor, and not merely read with the eye, but from a well-graced actor was a moving experience ... From its very first line ... to the last, the play is a symphony of that elegiac sadness which Grat [sic] captured for a few stanzas and Keats later more intensely in "Ode to the Nightingale".[58]

Such literary-minded reviews that lavished special praise on famous speeches and select scenes were an heirloom of earlier university tours. Wyse's 'lamentations for England's departed glories' was especially celebrated as it 'rose to the occasion and successfully put the action in its wider historical perspective ... his noble old-age wisdom was nobly projected, a sad, beautiful voice in the wilderness'.[59] William's own ability to convey the musicality of Shakespeare's poetry was seen as the expression of a courtly ideal epitomised by the character of Richard himself:

> Every mistake, every crime is forgotten when the king speaks, for he is instinct with poetry. Higher psychiatry may have harsh things to say of him. He may be said to be living on his emotions. He certainly delighted in the pageant of his downfall. That matters little ... Can we not draw some lessons from the fact that Shakespeare preferred to endow this weakling, this poseur with a gift which he denied to his all too successful rival? ... I revolved these thoughts in my mind as I watched.[60]

The depiction of King Richard as a sympathetic figure drew criticism in Sri Lanka, however. 'His fall is not tragic', Iago argued, because 'Richard's whole life is an outrage to divinity'. Attacking the way in which the production upheld the old 'cult of personality' tradition, the critic accused William of getting 'carried away by his own part'. 'There is more in this play than Richard. There is Richard's time and Richard's world to be shown'. Though the play had 'once roused a revolt in London ... Can one ... believe it now, after seeing the emasculated hash that is served up as Shakespeare? ... The present English Richard is quite a grand figure, seriously embodying the inalienable, divine right to rule'.[61]

William was at pains to assert that his *Richard II* steered clear of the issue 'of political authority', a theme that he admitted was prominent in England at the time but that he summarily dismissed as 'a craze just now'.[62] Despite William's insistence, Indian reviewers saw the production's impactful staging as 'a representative image' of ensemble practices that enabled more political interpretations of the play.[63] William's show appropriated the visual grammar of productions that sought to engaged with the play's socio-political concerns, while reducing them to aesthetic effects and stylistic ornaments. *Richard II*'s set was influenced by John Bury's design for the RSC's *The Wars of the Roses*, a production which itself built upon Joan Littlewood's trailblazing Theatre Workshop staging of 1955. 'Impeccably mounted' within a 'skeletal' wooden frame, the production's technical accomplishments were considered representative of what was 'coming more and more into fashion these days in historical productions'.[64] Alongside Bardon's 'economically monumental and serviceable' set, Brian Benn's 'shrewd lighting' enabled easy transition between scenes.[65] Such 'functional simplicity' was hailed as 'a planned masterpiece', with its 'simple lines of wooden scaffolding ... dominated by a single, rich, glowing tapestry' that appeared 'symbolic of England's throne'.[66] The set echoed Moiseiwitsch's design for Quayle's 1951 production with the 'unpainted weathered timber' of its 'rough and unfinished' wooden structure offsetting 'the rich colour of the costumes'.[67] Replete with levels and stairs, the flexible space accentuated 'the changing pattern of relationships' within, drawing audiences' attention to each character's passage 'across the stage to and from the throne'.[68] Overall, the production's open skeletal setting brought visual clarity to the political negotiation, intrigues, and factional formations that constituted the 'changing world order' of the play.

The press enthused about the precision of the actors' movements and at how the production 'manage[d] the transition from one scene to another?':

> The disposition of actors at any instant, standing or seated at varying elevations, constituted a spectacle to behold ... The lights would go out and one would hear music for a few seconds. The music would fade out, and the lights would return, disclosing a magical transformation of the scene. One hardly heard a sound.[69]

Such group work 'made for continuity and enhanced our enjoyment of the show'[70]. Contrary to William's claims, although the company 'conveyed to us the poetry of Shakespeare ... their achievement consisted in dramatizing it' through movement:

> In two and a half hours it is difficult to recall a sterile moment. Even moments when the actors stood transfixed communicated dramatic tension ... The regrouping of actors every minute had the effect of creating before our eyes a pageant of exquisite paintings'.[71]

Large sections of the Indian press were intrigued by the ways in which technical advances improved the theatre-going experience overall. As one journalist put it, 'starved as we in India are of the satisfaction that comes from witnessing mastery of the stage's demands, such technical staging was seen as something to be grateful for'.[72] Interest in the latest technical achievements, and enthusiasm for the ways in which international cultural exchanges could play a meaningful role in improving the Indian theatre industry itself, reflected the primacy of the developmental ethos of the time. Throughout India, regional theatres and local amateur dramatics societies played a leading role in hosting and assisting the NSC during their stay, thus providing an opportunity for the English visitors to examine' local technical know-how such as 'the new technique of panoramic stage' conceived by 'Anil Kumar, founder-president of the Bihar Arts Theatre'.[73]

Overall, despite adopting design elements that originally sought to expose the social forces moving through the world of the play, William's insistence that staged Shakespeare should not be used to comment on twentieth-century political concerns won favour with most Indian critics. One argued that although some

> could suggest that there was an obvious parallel between Bolingbroke and the Generals' plot against Hitler; or that the Theatre Workshop could present Bolingbroke as a modern revolutionary agitator; or that, in Queen Bess' own time, there was a Globe version which made Bolingbroke the hero ... [we] would hate to see a *Richard II* so contemporary and so timidly political that he would keep time to the tragi-comic dance of South Vietnam![74]

Such 'daringly provocative interpretations' were not for William who

> has allowed himself to be ruled by the poetry and I am with him in this. As Sir Walter Raleigh said many years ago, you cannot take sides against Richard unless you are prepared to take sides against the Poetry. To do so (Joan Littlewood notwithstanding) is to be perversely eccentric.[75]

The Taming of the Shrew in Pakistan and the Philippines

In its handling of smaller theatre companies, the British Council appeared to be fastidious and exacting sponsors. The organisation felt entitled to assess both the artistic quality of productions that toured under their auspices ('for which we depend on the professional advice of our Drama Advisory Committee'), and to gauge a show's suitability for the cultural sensitivities of the countries to be visited ('of which our own staff have expert knowledge'). Consequently, agreement as to whether *The Taming of the Shrew* was a suitable production to tour South and Southeast Asia was not arrived at easily.[76]

Prior to touring, prominent members of the British Council's Drama Advisory Committee including Norman Marshall, Michael Benthall, and Hugh 'binkie' Beaumont attended a performance of *The Taming of the Shrew* at Regent's Park. Given the fact that the upcoming tour had already been announced in the national press, and that Vladek Sheybal's spirited production was enjoying commercial and critical success that summer, the DAC's scathing assessment came as a great surprise. The committee's verdict was that the show was 'not suitable' in 'its present form' and that a 'very much higher standard of production' was expected for such an 'important and costly tour'. Conville was presented with a list of changes and a warning that 'if this is not achieved, we may have to consider cancelling the whole project'. The full list reads: '1. Improved verse speaking 2. Elimination of actions likely to offend the moral susceptibilities of Eastern audiences (especially in the Sly scenes) 3. Less horseplay 4. Clarification of the sub-plot 5. Reduction of the playing time by, say, 20 minutes'.[77] The committee warned that if Sheybal was not willing 'to make these modifications' it would 'consider appointing another producer to prepare the play for the tour'.[78] The advisory committee's assumption that it could take creative control over the production indicates that the British Council enjoyed a surprising degree of influence over smaller companies, suggesting that the Nottingham Player's *Macbeth* and the NSC's *The Tempest* were the unhappy product of such interference.

Conville countered the DAC's impulse to vet, censor, and control by mounting a spirited defence of Sheybal's production. He explained that the director had 'purposely use[d] an opera bouffa style' because, as 'one of the least lyrical of Shakespeare's plays', *The Taming of the Shrew* 'must be produced and acted with great guts and panache' to win audiences over, adding that it had proven 'very popular' and 'had generated great box office success'.[79] Sheybal's staging followed in the wake of John Barton's landmark RSC production of 1960 which, in setting out to undermine 'the rarefying effects of good taste', appealed to a new generation of theatregoers.[80] Carnivalesque approaches that deliberately sought to juxtapose the profane with the profound partly resolved the overall challenge of bringing a problematic text like *The Taming of the Shrew* successfully to the stage; a play which Graham Holderness characterises as 'a typical example of the 'impure' art of the Renaissance theatre', loaded with 'internal complexity', 'dizzying shifts', and a 'diversity of generic content'.[81] Conville admitted that the reception to Sheybal's *The Taming of the Shrew* was 'sharply divided' and that while some reviews 'were ecstatic' others from 'knowledgeable Shakespeareans' were quite 'the opposite'. Conville's comments nod towards a deeper schism between a scholastic tradition invested in fidelity to the Folio text attributed to Shakespeare, and a performance tradition that relied upon the 'corrupt' text of *The Taming of A Shrew* to bring the generically ambivalent play successfully to the stage.[82]

The DAC's main concern, however, was with the production's potential reception in South and Southeast Asia, rather than its popularity with London audiences, a view determined by cultural-diplomatic considerations. As Holderness points out, Shakespeare, 'the absent author' whose 'forbidding and ghostly mythological' presence the DAC sought to evoke whilst promoting Britain overseas, 'does not always bear with quite the same gravity' upon *The Taming of the Shrew* as it does on other texts.[83] With its heightened style of performance, and inclusion of the Sly frame from *A Shrew*, Sheybal's production raised issues of quality, attribution, and authenticity, and thus threatened to undermine the integrity and cultural-diplomatic value of Shakespeare itself. Indeed, during the tour questions were frequently raised as to why "Shrew' of all plays' had found a place 'in a microscopic repertoire sent out to India! ... If the object of an English company ... is to educate the Indian audiences in the Shakespeare canon, "shrew" is a ludicrous misfit'.[84] Despite being 'all fun and games', the production was dismissed by critics as being 'hardly material for art of any depth or plenitude'.[85] Some could only come to terms with its inclusion by reasoning that it 'must be an older play that Shakespeare merely revised' and was 'not, in any way, representative [of] his dramatic power', while others opined that the play 'seems to have a larger appeal to those who in Shakespeare's day were called the groundlings'.[86] On tour throughout South and Southeast Asia, the production went on to enjoy a mixed though largely positive reception that settled along the class-cultural lines indicated in some of the more disdainful Indian reviews.

Despite Conville's assurance to the DAC that the production would eliminate any actions 'likely to offend the moral susceptibilities of Eastern audiences', the NSC actors evidently stuck to their original intentions and chose iconoclasm over tradition. Critics in Pakistan greeted the production's 'robust, rowdy, virile and vigorous acting and horseplay' with 'ten curtain calls' and 'applause, applause and applause'. The 'broad and lusty production' was hailed as being 'endlessly inventive and visual' with audiences appreciating how it 'tool[ed] along at a fast clip, every moment of which is alive with humour, wit, or farcical business'.[87] The warm reception that the production enjoyed from the outset came as evident relief to Conville who wrote in his report back to London that 'Lahore audiences were excellent and surprisingly sophisticated', that it was 'astonishing to see a Pakistani audience taking every twist of the complicated plot and responding so spontaneously to jokes which are often difficult', and that although 'we were advised by the Drama Panel for the Tour that Asiatics and especially Indians did not particularly like comedy nor robust comedy business ... we found the opposite to be the case'.[88] Vindicated for defending Sheybal's production and for allowing his outdoor company to play to its strengths, Conville was delighted to discover a home from home in Lahore's Jinna Gardens. The tour manager confessed to local journalists that his company was primarily a comedy troupe because any 'open-air theatre' where 'birds may frequently make dramatic dives all around' is naturally 'more suited to comedy than tragedy'.[89]

Thanks to *The Taming of the Shrew*'s inclusion on the tour's itinerary in the Philippines, initial attempts at associating the visiting English company with high cultural values eventually gave way to efforts to align Shakespeare with the revival of Philippine popular theatre. Following its opening night in Manilla, the The Filipinescas Dance Company's director-choreographer, Leonor Orosa Goquingco, dismissed *The Taming of the Shrew* as a play 'classed with *Merry Wives of Windsor* and *The Comedy of Errors* as being among' Shakespeare's 'unfeeling farces'. Goquingco considered the play ill-suited for such an important diplomatic event because it failed to display the 'subtle variety of humour one had come to associate with some wonderful Britishers we have met and admired in Manila'.[90] As history would have it, the NSC inadvertently found themselves commemorating the recent passing of 'Winston Churchill – statesman, writer and painter' with a farce-like production of *The Taming of the Shrew* by 'William Shakespeare – poet, player and playwright'.[91] Despite the initial snub from the intelligentsia, the Cultural Foundation of the Philippines which co-sponsored the first visit by a professional English Shakespeare company to Manilla's Far Eastern University, stated a hope that the tour would help restore traditional Philippine drama 'to its former popularity'.[92]

Over time *The Taming of the Shrew* proved to be a popular production that garnered sincere appreciation, especially for the technical skills of the NSC's comic actors. Under Sheybal's 'deft touch for business and line emphasis', 'lightning-quick direction', and '"for-adults-only" lines', the performers were commended for playing *The Taming of the Shrew* for every laugh they could get, and 'for doing all who would be terrified of Shakespeare (thanks to timorous English teachers and pseudo-literary snobs) a tremendous favour: they made the man human. More than human. More than funny, tolerable'.[93] The production presented audiences with

> a world of pantomime horses, farcical boo-hooing and a continuous whirl of movement in which it is not at all clear what is happening except that everyone is in hot pursuit of everyone else – farcical pass-it-on nudging in which the last man to be nudged falls over, exaggerated collapses from entirely unconvincing fatigue, all the fun of the fair in fact.[94]

To the oft-repeated question as to whether any of this was 'authentic' Shakespeare or not, the collective response was often 'who cares?' As a touring show playing to audiences whose first language was not English, the production's physical exuberance, raucous energy, and expert comic timing, was judged overall to be 'a fault in the right direction'.[95] Debates on authenticity evolved into something of a punch line for journalists, with the production's 'facial mugging', 'water dousing', 'human horse', and 'caveman act' prompting the playful comment: 'and to think that Shakespeare wrote it four centuries ago!':[96]

> Shakespeare is fun. With a skip and a jump, a wink here and a naughty chuckle there, players of the New Shakespeare Company of London never let us forget how much fun ... The packed house caught line and gesture as tossed from the stage, disdainful of the fact that the funny lines are nearly 400 years old and some in passé English ... In fact the play teetered on the slapstick, but then who was pretending?[97]

The show's relentless tempo and expert comic timing were perfectly pitched, while 'the feed and punch lines induced roars of laughter time and again and the play reaches hilarious peaks'.[98] In exceeding audiences' expectations of what 'English Shakespeare' should be, the production appealed 'to the Filipino's funny bone' while evoking disappearing local comic-theatrical traditions.[99] 'Amidst the melee of head plunging and water dousing, of funny clothes and confused identities, of atrocious puns and naughty lines', the NSC actors appeared to be 'kin to Tugak and Pugak, twin to the nameless laugh-makers who strew the stage of the Manila Grand Opera House, kin to our long departed zarzuela'.[100]

Column inches filled with appreciation for cast members who performed 'with the slickness of the first-rate music hall comedy'.[101] With 'superb body movement', Atienza gave a fine physical performance as Biondello, offering a masterclass into the 'fine art of clowning' and providing invaluable insights into the 'secret of how these professional players keep Shakespeare ever alive, vivid and funny'.[102] 'Their trick is to couch the language, which may have become obscure with the gesture apt and in time. One is prepared for the laugh and yet is still delighted when it comes'.[103] Atienza seemed 'to be made of rubber both in the face and limbs' whilst maintaining 'superb control. His account of Petruchio's approach to the wedding was a masterpiece of virtuoso buffoonery'.[104] He 'talked with his body. An arm twisted like a heraldic flag to announce his master, two legs knocked in terrifying eloquence when he was in fright, a hurling missile when he had news to convey'.[105]

Though admiration for the art of comic acting helped renew appreciation for popular drama in the Phillipines, English journalists based in Singapore and Malaya grumbled that the physical comedy went too far. Even those who approved of Sheybal's efforts to keep the 'audience continually amused' wondered at times, 'as when a pantomime horse appeared', whether 'the slapstick had not been overdone'. A common criticism was that the company failed to deliver the verse with clarity and that, with 'so much to busy the eye, the ear has a hard time of it'.[106] The most appreciative reviewers conceded that, while 'the cheerfulness on the stage infected the audience', it was only 'from time to time' that 'the fine poetry broke through'.[107] Though 'pace in a play like this is admirable, in fact essential', 'it should not come first if the audience does not use English as its first language'.[108]

Physical comedy helped mitigate the play's problematic sexual politics to some degree. Though the text had been stretched 'upon the framework of a farce' it was clear that, as with most farces, *The Taming of the Shrew* 'has its basis in cruelty'. Brian St. Clair, writing in *The Tiger Standard* admitted that

> the more one thinks of this play the more unpleasant it is – for all that it is a comedy. It opens with a drink-stupefied lout being made a fool of by a lord and continues with a woman's spirit being apparently broken. Whilst this may be the stuff that farce has always been made of, it is by modern standards pretty unpalatable stuff.[109]

Others noted that the company's slap-stick approach was essential because 'to take this play in any way seriously' would be 'to make it slightly distasteful':

> to have a serious Petruchio, as physically violent as Dinsdale Landen's interpretation, taming a woman by beating her would turn the play into something different from what Shakespeare had intended. Or from what he seems to have intended.[110]

Landen's gusto performance as Petruchio 'dominated the entire orbit' of the stage from its first entrance, reaching such an elevated pitch of comic absurdity that it almost mitigated the play's troubling sexual politics singlehandedly.[111] Landen 'storm[ed] through the play' with an 'uproarious seriousness' that kept the audience 'in fits of laughter'.[112] His 'lusty, swash-buckling' portrayal 'skilfully sought the confidence of the audience much to their delight', though one critic 'seemed to feel that however unpleasant the taming of Katherine might be it would not mar his fun' and that Landen's 'performance analysed on the couch would be a turn-up for the psychiatric book'.[113]

Although farce brought the theme of coercion and control centre stage, it did so in a manner that failed to address the issue sincerely or resolve it satisfactorily. The inclusion of the Sly frame seemed to have the potential to open the play up to a more detailed interrogation, but ultimately left audiences with a sense of unease over its unresolved tensions. Katherina's closing speech, for instance, was delivered in a way that left little room to doubt her total conversion to patriarchal rule. Consequently, many critics were vocal in their disappointment that the production 'not only tames Katherina but makes her so much into an ornament of her sex that she, in her final speech, breaks out into a lyrical description of conjugal bliss, calculated to satisfy even the most demanding male ego'.[114] 'By surrendering entirely' Katherina deprived audiences 'of the gentle satire of her last speech'.[115] This sudden about-face was perplexing:

> what are we to make of the long speech – the only "speech" in the play – in which the tamed shrew preaches womanly submissiveness? It is a beautiful speech, in many ways. Sheila Ballantine, whom I thought an almost ideal Katherina, very rightly treated it seriously; so, what happened? We were suddenly aware, after two and a half hours of Katherina as a bad joke, that we were listening to a real woman and that she was meaning every word she said. The only possible reaction is to let it go and end the play in the same temper as it began.[116]

The production's deliberately downbeat conclusion suggests that Sheybal intended to jar audiences into questioning the nature of the performance they had just witnessed:

> The play is over: Sly, a plain tinker once more, is thrown out of the Lord's house. Mr Sheybal sent him away through the sound of a nasty English storm after the Italian sunlight of the play. Indeed "our revels now are ended". It was a thoughtful and ironic ending as Sly, without a trace of Petruchio's charm or virility, set off home through the storm announcing his intention of beating is wife.[117]

In an echo of Barton's RSC production, Sheybal's surprise ending aimed at stimulating an 'invigorated sceptical consciousness' of the 'enacted artifice' of the performance that the audience had just enjoyed.[118] Some reviewers felt that though the pointed irony was 'very nicely made' it failed to give Britain's cultural image much of a shine. 'If all Shakespeare plays except this one were totally destroyed, posterity might be forgiven for wondering what all the Shakespearean fuss had been about.'[119] On the whole, critics in Pakistan and the Philippines appreciated the production's bold theatricality and professional execution, but declined any invitation to praise it for its 'wide-awake scholarship' or for the manner in which it was ultimately incapable of resolving its own contradictions.[120]

The Tempest in Hong Kong, Singapore, Malaya, and Borneo

By the time the NSC reached its final destination of Sarawak in Northern Borneo, expectant theatre-goers were being warned that, though the chance 'to see a full professional company on a Kuching stage was most exhilarating and instructive', the 'long' 'arduous' 'exhaustive and probably exhausting tour' had made 'great demands on the players'.[121] In the final Southeast Asia leg of the tour, audiences were evidently disappointed by the 'threadbare' and 'earthbound' production of *The Tempest* that washed up on their shores. Opening night in the Philippines was plagued with technical hitches when 'the storm, like the play itself, took some time to get going'.[122] Even when things went to plan, the 'professional stagecraft, lighting, lavish costumes and masks' failed to get the show 'off the ground':[123]

> I fell asleep in a tempest ... a pity I thought. The New Shakespeare Company has come a long way from London to our town ... [but] Miranda comments on the play so well, "The strangeness of your story puts heaviness on me".[124]

With *Richard II* ending its run on the subcontinent, Conville realised with some concern that the 'very tatty' looking *Tempest* would go on to 'represent fifty-percent of our programme' in Southeast Asia. Due to 'the ravishes of time and Indian travel' the show 'had lost something' and 'was satisfactory and no more'.[125] Unbeknownst to most theatregoers in Southeast Asia, *The Tempest* was included in the tour because it was a set-text for English exams across India that year. Like the Nottingham Players' *Macbeth*, the NSC *Tempest* was performed in a strangely didactic and oversimplified manner, presumably for the 'benefit' of school audiences comprised of non-native English speakers. Despite its poetry being 'among the greatest in the English language', critics lamented the degree to which the NSC had managed to reduce *The Tempest* to 'a test of elocution rather than acting'.[126]

If the intention had been to 'bring Shakespeare to the young, the decision was fatally made'. Restless school and public audiences struggled through the production's 'tortoise pace' and 'talkativeness', while Prospero's long opening speech was 'rendered weaker by John Wyse's monotonous voice'.[127] To enthusiasts in the front rows, the veteran actor's delivery was 'a delight to the ear', but to most Wyse seemed 'out-of-sorts' with many of his lines coming across as 'a confusion of sounds'.[128] Prospero employed 'a style of verse-speaking which is only too often heard in the professional theatre, which might irreverently be characterised as "gasp-and-gabble"; and he was by no means the worst offender of the men'.[129] The veteran actor's voice had been impacted by the strain of touring and as a consequence there was felt to be 'too much bad temper in John Wyse's playing', a temperament which carried through into his character who 'never seemed to be in complete control, or if he was one wondered how'.[130] Though Wyse's Prospero appeared 'closest to the schoolboy's Shakespearean hero ... waving right and left hands, striding in giant steps hither and yon, brandishing a grand wand and swishing his magic robes' it was felt that his efforts were 'in vain' because 'with Shakespeare against him, how could he win? ... this Prospero wasn't even Mandrake the Magician'.[131]

After *Richard II* and *The Taming of the Shrew*, Indian reviewers were perplexed as to why the company had suddenly resorted to a 'fire and brimstone' style of acting that 'only added up to so much ham'.[132] The actors were accused of 'overacting', and 'enjoying every word' to the point that the audience were left 'in no doubt how important every word was'.[133] Some were left wondering whether the declamatory style of delivery had 'something to do with their 'open Air' habit''.[134] Just as *Macbeth* undermined faith in the Nottingham Player's professionalism, *The Tempest* led many to ask whether the NSC were not really an amateur troupe more used to performing in the park for 'American tourists', or hobbyists who found themselves 'in a limited environment on stage'.[135] With 'scarcely a player who seemed to know how to give anything like a context to his or her lines for the whole duration', the production came as 'a frightful anti-climax after the London troupe's superb *Shrew*'.[136] More generous reviewers suggested that the show

> should attract students and amateur actors alike. They are not so brilliant as to totally discourage the later, and students, who inevitably know Shakespeare as a "book" rather than as a playwright, must jump at the opportunity to see the plays brought to life.[137]

As the tour progressed, the actors appeared to lose all faith and confidence in the show and made 'less than half-hearted efforts to bring the spirit of the play to life'.[138]

Despite the inherent limitations of touring, William tried to replicate the technical effects audiences might expect in a well-equipped theatre building. It was 'evident that more love and care, and a more expensive wardrobe, were lavished' on *The Tempest* 'than on *The Taming of the Shrew* but that the décor weighed heavy on the eye'.[139] Although the music, props, and visual effects were 'rich and imaginative', the overall impact was hampered by Henry Bardon's 'spirit-level unit set' that was so 'cramped, barren, and literal' it hindered the audiences' imagination as much as it did the actors' movements.[140] Audiences 'did not have to sit back and imagine what Caliban's island looked like or what weird shapes the supernatural beings who peopled that isle possessed [as] director David William has done that imagining for you' (Figure 5.3).[141]

Figure 5.3   The banquet scene from *The Tempest*, III. 3.
The New Shakespeare Company, Regent's Park Theatre Company, 1964. Directed by David William. Photo by David Mordecai. Images held by the Shakespeare Institute, University of Birmingham DSH1/11/1/7/8. Used by permission of Regent's Park Theatre/Shakespeare Institute, University of Birmingham/Estate of David Mordecai.

William stated that his overall intention was to bring out 'the mysticism' of the play, a quality that he felt was sure to 'commend itself to the peoples of the East'. The theme was most prominent in the Masque of Juno, a scene that traditionally utilises all the technical wizardry that a theatre can muster to achieve a spectacular visual crescendo. The sheer effort required to accomplish something similar under cramped touring conditions, however, led the masque to collapse under the weight of its own ambitions. As one reviewer delicately put it, 'in certain of the airy scenes, the earthy is too obvious':[142]

> How awkward seems the intrusion of the masque with a whole host of celestial characters which, despite the liveliest choreography, fails to lift it from the ground![143]

The entrance of 'Iris, Ceres, Juno', replete with giant papier mâché heads was 'very much impeded by the clumsy set'.[144] 'All were heavily earthbound, their routines and movements naively ordinary, and became even amusingly so when three gaunt young men in straw hats appeared to dance with the nymphs!'[145]

Lacking firm direction, and without the unity and cohesion that comes with working as an ensemble, individual performers were left to fend for themselves. Where Wyse's ponderous Prospero came across as 'Shakespeare in Kipling's image of the retired Anglo-Indian civil servant', Arthur Howard's Trinculo and Ronald Herman's Stephano were 'played for laughs' in a manner that managed to 'leap the centuries' and cause even 'blasé Hong Kong to laugh'.[146] Many thanked them for redeeming the production 'from the rhetorical gloom which pervaded its atmosphere' while others dismissed the pair as 'buffoons' who 'kept destroying the dramatic spell'.[147] Traditionalists were dismayed when the comic actors 'forged a bond with our non-Elizabethan consciousness' and became impatient with modern audiences who appeared to have 'lost [their] ear for verse'.[148] In the final act, Trinculo, Stephano, Caliban, and Ariel indulged in 'some unasked for overacting' and 'overdid their parts' with 'extravagant gesticulations'.[149] As Caliban, Wolf Morris' gave one of 'the least satisfactory' performances in the show because, in one critic's view, 'if there is a character of truly tragic proportions in *The Tempest* it is he'.[150] The heaviness of Morris's costume deprived him of the 'means of communication with the audience' condemning Caliban to the status of a 'rank beast' that entirely failed to 'evoke sympathy'. *The Daily Mail* in Kuala Lumpur exclaimed, 'What a sight' it was to see such a monstrous Caliban, 'standing on a rock shouting out his new-found freedom'.[151]

Overall, the production failed to successfully adopt stale stage conventions from a previous era. From the choreography of the sprites that 'almost looked (and sometimes sounded) like a ballet', to Ariel's costume that allowed him to 'melt into the set', and Caliban's 'resemblance to Hollywood sea monsters from 20 thousand fathoms deep', the production appeared to be a pale imitation of Michael Benthall's Festival of Britain production of 1951–1952.[152] As Benthall was a member of the DAC subcommittee directly overseeing the NSC tour, it is possible that he had some indirect influence over the production. Iago disparaged William's for his emphasis on 'full-fledged superstitious mysticism', and for not exploring the colonial dimensions of the play. For him the crucial imperial power struggle enacted by Prospero and Caliban was entirely missing, replaced instead by a Prospero 'made to perform with a staff in the manner of a harassed bandmaster'.[153] Iago lambasted the NSC as the foot soldiers of a tired and dated British theatrical tradition that studiously avoided any engagement with the anti-colonial readings of the play that were available at the time.

As he emphatically put it, the innately conservative British theatre knows that 'all the scholarship does not entitle the bloody bookworms to lord it over us, dammit!'[154]

Handling the Press and Diplomatic Functions

The 'Esher Touring Contract' that each actor signed prior to travelling provides some insight into the demands and constraints placed upon the company. The tour was considered to be 'of a special and unique character in that the NSC will be regarded as representative both of this country and of the British Theatre'. Creating the right impression overseas was paramount and so strict rules governed the Company's interactions with the press from the outset. The actors signed an agreement that 'no interviews shall be granted, information given, or opinions expressed to the Press and/or Broadcasting and Television services' 'without the express permission of the Manager'.[155] Beyond press junkets and 'radio and television interviews', a busy schedule of diplomatic functions required careful navigation. Actors agreed to make themselves available at 'social and public events' many of which were 'on a government[al] level' to 'ensure that an adequate proportion of the Company is present at each'. The typical routine was for the road-weary troupe to give a press conference upon arrival, and then attend a diplomatic event immediately following the opening night's show. Acknowledging that social performances could be just as tiring as theatrical ones, it was agreed 'to keep such official functions to the minimum possible'.[156]

Though the degree of press control varied according to location, it generally relaxed as the tour progressed. Initially, in Pakistan, formal press conferences were the norm with press releases vetted by the British Information Services disseminated to the local press corps who were often happy to quote them verbatim. The Company soon tired of carefully stage-managed press conference that often descended into 'a monologue from the person being interviewed'. Conville was especially resentful at having to handle such 'grisly' and 'depressing' press junkets himself whenever the Functioning Officer from the local British Council institute was not available.

What struck the tour manager as inexplicably dull may have been considered perfectly adequate, and even satisfactory, by government officials on the ground. Press coverage was entirely avoided in some politically sensitive areas, though misunderstandings sometimes arose when the NSC's commercial instincts contradicted the British Council's discrete handling of local political concerns that the Company were not privy to. In the restive city of Rawalpindi, for instance, Conville was perplexed that although 'a considerable amount of private entertainment' was laid on for the company upon their arrival, including dinner with The British High Commissioner, the local press 'seemed unaware of our existence'.[157] With the BIS press release translated verbatim and published in its entirety, the tour leader sensed that 'some kind of "war"' was taking place 'between the press and the British Council', and took the initiative to drum up some local interest himself by giving a radio interview and broadcasting excerpts from *The Tempest*. When the company subsequently visited Gordon College their performance was interrupted by student protests which got 'very out of hand'. 'Whenever there was a black-out in any of the shows, the gallery would start shouting out political slogans', a phenomenon that 'unsettled the actors.'[158] These protests were linked to a recent visit to the region by the President of Pakistan, Muhammad Ayub Khan, a former Army general who had staged a military coup in 1958. The hostile reception suggests that the Foreign Office were deliberately keeping the company's visit low-key to avoid such incidents.

The rules on press engagement began to relax somewhat in India where Conville expressed appreciation for 'the Council's unwillingness to use the BIS in certain places'.[159] The tour manager appeared to win the argument that better publicity would come 'from private interviews arranged at the British Council reception where we [could] meet the more on the ball journalists'.[160] From their time in Bombay onwards, a more open and revealing exchange between the company and the press became the norm. Commercially speaking, the 'excellent idea' of conducting one-to-one interviews meant that 'there was an article nearly every day concerning us', though this press strategy also ran the risk of allowing actors to stray into subject areas that the BIS's tightly scripted line usually skirted. Questions on the commercial and political logic behind the touring mission began to crop up and, in one instance, Conville and William admitted to feeling 'a bit uneasy' about having to explain 'why the British Council always arranges tours of classical plays not the modern ones?' The pair could only reply by asking 'what would be the response' if they'd brought 'Pinter, Rattigan, Osborne and other new playwrights' instead?[161]

Unlike the days of Lewis Casson in Egypt or Anthony Quayle in Australia, the British Council were keen to steer the NSC actors away from politics, and to keep their public comment squarely in the realm of appreciative cultural exchange. When the British Council's Mr Dolby replaced the invalided Conville for the Southeast Asian leg of the tour, junior members of the company appeared more often in the press, where their fresh-faced enthusiasm served the tours cultural diplomatic mission well. Presented as simply being 'in love with life', the young actors expressed their enthusiasm for local cultures. The press in Malaysia, for instance, framed the company as happy-go-lucky tourists buying 'krises, hats and handicrafts – all souvenirs of their five-day stay in the Federal capital'. Conservative family values were often expressed, as when Amanda Reiss replied that Miranda was her favourite role because 'she stands for ideals which are fast disappearing'.[162] Malay audiences were praised for being 'sophisticated and receptive', with actors confessing themselves to be 'simply amazed at the love Asians have for Shakespeare'. Sticking to an old and trusted script, it was reported that the sight of 'hundreds of people' being 'turned away because of limited seats' just 'goes to show that Shakespeare is still very much in the hearts of his followers in this part of the world'.[163]

Trouble on the Road: An Equity Report

Things were not quite so idyllic behind the scenes. Overall, the company's actors felt that 'working conditions' on tour had been 'manifestly and unnecessarily below a tolerable standard' and consequently submitted a formal written complaint through their union, Equity. The report outlined several grievances, and though it was primarily 'aimed at protecting its members' rights it was also delivered in the spirit of making helpful recommendations for improving future touring endeavours:

> Bearing in mind that we have on occasion worked in places where British professional actors have never worked before and that our fellow-members may in the future be invited to work in similar places and conditions, we wish to present the following.[164]

'The Equity Members Report on The New Shakespeare Company – British Council Tour of Pakistan, India, Ceylon and The Far East, 1964–1965' reveals the actors' frequent illness and general exhaustion caused by extensive travel and a punishing workload in substandard theatres with grim backstage conditions. It added to the list the lack of reliable support on the ground, tiring social and diplomatic functions, dingy shared accommodation, and general disregard for the actors' welfare.[165] The Report argued that the conditions the company worked under directly impacted the quality of their performances thus undermining the entire cultural mission. The main thrust of the paper was that the company did not feel that they were made fully aware of the kind of venture they were signing up for, and that they were frequently called upon to make unreasonable personal sacrifices.[166] Its overall recommendation was that actors invited to undertake such an ambitious tour in future should be fully informed, better prepared, and more fairly treated. And that they be given full notice of the challenges involved 'before they sign the contract'.[167]

A meeting was arranged between the NSC, Equity, and a DAC sub-committee comprising Norman Marshall, Michael Benthall, Binky Beaumont, and Rees (one of the post-war governors of the Old Vic). Minutes show that the committee took a dim view of the criticism levelled at their organisation of the tour and were determined to counter each and every complaint. In retrospect most actors felt that they had little idea what they were letting themselves in for. Atienza thought that 'more information about professional conditions and the standard of living in the various places would have been welcome' and 'stressed the value' that would have come from being properly briefed 'both by officials and by actors with relevant experience'. Carter also felt that future ventures would benefit from having 'a talk by an actor who had taken part in a similar tour'. Conville, who played the role of moderator between the two parties, countered that the 'number of lectures given by Council staff with experience of the countries to be visited' had been 'perfectly adequate', while the British Council's Peter Dalby added that Christopher Burgess 'who was with the NSC and [had] also been a member of the Bristol Old Vic tour' had, on an anecdotal level at least, given the actors some indication of what to expect.[168]

Many problems were caused by a lack of forward planning. Preparation was undertaken by the NSC's Stage Manager, Griffith James, during a preliminary six-week tour of Pakistan, India, and Sri Lanka. As an employee of the Regent's Park Theatre rather than the British Council itself, however, James appeared to lack the local knowledge and expertise needed for the task and it remained unclear how much practical assistance he received during his visit.[169] Conville felt that throughout the circuit, the company would have benefitted from having a permanent 'advance man' on the ground, someone to arrive 'in a city a few days before the company' and prepare things. He also asserted that the NSC lacked sufficient day-to-day support 'due to the Council underestimating the size of the operation' especially with 'such a big company' laden with 'heavy sets' and 'a heavy wardrobe'.[170]

The company gave one hundred and twenty-eight performances during one hundred and forty-eight days of touring. The pace, length, and intensity of the schedule was debilitating. With twenty-five days dedicated solely to travel, the itinerary amounted to 'barely less than eight performances a week' 'in the tropics, on tour, in challenging conditions and supplemented by a programme of social obligations which made additional demands'.[171] The actors were given only nine days off over the twenty-one week period and, despite repeated requests prior to departure, no paid leave was permitted at the end of the tour as reward or compensation for the pressing workload. The additional travel required to fulfil some of the more diversionary legs of the tour was 'extremely exhausting' with the three-day whistle-stop visit to Hong Kong, for instance, requiring two flights, a hundred-and-forty-mile bus journey, and two shortened nights of rest.[172] To the overall complaint that 'the tour appeared to be excessively long' the British Council countered that Conville and the Company 'had wanted the Far East extension to take place so as to give as long a period of employment as possible'. Again, the Bristol Old Vic tour of the previous year was put forward as a counter argument, simply because they had achieved 'ninety performances in ninety-eight days' whilst the NSC gave 'only eighty performances in the same period'.

'Anxious not to sacrifice the artistic quality of the tour' Conville and William insisted on taking an elaborate load of sets, costumes, and technical equipment that resulted in the NSC baggage being '3 or 4 times heavier than [the] Bristol Old Vic's', despite Jane Edgehill's prior warning 'against so much freight'. Costumes became an area of significant contention. The company took well over a hundred on the road as it was felt that 'materials used in the Elizabethan period were necessary to give the correct fold, swinging movement, and effect in the light'. As soon as the tour began, it was recognised that the artistic management's decision to 'sacrifice nothing to the genuineness of effect' was a grave mistake that placed an 'intolerable strain on the actors' who 'all lost several pounds', suffered 'chills, and sometimes more serious ailments' as a consequence.[173] A rare interview with the wardrobe mistress, Elizabeth Penn, shone a revealing light on life behind the scenes and beneath the seams:

> washing and cleaning of clothes has been a constant headache. Mildew would develop happily in the heavy material and leath ... would brush off fairly easily leaving only a musty smell! ... At times, two performances were given ... Imagine donning a garment still wet with sweat from the previous performances.[174]

The 'wearing of wigs' was 'a particular ordeal' because, on top of the heat and humidity, the actors were baked under 'two rows of spotlights'.

On the wardrobe issue, Conville admitted that William and himself 'were completely responsible for any complaints from the Cast'.[175]

The tour had gotten off to a 'bad start' that created 'bad feeling' between the actors and the organisers from the outset, primarily because it opened in 'the worst hall that the company played in during the tour', the Jamshed Memorial Theatre in Karachi.[176] The October starting date had been determined by the Park's London season and as a consequence the company arrived in the middle of a heatwave that saw temperatures rising 10 degrees above the already high seasonal average. Given no time to acclimatise, the troupe soon found themselves struggling 'to get enough breath to speak their lines' in the 'great heat'.[177] The exertion of these opening performances resulted in rapid weight-loss throughout the entire cast, prompting a local doctor to tell Conville 'in strong terms' that 'it was stupid to perform at the Jamshed Hall in early October'.[178] The medical bill after only the first week of touring stood at over eight hundred rupees, a figure that Conville admitted 'tells its own story'. John Wyse was an early casualty who 'never completely recovered during the tour' but had to go on performing below par throughout. Medical reports on unspecified problems affecting a further six members of the Company were sealed and submitted separately, while the sheer array of 'minor' medical problems that the actors succumbed to illustrate some of the hidden perils of touring. The list included 'a cist, a quinsy, impetigo, sinusitis, an abscess, a collapse during the air flight from Madara to Delhi'. Two cases of hepatitis nearly brought the tour to a halt when the company electrician Brian Benn had to be flown home after becoming jaundiced. Thereafter the lighting was not 'always in the hands of people who knew the shows'.[179] Conville came down with hepatitis at the end of the India leg and, as he was unable to complete the Southeast Asian section, had to be replaced by the British Council's Peter Dalby.[180]

Bangladesh (then East Pakistan) was included in the itinerary, and though Conville understood that 'it is essential for political reasons that any company playing in Pakistan must play Dacca', the trip constituted a challenging and 'depressing week' as the old theatre's lack of air-conditioning, 'rough backstage conditions, and extreme humidity and heat' failed to make it 'conducive to enjoyable acting'.[181] Dilapidated colonial-era theatres provided the company with basic, and sometimes substandard, backstage areas. In Calcutta, the company resided in 'a filthy theatre', while in Delhi 'the only place where actors could rest between scenes or performances was on a stone staircase, haunted by a powerfully unpleasant smell'.[182]

Furthermore, Conville was never quite certain who was meant to be overseeing the myriad of practical day-to-day challenges that came with life on the road. Technically, as company manager he had ultimate responsibility, though a great deal of assistance was meant to be forthcoming from a variety of British Council Functional Officers, with one taking responsibility in each designated area. Given the fact that the Company were constantly on the move it quickly became apparent that if any Functional Officer's 'grasp of the problems involved' was 'unsure' the issue would 'only be revealed when it [was] too late to do anything about it'. Despite showing 'great interest in the productions', the Representative and Functional Officers in Karachi lacked the skills and experience required to undertake 'practical backstage organisation'. Conville suggested that a Functional Officer should have visited every theatre or hall during the morning when setting-up for that day's performance, and even more importantly 'state where he can be found' later in the day when further help would often be required. 'In a strange place and with no telephone available, stage management can waste valuable time attempting to find things for themselves.'[183] The few material comforts and backstage necessities that the company requested in advance could not be sourced if the Functional Officer had not prepared them in advance. Additionally, the occasional demand to perform two different shows in one day (usually a school matinee followed by a public performance) placed unnecessary strain on the already overburdened stage management 'who had to set and strike each play twice'.[184]

Though it was emphasised in the actors' contract that 'the social obligations of touring companies have considerable diplomatic value' the actors' baggage allowance was only 44lbs per person, thus making it impossible to include clothes that were smart enough to attend 'receptions in Singapore' and yet warm enough to visit venues likes Chandigarh in winter. Irrespective of the journalists and photographers awaiting them, it was not possible for the cast to arrive 'at an airport in a style suitable for a press reception'. Though 'the social side of the tour was naturally extremely enjoyable and interesting' it was also 'exhausting', especially 'after a performance' when 'all members of a Company are tired, most are hungry, and some very much want a drink'.[185]

The sub-committee countered each and every one of the above complaints. First of all, they reasoned that 'most of the difficulties described were of a kind which could and should have been forestalled or dealt with by the advance management and by the leader of the tour itself'. Secondly, that 'the management had firmly declined to accept the Council's advice in several important respects', thirdly that 'there were very few complaints which referred to the period when Mr. Dalby of the British Council was in charge of the Company', and finally that 'earlier tours to this territory had produced no such complaints'.[186] Behind the scenes Conville attempted to mediate between both parties in the dispute. In a personal report that was submitted for the DAC's eyes only, Conville stressed that when actors 'felt their work was appreciated, their problems understood, and the Council was doing everything possible for them' they 'seemed to give their best':

> On a tour like ours, the Company could become homesick, be frustrated sharing a room. Find the food, etc. disagreeable. As we all know, actors can be childish and temperamental. It is important that Council Officers realise this and make every effort to make the Company comfortable and feel important.[187]

Despite the persuasive evidence that the tour entailed unreasonable demands and a great deal of personal sacrifice, the sub-committee dismissed the complaints as 'fundamentally a matter of concern between the management of the New Shakespeare Company and Equity'. Responsibility ultimately rested with the NSC because

> the Council does not enter into contractual relations with the artists as regards terms and conditions of employment. In this respect the Council's policy and practice is simply to ensure that managements with which they are associated observe terms and conditions not less favourable to the artist than those agreed between the Theatrical Managers and Equity.[188]

In conclusion, the sub-committee were willing to admit that 'touring some parts of these territories is pioneering work' and that

> some degree of hardship and discomfort is inevitable. Any proposals which will lessen this are always very carefully considered here and many of those made by this Company and Mr. Conville in his report are already being taken into account in our future planning.[189]

Overall, the company were admonished for not appreciating the extent to which touring Shakespeare went beyond standard theatrical practices and that it constituted, in fact, a kind of national calling that inevitably required some degree of personal sacrifice. Regretting that 'there had not been time to go through the report in detail', but reasoning that 'the main points at issue had been covered' and 'that a further meeting would not be necessary', Duke concluded by stating:[190]

> how pleased we were to receive Mr Conville's appreciation of the help given to the Company by members of the Council's staff (and their wives) which

often went beyond the limits of their normal responsibilities and was sometimes given at great personal cost in time and money, and at the expense of other work for which they were also responsible ... many members of the Company had written appreciatively of the hospitality and help which they had received from members of the British Council staff, no reference was made to this in the Company's report.[191]

Such wounded comments suggest that the DAC viewed the actors' formal complaint dimly indeed, almost as if they were letting the side down.

Conclusion

Touring Shakespeare has disclosed numerous instances where Shakespeare productions played a prominent role in supporting Britain's foreign policy objectives overseas at the end of Empire and the start of the Cold War. At the outset, I identified my primary areas of concern as the evolution of touring practices, the performance and reception of individual English productions overseas, and the state–private networks and institutional formations that supported Shakespeare tours. The precise questions I raised were: how did the cultural projection of English Shakespeare begin and evolve over time, and what impact did it have on the post-war Shakespeare theatre? Secondly, why were certain plays and theatre companies selected for touring, and was the choice of play or the style of its adaptation determined by its cultural mission? Did productions ultimately support, contradict, or run adjacent to the broader diplomatic objectives they were sent out to accomplish? My third set of questions concerned the role that state–private networks played in commissioning and selecting touring theatre companies, supporting them overseas, and commemorating their endeavours back in the UK. All of the above have been addressed within each chapter, and we can now draw some general conclusions. Before going on to discuss the state-of-play regarding Shakespearean soft power today, let us conclude by identifying some of the main tensions and contradictions that arose when Shakespeare tours travelled overseas in service to British cultural diplomacy between 1939 and 1965.

In maintaining the illusion that it continued to be a major world power following the Second World War, Britain faced the dichotomy of celebrating liberal democracy at home whilst prolonging colonial modes of governance overseas. To achieve this balancing act, Britain called upon extensive state–private networks to perpetuate the near-infinite variety of political settlements that characterised the entrepreneurial core of the British Empire throughout its long history.[1] In administering the loss of

Empire with careful diplomacy, while aligning its own interests with America's advancing global hegemony, Britain could look forward to maintaining a considerable degree of global influence. On the cultural front, Shakespeare tours were an effective compensatory device for the loss of economic and political power because Shakespeare could help Britain maintain ethnic, linguistic, and cultural bonds at the exact moment when it faced a series of financial, political, and military reverses. Thanks to the new ethos of developmentalism, Shakespeare could even help Britain promote its own self-interest as the best choice for decolonising nations themselves.

Despite cultural diplomacy's increasing value to the state, Britain never formulated or adopted an official cultural policy during the period. Throughout this study we have seen how the act of cultural projection was characterised by contingency, informality, and improvisation. One of the main reasons why Britain was unwilling to settle on a formal cultural position was fear of being cornered into a coherent policy it would have to abide by at home as well as overseas.[2] Given its compromised position at the heart of a vast global empire, adopting a formal or consistent approach risked exposing the metropole to unforeseen domestic consequences, complicating the UK's own rapid social transformation during the post-war period. On the one hand, it made strategic sense to send English Shakespeare productions to newly independent countries where they could help maintain close cultural ties with 'the right people', ensure Britain's continuing presence in key commercial industries, and generally steer postcolonial nation states in directions favourable to Britain itself. On the other hand, the expectation of Commonwealth citizenry to visit, work, and study in the 'mother country' ran up against conflicting metropolitan attitudes that sought to curb non-white immigration.[3] For Britain then, cultural diplomacy worked best when its application was informal, improvised, and easily disavowed.

With the British Council acting as a conduit between the separate worlds of government and entertainment, theatre companies were able to maintain the necessary illusion that they were operating free from political interference or state control. Many of the artists and individuals involved shared the belief that the English national poet possessed a universal value and appeal; a common assumption that mitigated the need to reflect critically upon their role as cultural ambassadors, or raise concerns that they were lending personal support to dubious commercial or political initiatives.[4] It is worth stressing that the British state could always deny that it was using its national poet or theatre companies for propaganda

Conclusion

purposes because, formally speaking, the UK government did not consider cultural diplomacy to be a form of direct action. The very existence of covert organisations orchestrating Shakespeare tours to the Communist world like the CRD and the SRC was denied at the time.

Overall, it would be an excessive generalisation to assert that the British Council was a consistent or easily wielded weapon in the direct application of state power overseas. That said, this study has not found examples where the British Council's activities went counter to the spirit of UK foreign policy. The organisation was closely attuned to the needs of the Foreign Office, the Colonial Office, and the Commonwealth Relations Office, not least because these branches of Government provided much of its funding. Many tours were only undertaken because of direct requests from various Departments of State, and the historical evidence points to the fact that Shakespeare tours most often occurred at decisive moments in the history of UK foreign policy. In times of need, government could ask the British Council to call upon its extensive network of theatrical 'experts' and partners, prompting the organisation to marshal a wide-enough range of state-private resources to allow Britain to compete effectively against better-funded and more state-centralised cultural-diplomatic adversaries.

Financing was a major issue for both the British Council and the theatre companies that toured under its auspices. Arguably, the lack of adequate institutional funding constituted a form of political control, allowing governmental departments to channel money into the specific cultural undertakings that were closest to their diplomatic concerns at any given period. *Titus Andronicus* in Eastern Europe and *Macbeth* in West Africa are two instances where the Foreign Office and the Commonwealth Relations Office provided additional funds to enable touring endeavours they considered politically urgent. Generally speaking, however, the lack of adequate funding significantly limited the range and amount of English Shakespeare tours that the British Council was able to project overseas. Although there was a massive post-war appetite for UK theatrical manifestations throughout the world, and though Embassies made frequent requests for the British Council to satisfy local demands for the betterment of British interests, tours were only intermittently deployed. There was always a significant gap between demands for cultural manifestations made by Embassies and Representatives in the field, and the occasional cultural initiatives the inadequately funded British Council was able to respond with. Viewed up close then, the practice of cultural diplomacy appears to be rife with contradictions and inconsistencies, with individual touring missions determined by the complex variety of internal and external contingencies that each era and undertaking presented. In stark contrast to cultural diplomacy's central and valued position within Soviet Russian and American strategic thinking, for instance, the arms-length relationship between the UK government and the British Council, the absence of a formal and coherent cultural policy, and the lack of adequate or consistent funding, suggests that culture's political value was viewed with a degree of scepticism by successive UK governments.

The British Council routinely chose professionally staged Shakespeare to represent the best of British theatrical culture abroad, a habit of mind that led to an excessive reliance on a handful of flagship companies like the Old Vic and the Shakespeare Memorial Theatre, and a select number of influential practitioners like Tyrone Guthrie, Lawrence Olivier, and Anthony Quayle. While this unthinking bias towards the playwright affirmed the capaciousness of Shakespeare's works, it also spoke to a poverty of the national imagination, and an evident lack of interest in new and emerging post-war drama. The close-knit working relationship that existed between leading industry figures and the British Council gravitated the post-war British theatre towards more conventional notions of national heritage. Unlike the Arts Council, providing financial aid to support UK theatre companies was never part of the British Council's remit. The DAC routinely refused to provide financial guarantees-against-loss to small companies of the highest artistic standards that had been invited to play overseas through international contacts of their own. Financial support was routinely denied to innovative left-wing companies like Joan Littlewood's Theatre Workshop, and even to prominent conservative playwrights like T.S. Eliot.[5] The fact that many of the DAC's members had worked for the flagship theatre companies receiving regular financial assistance is another astonishing feature of the state–private networks that flourished in the early post-war period.

Britain had much to gain from promoting the notion of Shakespeare's universality throughout the world whilst maintaining an exclusive claim on his native genius. This ideological stance, like the ad hoc institutional arrangements and state–private networks that enabled it, was as mutable as it was tactical. In the field, the British Council often ignored competing local claims on Shakespeare while promoting Britain's supposedly unique insights and expertise. In Australia, for example, the British Council dismissed John Alden's successful touring productions that performed Shakespeare in Australian accents, while promoting Quayle's English productions as a rare opportunity to experience Shakespeare as a 'living language' and even as the white racial embodiment of some Greater-British ideal. Such ideological claims were partial and flexible because they were inherently tactical and contingent on the political expediency of time and place. Where non-English claims could be of use to the British state they were enthusiastically embraced. In the Eastern Bloc, for instance, local Shakespeare productions affirmed a shared European cultural heritage that stretched beyond the immediate and temporal horizons of Soviet rule. Polish Shakespeare's anti-Stalinist gestures were lauded, imported back to Britain via the work of border-crossing experts like Jan Kott, and then absorbed into Britain's theatrical mainstream, thus undermining communist sympathies within the UK itself. Nigeria's entire theatrical culture, let alone its stake in Shakespeare, was dismissed until it could be hailed as evidence of Shakespeare's global appeal and relevance during the 1964 quatercentenary. 'Pioneering' English companies benefited directly from new and emerging local initiatives like the practice-based research into Yoruba-style adaptations of Shakespeare undertaken by the University of Ibadan's Drama department, and then began drawing up plans to appropriate these syncretic adaptations further still for later visits to the region.

In relying so heavily on Shakespeare, Britain played to historical strengths that gradually became something of a limitation within the post-war context. The decisive role that English literature played in the British Empire's civilising mission, primarily in instilling an English sensibility amongst collaborating elites within exclusive educational settings, became increasingly anachronistic in comparison to the developmentalist ideas that were the handmaiden to post-imperial independence.[6] Although the burgeoning field of ELT offered Britain enormous commercial and cultural diplomatic advantages throughout its former Empire, America's developmentalist approach undermined the traditional association of the English language with English literature; a shift in educational emphasis that drained dominant literary figures like Shakespeare of their social prestige and relevance in the eyes of the earliest generations to enjoy the fruits of full independence.

Though Embassies, Consulates, and British Council Representatives stationed throughout the world demonstrated a preference for Shakespeare's most canonical works, in practice they often had to accept whatever plays were being staged when touring opportunities arose. Where preferred plays were available, the polyvalent nature of Shakespeare's works meant that they could be enlisted into promoting the political message of the cultural mission at hand. The stress on 'youth' in the Old Vic *Hamlet* to fascist Europe, or *Richard III*'s examination of 'tyranny' in Australia, are examples of this. As we saw with Quayle's *Othello*, attempts at asserting Shakespeare's topicality could be driven by commercial concerns as much as political ones. That said, ubiquitous press images of Quayle performing Othello in blackface during the Australian tour supported the broader identification of Shakespeare with legacies of white-settler colonialism and chimed with debates about the exclusionary immigration policies that were prevalent in Australia at the time. Overall, the production's actual engagement with the issue of racial politics registered more forcefully off-stage than on; in speeches, interviews, and commemorative events that implicitly linked Shakespeare with the continuation of imperial racial hierarchies privileging whiteness. Brook's staging of *Titus Andronicus* on the other hand, was purposefully adapted to its Cold War mission and actively sought to expose the lie of communism within its own sphere of influence via performance.

***

Should we consign the history of touring Shakespeare to the past and bracket it exclusively within the volatile era of the Cold War and the end of Empire? In fact, debates on Shakespeare's utility to the state, and competing calls for a better understanding of the role that Shakespeare has played in Britain's imperial history, are becoming increasingly prevalent today. Even before Britain's exit from the European Union in 2020, and the major disruption to the theatre sector brought about by the Covid pandemic from 2019 onwards, publications like the British Council's *All the World's: How Shakespeare is Viewed Around the Globe and the Role his Work Can Play to Support the UK's Soft Power* (2016) advocated for the continuing deployment of Shakespeare tours in service to British cultural diplomacy. Published during the Shakespeare quatercentenary of 2016, *All the World's* highlights the various ways in which Shakespeare could 'pay dividends' to Britain when projected 'internationally' as a 'potential envoy for the UK's wider tourism and creative industries' or as a 'powerful cultural facilitator' in 'emerging economies'.[7] The brochure's instrumental approach to Shakespeare extends to the plays themselves, reducing the canon to an inventory of tired interpretations and well-worn themes that it claims 'resonate powerfully with contemporary audiences and address issues all too familiar in today's world'.[8] If you intended to stage a production addressing the topical issue of 'Refugees and Shipwrecks', for instance, you might want to consider staging *Comedy of Errors*, *Twelfth Night*, *The Winter's Tale*, or *Pericles*. For something gesturing more towards the 'clash of civilisations' you could do worse than mount a production of *Troilus and Cressida* or *Anthony and Cleopatra*.[9] The list continues:

> The Morality and Nature of International and Civil War (*King John, Henry IV, V,* and *VI*). Political Legitimacy, Tyranny, and Resistance (*As You Like It, Richard II,* and *III, Macbeth*), Political Violence And Assassination (*Julius Caesar*), Political Revolution and Counter-Revolution (*Coriolanus*), Gang Violence (*Romeo and Juliet*), Racism and Prejudice (*Merchant of Venice, Othello*), Servitude and Slavery (*Taming of the Shrew, The Tempest*), Punishment and Imprisonment (*Two Noble Kinsmen, Measure for Measure*), Debt and Poverty (*Merchant of Venice, Timon of Athens*).[10]

In coupling Shakespeare's global ubiquity with the canon's capacious ability to 'speak to' a range of evergreen socio-political issues, *All the World's* commends Shakespeare as Britain's ideal cultural ambassador. In presenting Shakespeare's utility as a new and emerging opportunity, however, the publication barely acknowledges the British Council's active role in establishing and maintaining the profile of England's national poet upon the world stage over the last 80 years.

More recently, dubious claims about what Shakespeare 'ought to be' and who Shakespeare 'really belongs to' have become a regular feature in a government-led culture war launched in response to the Black Lives Matter movement's success in prompting the UK Shakespeare industry to address the legacies of its own imperial history.[11] At a time when the grants awarded to help Shakespearean theatres survive their forced closure during the Covid pandemic are justified in part by characterising the sector as an 'irreplaceable part of our heritage' that makes Britain a 'cultural superpower', and when important national debates aimed at rectifying ongoing structural inequalities are misrepresented as a besieged heritage sector heroically resisting attempts to put Britain down, it seems that the Shakespearean stage is destined to remain a site of significant political contestation.[12] At the very moment when it seeks to address its own imperial legacies then, will the Shakespeare industry be called upon to justify its subsidy by demonstrating its value in enhancing the UK's image overseas? It is hard to conceive how theatre companies engaging with Shakespeare to address issues of racism, inequality, and social justice could simultaneously be involved in promoting Britain's geo-political and economic interests overseas through the kinds of cultural diplomatic touring practices we have examined in this study. A key question for the future, then, is whether such instrumental uses can square with the widespread demands to decolonise Shakespeare coming from within the theatre industry itself.

In a 2020 Shakespeare's Globe event titled 'Reckoning with Our Past', the novelist and academic Preti Taneja addressed the question of how we can decolonise Shakespeare and make the theatre a more equitable and inviting space for all. Taneja called for more understanding not only into 'how Shakespeare is done in different parts of the world' but 'why', arguing that 'we need to learn about the politics of dissemination and consider how Shakespeare travelled out of this globe into that globe because you cannot separate such a history from his 'Genius''.[13] Priyamvada Gopal argues that to address the issue of decolonisation meaningfully, Europe must begin 'with the world as it undertakes an unflinchingly truthful engagement with the pivotal role of empire and colonialism in its own making'.[14] As decolonisation cannot occur 'independently of society and [the] economy' the theatre seems well placed to register how Empire has shaped metropolitan culture throughout history. Were the Shakespearean stage to take up Taneja and Gopal's challenge, it could be a significant arena for confronting and changing entrenched 'habits of mind' and for the promotion of wider societal change.[15] That said, it is difficult to envisage how the pursuit of national self-interests that is the driving force behind cultural diplomacy can be compatible with the impetus to decolonise Shakespeare today. At the very least it would require transparency into the practices and purposes of cultural diplomacy, a meaningful acknowledgement and engagement with its own history, and recognition that the British theatre industry is inseparable from the material and discursive practices of a long imperial history whose legacies persists to this day.[16] The task seems especially urgent at a time when public advocacy for Shakespeare's use in British cultural diplomacy is growing.

It is germane then, to conclude by identifying and critiquing the key features of a new and emerging myth that we might term 'Shakespearean soft power'. In June 2021 the Shakespeare Beyond Borders Alliance (SBBA) brought together 'Shakespeare practitioners, directors, government representatives, scholars, and institutions with the aim of fostering dialogue, collaboration and mutual learning across national, social, and disciplinary borders'.[17] The first day of the SBBA's inaugural conference was dedicated to the theme of 'Shakespeare Beyond National Borders' and featured a roundtable event debating the question 'Is Shakespeare "Soft Power"'? Much of the discussion focused on defining the term to then justify the practice as a new and emerging opportunity that Britain has recently arrived at by some fortuitous historical accident.[18] The British High Commissioner to Cyprus, for instance, acknowledged that Shakespeare is 'absolutely' a tool of British soft power today, acting as a 'convening force' 'creating opportunities to bring different groups together' across the divided island. A former British Ambassador to Germany and China adopted the definition provided by the influential 1980s US international relations expert Joseph Nye, that soft power is essentially the art of co-opting others into wanting what you want. The Ambassador expressed the pragmatic view adopted within diplomatic circles that 'you make the most of your national strengths which is fair enough'.[19] In regard to recent exchanges between the RSC and China, Shakespearean soft power is no longer expressed in the language of imperial projection but rather in terms of more equal and bilateral cultural exchanges. The idea that Shakespeare has become Britain's official cultural ambassador by some historical accident was frequently expressed. Although assertions of Shakespeare's universality are now admitted as belonging to a bygone imperial era, the national poet is still said to map out 'the emotions we all share and express them uniquely'. The prospect was raised that Shakespeare might soon be 'de-linked from the UK' altogether and be presented more as 'part of our British world heritage'. Ultimately, Shakespeare's global status seems more than assured, as efforts are currently underway to have UNESCO officials recognise the Elizabethan playwright as part of the world's 'intangible cultural heritage'.[20]

Three of the more problematic characteristics of the debate were reiterations of beliefs and practices that we have already outlined in this study and could be summarised as: a reliance on euphemistic terms like 'soft power', historical amnesia with regards to Empire and decolonisation, and institutional denial. First, the bland and somewhat oxymoronic term 'soft power' encourages a peculiarly narrow and overly optimistic view of what cultural diplomacy actually is. Nowhere does the debate acknowledge that soft power is just one tool in a range of diplomatic instruments, neither is any consideration given to the fact that Shakespeare tours would almost certainly be deployed in concert with more conventional forms of state power. Though 'soft power' is the preferred term today it is simply the latest variant of 'cultural projection', the phrase that Rex Leeper coined to obscure, sanitise, and distinguish British propaganda when establishing the British Council almost a century ago. The fact that debates on 'soft power' spend a great deal of time and energy equivocating over the meaning of this slippery term betrays a fundamental unease, primarily because a detailed consideration of the role that cultural diplomacy has played throughout history would inevitably draw our attention back to the imperial power politics that have been the driving force behind Britain's global prominence for centuries.

Secondly, historical amnesia gives rise to an enabling innocence with regards to cultural diplomatic practices past and present, removing the need to acknowledge how cultural diplomacy has long played a decisive role in maintaining Shakespeare's cultural pre-eminence on the world stage throughout history. The notion that Shakespeare has become Britain's cultural ambassador by historical accident perpetuates an effective post-war strategy used to promote British cultural exceptionalism within a larger European framework after the Second World War, effectively divorcing it from its numerous imperial entanglements. This formulation was laid out in T. S. Eliot's *Notes Towards a Definition of Culture*, which was initially broadcast throughout occupied Germany in 1946.[21] According to Graham MacPhee, Eliot's thesis managed to 'extract the claim of the transcendental value of English culture from the unsustainable commitment to universality ventured by British imperial ideology'.[22] Today Britain not only celebrates its exemplarity while excising the imperial history upon which it was first erected, but seeks to enjoy a preeminent international cultural role without reference to the intervening decades of Cold War brinkmanship, decolonisation, neo-colonialism, and the triumph of free-market politics and competitive global capitalism.

Finally, institutional denial allows the cultural bodies most invested in the promotion of Shakespearean soft power to overlook the active historical role that they themselves have played in the field of cultural diplomacy since the mid-twentieth century. Although the Shakespeare Birthplace Trust is tasked with promoting Shakespeare globally through events like the International Shakespeare Association and the World Shakespeare Congress, its representatives at the SBBA claimed that if its activities 'sound like soft power, and I suspect it does, then we are not doing it deliberately'. In fact, such institutions can be seen as part of the extensive network of international expertise that America established in the early post-war period to achieve 'cultural and intellectual penetration' on a vast global scale.[23] More broadly, the rich cultural history lying dormant within the extensive administrative archives of prominent mid-twentieth-century cultural organisations, like the British Council, the International Theatre Institute, and the 'big three' American Foundations of Ford, Rockefeller, and Carnegie, almost certainly contain undisclosed insights into the global dissemination of Shakespeare over the last century. Overall, our denial of the consequential role played by prominent cultural institutions that operate on a global scale plays a significant role in sustaining the present-day myth of Shakespearean soft power.[24]

Conclusion

Although it has been beyond the scope of this study to examine what political and economic concerns underlie present-day cultural projections, the reductive approaches outlined in *All the World's* evidently continue in updated forms and reiterations. Framing Shakespeare's international popularity as a fortuitous side effect of history, while ignoring the kind of material and institutional practices we have explored throughout this book, distorts our sense of what has made Shakespeare global and limits our understanding of how cultural diplomatic practices continue to shape the UK theatre industry today. A necessary step in the process of decolonising Shakespeare would be to acknowledge this previously hidden history and recognise how its erasure helps sustain new myths of Shakespearean soft power. *Touring Shakespeare* has provided plenty of evidence that undermines the notion that Shakespeare's global pre-eminence is somehow natural, fortuitous, or inevitable.

Notes

Introduction

1 The National Archives [TNA] BW 52/1 'British Institute at Lisbon 1938–1939', 'Lord Lloyd's Speech', 23 November 1938.
2 Ibid.
3 Ibid.
4 Ibid.
5 Ibid.
6 Frances Donaldson, *The British Council: The First Fifty Years* (London: Jonathan Cape, 1984), pp. 46–47. Lloyd served as the British Council's second Chairman from 1937 to 1941. Within the historical scope of this study, the total expenditure for the British Council grew from £178,466 in 1938–39 to £13,036,514 by 1964–65. See 'Appendix 5: Income and Expenditure 1934–1984' in Donaldson, *The British Council*, p. 383.
7 Britain managed to get 36,000 troops on the ground in Egypt before Italy joined the conflict in June 1940. James Whidden, *Egypt: British Colony, Imperial Capital* (Manchester: Manchester University Press, 2017), pp. 164–65; John Darwin, *The Empire Project: The Rise and Fall of the British World-System, 1830–1970* (Cambridge: Cambridge University Press, 2009), p. 71.
8 J. M. Lee, 'British Cultural Diplomacy and the Cold War: 1946–1961', *Diplomacy and Statecraft*, 9.1 (1998), 112–34 (p. 112).
9 On these methodological challenges see Christopher B. Balme, 'The Bandmann Circuit: Theatrical Networks in the First Age of Globalization', *Theatre Research International*, 40.1 (2015), 19–36 (p. 22); and Sonia Massai, 'Networks: Researching Global Shakespeare', in *The Arden Research Handbook of Shakespeare in Contemporary Performance*, ed. by Peter Kirwan and Kathryn Prince (London: Bloomsbury Publishing, 2021), pp. 114–31. For an early overview of Shakespeare tours, see Peter Holland, 'Touring Shakespeare' in *The Cambridge Companion to Shakespeare on Stage*, ed. by Stanley Wells and Sarah Stanton (Cambridge: Cambridge University Press, 2002), pp. 194–211.
10 Christopher B. Balme and Berenika Szymanski-Düll, eds., *Theatre, Globalization, and the Cold War* (London: Palgrave Macmillan, 2017), pp. 3–6.

11 John Goodwin, ed., *Shakespeare Memorial Theatre Annual Programme, 1957* (Evesham: Journal Press, 1957), pp. 39–42.
12 Michael Blakemore, *Arguments with England* (London: Faber and Faber, 2005), pp. 161–71.
13 Paul Menzer, *Anecdotal Shakespeare: A New Performance History* (London: Bloomsbury, 2015), p. 6.
14 On post-war travel writing, see Patrick Holland and Graham Huggan, *Tourists with Typewriters: Critical Reflections on Contemporary Travel Writing* (Ann Arbor, MI: University of Michigan Press, 2000); and Carl Thompson, *Travel Writing* (Abingdon: Routledge, 2011).
15 The British Council, 'Our Organisation', www.britishcouncil.org/organisation [Accessed 1 April 2023].
16 Sophie Bush, 'Valerie West Interview Transcript' (London: British Library Theatre Archive Project, 2010), p. 12.
17 For a comprehensive overview of the available holdings, see The National Archives, 'Records of the British Council'. www.discovery.nationalarchives.gov.uk/details/r/C40 [Accessed 28 April 2017].
18 Although the notion of a post-war 'theatre establishment' is problematic, the prevalence of the same names across both creative and administrative archives indicates a coherent, identifiable, and closely knit network with strong class, cultural, and personal links. The phrase is widely used in histories of Britain's post-war cultural consensus. See, for example, Robert Hewison, *Culture and Consensus: England, Art, and Politics since 1940* (London: Methuen, 1995), pp. 75–79; Alan Sinfield, *Literature, Politics and Culture in Post-war Britain* (London: Continuum, 2004), pp. 89–90, 322–26.
19 Robert Phillipson, *Linguistic Imperialism* (Oxford: Oxford University Press, 1992), p. 143.
20 Clifford Geertz, *The Interpretation of Cultures: Selected Essays* (New York: Basic Books, 1973).
21 Between 1945 and 1965, decolonisation saw United Nations membership grow from 51 to 117 member states. Mark Philip Bradley, 'Decolonisation, the Global South, and the Cold War, 1919–1962', in *The Cambridge Companion to the Cold War, Volume I: Origins*, ed. by Melvyn P. Leffler and Odd Arne Westad (Cambridge: Cambridge University Press, 2012), pp. 464–85 (p. 464).
22 James Belich defines recolonisation as a second phase, following an initial period of 'explosive colonisation' and 'supercharged growth', where settler colonies are culturally and economically reintegrated back towards the metropolis despite their political divergence. James Belich, *Replenishing the Earth. The Settler Revolution and the Rise of the Anglo-world, 1780s–1920s* (Oxford: Oxford University Press, 2011) pp. 9, 179–80. I use the contentious term 'Third World' in its Cold War sense, as a means of defining the ambitions of decolonising nations away from the binary outlook of the Western 'First World' and the Soviet 'Second World'.
23 Kenneth M. Jensen, ed., *Origins of the Cold War* (Washington, DC: US Institute of Peace Press, 1993), p. 18; David C. Engerman, 'Ideology and the

Origins of the Cold War, 1917–1962', in *The Cambridge Companion to the Cold War, Volume I: Origins*, ed. by Melvyn P. Leffler and Odd Arne Westad (Cambridge: Cambridge University Press, 2012), pp. 20–43 (pp. 34–35).
24 Odd Arne Westad, *The Global Cold War* (Cambridge: Cambridge University Press, 2007), pp. 1, 15–17, 79–80. Westad's influential study examines how the Cold War was a constitutive force in the formation of postcolonial nation-states from the outset.
25 Balme and Szymanski-Düll, *Theatre, Globalization, and the Cold War*, pp. 1, 6–9, 14.
26 Irena R. Makaryk and Joseph G. Price, eds., *Shakespeare in the Worlds of Communism and Socialism* (Toronto: University of Toronto Press, 2006); Alexandr Parfenov and Joseph G. Price, eds., *Russian Essays on Shakespeare and His Contemporaries* (Newark, DE: University of Delaware Press, 1998).
27 Irena R. Makaryk and Marissa McHugh, eds., *Shakespeare and the Second World War: Theatre, Culture, and Identity*, (Toronto: University of Toronto Press, 2012); Keith Gregor, ed., *Shakespeare and Tyranny: Regimes of Reading in Europe and Beyond* (Newcastle-upon-Tyne: Cambridge Scholars Publishing, 2014).
28 For Shakespeare's role throughout Europe's political history see, Dirk Delabastita, and others, eds., *Shakespeare and European Politics* (Newark, DE: University of Delaware Press, 2008).
29 Erica Sheen and Isabel Karremann, eds., *Shakespeare in Cold War Europe: Conflict, Commemoration and Celebration* (Basingstoke: Palgrave Pivot, 2016).
30 Alexander C. Y. Huang, 'Global Shakespeares as Methodology', *Shakespeare*, 9.3 (2013), 273–90; Jill L. Levenson and Robert Ormsby, eds., *The Shakespearean World* (Abingdon: Routledge, 2017).
31 Aneta Mancewicz, and Alexa Alice Joubin, eds. *Local and Global Myths in Shakespearean Performance* (London: Palgrave Macmillan, 2018), p. 1.
32 Ibid., p. 17.
33 Bill Ashcroft, Gareth Griffiths, and Helen Tiffin, 'Introduction to Diaspora', in *The Post-Colonial Studies Reader*, ed. by Bill Ashcroft, Gareth Griffiths, and Helen Tiffin (Abingdon: Routledge, 1995), pp. 425–27, (p. 426). Stephen Alomes describes the cultural cringe as the idea that 'Australian culture and achievement is inferior', a belief which stems from deep 'settler/invader' anxieties rooted in 'dual colonialism'. For Alomes' full definition see his entry 'Colonial Cultural Cringe: Australia', in Prem Poddar and David Johnson, eds., *A Historical Companion to Postcolonial Literatures in English* (Edinburgh: Edinburgh University Press, 2005), pp. 104–5.
34 Christopher Mayhew, *Time to Explain: An Autobiography* (London: Hutchinson, 1987), p. 139.

Chapter 1

1 For Shakespeare's mobilisation on the home front during the First World War, for instance, see Jonathan Bate, 'Shakespeare Nationalised, Shakespeare Privatised', *English*, 42 (1993), 1–18; Mathew C. Hendley, 'Cultural Mobilisation

and British Responses to Cultural Transfer in Total War: Shakespeare Tercentenary of 1916', *First World War Studies*, 3.1 (2012), 25–49; Monika Smialkowska, 'Introduction: Mobilising Shakespeare during the Great War', *Shakespeare*, 10.3 (2014), 225–29.
2 For the history of the British Council, see Donaldson, *The British Council*. For the interwar origins of British propaganda overseas, see Philip M. Taylor, *The Projection of Britain: Propaganda during the Second World War* (Cambridge: Cambridge University Press, 1981).
3 Philip M. Taylor, *British Propaganda in the Twentieth Century: Selling Democracy* (Edinburgh: Edinburgh University Press, 1999), p. 77.
4 Ibid., p. 77.
5 In Donaldson, *The British Council*, pp. 55–56.
6 Ibid., pp. 15–19.
7 Darwin, *The Empire Project*, pp. 418–75; Piers Brendon, *The Dark Valley: A Panorama of the 1930s* (London: Pimlico, 2001), pp. 353–73.
8 John Darwin, 'A Third British Empire? The Dominion Idea in Imperial Politics', in *The Oxford History of the British Empire: Volume IV: The Twentieth Century*, ed. by Judith Brown and Wm Roger Louis (Oxford: Oxford University Press, 1999), pp. 64–87.
9 In Stephen Constantine, *Buy and Build: The Advertising Posters of the Empire Marketing Board* (London: Public Records Office, 1986), p. 1; Stephen Constantine, '"Bringing the Empire Alive": The Empire Marketing Board and Imperial Propaganda, 1926–1933', in *Imperialism and Popular Culture*, ed. by John M. MacKenzie (Manchester: Manchester University Press, 1986), pp. 192–231 (p. 192).
10 Stephen Tallents, *The Projection of England* (London: Faber & Faber, 1933), p. 76.
11 Scott Anthony, *Public Relations and the Making of Modern Britain: Stephen Tallents and the Birth of a Progressive Media Profession* (Manchester: Manchester University Press, 2012), pp. 8–17.
12 On the shifting fortunes of cultural diplomacy within the decentralised structure of Britain's Information Services, see Richard J. Aldrich, *The Hidden Hand: Britain, America, and Cold War Secret Intelligence* (London: John Murray, 2001).
13 Israel Gershoni and James P. Jankowski, *Confronting Fascism in Egypt: Dictatorship versus Democracy in the 1930s* (Stanford, CA: Stanford University Press, 2010), pp. 15–17. See also, John M. MacKenzie, '"In Touch with the Infinite": The BBC and Empire, 1923–53', in *Imperialism and Popular Culture*, ed. by John M. MacKenzie (Manchester University Press: Manchester, 1986), pp. 192–231; Simon J. Potter, *Broadcasting Empire: The BBC and the British World, 1922–1970* (Oxford: Oxford University Press, 2012), pp. 169–91.
14 On the political and intellectual character of the BBC and Bush House in the 1930s and 1940s, see Marie Gillespie, 'Writers at Bush House', *Wasafiri*, 26.4 (2011), 1–3.

15 In Donaldson, *The British Council*, p. 47.
16 Piers Brendon, *The Decline and Fall of the British Empire, 1781–1997* (London: Jonathan Cape, 2007), p. 325.
17 Donaldson, *The British Council*, pp. 46–51; Taylor, *Projection of Britain*, p. 168.
18 In Taylor, *Projection of Britain*, pp. 177–78.
19 Colin Forbes Adam, *Life of Lord Lloyd* (London: Macmillan, 1948), p. 282.
20 Lloyd drew Franco's attention to Britain and Spain's commitment to anti-communism, comparing it with Germany's recent accommodation with Russia. John Charmley, *Lord Lloyd and the Decline of the British Empire* (London: Weidenfeld & Nicolson, 1987), p. 230.
21 Charmley, *Lord Lloyd*, pp. 217–41.
22 Ibid., pp. 251–62.
23 Churchill stated that the British Council's 'usefulness ended with the death of Lord Lloyd'. In Donaldson, *The British Council*, p. 79.
24 Edward Corse, *A Battle for Neutral Europe: British Cultural Propaganda during the Second World War* (London: Bloomsbury, 2014), p. 27; Donaldson, *The British Council*, p. 46.
25 In Donaldson, *The British Council*, p. 65.
26 Ibid.
27 Taylor, *Selling Democracy*, p. 52.
28 Ibid., p. 27.
29 Ibid., p. 52.
30 On the Allied press' representation of 'German Atrocities' in the First World War, see John Horne and Alan Kramer, *German Atrocities 1914: A History of Denial* (New Haven, CT: Yale University Press, 2001), pp. 204–11.
31 Donaldson, *The British Council*, p. 66.
32 Short residency visits, such as the John Gielgud Company's 1939 performance of *Hamlet* at Kronborg Castle, Denmark were the norm prior to the Old Vic's Mediterranean tour. Jonathan Croall, *John Gielgud, Matinee Idol to Movie Star* (London: Methuen Drama, 2012), pp. 261–63.
33 Daniel Rosenthal, *The National Theatre Story* (London: Oberon Books, 2013), p. 112. Bridge-Adams established the international status of the Stratford-upon-Avon festival between 1919 and 1934, before going on to become dramatic advisor to the British Council from 1937 to 1944. Robert Speaight, ed., *A Bridge-Adams Letter Book* (London: The Society for Theatrical Research Press, 1971), pp. 11–28.
34 The company also played Richard Sheridan's *The Rivals* (1775), George Bernard Shaw's *Man and Superman* (1903), J. B. Priestley's *I Have Been Here Before* (1937), Arthur Wing Pinero's *Trelawny of the 'Wells'* (1898), Norman Ginsbury's *Viceroy Sarah* (1936), and Edward Wooll's *Libel* (1934).
35 Anthony Quayle, *A Time to Speak* (London: Barrie & Jenkins, 1990), p. 192.
36 Anthony B. Dawson, *Shakespeare in Performance: Hamlet* (Manchester: Manchester University Press, 1995), p. 83.
37 Ibid., p. 96.

Notes to pages 22–29

38 In Paul Read, *Alec Guinness: The Authorised Biography* (London: Simon & Schuster, 2003), p. 83.
39 Kenneth Tynan, *Alec Guinness* (London: Salisbury Square, 1953), p. 33.
40 Dawson, *Hamlet*, p. 117.
41 Gregor, *Shakespeare and Tyranny*, p. 10.
42 *Cesare* (1939) premiered just after the Old Vic visit and was due to tour internationally at the outbreak of the Second World War. Michele De Benedictis, 'Crossing the Rubicon in Fascist Italy: Mussolini and Theatrical Caesarism from Shakespeare's *Julius Caesar*', in *Shakespeare and Tyranny*, pp. 105–26 (pp. 114–15).
43 Ibid., pp. 116–17.
44 In Diana Devlin, *A Speaking Part: Lewis Casson and the Theatre of His Time* (London: Hodder & Stoughton, 1982), pp. 195–96.
45 The British Library Archives [BL] MS 89015/1/4/1 'Merula Guinness' Old Vic Tour Diary 1939', Vol. 1, 4 February 1939.
46 In Read, *Alec Guinness*, p. 86.
47 Quayle, *A Time to Speak*, p. 192.
48 Alec Guinness, *Blessings in Disguise* (London: Hamish Hamilton, 1985), pp. 18–19.
49 Ibid., p. 19.
50 Devlin, *Speaking Part*, p. 195; Guinness, *Blessings*, p. 19.
51 Guinness, *Blessings*, p. 19.
52 BL MS 89015/1/4/1 'Old Vic Tour Diary 1939', Vol. 1, 25 January, 28 January 1939.
53 Ibid., 28 January, 27 January 1939.
54 Read, *Guinness*, p. 88.
55 Ibid.
56 On bohemianism, see Virginia Nicholson, *Among the Bohemians: Experiments in Living 1900–1939* (London: Penguin Books, 2003).
57 BL MS 89015/1/4/1 'Old Vic Tour Diary 1939', Vol. 1, 4 February, 8 February 1939.
58 Anon, 'Address to the Artists of the Old Vic Company by the President of the Federazione Nazionale Fascista', 6 February 1939, in BL MS 89015/1/4/1 'Old Vic Tour Diary 1939', Vol. 1.
59 Anon, 'Address to the Artists', in BL MS 89015/1/4/1 'Old Vic Tour Diary 1939', Vol. 1.
60 BL MS 89015/1/4/1 'Old Vic Tour Diary 1939', Vol. 1, 6 February 1939.
61 Guinness, *Blessings*, p. 19.
62 Devlin, *Speaking Part*, pp. 195–97.
63 Besides Shakespeare and Shaw, all British playwrights were boycotted on the Italian stage at the time. Richard Halpern, *Shakespeare Among the Moderns* (Ithaca, NY: Cornell University Press, 1997), p. 52.
64 Devlin, *Speaking Part*, p. 197.
65 Quayle, *A Time to Speak*, p. 194. Giuseppe Blanc's *Giovinezza* (1909) had been appropriated as a Fascist hymn and became the unofficial Italian national

anthem between 1924 and 1943. George Stanley Payne, *A History of Fascism, 1914–1945* (Abingdon: Routledge, 1995), p. 92.
66 Quayle, *A Time to Speak*, p. 194.
67 Darwin, *The Empire Project*, p. 71.
68 Tarek Osman, *Egypt on the Brink: From Nasser to the Muslim Brotherhood* (New Haven, CT: Yale University Press, 2010), p. 33; Darwin, *The Empire Project*, p. 72.
69 Whidden, *Egypt*, pp. 38–40.
70 Darwin, *The Empire Project*, pp. 75–78.
71 Osman, *Egypt on the Brink*, p. 33; Darwin, *The Empire Project*, p. 72.
72 Whidden, *Egypt*, pp. 164–65.
73 Quayle, *A Time to Speak*, pp. 195–96.
74 Gershoni and Jankowski, *Confronting Fascism in Egypt*, pp. 59–63.
75 Freya Stark, *Dust in the Lion's Paw* (London: Arrow Books, 1990), pp. 52–3.
76 Whidden, *Egypt*, pp. 123–4.
77 Margaret Litvin, *Hamlet's Arab Journey: Shakespeare's Prince and Nasser's Ghost* (Princeton, NJ: Princeton University Press, 2011), p. 61; M. M. Badawi, 'Shakespeare and the Arabs', in *Cairo Studies of English* (Cairo: Al-Maktaba al-Anjlu al-Misriyya, 1966), pp. 181–96.
78 Litvin, *Hamlet's Arab Journey*, pp. 59–60.
79 Ibid., p. 64.
80 Ibid., pp. 62–64, 71.
81 BL MS 89015/1/4/1 'Old Vic Tour Diary 1939', Vol. 2, 21 February 1939.
82 In Whidden, *Egypt*, p. 7,
83 Whidden, *Egypt*, pp. 9–10, p. 141; Osman, *Egypt on the Brink*, p. 27; Darwin, *The Empire Project*, p. 71.
84 BL MS 89015/1/4/1 'Old Vic Tour Diary 1939', Vol. 2, 4 February 1939.
85 Ibid.
86 The Old Vic's association of Shakespeare with education and a modicum of state support strengthened the sense that, despite the commercial risks involved, the canon was a 'worthy cause' to disseminate down to 'the masses'. J. C. Trewin, *Shakespeare on the English Stage 1900–1964* (London: Barrie and Rockliff, 1964), p. 189.
87 BL MS 89015/1/4/1 'Old Vic Tour Diary 1939', Vol. 2, 27 February 1939.
88 Ibid., 4 February 1939.
89 In Read, *Guinness*, p. 80, pp. 87–88.
90 Ibid., pp. 89–90.
91 Paul Gilroy, *After Empire* (Abingdon: Routledge, 2004), p. 95.
92 Jörn Weingärtner, *The Arts as a Weapon of War: Britain and the Shaping of National Morale in the Second World War* (London: Taurus Academic Studies, 2006), pp. 1–34.
93 Andy Merriman, *Greasepaint and Cordite: How ENSA Entertained the Troops During World War II* (London: Aurum Press, 2014), p. 59.
94 In Weingärtner, *Arts as a Weapon*, pp. 162–63.
95 James Forsyth, *Tyrone Guthrie* (London: Hamish Hamilton, 1976), p. 181.

96 Weingärtner, *Arts as a Weapon*, p. 164.
97 Laurence Olivier, 'From Gin Palace to National Theatre', in *Five Seasons of the Old Vic Theatre Company: A Scrapbook Record of Production for 1944–1949* (London: Saturn Press, 1949), p. 5.
98 See Andrew Sinclair, *Arts and Cultures: The History of the Fifty Years of the Arts Council in Great Britain* (London: Sinclair-Stevenson, 1995).
99 Richard Fawkes, *Fighting for a Laugh: Entertaining the British and American Armed Forces, 1939–1946* (London: Macdonald and Jane's, 1978), pp. 11–24.
100 Basil Dean, *Theatre at War* (London: Harrap & Co, 1956), pp. 500–2.
101 Donald Wolfit, *First Interval* (London: Odhams Press Limited, 1954), p. 229.
102 Ronald Harwood, *Sir Donald Wolfit: His Life and Work in the Unfashionable Theatre* (London: Secker and Warburg, 1971), p. 188.
103 On the politics surrounding demobilisation see, Angus Calder, *The People's War: Britain 1939–1945* (London: Pimlico, 1992), pp. 570–71.
104 Ronald Harwood, *The Dresser* (London: Amber Lane Press, 1984).
105 Dean, *Theatre at War*, pp. 501–2.
106 Wolfit, *First Interval*, pp. 227.
107 Ibid., pp. 227–28.
108 Ibid., p. 230.
109 In Harwood, *Donald Wolfit*, p. 191.
110 Harwood, *Donald Wolfit*, p. 177; Laurence Raw, 'People's Theatre and Shakespeare in Wartime: Donald Wolfit's *King Lear* in London and Leeds, 1944–1945', *Shakespeare*, 12.1 (2016), 55–66, (p. 56).
111 Harwood, *Donald Wolfit*, p. 152.
112 Wolfit, *First Interval*, p. 231.
113 John Springhall, *Decolonisation Since 1945* (Basingstoke: Palgrave Macmillan, 2001), pp. 87–91.
114 Wolfit, *First Interval*, p. 230.
115 Ibid.
116 At the time Britain owed Egypt around £400,000,000 for 'services rendered' during the war. Darwin, *The Empire Project*, p. 525.
117 Stark, *Dust*, p. 60.
118 Ibid.; Laurence Grafftey-Smith, *Bright Levant* (London: Stacey International, 2002), p. 221.
119 Grafftey-Smith, *Bright Levant*, p. 222.
120 Croall, *Gielgud*, p. 315.
121 Dean, *Theatre at War*, p. 498.
122 Croall, *Gielgud*, p. 261.
123 Richard Huggett, *Binkie Beaumont: Eminence Grise of the West End Theatre 1933–1973* (London: Hodder and Stoughton, 1989), p. 246.
124 Croall, *Gielgud*, p. 317.
125 Ibid., p. 320.
126 Richard Mangan, ed., *Gielgud's Letters* (London: Weidenfeld and Nicolson, 2004), pp. 82–86.

127 Afaf Lutfi Al-Sayyid-Marsot, *Egypt's Liberal Experiment* (Berkeley, CA: University of California Press, 1978), p. 232.
128 Springhall, *Decolonisation*, pp. 87–91.
129 Selman Botman, *Egypt From Independence to Revolution, 1919–1952* (Syracuse, NY: Syracuse University Press, 1991), p. 154.
130 Al-Sayyid-Marsot, *Egypt's Liberal Experiment*, p. 229; Darwin, *The Empire Project*, p. 218; Osman, *Egypt on the Brink*, pp. 44–45. Many of the Free Officers who eventually seized power in July 1952 came into political activism as high school students during the 1946 uprising. Ahmed Abdalla, *The Student Movements and National Politics in Egypt, 1923–1973* (Cairo: The American University of Cairo Press, 2008), pp. 62–79.
131 Dean, *Theatre at War*, p. 503.
132 Abdalla, *Student Movements*, p. 64.
133 Dean, *Theatre at War*, p. 504.
134 Ibid., p. 504; Croall, *Gielgud*, p. 325.
135 Dean, *Theatre at War*, pp. 506–7.
136 In Abdalla, *Student Movements*, p. 66.
137 Dean, *Theatre at War*, p. 508.
138 Whidden, *Egypt*, p. 169.
139 Stark, *Dust*, pp. 68–71.
140 Whidden, *Egypt*, p. 169.
141 Ibid., p. 206. Stark, *Dust*, p. 63. 'The Brotherhood of Freedom' was based on Stark's own three-point 'theory of persuasion': that one had to 'believe one's own sermon', that the message 'must be advantageous not only to one's own side but to that of the listeners also', and that it was better 'to influence indirectly, making one's friends among the people of the country distribute and interpret one's words' for you. Stark, *Dust*, p. 65.
142 Aldrich, *The Hidden Hand*, p. 12; Abdalla, *Student Movements*, p. 69–79.
143 Dean, *Theatre at War*, p. 509.
144 In Whidden, *Egypt*, p. 104.
145 In contrast to Britain's laissez-faire approach, Sir Charles Mendl (Press Attaché at the British Embassy in Paris), recognised that the Alliance française was becoming 'by far the largest, best organised and most powerful instrument of cultural propaganda that France possessed'. In Donaldson, *British Council*, p. 3.
146 In Donaldson, *The British Council*, p. 79.
147 In Taylor, *Projection of Britain*, p. 169.
148 In Donaldson, *The British Council*, p. 3.
149 Whidden, *Egypt*, pp. 11, 103, 110. When British Council Institutes opened in Cairo and Alexandria in 1938, 30,000 Maltese and Cypriot children and 7,000 British children were in immediate need of unavailable school places. Taylor, *Projection of Britain*, pp. 169–70.
150 TNA BW 72 'British Council: Sub-Committee on British Education in the Near East: Minutes 1935–1939', 20 November 1935.

151 Whidden, *Egypt*, p. 103.
152 Forbes Adam, *Lord Lloyd*, p. 282.
153 In Whidden, *Egypt*, p. 103.
154 Ibid.
155 Ibid., p. 104.
156 Said found colonial schooling at Victoria College 'more serious' than 'any I had attended, the pressure greater, the teachers harsher, the students more competitive, and sharp, the atmosphere bristling with challenges, punishments, bullies, and risks'. Sahar Hamouda and Colin Clement, eds., *Victoria College: A History Revealed* (Cairo: The American University of Cairo Press, 2002), p. xiii.
157 Edward Said, *Out of Place: A Memoir* (London: Granta Books, 1999), p. 51.
158 Ibid., pp. 51–52.
159 Ibid., p. 53.
160 Ibid.
161 Ibid.
162 Mahmoud F. Al-Shetawi, '*Hamlet* in Arabic', *Journal of Intercultural Studies*, 20.1 (1999), 43–63.
163 'Abdel-qadir Al-Samahi, 'Hamlit', *Al-Thaqafah*, 384 (1946), 18–21.
164 Andrew Murphy, *Shakespeare for the People: Working-Class Readers, 1800–1900* (Cambridge: Cambridge University Press, 2010), p. 173.
165 Nicolas, J. Cull, *The Cold War and the United States Information Agency: American Propaganda and Public Diplomacy, 1945–1989* (Cambridge: Cambridge University Press, 2008), p. 19.
166 TNA BW 29/47 'General Policy: Propaganda War in Egypt during 1939–1940', 'Brian Jones to Furness', 21 February 1946.
167 TNA BW 29/47 'Brian Jones to Furness', 21 February 1946.
168 On CRD responses to Soviet propaganda activities during the Cold War interregnum period, see Richard J. Aldrich, 'Putting Culture into the Cold War: The Cultural Research Department and British Covert Information Warfare', *Intelligence and National Security*, 18.2 (2003), 109–33.
169 Whidden, *Egypt*, p. 207.
170 Grafftey-Smith, *Bright Levant*, pp. 217, 219.
171 Whidden, *Egypt*, pp. 129, 127.
172 Aldrich, 'Putting Culture into the Cold War', p. 109.
173 Dean, *Theatre at War*, p. 507.
174 Alfred Harbage, *Shakespeare's Audience* (New York: Columbia University Press, 1969). John Drakakis describes Harbage's 'harmonious integration' as 'a picture of the Elizabethan theatre as an institution in which different social groups relinquished their mutual antagonisms in favour of a corporate activity that was both festive and anticipated the modern spirit of democracy'. John Drakakis, ed., *Alternative Shakespeares* (Abingdon: Routledge, 1985), p. 13.
175 F. R. Leavis, *For Continuity* (Cambridge: Minority Press, 1933), p. 216.

Chapter 2

1. In Terry Coleman, *Olivier: The Authorised Biography* (London: Bloomsbury, 2005), p. 204.
2. Forsyth, *Tyrone Guthrie*, pp. 200–1; Garry O'Connor, *Darlings of the Gods: One Year in the Lives of Laurence Olivier and Vivien Leigh* (London: Hodder and Stoughton, 1984), p. 116.
3. In Coleman, *Olivier*, p. 204.
4. O'Connor, *Darlings*, p. 100.
5. Ibid.
6. Quayle had been appointed Artistic Director of the Shakespeare Memorial Theatre in 1948 and was quick to expand upon the institutional changes brought about by his two predecessors Robert Atkins (1944–45) and Barry Jackson (1945–48). Sally Beauman, *The Royal Shakespeare Company: A History of Ten Decades* (Oxford: Oxford University Press, 1982), pp. 193–95, 200.
7. Ivor Brown and Anthony Quayle, *Shakespeare Memorial Theatre 1948–1950: A Photographic Record* (London: Reinhardt and Evans, 1951), p. 15.
8. On Australia's enormous appetite for British culture and patterns of post-war migration between Australia and London, see Kate Darian-Smith and Patricia Grimshaw, eds., *Britishness Abroad: Transnational Movements and Imperial Cultures* (Melbourne: Melbourne University Press, 2007).
9. Belich, *Replenishing the Earth*, p. 460.
10. Ibid., p. 9.
11. Ibid., p. 464. See also Stuart Ward, *Australia and the British Embrace: The Demise of the Imperial Ideal* (Melbourne: Melbourne University Press, 2001), pp. 13–27.
12. Lee, 'British Cultural Diplomacy', p. 112.
13. Andrew Defty, *Britain, America, and Anti-Communist Propaganda 1945–1953: The Information Research Department* (Abingdon: Routledge, 2003), pp. 28–29.
14. TNA BW 12/4 'Australia: Reports, 1947–1953', 'Sydney Press Release', 24 April 1947.
15. See, Boyd Neel and J. David Finch, *My Orchestra and Other Adventures: The Memoirs of Boyd Neel* (Toronto: The University of Toronto Press, 1985).
16. Taylor, *Projection of Britain*, p. 9.
17. Belich suggests that nineteenth-century patterns of shared industrial growth and identity across Britain's white-settler Empire and the US led to the creation of a recognisable 'Anglo-world' or Anglosphere, a 'sub-global, yet transnational, intercontinental … melange of partners and subjects' characterised by the transfer of 'things, thoughts, and people, lubricated by shared language and culture'. Belich, *Replenishing the Earth*, pp. 49–51.
18. Blakemore, *Arguments*, pp. 148–49.
19. Anon, 'Meat Coupons for British Food Appeal Fund', *Morning Bulletin*, 28 May 1947, p. 10.

20 Springhall, *Decolonisation*, pp. 31–64.
21 On the domino theory, see Peter T. Leeson and Andrea Dean, 'The Democratic Domino Theory', *American Journal of Political Science*, 53.3 (2009), 533–51. On imperial security and anti-communist intelligence sharing between Britain and the United States during the early Cold War see, Calder Walton, *Empire of Secrets: British Intelligence, The Cold War, and The Twilight of Empire* (London: Harper Press, 2013), pp. 141–42, 153–55.
22 On the strategic importance of Commonwealth Security for Britain's post-war status, especially in the broader terms of Anglo-American Intelligence sharing, see Aldrich, *The Hidden Hand*, pp. 103–13. On Britain's rush to establish the Australian Security Intelligence Organisation (ASIO) in response to Soviet infiltration, see Aldrich, *The Hidden Hand*, pp. 111–15. See also, Nigel West, 'ASIO Opens its Books', *International Journal of Intelligence and Counterintelligence*, 28.3 (2014), 620–29.
23 TNA BW 12/4 'General Report March to June 1947', 'Notes on the First Meeting of the Inter-Departmental Committee set up to advise and Assist the British Council on its Relations with the External Territories of Australasia', 18 June 1947. In March 1949 a US National Security Council paper stated that '19th century imperialism is no longer a practicable system in SEA [Southeast Asia] excepting in the short run in Malaya'. In Westad, *Global Cold War*, p. 113.
24 Darwin, *The Empire Project*, pp. 559–60. Mark Curtis, *Web of Deceit: Britain's Real Role in the World* (London: Vintage Books, 2003), pp. 334–45. See also, Robert Jackson, *The Malayan Emergency and Indonesian Confrontation: The Commonwealth's Wars 1948–1966* (London: Pen and Sword Aviation, 2008).
25 This cultural service carried 'identity as well as information' with the Australian book trade, for instance, being 'almost entirely in British hands' before the war. Belich, *Replenishing the Earth*, pp. 460–61. Although Benedict Anderson's original phrase refers to the formation of nation-states, my use here exceeds this to incorporate metropolitan and white settler-colonial citizenry. Benedict Anderson, *Imagined Communities* (London: Verso Books, 2006), pp. 5–7.
26 Donald Read, *The Power of the News: The History of Reuters* (Oxford: Oxford University Press, 1992), p. 259.
27 TNA BW 12/4 'General Report March to June 1947', 24 April 1947. Charles Wilmot set up advance British Council administrative units in each area to be visited during the tour. O'Connor, p. 84.
28 TNA BW 12/4 'Representative's Report for January to August 1948'.
29 TNA BW 12/4 'Report of British Council Representative in Australia for Period 10 January to 5 February 1947', p. 5.
30 TNA BW 12/4 'Representative's Report for January to August 1948'.
31 TNA BW 12/4 'General Report March to June 1947'.
32 In autumn 1942 Olivier was temporarily released from the Navy by the Ministry of Information to 'make two pictures, one of which was *Henry V*. Olivier, *Five Seasons*, p. 5.

33 Michael W. Boyce, *The Lasting Influence of the War on Post-War British Film* (Basingstoke: Palgrave Macmillan, 2012), p. 119.
34 Emma Smith, *Shakespeare in Production: Henry V* (Cambridge: Cambridge University Press, 2002), pp. 50–62. On Olivier's film version of *Henry V*, see Maurice Hindle, *Studying Shakespeare on Film* (Basingstoke: Palgrave Macmillan, 2007), pp. 140–46.
35 Tyrone Guthrie, *A Life in the Theatre* (London: Hamish Hamilton, 1960), p. 203.
36 Ibid., pp. 188–89.
37 Julie Hankey, ed., *Richard the Third: Plays in Performance* (Bristol: Bristol Classical Press, 1988), p. 67.
38 Wolfit, *First Interval*, p. 205.
39 Hugh M. Richmond, *King Richard III: Shakespeare in Performance* (Manchester: Manchester University Press, 1991), p. 56.
40 Ibid., p. 57.
41 Ibid., p. 58.
42 Hankey, *Richard the Third*, p. 68.
43 Jonathan Rose, *The Literary Churchill: Author, Reader, Actor* (New Haven, CT: Yale University Press, 2014), p. 315.
44 In O'Connor, *Darlings*, p. 162.
45 Hankey, *Richard the Third*, p. 63.
46 In Jonathan Croall, *Sybil Thorndike: A Star of Life* (London: Haus Books, 2008), p. 345.
47 In Croall, *Sybil Thorndike*, p. 345.
48 Robert Collis, *To Be a Pilgrim* (London: Secker and Warburg, 1975), p. 103; Croall, *Thorndike*, p. 348–49.
49 Croall, *Thorndike*, p. 350.
50 The planned tour itinerary was, *School For Scandal* at Perth's Capitol Theatre, 20–28 March; *Richard III* and *Skin of Our Teeth* at Adelaide's Theatre Royal, 3–18 April; *School for Scandal, Richard III* and *Skin of Our Teeth* at Melbourne's Princess Theatre, 20 April to 12 June; *School for Scandal* at Hobart's Theatre Royal, 14–20 June; *School for Scandal, Richard III* and *Skin of our Teeth* at Sydney's Tivoli Theatre, 29 June to 21 July; *School for Scandal* at Brisbane's His Majesty's, from 21 August to 3 September.
51 Anthony Holden, *Olivier* (London: Little Books, 2007), p. 232.
52 O'Connor, *Darlings*, p. 109.
53 James Lawrence, *Churchill and Empire: Portrait of an Imperialist* (London: Phoenix, 2013), p. 276, p. 287.
54 Holden, *Olivier*, p. 225.
55 Ibid., p. 233.
56 Ibid., p. 234.
57 In Coleman, *Olivier*, p. 208.
58 O'Connor, *Darlings*, pp. 122–23.
59 Holden, *Olivier*, p. 238.
60 O'Connor, *Darlings*, pp. 113–14.

61 Felix Barker, *The Oliviers: A Biography* (London: Hamish Hamilton, 1953), p. 283; O'Connor, *Darlings*, p. 158.
62 O'Connor, *Darlings*, p. 124.
63 Peter Cushing, *The Complete Memoirs* (Cambridge: Signum Books, 2013), p. 141.
64 Forsyth, *Guthrie*, pp. 200–1.
65 TNA BW 12/4 'Report on British Council Activities in Australia, January to September 1949', p. 2.
66 Tyrone Guthrie, 'Report on Australian Theatre', *The Australian Quarterly*, 21.2 (1949), 78–83. For the original coinage of the term and a detailed discussion on 'the cultural cringe' see A. A. Phillips, *The Australian Tradition: Studies in a Colonial Culture* (Melbourne: Cheshire Press, 1958); Stephen Alomes, *When London Calls: The Expatriation of Australian Creative Artists to Britain* (Cambridge: Cambridge University Press, 2000), pp. 4–11, 19–23.
67 'Representative's Report January to August 1948', p. 5.
68 Alomes, *When London Calls*, p. 22.
69 TNA BW 12/4 'October 1949 to September 1950'.
70 Penny Gay, 'International Glamour or Home-Grown Entertainment? 1948–1964', in *O Brave New World: Two Centuries of Shakespeare on the Australian Stage*, ed. by John Golder and Richard Madelaine (Sydney: Currency Press, 2001), pp. 180–99 (p. 182). The 1949 touring production of *Much Ado About Nothing* was directed by John Gielgud. Both it and *Macbeth* starred Anthony Quayle and Diana Wynyard.
71 Geoffrey Milne, *Theatre Australia (Un)Limited: Australian Theatre Since the 1950s* (Amsterdam: Rodopi Press, 2004), p. 80.
72 TNA BW 12/4 'General Report on Activities for Six Months ending March 1950', p. 2.
73 David Addenbrooke, *The Royal Shakespeare Company: The Peter Hall Years* (London: William Kember, 1974), p. 12. During his tenure, Quayle took the company on six tours, performing eleven productions in total: Australia in 1949–50, West Germany in 1950, New Zealand and Australia in 1953, Continental Europe in 1953–54, 1955 and 1957, and the USSR in 1958. Addenbrooke, *Peter Hall Years*, p. 283.
74 TNA BW 12/4 'October 1949 to September 1950'.
75 Quayle, *A Time to Speak*, p. 321.
76 Hewison, *Culture and Consensus*, p. 80.
77 Ibid., p. 23. See also, Angus Calder, *The Myth of the Blitz* (London: Jonathan Cape, 1991), pp. 180–208; Patrick Wright, *On Living in an Old Country: The National Past in Contemporary Britain* (Oxford: Oxford University Press, 2009), pp. 77–83.
78 For the spread of the place name 'Stratford' throughout the anglosphere, see Katherine Scheil, 'Importing Stratford', in *Critical Survey*, 24.2 (2012), 71–87.
79 Quayle, *A Time to Speak*, pp. 318–19.

80 In Heather Wiebe, *Britten's Unquiet Pasts: Sound and Memory in Post-war Reconstruction* (Cambridge: Cambridge University Press, 2012), p. 303; Darwin, 'A Third British Empire?', pp. 64–87.
81 See, for instance, A. L. Rowse, *An Elizabethan Garland* (London: Macmillan, 1953).
82 For links between New Elizabethanism and Britain's anthropological turn see Jed Esty, *A Shrinking Island: Modernism and National Culture in England* (Princeton, NJ: Princeton University Press, 2003).
83 Brown and Quayle, *A Photographic Record*, p. 11.
84 The tour played Auckland, Christchurch, Dunedin, and Wellington from 2 February, and then Sydney, Brisbane, Melbourne, Adelaide, and Perth from 21 April. With a two-months sea voyage at either end, the protracted international circuit required the SMT to be split into two interchangeable companies. *Henry IV (Part I)* was a revival of the 1951 staging, while both *As You Like It* and *Othello* were new productions destined to enter the Stratford-upon-Avon repertoire the following season.
85 Anon, 'It's the Bard – But Without Tears', *Brisbane Sunday Mail*, 26 April 1953; Anon, 'Shakespeare Players Strong Empire Bond', *Weekly Radio and Music Records*, 11 May 1953.
86 Anon, 'Anthony Quayle', *People*, 17 June 1953.
87 Elizabeth Stead, 'Shakespeare Company Moves Like an Army', *Launceston Examiner*, 22 August 1953.
88 Arthur Polkinghorne, 'Sydney Will Drink a Toast to W. Shakespeare', *The Sun*, 20 April 1953.
89 Anon, 'A Glance at Some New Elizabethans' *The Geelong Advertiser*, 25 July 1953.
90 Ibid.
91 Ibid.
92 Polkinghorne, 'Sydney Will Drink a Toast'.
93 Ibid.
94 Ibid. Phillip Knightley, *Australia: A Biography of a Nation* (London: Vintage Books, 2001), p. 47. See also, Wendy Webster, *Englishness and Empire 1939–1965* (Oxford: Oxford University Press, 1996).
95 Anon, '"Operation Theatre" Makes Big Demands on Off-Stage Planners', *The ABC Weekly*, 28 March 1953.
96 Stead, 'Shakespeare Company'.
97 Anon, 'Operation Theatre'.
98 Anon, 'Travel', *Melbourne Age*, 10 August 1953.
99 Jim Macdougall, 'Contact', *The Sun*, 22 April 1953.
100 Anon, 'Top Hats at Othello', *The Daily Telegraph*, 22 April 1953; Wiebe, *Britten's Unquiet Pasts*, p. 302.
101 Macdougall, 'Contact'.
102 Anon, 'Stratford Othello at the Tivoli', *The Herald*, 22 April 1953.
103 Anon, 'Passion, Colour, seen in Othello', [No Publication], 22 April 1953. All *Othello* reviews can be found in the Shakespeare Birthplace Trust's [SBT]

RSC/Theatre Records/Series B/Vols.69–79 'Press Books: Tour to Australia and New Zealand'. Gaps in attribution are indicated with [No Title], [No Author], [No Publication], or [No Date]. Anon, 'Shakespeare May Be Seen Here in a New Light', *The Western Australian*, 18 September 1953.
104 Anon, 'Othello is Enthralling', *Telegraph*, 22 April 1953; Anon, 'Othello at Tivoli', [No Publication], May 1953.
105 Anon, 'Passion'.
106 Frank Murphy, 'Othello', *Melbourne Advocate*, 7 July 1953.
107 Anon, 'Othello at Tivoli'.
108 Anon, 'Othello Is Too Smooth and Quiet', *The Sun*, 26 April 1953.
109 Anon, 'Stratford Othello'.
110 Macdougall, 'Contact'.
111 Anon, 'Stratford Othello'.
112 Anon, 'Othello Is Too Smooth'.
113 Leo McKern, *Just Resting* (London: Methuen, 1983), p. 87.
114 Ibid., p. 87.
115 Ibid., p. 86.
116 Ibid., p. 87.
117 Anon, 'Passion'.
118 Anon, 'Sydney Diary', *The Sun*, 24 April 1953; Anon, 'Stratford Othello'.
119 Anon, 'Othello at Tivoli'.
120 McKern, *Just Resting*, p. 87.
121 George Whaley, *Leo 'Rumpole' McKern: The Accidental Actor* (Sydney: University of New South Wales Press, 2009), pp. 83, 78.
122 For Whaley, McKern's journey from obscurity to third billing with the prestigious SMT company was not only 'a leg-up almost into the ranks of British theatre nobility', but a promotion so rapid it was 'almost beyond belief'. Whaley, *Leo 'Rumpole' McKern*, p. 70.
123 Murphy, 'Othello'.
124 Ibid.
125 Anon, 'Othello is Enthralling'.
126 Hugh M. Richmond, 'The Audience's Role in *Othello*', in *Othello: New Critical Essays*, ed. by Philip Kolin (Abingdon: Routledge, 2016), p. 91.
127 Ibid., p. 91.
128 Richard Halpern states that the sheer weight of historical comparisons made during the 1953 Coronation promoted 'a juxtaposition of losses' that saw in the early-modern period 'a sufficiently dark reflection of its own catastrophes'. Halpern, *Shakespeare among the Moderns*, p. 9.
129 John Sumner, *Recollections at Play: A Life in Australian Theatre* (Melbourne University Press: Melbourne, 1993), p. 9.
130 Zelie McLeod, 'The Theatre in Australia Faces a Crisis', *Daily Telegraph*, 16 May 1953.
131 Ibid.
132 Anon, 'Editorial: Australia Needs a National Theatre', *The Sun*, 5 June 1953.

133 McLeod, 'The Theatre in Australia'.
134 Sumner, *Recollections*, p. 9.
135 Anon, 'Could Play Shakespeare in a Swimsuit', *Courier Mail*, 26 June 1953.
136 Anon, 'How to Get the Most Out of Shakespeare', *Western Australian*, 19 September 1953.
137 Anon, [No Title], [No Publication], 26 April 1953.
138 Anon, [No Title], *Sunday Sun*, 7 June 1953.
139 Anon, 'Shakespeare Queue Began at 4.50 A.M.' [No Publication], 14 March 1953.
140 Anon, 'Brawn Called for In This Act', *Telegraph*, 15 April 1953. Webster, *Englishness and Empire*, pp. 119–135.
141 Anon, 'News of the Day', *Age*, 19 August 1953.
142 Anon, 'Play Festival Age', *Melbourne*, 20 July 1953; Anon, 'Directors Wife Is Talent Scout', *Age* 27 June 1953.
143 TNA BW 12/6 'Representative's Annual Report for 1951–1952', 'Representative's Annual Report for 1952/53', p. 9.
144 Reg Luckie, 'Australian Actor for Stratford', *Women's Weekly*, 18 July 1953.
145 Anon, 'Shakespearean Visit Coronation Gesture', *Brisbane Telegraph*, 23 May 1953.
146 Elizabeth Stead, 'Shakespeare Under the Southern Cross', *Melbourne Sun*, 20 June 1953.
147 Coral Craig, 'Stratford Players at Their Best', *Women's Day*, 9 February 1953. Other Australian and New Zealand members of the company were Robert Stead, Rosalind Atkinson, Max Hillier, Jane Holland, and Antony Riddell. Hazel Tully, 'Our Four Shakespeareans', *Women*, 15 September 1953.
148 Robert Kennedy, 'Town Talk', [No Publication], 25 April 1953; Craig, 'Stratford Players'.
149 Anon, 'Eating, Sleeping – In Unrefined Way', *Melbourne Age*, 7 August 1953.
150 Though the ABC Play Unit provided an essential outlet for Australian acting talent it restricted local accents in broadcasting well into the 1960s. In Phillips, *The Australian Tradition*, p. 92.
151 Anon, 'Neutral Accent is 'Must' in London', *The Listener In*, 15 August 1953.
152 Anon, 'For Home Service', *The Listener In*, [No Date].
153 John Scarlett, 'Talk Too Much Nonsense on Shakespeare', *The Sunday Times*, 27 September 1953.
154 Ibid.
155 Anon, 'Ban Shakespeare from Schools', *The Argus*, 7 July 1953.
156 Anon, 'They Live, Breath Shakespeare', *Melbourne Sun*, 19 June 1953.
157 Anon, 'Shakespeare and "Snobs"', [No Publication], 23 April 1953.
158 Anon, 'Playgoers are 'Critics First' Says Actress', *Age Melbourne*, 1 August 1953.
159 Anon, 'Big Contrasts in Our Audience', *Perth Daily News*, 18 September.

160 Anon, 'Let us Pep Up Shakespeare!', *Melbourne Argus*, 1 August 1953.
161 Alec King, 'Letters to the Editor: A Play in Perth', *The Western Australian*, 8 October 1953.
162 J. H. Reynolds, 'Letters to the Editor: Opportunity', *The Western Australian*, 8 October 1953; Anon, 'What's on in Town', *Perth Mirror*, 10 October 1953; Frank Doherty, 'Must We Be Told What to See', *Melbourne Argus*, 19 August 1953.
163 Lennard Crooks, 'Too Lazy to Dig Out 21/for a Seat', *Melbourne Argus*, 22 August 1953. Anon, 'Melbourne Audiences 'Lazy': Quayle', *Melbourne Argus*, 19 August 1953; Anon, [No Title], *Melbourne Argus*, 19 August.
164 Paterfamilias, 'Letters to the Editor: Play Audience', [No Publication], 12 October 1953.
165 Ibid.
166 Had It, 'Letters to the Editor: Play Audiences', 12 October 1953.
167 J. Chaplin, 'Letters to the Editor: Play Audiences', [No Publication], 12 October 1953.
168 Anon, '"Appalling" Says Quayle', *Sydney Sunday Times*, 18 October 1953.
169 Nomad, 'Letters to the Editor: Theatre Seats', *The Western Australian*, 15 October 1953.
170 Nomad, 'Theatre Seats'.
171 Anon, '"Appalling" Says Quayle'.
172 McKern, *Just Resting*, p. 86.
173 Anon, '"Appalling" Says Quayle'.
174 Anon, 'Music and Theatre World', *Western Australian*, 14 October 1953.
175 Ibid.
176 O'Connor, *Darlings*, pp. 113–14. For an example of similar cultural-diplomatic tactics being used in the United States, see M. G. Aune, 'Importing Shakespeare: Tyrone Guthrie and British Cold War Cultural Colonialism', in *Shakespeare*, 5.4 (2009), 423–40.
177 The Third British Empire scuppered American hopes that Britain's future lay in a greater European project. See, Richard J. Aldrich, 'OSS, CIA and European Unity: The American Committee of United Europe, 1948–60', *Diplomacy and Statecraft*, 8.1 (1997), 184–227.
178 In Belich's words, when Britain joined the EEC 'Greater Britain was no more, and mourning was short-circuited by the growing pretence that it had never existed'. Belich, *Replenishing*, pp. 471–72.
179 Donaldson, *The British Council*, pp. 191–92.
180 TNA BW 12/6 'Representative's Annual Report for April 1954 to March 1955'.
181 Ernest W. Burbridge, 'The British Council', *Sydney Morning Herald*, 5 March 1954.
182 Alistair Morrison, 'The British Council', *Morning Herald*, 12 March 1954.
183 Anon, 'End of the British Council', *Sydney Morning Herald*, 4 March 1954.
184 Peter H. Hansen, 'Coronation Everest: The Empire and Commonwealth in the 'Second Elizabethan Age", in *British Culture and the End of Empire*, ed.

by Stuart Ward (Manchester: Manchester University Press: 2001), pp. 57–72 (pp. 60–62); TNA BW 12/6 'Representative's Annual Report for April 1954 to March 1955'.
185 TNA BW 12/6 'Representative's Annual Report for April 1954 to March 1955'.
186 Gay, 'International Glamour', p. 190.
187 John Rickard, 'John Alden (1908–1962)', *The Australian Dictionary of Biography Online*. www.adb.anu.edu.au/biography/alden-john-9323 [Accessed 13 November 2018].
188 TNA BW 12/6 'Representative's Annual Report for 1952/53', p. 9.
189 In Phillipson, *Linguistic Imperialism*, p. 145.
190 Defty, *Information Research Department*, pp. 163–71.

Chapter 3

1 TNA BW 120/1 'Drama Advisory Committee: Minutes of Meetings, 1939–1957', 'Paper on Theatre Export', 28 February 1956.
2 TNA BW 120/1 'Paper on Theatre Export'.
3 See, for example, David Monod, '"He is a Cripple an' Needs my Love": *Porgy and Bess* as Cold War Propaganda', in *The Cultural Cold War in Western Europe, 1945–1960*, ed. by Giles Scott-Smith and Hans Krabbendam (London: Frank Cass, 2003), pp. 300–12.
4 TNA BW 120/1 'DAC Minutes 1939–1957', 13 September 1955.
5 Defty, *Information Research Department*, pp. 163–71.
6 Aiko Watanabe, 'Cultural Drives by the Periphery: Britain's Experiences', *History in Focus*, 10 (2006), p. 1. www.history.ac.uk/ihr/Focus/cold/articles/watanabe.html [Accessed 30 March 2021].
7 The fifty-seven cast members included Laurence Olivier (Titus), Vivien Leigh (Lavinia), Anthony Quayle (Aaron), Maxine Audrey (Tamora), Alan Webb, Frank Thring, Kevin Miles, Lee Montague, Edward Atienza, Basil Hoskine, Ralph Michael, Rosalind Atkinson, Ian Holm, and Michael Blakemore. Blakemore, *Arguments*, p. 148.
8 On the Cultural Cold War, see David Caute, *The Dancer Defects: The Struggle for Cultural Supremacy During the Cold War* (Oxford: Oxford University Press, 2003); Walter L. Hixson, *Parting the Curtain: Propaganda, Culture, and the Cold War, 1945–1951* (London: Macmillan, 1997); Frances Stonor Saunders, *Who Paid the Piper?: The CIA and the Cultural Cold War* (London: Granta, 1999).
9 Blakemore, *Arguments*, p. 170; *Henry V*, IV. 8. 126, in Gary Taylor and Stanley Wells, eds., *William Shakespeare: The Complete Works*, 2nd edn (Oxford: Clarendon Press, 2005), pp. 595–626.
10 Blakemore, *Arguments*, p. 171.
11 J. C. Trewin, *Peter Brook: A Biography* (London: Macdonald, 1971), p. 101.
12 Royal Shakespeare Company productions influenced by Kott's ideas include Peter Brook's *King Lear* (1962), Peter Hall and John Barton's *War of the Roses* (1963–4), and Peter Hall's *Hamlet* (1965).

13 John Elsom, ed., *Is Shakespeare Still Our Contemporary?* (Abingdon: Routledge, 1990), p. 98.
14 Alan Sinfield, 'Royal Shakespeare: Theatre and the Making of Ideology', in *Political Shakespeare: Essays in Cultural Materialism*, ed. by Jonathan Dollimore and Alan Sinfield (Manchester: Manchester University Press, 1985), pp. 182–205.
15 For a wide-ranging discussion on the impact that conservative continental political dissidents such as Kott had in shaping twentieth-century British intellectual life, see Perry Anderson, 'Components of the National Culture', *New Left Review*, 50 (1968), 3–57.
16 In Mark G. Toulouse, *The Transformation of John Foster Dulles* (Macon, GA: Mercer University Press, 1985), p. 161.
17 In 1961 the American Secretary of State announced that the Cold War was becoming 'a genuine contest for the underdeveloped countries ... not on a military plane ... but for influence, prestige, loyalty, and so forth'. In Robert J. McMahon, *The Cold War: A Very Short Introduction* (Oxford: Oxford University Press, 2003), pp. 60–64.
18 For a classic critique of the limitations that Stalinism placed on the anti-imperial struggle, see C. L. R. James, *World Revolution, 1917–1937: The Rise and Fall of the Communist International* (London: Seeker and Warburg, 1937).
19 Czech arms sales to Nasser's Egypt in the mid-1950s were a prominent example. See, Vijay Prashad, *The Darker Nations: A People's History of the Third World* (New York: The New Press, 2007), pp. 47–50, p. 99.
20 Arch Puddington, *Broadcasting Freedom: The Cold War Triumph of Radio Free Europe and Radio Liberty* (Lexington, KY: The University Press of Kentucky, 2000), p. 111.
21 Prashad, *Darker Nations*, pp. 97–100.
22 McMahon, *The Cold War*, p. 64.
23 Saunders, *Who Paid the Piper*, pp. 302–06.
24 Ibid., p. 305.
25 Ibid., p. 304.
26 Krystyna Kujawinska Courtney, 'Krystyna Skuszanka's Shakespeare of Political Allusions and Metaphors in Communist Poland', in *Shakespeare in the Worlds of Communism and Socialism*, ed. By Irena R. Makaryk and Joseph G. Price (Toronto: University of Toronto Press, 2006), pp. 228–45 (p. 235).
27 Misha Glenny, *The Balkans: Nationalism, War, and the Great Powers 1804–2012* (London: Granta, 2012), p. 570.
28 Mark Atwood Lawrence, 'The Rise and Fall of Nonalignment', in *The Cold War in the Third World*, ed. By Robert J. McMahon (Oxford: Oxford University Press, 2013), pp. 139–155 (pp. 144–45); Christopher J. Lee, ed., *Making a World after Empire: The Bandung Moment and Its Political Afterlives* (Athens, OH: Ohio University Press, 2010), pp. 17–22.
29 Lawrence, 'Nonalignment', p. 140.
30 Watanabe, 'Cultural Drives', p. 1.

31 Christopher Mayhew, *War of Words: A Cold War Witness* (London: I. B. Tauris, 1998), p. 51.
32 A 'mammoth portrait of Shakespeare' hung over the All-Union Congress of Soviet Writers in 1934 where Maxim Gorki urged Soviet writers to imitate 'the world's greatest writer'. Makaryk and Price, p. 3.
33 Parfenov and Price, *Russian Essays on Shakespeare*, p. 12.
34 Ibid.
35 Ibid., p. 13.
36 Dmitri Shostakovich, *Testimony: Memoirs as Related to Solomon Volkov* (London: Faber and Faber, 2005) p. 65; Caute, *The Dancer Defects*, p. 80.
37 Mayhew, *Time to Explain*, pp. 108–12.
38 Ibid., p. 139.
39 Ibid., p. 139.
40 Watanabe, 'Cultural Drives', p. 1.
41 Ibid.
42 Coleman, *Olivier*, p. 297.
43 'DAC Minutes 1939–1957', 13 September 1955.
44 Kenneth Tynan, 'King's Rhapsody: *Hamlet* with Paul Schofield, Directed by Peter Brook', *Observer*, 11 December 1955. For a prior example of the British Council turning a lack of preparation and funding to their diplomatic advantage, see Noel Annan's account of the Marlowe Society visit to Berlin in 1948. Noel Annan, *Changing Enemies* (London: Harper Collins, 1996), pp. 237–39. See also, Erica Sheen, 'Mystery in the Soul of State: Shakespeare in Airlift Berlin', in *Shakespeare in Cold War Europe: Conflict, Commemoration, and Celebration*, ed. by Erica Sheen and Isabel Karremann (Basingstoke: Palgrave Pivot, 2016), pp. 9–22.
45 Laurence Senelick, '"Thus conscience doth make cowards of us all": New Documentation on the Okhlopkok *Hamlet*', in *Shakespeare in the Worlds of Communism and Socialism*, pp. 136–56 (p. 153).
46 Ibid., pp. 136–37.
47 Ibid., p. 139.
48 Kenneth Tynan, 'The Russian Way', *Observer*, November 1955.
49 Michael Kustow, *Peter Brook: A Biography* (London: St Martin's Press, 2005), pp. 199–200.
50 Senelick, 'Okhlopkok *Hamlet*', p. 153.
51 Alan. C. Dessen, *Titus Andronicus: Shakespeare in Performance* (Manchester: Manchester University Press, 1990), p. 3.
52 Brian Vickers, *Shakespeare, Co-Author: A Historical Study of Five Collaborative Plays* (Oxford: Oxford University Press, 2002), pp. 150–52.
53 Ibid., p. 242, table 3.19.
54 Ibid., p. 243.
55 Michael D. Friedman and Alan Dessen, *Titus Andronicus: Shakespeare in Performance* (Manchester: Manchester University Press, 2013), pp. 16–17.
56 George W. Bishop, 'Stratford Does Shakespeare's Horror Comic', *Daily Telegraph*, 15 August 1955.

57 David Lewin, 'Horror Comic', *Daily Express*, 15 August 1955.
58 John Coe, 'Impressive – But Still Revolting', *Bristol Evening Post*, 17 August 1955.
59 Trewin, *Peter Brook*, p. 100; Beauman, *The Royal Shakespeare Company*, p. 224.
60 Sinfield, *Political Shakespeare*, p. 199.
61 Trewin, *Peter Brook*, p. 80.
62 Ibid., p. 83.
63 Beauman, *The Royal Shakespeare Company*, p. 224.
64 Anon, *Souvenir Programme for the Shakespeare Memorial Theatre, Stratford-upon-Avon, 1955* (London: Reinhardt and Evans, 1955), p. 7.
65 Sinfield, *Political Shakespeare*, p. 187.
66 Beauman, *The Royal Shakespeare Company*, p. 224; Trewin, *Peter Brook*, p. 83.
67 Anon, 'Search for a Hunger', *Encore*, July–August 1961, pp. 16–17; Jack E. Reese, 'The Formalisation of Horror in *Titus Andronicus*', *Shakespeare Quarterly*, 21:1 (1970), 77–84.
68 Bernard Levin, 'Titus Review', *The Truth*, 26 August 1955.
69 In Beauman, *The Royal Shakespeare Company*, p. 224.
70 Trewin, *Peter Brook*, p. 83.
71 Hugo Vickers, *Vivien Leigh* (London: Hamish Hamilton, 1988), p. 227.
72 Ian Holm, *Acting My Life* (London: Corgi Books, 2004), p. 53.
73 Louis Niebur, *Special Sound: The Creation and Legacy of the BBC Radio-phonic Workshop* (Oxford: Oxford University Press, 2010), pp. 64–119.
74 Francis Martin, 'Mr Brook Decided to Make His Own Primitive Roman Music', *Edinburgh Evening Dispatch*, 27 August 1955.
75 Niebur, *Special Sound*, p. 97; Timothy D. Taylor, *Strange Sounds: Music, Technology and Culture* (Abingdon: Routledge, 2001), pp. 45–60; Ross Brown, *Sound: A Reader in Theatre Practice* (Basingstoke: Palgrave Macmillan, 2010), pp. 190–98.
76 Trewin, *Peter Brook*, pp. 87, 100.
77 Dessen, *Titus Andronicus*, p. 17.
78 Trewin, *Peter Brook*, p. 82.
79 Beauman, *The Royal Shakespeare Company*, p. 224.
80 Harold Hobson, 'A Modern Play', *The Sunday Times*, 21 August 1955.
81 Caute, *The Dancer Defects*, p. 1.
82 Scott Lucas, 'Beyond Freedom, Beyond Control: Approaches to Culture and the State–Private Network in the Cold War', in *The Cultural Cold War in Western Europe, 1945–1960*, ed. by Giles Scott-Smith and Hans Krabbendam (London: Frank Cass Publishers, 2003), pp. 53–108.
83 On the unwitting enlistment of many writers and artists into CIA funded anti-Communist cultural activities, see Saunders, *Who Paid the Piper*; Andrew N. Rubin, *Archives of Authority: Empire, Culture, and the Cold War* (Princeton, NJ: Princeton University Press, 2012).
84 TNA BW 120/1 'DAC Minutes 1939–1957', 23 January 1951.
85 Ibid., 21 January 1952.

86 Ibid., 9 February 1955.
87 Defty, *Information Research Department*, p. 49.
88 TNA BW 120/1 'DAC Minutes 1939–1957', 25 July 1956.
89 Ibid., 24 October 1956.
90 Ibid., 24 October 1956.
91 Watanabe, 'Cultural Drives', p. 1.
92 TNA BW 120/1 'DAC Minutes 1939–1957', 29 January 1957.
93 Blakemore, *Arguments*, p. 162; Coleman, *Olivier*, p. 299; Holm, *Acting*, p. 59; Vickers, *Vivien Leigh*, p. 241; Robert L. Ivie, 'Metaphor and the Rhetorical Invention of Cold War "Idealists"', in *Cold War Rhetoric: Strategy, Metaphor and Ideology*, ed. by Martin J. Medhurst, and others (Ann Arbor, MI: University of Michigan Press, 1990), pp. 103–27.
94 Vickers, *Vivien Leigh*, p. 244.
95 Ibid., p. 245.
96 Holm, *Acting*, p. 61.
97 Ibid., pp. 60–61.
98 Ibid., pp. 59–61.
99 Mary Louise Pratt, *Imperial Eyes: Travel Writing and Transculturation* (Abingdon: Routledge, 1992), pp. 37–83. Although Pratt concentrates on travel writing of the eighteenth and nineteenth centuries, I extended her terms to later periods here.
100 Blakemore, *Arguments*, p. 164; Vickers, *Vivien Leigh*, p. 244.
101 Blakemore, *Arguments*, p. 169.
102 Ibid., p. 161.
103 Ibid., p. 165.
104 Hans Weigel, 'Titus Review', [No Publication], 13 June 1957, in TNA BW 1/235. 'Sir Laurence Olivier and Shakespeare Memorial Theatre's Tour of "Titus Andronicus" to Paris, Venice, Belgrade, Zagreb, Vienna and Warsaw 1957–1958'. All Viennese reviews are taken from the British Council's own English translations held within TNA BW 1/235. Though dates are provided, many articles are not attributed to specific newspapers or periodicals. These gaps are indicated with [No Publication].
105 Friedrich Heer, 'A Moment of History in the Theatre', [No Publication], 22 June 1957.
106 Ibid.
107 Ibid.
108 Anon, 'Sir Laurence Olivier in the Burgtheater', *Die Fresse*, 14 June 1957.
109 TNA BW 1/436, 'Shakespeare Memorial Theatre Company Tour of *Titus Andronicus* to Europe (Sir Laurence Olivier)', 14 July 1957.
110 Coleman, *Olivier*, p. 241.
111 TNA BW 120/1 'DAC Minutes 1939–1957', 9 July 1957.
112 TNA BW 1/436 'Tour of *Titus Andronicus*', 14 July 1957.
113 Ibid.
114 Ibid.
115 TNA BW 1/436 'Tour of *Titus Andronicus*', 14 July 1957.

116 Judi Dench, *And Furthermore* (London: Pheonix Press, 2010), pp. 23–27.
117 Steve Wilson, *The Making of Gone with the Wind* (Austin, TX: University of Texas Press, 2004), pp. xi–xii.
118 Coleman, *Olivier*, p. 299.
119 In the mid-to-late 1950s, Yugoslav film production 'approximated world norms' while 'domestic films found an export market and received their first prizes at international film festivals'. Daniel J. Goulding, *Liberated Cinema: The Yugoslav Experience 1945–2001* (Bloomington, IN: Indiana University Press, 2002), p. 38.
120 Goulding, *Liberated Cinema*, p. 37.
121 Ibid., p. 38.
122 Jan Kott, *Shakespeare Our Contemporary* (London: Methuen, 1964), p. 1.
123 Ibid., p. 2.
124 Ibid., pp. 14–17.
125 Ibid., p. 19.
126 Jan Kott, *Still Alive: An Autobiographical Essay* (New Haven, CT: Yale University Press, 1994), p. 187.
127 Ibid., p. 165.
128 Ibid., p. 187.
129 Ibid., p. 188.
130 Fredric Jameson, *Marxism and Form* (Princeton, NJ: Princeton University Press, 1971), p. 80.
131 For a detailed survey and analysis of Lukács's ideas on Realism, see Jameson, *Marxism and Form*, pp. 191–205.
132 Michael Kustow, 'Jan Kott: An Obituary', *The Guardian*, 10 January 2002.
133 Kott, *Still Alive*, pp. 182–83.
134 Ibid., p. 186.
135 Ibid., p. 161. On the Eastern Bloc purges at the time see, Jonathan Brent and Vladimir P. Naumov, *Stalin's Last Crime: The Doctor's Plot* (London: John Murray, 2004); Mikhail Heller and Aleksandr Nekrich, *Utopia in Power: The History of the Soviet Union from 1917 to the Present* (New York: Summit Books, 1986), pp. 502–04.
136 Kott, *Still Alive*, p. 190.
137 Kustow, 'Jan Kott'.
138 Marci Shore, *Caviar and Ashes: A Warsaw Generation's Life and Death in Marxism, 1918–1968* (New Haven, CT: Yale University Press, 2006), p. 309.
139 See Jan Nowak, *Courier from Warsaw* (Detroit: Wayne State University Press, 1982); Kott, *Still Alive*, p. 209.
140 Kott, *Still Alive*, p. 220.
141 Defty, *Information Research Department*, p. 171.
142 Kott, *Shakespeare Our Contemporary*, p. 9.
143 Ibid., p. 347.
144 Ibid., p. 348.
145 Ibid., pp. 352–53.
146 Bertolt Brecht, 'The Popular and the Realistic', in *Brecht on Theatre*, ed. by John Willett (London: Methuen, 1964), pp. 107–15 (p. 114).

147 Bertolt Brecht, 'Against Georg Lukács', in Theodor Adorno et al., *Aesthetics and Politics* (London: Verso, 1977), pp. 68–85.
148 Eugene Lunn, *Marxism and Modernism: An Historical Study of Lukács, Brecht, Benjamin, and Adorno* (Berkeley, CA: University of California Press, 1992), p. 90.
149 See for example, Leanore Lieblein, 'Jan Kott, Peter Brook, and *King Lear*', in *Journal of Dramatic Theory and Criticism*, 1:2 (1987), 39–50; Carl Tighe 'Jan Kott: The Revisionist', *Journal of European Studies*, 26.3 (1996), 267–97.
150 Jonathan Dollimore and Alan Sinfield, 'History and Ideology: The Instance of *Henry V*', in *Alternative Shakespeares*, pp. 210–231 (p. 211).
151 Sinfield, *Political Shakespeare*, p. 185; Kott, *Shakespeare Our Contemporary*, p. 47.
152 Zofia Sawicka, 'Jan Kott: The Road to Shakespeare', *Culture.pl* (March 2009). www.culture.pl/en/article/jan-kott-the-road-to-shakespeare [Accessed 10 May 2023].
153 Ibid.
154 Krytyna Kujawinska Courtney, 'Celebrating Shakespeare Under the Communist Regime in Poland', in *Shakespeare in Cold War Europe : Conflict, Commemoration, Celebration*, ed. by Erica Sheen and Isabel Karremann (Basingstoke: Palgrave Macmillan, 2016), pp. 23–35.
155 Ibid., pp. 228–45.
156 Ibid., p. 235.
157 Sinfield, *Political Shakespeare*, p. 174.
158 Kott, *Still Alive*, p. 201.
159 Ibid.

Chapter 4

1 TNA BW 120/3 'Drama Advisory Committee: Minutes and Papers of Meetings, 1961–1965', 11 July 1962. The committee at that time included Michael Benthall, Hugh Beaumont, Philip Hope-Wallace, Ivor Brown, Kenneth Tynan, and Peter Ustinov.
2 TNA BW 120/3 'DAC Minutes 1961–1965', 11 July 1962.
3 Ibid.
4 The West Africa Tour itinerary was, Nigeria: Lagos (6–15 January), Kaduna and Zaria (16–20 January), Kano (21–24 January), Nsukka, Enugu, and Port Harcourt (25 January–4 February), Ibadan (5–12 February). Ghana: Cape Coast (13–16 February), Takoradi (17–19 February), Accra (24 February - 6 March). Sierra Leone: Freetown (6–15 March).
5 TNA BW 120/3 'DAC Minutes 1961–1965', 11 July 1962. The acting company comprised John Neville, Polly Adams, Peter Blythe, James Cairncross, Simon Carter, Paul Daneman, Judi Dench, Marielaine Douglas, Patrick Duffy, Jill Gascoine, Richard Hampton, Terence Knapp, Terence Palmer, John Toye, and Peter Wilkins.

6 Bush, 'Valerie West', p. 12.
7 Ibid. For a critical account of the British Council's role in English Language Teaching (ELT), see Phillipson, *Linguistic Imperialism*. For a general history of ELT see A. P. R. Howatt and H. G. Widdowson, *A History of Second Language Teaching* (Oxford: Oxford University Press, 2004).
8 Bush, 'Valerie West', p. 12.
9 Phillipson, *Linguistic Imperialism*, p. 138.
10 Caroline Davis, 'Creating a Book Empire: Longmans in Africa', in *The Book in Africa: Critical Debates*, ed. by Caroline Davis and David Johnson (Basingstoke: Palgrave Macmillan, 2015), pp. 128–152.
11 Richard Bourne, *Nigeria: A New History of a Turbulent Century* (London: Zed Books, 2015), p. 105.
12 TNA BW 120/3, 'DAC Minutes 1961–1965', 'Report on Tours', 17 April 1964.
13 On Soviet involvement in post-independence West Africa, see Sergey Mazov, *A Distant Front in the Cold War: The USSR in West Africa and the Congo, 1956–1964* (Palo Alto, CA: Stanford University Press, 2010); Miriam Neirick, *When Pigs Could Fly and Bears Could Dance: A History of the Soviet Circus* (Madison, WI: The University of Wisconsin Press, 2012).
14 Anon, 'Playhouse Choose Cast for Their West African Tour', *Nottingham Evening Post*, 27 November 1962; Springhall, *Decolonisation*, pp. 146–56.
15 TNA BW 128/9 'British Council Northern Nigeria Annual Report 1962/63', p. 1.
16 Penny M. Von Eschen, *Satchmo Blows up the World: Jazz Ambassadors Play the Cold War* (Cambridge MA: Harvard University Press, 2004), p. 78.
17 See Carol Anderson, 'The Histories of African Americans' Anti-Colonialism During the Cold War', in *The Cold War in the Third World*, ed. by Robert J. McMahon (Oxford: Oxford University Press, 2013), pp. 178–91 (p. 179).
18 TNA BW 128/9 'Northern Nigeria Annual Report 1962/63', p. 1.
19 Kunibert Raffer and H. W. Singer, *The Economic North–South Divide: Six Decades of Unequal Development* (Northampton, MA: Edward Elgar, 2001), pp. 64–78; Westad, *Global Cold War*, pp. 152–157.
20 Edward H. Berman, 'The Foundations' Role in American Foreign Policy: The Case of Africa, post 1945', in *Philanthropy and Cultural Imperialism: The Foundations at Home and Abroad*, ed. by Robert F. Arnove (Bloomington, IN: Indiana University Press, 1982), pp. 203–32 (p. 204).
21 Ibid, p. 204.
22 In ibid, pp. 209–10; Walter Schwarz, *Nigeria* (London: Frederick A. Praeger Publishers, 1968), pp. 114–117.
23 On the role that Shakespeare played in educational setting in South Africa, for instance, see David Johnson, 'From the Colonial to the Post-Colonial: Shakespeare and Education in Africa', in *Post-Colonial Shakespeares*, ed. by Ania Loomba and Martin Orkin (Abingdon: Routledge, 1998), pp. 218–234; and David Johnson, *Shakespeare and South Africa* (Oxford: Clarendon Press, 1996).

24 In Bergman, 'The Foundations', pp. 209–210. For precise details on foundation funding for the University of Ibadan at the time, see E. Jefferson Murphy, *Creative Philanthropy: Carnegie Corporation and Africa, 1953–1973* (New York: Carnegie Corporation Publishing, 1976), pp. 164–167.
25 In Donaldson, *The British Council*, p. 155.
26 Ibid, p. 154.
27 Harold Macmillan's new Department for Technical Co-operation would have 1000 of its 1,050 staff members made up of 'job-perpetuating ex-Colonial personnel'. Donaldson, *The British Council*, pp. 218–222.
28 At the end of the 1940s, Ghana had an estimated 32 journalists, 38 medical doctors, and 114 lawyers out of a population of 4.5 million. Nigeria had 150 lawyers and 160 doctors for a population of 40 million. By 1955 only 3000 British West African colonial subjects were studying at UK universities. T. E. Vadney, *The World Since 1945* (London: Penguin Books, 1998), pp. 134–135.
29 Lee, 'Cultural Diplomacy and the Cold War', pp. 125–126.
30 Donaldson, *The British Council*, p. 227.
31 Phillipson, *Linguistic Imperialism*, p. 133; A. H. King 'The Nature and Demand for English in the World Today, as it effects British Universities', in *English Teaching Abroad and the British Universities*, ed. by H. G. Wayment (London: Methuen, 1961), pp. 22–25. 1960 saw the Universities of London, Leeds, and others post around 850 ELT professionals and 50 British lecturers throughout the Commonwealth. Donaldson, *The British Council*, p. 217.
32 Phillipson, *Linguistic Imperialism*, p. 151.
33 Donaldson, *The British Council*, p. 216. On the Makerere Conference see, Howatt and Widdowson, *Second Language Teaching*, pp. 310–314.
34 For an overview of Oxford University Press' development of English Language Courses' publications across Africa, see Caroline Davis, *Creating Postcolonial Literature* (Basingstoke: Palgrave Macmillan, 2013), pp. 17–31. For the British Council's role in the Makerere Conference, see Donaldson, *The British Council*, pp. 214–216.
35 Dench, *And Furthermore*, p. 35.
36 Having completed his graduate degree at the University of Leeds, written and performed at the Royal Court Theatre, and had two successful UK productions restaged in Nigeria, Wole Soyinka returned to the University of Ibadan in 1960 to assist Geoffrey Axworthy at the Arts Theatre. Robert W. July, *An African Voice: The Role of the Humanities in African Independence* (Durham, NC: Duke University Press, 1987), p. 68.
37 Dench, *And Furthermore*, p. 35.
38 On the University of Ibadan's Drama Department and University Travelling Theatre, see July, *An African Voice*, pp. 62–73.
39 Dapo Adelugba, Olu Obafemi, and Sola Adeyemi, 'Nigeria', in *A History of Theatre in Africa*, ed. by Martin Banham (Cambridge: Cambridge University Press, 2004), pp. 138–58 (p. 140). On Yoruba Travelling Theatre see, J. A.

Adedeji, 'Oral Tradition and the Contemporary Theatre in Nigeria', *Research in African Literatures*, 2.2 (1971), 196–200.
40 Dele Layiwola, ed., *African Theatre in Performance: A Festschrift for Martin Banham* (Amsterdam: Harwood Academic Press, 2000), p. xiii.
41 Amos Tutuola, *The Palm-Wine Drinkard* (London: Faber and Faber, 1952).
42 The Drama Department was established in 1960 thanks to a large grant from the Rockefeller Foundation. Martin Banham, Errol Hill, and George Woodyard, eds., *The Cambridge Guide to African and Caribbean Theatre* (Cambridge: Cambridge University Press, 1994), p. 87.
43 Ahmed Yerima, *Modern Nigerian Theatre: Geoffrey Axworthy Years, 1956–1967* (Ibadan: Kraft Books, 2005), p. 61.
44 Adelugba et al., 'Nigeria', p. 147.
45 Emmanuel Obiechina, *An African Popular Literature: A Study of Onitsha Market Literature* (Cambridge: Cambridge University Press, 1971), p. 105.
46 Yerima, *Axworthy Years*, p. 61.
47 Ibid, pp. 61–62.
48 Ibid, p. 33.
49 Deji Oguntoyinbo, 'Review of Ahmed Yerima's *Modern Nigerian Theatre: Geoffrey Axworthy Years, 1956–1967*', *California Linguistic Notes*, 37.2 (2012), 167–71 (p. 169).
50 Davis, *Creating Postcolonial Literature*, p. 39.
51 Caroline Davis, 'Publishing Wole Soyinka: Oxford University Press and the creation of 'Africa's own William Shakespeare'', *Journal of Postcolonial Writing*, 48.4 (2011), 344–358 (p. 344).
52 Davis, *Creating Postcolonial Literature*, p. 47.
53 Ibid.
54 James Currey, *Africa Writes Back: The African Writers Series and the Launch of African Literature* (Athens, OH: Ohio University Press, 2008), p. 9. See also, James Currey, 'Literary Publishing after Nigerian Independence: Mbari as Celebration', *Research in African Literatures*, 44.2 (2013), 8–16.
55 Adelugba et al., 'Nigeria', pp. 152–153.
56 Ibid, p. 152.
57 TNA BW 128/9 'Representative's Annual Report – 1 April 1962 to 31 March 1963', p. 4.
58 Ibid.
59 Anon, 'Three Plays for West Africa', *Stage and Television Today*, 27 September 1962.
60 Anon, 'Honoured Playhouse Will Keep the Home Shows Going', *Nottingham Evening News*, 28 September 1962.
61 For a history of the Nottingham Playhouse see, John Bailey, *A Theatre for All Seasons: Nottingham Playhouse* (Stroud: Alan Sutton Publishing, 1994); and George Rowell and Anthony Jackson, *The Repertory Movement: A History of Regional Theatre in Britain* (Cambridge: Cambridge University Press, 1984), pp. 131–37.

62 Anon, 'Macbeth Goes on Tour of County Schools', *Nottingham Guardian*, 24 March 1962.
63 Anon, 'Theatre', *Nottingham Observer*, January 1963.
64 Nottingham County Council Archives [NCCA] GB 0157 DD/NP/1/3/1 'Nottingham Playhouse Minutes, 1948–1988', 7 July 1961.
65 NCCA GB 0157 DD/NP/1/3/1 'Nottingham Playhouse Minutes, 1948–1988', 6 November 1961.
66 Anon, 'Theatre'; Bailey, *Nottingham Playhouse*, p. 75. Frank Dunlop directed *Macbeth* and *Twelfth Night* and John Neville directed *Arms and the Man*.
67 E. A. B., 'Macbeth with an Oriental Twist', *Nottingham Evening Post*, 19 December 1962.
68 Anon, 'Playhouse Preview of Tour 'Macbeth'', *Guardian Journal*, 12 December 1962.
69 Louise Rhoades, 'Acting Their Way from Nottingham to Africa', *Daily Telegraph*, 12 December 1962.
70 NCCA GB 0157 DD/NP/2/2/10, 'Overseas Productions', photograph 4.
71 E. A. B., 'Macbeth'.
72 Having won the best film award for *Rashomon* at the Venice Film Festival of 1951, Kurosawa's global fame and reputation was firmly established by 1963. See Daniel Martin, 'Subtitles and Audiences: The Translation and Global Circulation of the Films of Akira Kurosawa', *Journal of Film and Video*, 69.2 (2017), 20–33.
73 Anon, 'Strange Setting in 'Macbeth': Tour Preview', *Nottingham Evening News*, 18 December 1962.
74 E. A. B. 'Macbeth'.
75 Anon, 'Japanese 'Macbeth' for Africa', *Nottingham News*, 19 December 1962.
76 E. A. B. 'Macbeth'.
77 Ibid.
78 Anon, 'Playhouse Was Finest on NTS', *Nigeria Morning Post*, 19 January 1963.
79 Anon, 'The Formidable Force from Nottingham', *Nigeria Outlook*, 23 January 1963.
80 Sam Imayu, 'Nottingham Players not Impressive', *Sunday Express*, 20 January 1963.
81 Dench, *And Furthermore*, p. 36.
82 Imayu, 'Nottingham Players'.
83 Anon, 'Playhouse Defeated the Motive', *Nigeria Daily Express*, 16 January 1963.
84 Anon, 'Macbeth Is Always New', *Nigerian Outlook*, 6 February 1963.
85 Peter Pan, 'One Miserable Night I'll Never Forget', *Daily Times*, 15 January 1963.
86 Obiechina, *Onitsha Market Literature*, pp. 72–88.
87 Ibid, pp. 72–73.
88 Thomas Iguh's *The Last Days of Lumumba* (1961) and other 'Congo dramas' were rich in Shakespearian allegories as well as political references to *Julius*

Caesar, *Hamlet*, and *The Merchant of Venice*. Obiechina, *Onitsha Market Literature*, p. 74.
89 Obiechina, *Onitsha Market Literature*, p. 86.
90 Pan, 'One Miserable Night'.
91 Ibid.
92 Ibid.
93 Jane West, 'Macbeth in Lagos', *West African Pilot*, 19 January 1963.
94 Pan, 'One Miserable Night'.
95 Dench, *And Furthermore*, p. 36.
96 Ibid.
97 Kole Omotoso, 'Concepts of History and Theatre in Africa', in *A History of Theatre in Africa*, pp. 1–12 (p. 9).
98 TNA BW 128/9 'Representative's Annual Report – 1 April 1962 to 31 March 1963'.
99 Pan, 'One Miserable Night'.
100 TNA BW 128/9 'Representative's Annual Report – 1 April 1962 to 31 March 1963'.
101 Ibid.
102 Bush, 'Valerie West', p. 13.
103 Nottingham University Archives (NUA) MS 679/1/11 '*Arms and the Man* Theatre Programme, (Nottingham Playhouse, April 1964)', p. 7.
104 Anon, 'Shakespeare and Shaw in the Sun: Nottingham Conquers Africa', *Stage and Television Today*, 4 April 1963.
105 TNA BW 128/9 'Representative's Annual Report – 1 April 1962 to 31 March 1963'.
106 Ibid.
107 Anon, 'Nottingham Conquers Africa'.
108 Ibid.
109 Terence Knapp, *Hawaii's Adopted World-Class Actor* (Bloomington, IN: Xlibris Press, 2000), pp. 56–57.
110 Holland and Huggan, *Tourists with Typewriters*, p. 31.
111 Patrick Brantlinger, *Rule of Darkness: British Literature and the Imperialism, 1830–1914* (Ithaca, NY: Cornell University Press, 1988), pp. 227–254.
112 Gareth Armstrong, *A Case for Shylock: Around the World with Shakespeare's Jew* (London: Nick Horn Books, 2004), pp. ix–x.
113 Thompson, *Travel Writing*, p. 145.
114 Anon, 'Tour When Line of Vultures Sat on the Back of the Stage', *Evening Post*, 6 December 2008; Dench, *And Furthermore*, p. 36.
115 Knapp, *Hawaii's Adopted*, p. 135.
116 Holland and Huggan, *Tourists with Typewriters*, p. 31.
117 TNA BW 120/3, 'DAC Minutes 1961–1965', 'Kano Regional Director's Report', 29 January 1963, 17 April 1963.
118 TNA: BW 128/9, 'High Commissioner's Comments on Representative's Annual Report', 8 August 1963.

119 TNA BW 120/3, 'DAC Minutes 1961–1965', 'Kano Regional Director's Report', 29 January 1963, 17 April 1963.
120 TNA BW 128/9, 'Eastern Nigeria Regional Representative's Annual Report for 1962/63'.
121 Ibid.
122 TNA BW 120/3 'Report on the University of Ibadan Travelling Theatre tour of Nigeria, March 1964'.
123 Ibid.
124 Ibid.
125 Ibid; TNA BW 120/3, 'Report on Tours', 17 April 1964.
126 Knapp, *Hawaii's Adopted*, p. 136.
127 Ibid, pp. 136–137.
128 Ibid, p. 137.
129 Bourne, *Nigeria*, pp. 111–129; Knapp, *Hawaii's Adopted*, pp. 137–138.
130 Knapp, *Hawaii's Adopted*, p. 139.

Chapter 5

1 Our Theatre Reporter, 'Shakespeare 'Exports' to 80 Countries', *The Daily Telegraph*, 12 February 1964. All NSC reviews can be found in the Shakespeare Institute Archive [SIA] DSH1/5/8/14-22 'Press Cuttings from Tour of Asia'. Gaps in attribution are indicated by [No Title], [No Publication], or [No Date].
2 Anon, 'A Shakespearean Saga', *Dawn*, 4 October 1964.
3 N. S. Ramaswami, 'Richard II', [No Title], [No Date].
4 A. G. Hopkins, *American Empire* (New Jersey, NJ: Princeton University Press, 2018), p. 696. Hopkins comments that 'By 1964 the noted economist Gotfried Haberler, could describe 'the third wave of world-wide integration and growth' that had begun after World War II, using language that today would be phrased in terms of globalisation'. Hopkins, *American Empire*, p. 701.
5 Hopkins, *American Empire*, p. 699.
6 Ibid, p. 706.
7 Bradley, 'Decolonisation, the Global South, and the Cold War, 1919–1962' p. 464. Independence was gained later by Barbados, Botswana, Lesotho (1966), Aden (1967), Bahrain (1971), Muscat and Oman (1971), and Belize (1981). Graham MacPhee, *Postwar British Literature and Postcolonial Studies* (Edinburg: Edinburg University Press, 2011), pp. x–xviii. On the International Theatre Institute see Hanna Korsberg, 'Creating an International Community during the Cold War', in Balme and Szymanski-Düll, *Theatre, Globalization, and the Cold War*, pp. 151–163. Traditional dance and theatre troupes from Sri Lanka and India, for instance, began competing at the Théâtre des Nations in Paris from 1958 onwards. Daniela Peslin, *Le Théâtre des Nations: Une aventure théâtrale à redécourir* (Paris: L'Harmattan, 2009).

8 Hopkins, *American Empire*, p. 698.
9 Anon, 'A Shakespearean Saga'.
10 SIA DSH1/5/8/14-22 'The Equity Members Report on The New Shakespeare Company – British Council Tour of Pakistan, India, Ceylon and The Far East, 1964–65', 'Attached Minutes of Meeting Held on 16/7/64'.
11 Ravi, 'A Surfeit of Shakespeare', *The Sun*, 6 January 1965.
12 Ibid.
13 Ravi, 'A Surfeit of Shakespeare', *The Sun*, 6 January 1965.
14 Ibid.
15 George W. Bishop, 'Plays and Players', *The Daily Telegraph*, 8 August 1964.
16 David Conville, *The Park: The Story of the Open-Air Theatre, Regents Park* (London: Oberon Books, 2007), pp. 34–36.
17 Anon, [No Title], *The Lady*, 11 June 1964.
18 J. C. Trewin, [No Title], *Pakistan Observer*, 12 October 1964. British Information Services (BIS) translated and disseminated Trewin's piece to numerous press outlets throughout the tour.
19 Trewin, *Pakistan Observer*.
20 Ibid. The offer of an extensive British Council circuit followed a short trial tour of *Twelfth Night* to Portugal and Middle Temple Hall as part of the 1964 City of London Festival. SIA DSH1/9/3/1 'Show Reports for Tour of Asia', 'Unmarked Interview Transcript'.
21 Blakemore, *Arguments*, p. 283.
22 Ibid, pp, 281–283.
23 Ibid, p. 296.
24 Ibid.
25 Ibid, p. 281.
26 *The Stage*, "Obituaries: Christopher Burgess', 2013. www.thestage.co.uk/features/obituaries/2013/christopher-burgess/ [Accessed 12 September 2018].
27 SIA DSH1/5/8/13 'Scrapbook for Tour of Asia', 'NSC South and Southeast Asia Tour Programme'.
28 In Donaldson, *The British Council*, p. 157.
29 Ibid.
30 Our Drama Critic, 'New Shakespeare Company in Capital', *Times of India*, 27 November 1964.
31 Our Drama Critic, 'Richard II Has Many Memorable Moments', *Hindustan Times*, 30 November 1964.
32 A Special Correspondent, 'They Who Play Shakespeare Always Welcome', *Amrita Bazar Patrika*, 17 December 1964.
33 SIA DSH1/5/8/13 'NSC South and Southeast Asia Tour Programme'. The quote is taken from Tagore's contribution to the *Book of Homage to Shakespeare* published to mark the 300th anniversary of Shakespeare's death in 1916.
34 A Special Correspondent, 'They Who Play Shakespeare Always Welcome', *Amrita Bazar Patrika*, 17 December 1964.

35 The Shakespeare Birthplace Trust, 'The Bust of Rabindranath Tagore at Shakespeare's Birthplace', www.shakespeare.org.uk/explore-shakespeare/blogs/bust-tagore-shakespeares-birthplace/ [Accessed 26 May 2020].
36 Graham Holderness argues that Peter Hall and John Barton's 'preoccupation with verbal delivery' and emphasis on 'textual rather than psychological understanding' was 'a common inheritance of Cambridge English studies' and 'the product of a vigorous theatrical culture in post-war Cambridge'. Graham Holderness, *Shakespeare in Performance: The Taming of the Shrew* (Manchester: Manchester University Press, 1989), pp. 29–30; Eric Johns, 'Shakespeare for the Orient', *Theatre World*, September 1964.
37 Christopher J. McCullough, 'The Cambridge Connection: Towards a Materialist Theatre Practice', in *The Shakespeare Myth*, ed. by Graham Holderness (Manchester: Manchester University Press, 1988), pp. 112–121.
38 Johns, 'Shakespeare for the Orient'.
39 See, for example, Norman Marshall, 'Shakespeare Abroad', in *Talking of Shakespeare*, ed. by John Garrett (London: Hodder and Stoughton, 1954), pp. 91–110.
40 Anon, 'William on Shakespeare', *Hindustan Times*, 30 November 1964.
41 Ibid. See for example Anthony Quayle's stage adaptation of 1951, Joan Littlewood's of 1955, and Peter Hall's of 1963.
42 Anon, 'William on Shakespeare'.
43 Ibid.
44 Anon, 'Director', *Times of Indian*, 8 November 1964.
45 Anon, 'William on Shakespeare'.
46 Iago, 'The New Shakespeare Company', [No Title], 1 January 1965.
47 Ibid.
48 Ibid.
49 Blakemore, *Arguments*, p. 299.
50 SIA DSH1/5/8/14-22 'From Lighthill to Conville', 28 November 1963.
51 Ibid.
52 Our Staff Correspondent, 'David William as Richard II', *Pakistan Times*, [No Date].
53 Margaret Shewring summarises Gielgud's approach to acting Shakespeare, which became central to the Cambridge tradition, as 'a kind of authenticity rooted in a new scholarly tradition of fidelity to the language in which the play was originally written'. Margaret Shewring, *Shakespeare in Performance: King Richard II* (Manchester: Manchester University Press, 1996), p. 70.
54 Shewring, *King Richard II*, p. 4.
55 B. Chandrasekhara, 'The Crowning Performance', *Deccan Herald*, 20 November 1964.
56 Ibid.
57 Ibid.
58 Ramaswami, 'Richard II'.
59 N. E., 'Theatre', Imprint, December 1964.
60 Ramaswami, 'Richard II'.

61 Iago, 'The New Shakespeare Company'.
62 Shewring, *King Richard II*, p. 63; Anon, 'William on Shakespeare'.
63 Ensemble approaches helped directors like Littlewood, and later Hall, rethink 'the place of the King in a wider context of political relevance (rather than an opportunity for great actors to indulge themselves in the personality cult of the eponymous role)'. Shewring, *King Richard II*, p. 103.
64 Anon, [No Title], *Indian Express*, 4 November 1964; Anon, [No Title], *Financial Express*, 8 November 1964.
65 N. E., 'Theatre'.
66 Anon, [No Title], *She Magazine*, 15 October 1964; Anon, [No Title], *Examiner*, 14 November 1964.
67 In Shewring, *King Richard II*, p. 94.
68 Ibid, p. 102.
69 Ramaswami, 'Richard II'.
70 Ibid.
71 Ibid.
72 A Special Correspondent, 'They Who Play'; Staff Correspondent, 'Talking Massive Success', *The Indian Nation*, 16 December 1964; Atri, [No Title], *The Hindu*, 6 December 1964.
73 Ibid.
74 Chandrasekhara, 'Crowning Performance'.
75 Ibid.
76 SIA DSH1/3/2/3 'Production Administration File for Tour of Asia', 'Correspondence from Duke to Conville, 22nd July 1964'.
77 SIA DSH1/3/2/3 'Correspondence from Duke to Conville, 22nd July 1964'.
78 Ibid.
79 Ibid.
80 In Blakemore, *Arguments*, p. 293.
81 Holderness, *Shrew*, pp. 19–20.
82 SIA DSH1/3/2/3 'Conville to Duke, 23rd July 1964'.
83 Holderness, *Shrew*, p. 4.
84 Iago, 'The New Shakespeare Company'.
85 N. E., 'Theatre'.
86 Anon, [No Title], *Deccan Herald*, 19 November 1964.
87 Anon, [No Title], *Manilla Times*, 30 January 1965.
88 SIA DSH1/9/3/1 'David Conville's Asia Tour Report', p. 3, 25.
89 Staff Correspondent, 'Srinagar Lad Comes Back to Stage Shakespeare', *Hindustan Times*, 27 November 1964.
90 Leonor Orosa Goquingco, 'Two Great Englishmen Remembered as Shakespeare Group Performs', *The Manila Bulletin*, 30 January 1965.
91 Monina A. Mercado, 'Taming of the Shrew: It Teetered on the Slapstick', *Manila Herald*, 29 January 1965.
92 Mercado, 'Taming'.
93 Anon, *She Magazine*; A Staff Reporter, 'The Shrew Duly Tamed', *Sunday Hindustan Standard*, 27 December 1964; Mercado, 'Taming'.

94 Mary Visick, 'Taming of the Shrew: Time Flies and its Good Box Office', *South China Morning Post*, 25 January 1965.
95 Anon, [No Title], *Singapore Sunday Mail*, 21 February 1965.
96 C. H. Valenzuela, "Shakespeare Comes to Life: Bard's Shrew Tickles Filipino Funny Bone', *Evening News*, 9 January 1965.
97 Mercado, 'Taming'.
98 Anon, 'A Shakespearean Saga'.
99 Mercado, 'Taming'.
100 Ibid.
101 Anon, [No Title], *Today*, 9 November 1964.
102 Anon, *She Magazine*; Anon, *Financial Express*.
103 Mercado, 'Taming'.
104 Anon, 'Shakespeare in Kuching', *The Sarawak Tribune*, 2 February 1965.
105 Mercado 'Taming'.
106 Brian St. Clair, 'The Taming of the Shrew', *Tiger Standard*, 25 January 1965; Anon, [No Title], *Hindu*, 24 November 1964.
107 Anon, *Hindu*.
108 Anon, [No Title], *Tiger Standard*, 25 January 1965.
109 St. Clair, 'The Taming of the Shrew'.
110 Visick, 'Taming of the Shrew'.
111 Anon, [No Title], *Morning News*, 4 October 1964.
112 Kaier-e-Hind, [No Title], [No Publication], 15 November 1964.
113 Anon, *She Magazine*; Anon, [No Title], *The Indian Nation*, 16 December 1964; St. Clair, 'The Taming of the Shrew'.
114 Anon, [No Title], *Hindu*.
115 Kaier-e-Hind, [No Title].
116 Visick, 'Taming of the Shrew'.
117 Ibid.
118 Holderness, *Shrew*, p. 7.
119 Visick, 'Taming of the Shrew'.
120 'Wide-awake scholarship' was Kenneth Tynan's description of John Barton's landmark approach to the play. In Holderness, *Shrew*, p. 32.
121 Anon, [No Title], *The Sarawak Tribune*, 26 February 1964.
122 Mary Visick, 'The Tempest: Orthodox Performance by Shakespeare Company', *South China Morning Post*, 23 January 1965.
123 Anon, *Examiner*.
124 Monina A. Mercado, "The Tempest That Wasn't', *The Philippine Herald*, 3 February 1965.
125 SIA DSH1/9/3/1 'Conville's Asia Tour Report', pp. 19–20.
126 John Luff, 'The Tempest: Something of the Beauty of the Lines Was Lost', *China Mail*, 23 January 1965.
127 Anon, *Today*.
128 Kaier-e-Hind, [No Title]; Anon, [No Title], *Eve's Weekly*, 7 November 1964.

129 Visick, 'The Tempest'.
130 Kaier-e-Hind, [No Title].
131 Mercado, "The Tempest that Wasn't'.
132 Our Drama Critic, 'A Tame Tempest', *Indian Express*, 7 December 1964.
133 Our Drama Critic, 'The Tempest is a Botticellian Extravaganza', *The Statesman*, [No Date].
134 Anon, [No Title], *South China Morning Post*, 23 January 1964.
135 Anon, [No Title], *Eve's Weekly*.
136 Our Drama Critic, 'A Tame Tempest'.
137 Visick, 'The Tempest'.
138 Our Drama Critic, 'A Tame Tempest'.
139 Goquingco, 'The Bard Shines'; Anon, [No Title], *Times of India*, [No Date]; Anon, [No Title], *Pakistan Times*, 11 October 1964.
140 Anon, 'The Tempest', *The Statesman*, 20 December 1964; Anon, [No Title], *Onlooker*, 15 November 1964; A Special Correspondent, 'They Who Play'; Visick, 'The Tempest'.
141 Guttila, 'The Magic of the Tempest', *The Times*, 2 January 1965.
142 Arts Critic, 'Brave Effort to Create Atmosphere: The Tempest Staged', *The Star*, 2 October 1964.
143 Our Drama Critic, 'David William's Tempest Is Neat and Competent', *Indian Express*, 2 November 1964.
144 Visick, 'The Tempest'.
145 Neville Weeraratne, 'A Common Monsoon', [No Publication], [No Date].
146 N. E., 'Theatre'; Luff, 'The Tempest'.
147 Anon, *South China Morning Post*; Visick, 'The Tempest'.
148 Our Drama Critic, 'David William's Tempest'.
149 Anon, 'The Tempest'.
150 Iago, 'The New Shakespeare Company'.
151 Anon, 'Shakespeare Players Score Big Success in the Tempest', *Daily Mail*, 10 February 1965.
152 Anon, 'The Tempest'.
153 Iago, 'The New Shakespeare Company'.
154 Ibid.
155 SIA DSH1/3/2/3 'The Actors' Contract'.
156 Ibid.
157 SIA DSH1/9/3/1 'Conville's Asia Tour Report', p. 4.
158 Ibid.
159 Ibid.
160 Ibid.
161 Anon, "The Tempest' Tomorrow: NSC in City', [No Publication], [No Date].
162 Anon, 'Amanda Who Plays Miranda', *The Hindustan Times*, 2 December 1964.
163 Anon, 'Malaysian Audiences Lauded by a Top London Actor', *Straits Times*, 13 February 1965.

164 SIA DSH1/5/8/14-22 'The Equity Members Report on The New Shakespeare Company – British Council Tour of Pakistan, India, Ceylon and The Far East, 1964–65'.
165 SIA DSH1/5/8/14-22 'The Equity Members Report'.
166 Ibid.
167 Ibid.
168 SIA DSH1/9/3/1 'Attached Minutes of Meeting Held on 16/7/64'.
169 SIA DSH1/9/3/1 'Conville's Asia Tour Report'.
170 Ibid.
171 SIA DSH1/5/8/14-22 'The Equity Members Report'.
172 Ibid.
173 SIA DSH1/5/8/14-22 'Attached Minutes of Meeting Held on 16/7/64'.
174 Jeannie Stephens, 'A Back-Stage View', *Sunday Tribune*, 21 February 1965.
175 SIA DSH1/9/3/1 'Conville's Asia Tour Report'.
176 Ibid.
177 SIA DSH1/5/8/14-22 'The Equity Members Report'; 'Attached Minutes of Meeting Held on 16/7/64'.
178 SIA DSH1/9/3/1 'Conville's Asia Tour Report'.
179 SIA DSH1/5/8/14-22 'The Equity Members Report'.
180 Ibid.
181 SIA DSH1/9/3/1 'Conville's Asia Tour Report'.
182 SIA DSH1/5/8/14-22 'The Equity Members Report'.
183 Ibid.
184 Ibid.
185 Ibid; SIA DSH1/9/3/1 'Conville's Asia Tour Report'.
186 SIA DSH1/3/2/3 'Correspondence from Oxbury (Deputy Director-General) to Conville', 22 February 1965.
187 SIA DSH1/9/3/1 'Conville's Asia Tour Report'.
188 SIA DSH1/5/8/14-22 'Attached Minutes of Meeting Held on 16/7/64'.
189 Ibid.
190 Ibid.
191 Ibid.

Conclusion

1 John Gallagher and Ronald Robinson, 'The Imperialism of Free Trade', in *The Decline, Revival and Fall of the British Empire*, ed. by John Gallagher (Cambridge: Cambridge University Press, 1982) pp. 1–18.
2 Lee, 'British Cultural Diplomacy', pp. 122–26.
3 See Kathleen Paul, *Whitewashing Britain: Race and Citizenship in the Postwar Era* (Ithaca, NY: Cornell University Press, 1997), pp. 111–130.
4 Lee, 'British Cultural Diplomacy', p. 126.
5 See Smith, 'MI5 Surveillance and British Cold War Theatre', pp. 133–150.
6 Gauri Viswanathan details how 'the humanistic functions' of literary study were 'vital in the process of socio-political control' in colonial India, with 'the

English literary text' operating as 'a surrogate Englishman in his highest and most perfect state'. Gauri Viswanathan, *Masks of Conquest: Literary Study and British Rule in India* (London: Faber and Faber, 1990), pp. 2, 23.
7 Alasdair Donaldson, *All the World's: How Shakespeare is Viewed Around the Globe and the Role his Work can Play to Support the UK's Soft Power* (London: British Council Press, 2016), p. 2, pp. 30–32.
8 Ibid, p. 22.
9 Ibid, p. 22.
10 Ibid, p. 22.
11 See, for example, Anon, 'Hamlet Holds "Racist" Views of Black People, Globe Claims in Drive to Decolonise Shakespeare's Work', *The Daily Telegraph*, 11 February 2022.
12 Oliver Dowden, 'We Won't Allow Britain's History to be Cancelled', *The Telegraph*, 16 May 2021.
13 Preti Taneja in conversation with Professor Farah Karim-Cooper, Margot Finn, and Elliot Barnes-Worell, 'In Conversation: Reckoning with Our Past', Shakespeare's Globe, 24 August 2020. www.shakespearesglobe.com/whats-on/in-conversation-reckoning-with-our-past-2020/ [Accessed 17 May 2020].
14 Priyamvada Gopal, 'On Decolonisation and the University', *Textual Practice*, 35.6 (2021), 873–899, p. 879.
15 Ibid, p. 883.
16 Ibid, p. 879, p. 883.
17 University of Birmingham, 'The Shakespeare Beyond Borders Launch Event', www.birmingham.ac.uk/schools/edacs/departments/shakespeare/events/2021/shakespeare-beyond-borders-alliance.aspx [Accessed online 21 June 2021].
18 The roundtable on soft power featured speakers from the University of Birmingham's Shakespeare Institute, and the Shakespeare Birthplace Trust, 'in conversation with representatives from government bodies, theatre projects, curatorial and arts institutions, and the Royal Shakespeare Company'.
19 See Joseph Nye, *Soft Power: The Means to Success in World Politics* (New York NY: Public Affairs, 2004).
20 As this was a live conference debate, I have left quotes unattributed but have sought to indicate the range of separate views expressed.
21 T. S. Eliot, *Notes Towards a Definition of Culture* (London: Faber and Faber, 1948).
22 MacPhee, *Postwar British Literature and Postcolonial Studies*, p. 40.
23 Inderjeet Parmar, *Foundations of the American Century: The Ford, Carnegie, and Rockefeller Foundations in the Rise of American Power* (Columbia University Press: New York, 2012), pp. 2–3. For an example of the role global theatrical networks played in the cultural Cold War, see Christopher B. Balme and Nic Leonhardt, 'The Rockefeller Connection: Visualizing Theatrical Networks in the Cultural Cold War', *Comparatio*, 12.2 (2020) 127–144.
24 For a recent debate on institutional memory and official histories, see Patrick Salmon, *The Control of the Past: Herbert Butterfield and the Pitfalls of Official History* (London: University of London Press, 2021).

Bibliography

Primary Sources

The British Library (BL), Manuscripts Collection (MS)
BL MS 89015/1/4/1 'Merula Guinness' Old Vic Tour Diary, 1939', 2 Vols.

The National Archives of the UK (TNA), British Council Records (BW)
TNA BW 1/235 'Sir Laurence Olivier and Shakespeare Memorial Theatre's Tour of *Titus Andronicus* to Paris, Venice, Belgrade, Zagreb, Vienna and Warsaw, 1957–1958'
TNA BW 1/436 'Shakespeare Memorial Theatre Company Tour of *Titus Andronicus* to Europe (Sir Laurence Olivier)'
TNA BW 12/4 'Australia: Reports 1947–1953'
TNA BW 12/6 'Australia: Annual Reports 1947–1958'
TNA BW 29/47 'General Policy: Propaganda War in Egypt during 1939–1940'
TNA BW 52/1 'British Institute at Lisbon 1938–1939'
TNA BW 72 'British Council: Sub-Committee on British Education in the Near East: Minutes 1935–1939'
TNA BW 120/1 'Drama Advisory Committee: Minutes of Meetings 1939–1957'
TNA BW 120/3 'Drama Advisory Committee: Minutes and Papers of Meetings 1961–1965'
TNA BW 128/9 'Representative's Annual Reports, 1959–1963'

Nottinghamshire County Council Archives (NCCA)
NCCA GB 0157 DD/NP/1/3/1 'Minutes, 1848–1988'
NCCA GB 0157 DN/NP/2/2/10 'Overseas Productions'

Nottingham University Archives (NUA)
NUA MS 679/1/11 '*Arms and the Man* Theatre Programme, (Nottingham Playhouse, April 1964)'

The Shakespeare Birthplace Trust, Stratford-upon-Avon (SBT)
SBT RSC/SM/2/1953/6 'Australian and New Zealand Production Records: Shakespeare Memorial Theatre, 1953 (All Productions)'
SBT RSC/SM/2/1953/9 'Production Records for *Othello* Australian and New Zealand Tour'

SBT RSC/Theatre Records/Series B/Vols. 69–79 'Press Books: Tour to Australia and New Zealand'

The Shakespeare Institute, Birmingham University Archives (SIA)
SIA DSH1/3/2/3 'Production Administration File for Tour of Asia'
SIA DSH1/5/8/13 'Scrapbook for Tour of Asia'
SIA DSH1/5/8/14-22 'Press Cuttings from Tour of Asia'
SIA DSH1/9/3/1 'Show Reports for Tour of Asia'

Websites

The Australian Dictionary of Biography Online, 'John Alden (1908–1962)'. www.adb.anu.edu.au/biography/alden-john-9323 [Accessed 13 November 2018]
The British Council, 'Our Organisation'. www.britishcouncil.org/organisation [Accessed 1 April 2023]
The National Archives, 'Records of the British Council'. www.discovery.nationalarchives.gov.uk/details/r/C40 [Accessed 28 April 2017]
The Shakespeare Birthplace Trust, 'The Bust of Rabindranath Tagore at Shakespeare's Birthplace'. www.shakespeare.org/explore-shakespeare/blogs/bust-tagore-shakespeares-birthplace/ [Accessed 26 May 2020]
Shakespeare's Globe, 'In Conversation: Reckoning With Our Past', 24 August 2020. www.shakespearesglobe.com/whats-on/in-conversation-reckoning-with-our-past-2020/ [Accessed 17 May 2021]
The Stage, 'Obituaries: Christopher Burgess', 2013. www.thestage.co.uk/features/obituaries/2013/christopher-burgess/ [Accessed 12 September 2018]
University of Birmingham, 'The Shakespeare Beyond Borders Launch Event'. www.birmingham.ac.uk/schools/edacs/departments/shakespeare/events/2021/shakespeare-beyond-borders-alliance.aspx [Accessed Online 21 June 2021]

Newspapers

A Special Correspondent, 'They Who Play Shakespeare Always Welcome', *Amrita Bazar Patrika*, 17 December 1964
A Staff Reporter, 'The Shrew Duly Tamed', *Sunday Hindustan Standard*, 27 December 1964
Anon, 'A Glance at Some New Elizabethans' *The Geelong Advertiser*, 25 July 1953
Anon, 'A Shakespearean Saga', *Dawn*, 4 October 1964
Anon, 'Amanda Who Plays Miranda', *The Hindustan Times*, 2 December 1964
Anon, 'Anthony Quayle', *People*, 17 June 1953
Anon, "Appalling" Says Quayle', *Sydney Sunday Times*, 18 October 1953
Anon, 'Ban Shakespeare from Schools', *The Argus*, 7 July 1953
Anon, 'Big Contrasts in Our Audience', *Perth Daily News*, 18 September 1953
Anon, 'Brawn Called for in This Act', *Telegraph*, 15 April 1953

Anon, 'Could Play Shakespeare in a Swimsuit', *Courier Mail*, 26 June 1953
Anon, 'Director', *Times of India*, 8 November 1964
Anon, 'Director's Wife Is Talent Scout', *Age*, 27 June 1953
Anon, 'Eating, Sleeping – In Unrefined Way', *Melbourne Age*, 7 August 1953
Anon, 'Editorial: Australia Needs a National Theatre', *The Sun*, 5 June 1953
Anon, 'End of the British Council', *Sydney Morning Herald*, 4 March 1954
Anon, 'Honoured Playhouse Will Keep the Home Shows Going', *Nottingham Evening News*, 28 September 1962
Anon, 'For Home Service', *The Listener In*, [No Date] (in SBT RSC/Theatre Records/Series B/Vols. 69–79)
Anon, 'Hamlet Holds "Racist" Views of Black People, Globe Claims in Drive to Decolonise Shakespeare's Work', *The Daily Telegraph*, 11 February 2022
Anon, 'How to Get the Most Out of Shakespeare', *Western Australian*, 19 September 1953
Anon, 'It's the Bard – But without Tears', *Brisbane Sunday Mail*, 26 April 1953
Anon, 'Japanese 'Macbeth' for Africa', *Nottingham News*, 19 December 1962
Anon, 'Let Us Pep Up Shakespeare!', *Melbourne Argus*, 1 August 1953
Anon, 'Macbeth Goes on Tour of County Schools', *Nottingham Guardian*, 24 March 1962
Anon, 'Macbeth Is Always New', *Nigerian Outlook*, 6 February 1963
Anon, 'Malaysian Audiences Lauded by a Top London Actor', *Straits Times*, 13 February 1965
Anon, 'Meat Coupons for British Food Appeal Fund', *Morning Bulletin*, 28 May 1947
Anon, 'Melbourne Audiences 'Lazy': Quayle', *Melbourne Argus*, 19 August 1953
Anon, 'Music and Theatre World', *Western Australian*, 14 October 1953
Anon, 'News of the Day', *Age*, 19 August 1953
Anon, [No Title], *Deccan Herald*, 19 November 1964 (in SIA DSH1/5/8/14-22)
Anon, [No Title], *Eve's Weekly*, 7 November 1964 (in SIA DSH1/5/8/14-22)
Anon, [No Title], *Examiner*, 14 November 1964 (in SIA DSH1/5/8/14-22)
Anon, [No Title], *Financial Express*, 8 November 1964 (in SIA DSH1/5/8/14-22)
Anon, [No Title], *Hindu*, 24 November 1964 (in SIA DSH1/5/8/14-22)
Anon, [No Title], *Indian Express*, 4 November 1964 (in SIA DSH1/5/8/14-22)
Anon, [No Title], *Manilla Times*, 30 January 1965 (in SIA DSH1/5/8/14-22)
Anon, [No Title], *Melbourne Argus*, 19 August 1953 (in SBT RSC/Theatre Records/Series B/Vols. 69-79)
Anon, [No Title], *Morning News*, 4 October 1964 (in SBT RSC/Theatre Records/Series B/Vols. 69-79)
Anon, 'Neutral Accent Is 'Must' in London', *The Listener In*, 15 August 1953
Anon, [No Title], *Onlooker*, 15 November 1964 (in SIA DSH1/5/8/14-22)
Anon, [No Title], *Pakistan Times*, 11 October 1964 (in SIA DSH1/5/8/14-22)
Anon, [No Title], *Singapore Sunday Mail*, 21 February 1965 (in SIA DSH1/5/8/14-22)
Anon, [No Title], *She Magazine*, 15 October 1964 (in SIA DSH1/5/8/14-22)

Anon, [No Title], *South China Morning Post*, 23 January 1964 (in SIA DSH1/5/8/14-22)
Anon, [No Title], *Sunday Sun*, 7 June 1953 (in SBT RSC/Theatre Records/Series B/Vols. 69-79)
Anon, [No Title], *The Lady*, 11 June 1964 (in SIA DSH1/5/8/14-22)
Anon, [No Title], *The Indian Nation*, 16 December 1964 (in SIA DSH1/5/8/14-22)
Anon, [No Title], *The Sarawak Tribune*, 26 February 1964 (in SIA DSH1/5/8/14-22)
Anon, [No title], *Times of India*, [No Date], (in SIA DSH1/5/8/14-22)
Anon, [No Title], *Tiger Standard*, 25 January 1965 (in SIA DSH1/5/8/14-22)
Anon, [No Title], *Today*, 9 November 1964 (in SIA DSH1/5/8/14-22)
Anon, "Operation Theatre' Makes Big Demands on Off-Stage Planners', *The ABC Weekly*, 28 March 1953
Anon, 'Othello at Tivoli', [No Publication], May 1953 (in SBT RSC/Theatre Records/Series B/Vols. 69-79)
Anon, 'Othello Is Enthralling', *Telegraph*, 22 March 1953
Anon, 'Othello Is Too Smooth and Quiet', *The Sun*, 26 April 1953
Anon, 'Passion, Colour, Seen in Othello', [No Title], 22 April 1953 (in SBT RSC/Theatre Records/Series B/Vols. 69–79)
Anon, 'Play Festival Age', *Melbourne*, 20 July 1953
Anon, 'Playgoers are "Critics First" says Actress', *Age Melbourne*, 1 August 1953
Anon, 'Playhouse Choose Cast for Their West African Tour', *Nottingham Evening Post*, 27 November 1962
Anon, 'Playhouse Defeated the Motive', *Nigeria Daily Express*, 16 January 1963
Anon, 'Playhouse Preview of Tour "Macbeth"', *The Guardian Journal*, 12 December 1962
Anon, 'Playhouse Was Finest on NTS', *Nigeria Morning Post*, 19 January 1963
Anon, 'Search for a Hunger', *Encore*, July–August 1961
Anon, 'Shakespeare and Shaw in the Sun: Nottingham Conquers Africa', *Stage and Television Today*, 4 April 1963
Anon, 'Shakespeare and "Snobs"', [No Publication], 23 April 1953 (in SBT RSC/Theatre Records/Series B/Vols. 69-79)
Anon, 'Shakespeare in Kuching', *The Sarawak Tribune*, 2 February 1965
Anon, 'Shakespeare May Be Seen Here in a New Light', *The Western Australian*, 18 September 1953
Anon, 'Shakespeare Players Score Big Success in the Tempest', *Daily Mail*, 10 February 1965
Anon, 'Shakespeare Players Strong Empire Bond', *Weekly Radio and Music Records*, 11 May 1953
Anon, 'Shakespeare Queue Began at 4.50 A.M.', [No Publication], 14 March 1953 (in SBT RSC/Theatre Records/Series B/Vols. 69–79)
Anon, 'Shakespearean Visit Coronation Gesture', *Brisbane Telegraph*, 23 May 1953
Anon, 'Sir Laurence Olivier in the Burgtheater', *Die Fresse*, 14 June 1957

Anon, 'Strange Setting in "Macbeth": Tour Preview', *Nottingham Evening News*, 18 December 1962
Anon, 'Stratford Othello and the Tivoli', *Herald*, 22 April 1953
Anon, 'Sydney Diary', *The Sun*, 24 April 1953
Anon, 'The Formidable Force from Nottingham', *Nigeria Outlook*, 23 January 1963
Anon, 'The Tempest', *The Statesman*, 20 December 1964
Anon, '"The Tempest" Tomorrow: NSC in City', [No Title], [No Date], (in SIA DSH1/5/8/14-22)
Anon, 'Theatre', *Nottingham Observer*, December 1962
Anon, 'Theatre', *Nottingham Observer*, January 1963
Anon, 'They Live, Breath Shakespeare', *Melbourne Sun*, 19 June 1953
Anon, 'Three Plays for West Africa', *Stage and Television Today*, 27 September 1962
Anon, 'Top Hats at Othello', *The Daily Telegraph*, 22 April 1953
Anon, 'Tour When Line of Vultures Sat on the Back of the Stage', *Evening Post*, 6 December 2008
Anon, 'Travel', *Melbourne Age*, 10 August 1953
Anon, 'What's on in Town', *Perth Mirror*, 10 October 1953
Anon, 'William on Shakespeare', *Hindustan Times*, 30 November 1964
Arts Critic, 'Brave Effort to Create Atmosphere: The Tempest Staged', *The Star*, 2 October 1964
Atri, [No Title], *The Hindu*, 6 December 1964 (in SIA DSH1/5/8/14-22)
Bishop, George W., 'Plays and Players', *The Daily Telegraph*, 8 August 1964
Bishop, George W., 'Stratford Does Shakespeare's Horror Comic', *Daily Telegraph*, 15 August 1955
Burbridge, Ernest W., 'The British Council', *Sydney Morning Herald*, 5 March 1954.
Chandrasekhara, B., 'The Crowning Performance', *Deccan Herald*, 20 November 1964
Chaplin, J., 'Letters to the Editor: Play Audiences', 12 October 1953
Coe, John, 'Impressive - But Still Revolting', *Bristol Evening Post*, 17 August 1955
Craig, Coral, 'Stratford Players at Their Best', *Women's Day*, 9 February 1953
Crooks, Lennard, 'Too Lazy to Dig Out 21/ For A Seat', *Melbourne Argus*, 22 August 1953
Doherty, Frank, 'Must We Be Told What to See', *Melbourne Argus*, 19 August 1953
E. A. B., 'Macbeth with an Oriental Twist', *Nottingham Evening Post*, 19 December 1962
Heer, Friedrich, 'A Moment of History in the Theatre', [No Publication], 22 June 1957 (in TNA BW 1/235)
Hobson, Howard, 'A Modern Play', *Sunday Times*, 21 August 1955
Goquingco, Leonor Orosa, 'Two Great Englishmen Remembered as Shakespeare Group Performs', *The Manila Bulletin*, 30 January 1965
Guttila, 'The Magic of the Tempest', *The Times*, 2 January 1965

Iago, 'The New Shakespeare Company', [No Publication], 1 January 1965 (in SIA DSH1/5/8/14-22)
Imayu, Sam, 'Nottingham Players not Impressive', *Sunday Express*, 20 January 1963
Johns, Eric, 'Shakespeare for the Orient', *Theatre World*, September 1964
Kennedy, Robert, 'Town Talk', [No Title], 25 April 1953 (in SBT RSC/Theatre Records/Series B/Vols. 69–79)
King, Alec, 'Letters to the Editor: A Play in Perth', *The Western Australian*, 8 October 1953
Kustow, Michael, 'Jan Kott: An Obituary', *The Guardian*, 10 January 2002
Lewin, David, 'Horror Comic', *Daily Express*, 15 August 1955
Levin, Bernard, 'Titus Review', *The Truth*, 26 August 1955
Luckie, Reg, 'Australian Actor for Stratford', *Women's Weekly*, 18 July 1953
Luff, John, 'The Tempest: Something of the Beauty of the Lines Was Lost', *China Mail*, 23 January 1965
Macdougall, Jim, 'Contact', *The Sun*, 22 April 1953
Martin, Francis, 'Mr Brook Decided to Make His Own Primitive Roman Music', *Edinburgh Evening Dispatch*, 27 August 1955
McLeod, Zelie, 'The Theatre in Australia Faces a Crisis', *Daily Telegraph*, 16 May 1953
Mercado, Monina A., '"Taming of the Shrew": It Teetered on the Slapstick', *Manila Herald*, 29 January 1965
Mercado, Monina A., '"The Tempest That Wasn't', *The Philippine Herald*, 3 February 1965
Morrison, Alistair, 'The British Council', *Morning Herald*, 12 March 1954
Murphy, Frank, 'Othello', *Melbourne Advocate*, 7 July 1953
N. E., 'Theatre', *Imprint*, December 1964
Nomad, 'Letters to the Editor: Theatre Seats', *The Western Australian*, 15 October 1953
Our Drama Critic, 'A Tame Tempest', *Indian Express*, 7 December 1964
Our Drama Critic, 'New Shakespeare Company in Capital', *Times of India*, 27 November 1964
Our Drama Critic, 'Richard II Has Many Memorable Moments', *Hindustan Times*, 30 November 1964
Our Drama Critic, 'The Tempest Is a Botticellian Extravaganza', *The Statesman*, [No Date] (in SIA DSH1/5/8/14-22)
Our Staff Correspondent, 'David William as Richard II', *Pakistan Times*, [No Date] (in SIA DSH1/5/8/14-22)
Our Theatre Reporter, 'Shakespeare 'Exports' to 80 Countries', *The Daily Telegraph*, 12 February 1964
Pan, Peter, 'One Miserable Night I'll Never Forget', *Daily Times*, 15 January 1963
Paterfamilias, 'Letters to the Editor: Play Audiences', [No Publication], 12 October 1953
Polkinghorne, Arthur, 'Sydney Will Drink a Toast to W. Shakespeare', *The Sun*, 20 April 1953

Ramaswami, N. S., 'Richard II', [No Publication], [No Date] (in SIA DSH1/5/8/14-22)
Ravi, 'A Surfeit of Shakespeare', *The Sun*, 6 January 1965
Reynolds, J. H., 'Letters to the Editor: Opportunity', *The Western Australian*, 8 October 1953
Rhoades, Louise, 'Acting Their Way from Nottingham to Africa', *Daily Telegraph*, 12 December 1962
Scarlett, John, 'Talk Too Much Nonsense on Shakespeare', *The Sunday Times*, 27 September 1953
St. Clair, Brian, 'The Taming of the Shrew', *Tiger Standard*, 25 January 1965
Staff Correspondent, [No Title], *The Indian Nation*, 17 December 1964 (in SIA DSH1/5/8/14-22)
Staff Correspondent, 'Srinagar Lad Comes Back to Stage Shakespeare', *Hindustan Times*, 27 November 1964
Staff Correspondent, 'Talking Massive Success', *The Indian Nation*, 16 December 1964
Stead, Elizabeth, 'Shakespeare Company Moves Like an Army', *Launceston Examiner*, 22 August 1953
Stead, Elizabeth, 'Shakespeare under the Southern Cross', *Melbourne Sun*, 20 June 1953
Stephens, Jeannie, 'A Back-Stage View', *Sunday Tribune*, 21 February 1965
Trewin, J. C., [No Title], *Pakistan Observer*, 12 October 1964 (in SIA DSH1/5/8/14-22)
Tully, Hazel, 'Our Four Shakespeareans', *Women*, 15 September 1953
Tynan, Kenneth, 'King's Rhapsody: Hamlet with Paul Schofield, Directed by Peter Brook', *Observer*, 11 December 1955
Tynan, Kenneth, 'The Russian Way', *Observer*, November 1955
Valenzuela, C. H., 'Shakespeare Comes to Life: Bard's Shrew Tickles Filipino Funny Bone', *Evening News*, 9 January 1965
Visick, Mary, 'Taming of the Shrew: Time Flies and Its Good Box Office', *South China Morning Post*, 25 January 1965
Visick, Mary, 'The Tempest: Orthodox Performance by Shakespeare Company', *South China Morning Post*, 23 January 1965
Weeraratne, Neville, 'A Common Monsoon', [No Publication], [No Date] (in SIA DSH1/5/8/14-22)
Weigel, Hans, 'Titus Review', [No Publication], 13 June 1957 (in TNA BW 1/235)
West, Jane, 'Macbeth in Lagos', *West African Pilot*, 19 January 1963
Wickenburg, Eric G., 'A Victory and a Lost Battle', [No Publication], 14 June 1957 (in TNA BW 1/235)

Secondary Sources

Abdalla, Ahmed, *The Student Movement and National Politics in Egypt, 1923–1973* (Cairo: The American University of Cairo Press, 2008).
Adam, Colin Forbes, *Life of Lord Lloyd* (London: Macmillan, 1948).

Addenbrooke, David, *The Royal Shakespeare Company: The Peter Hall Years* (London: William Kember, 1974).
Adedeji, J. A., 'Oral Tradition and the Contemporary Theatre in Nigeria', *Research in African Literatures*, 2.2 (1971), 196–200.
Adelugba, Dapo, Olu Obafemi, and Sola Adeyemi, 'Nigeria', in *A History of Theatre in Africa*, ed. by Martin Banham (Cambridge: Cambridge University Press, 2004), pp. 138–158.
Aldrich, Richard J., *The Hidden Hand: Britain, America, and Cold War Secret Intelligence* (London: John Murray, 2001).
  'OSS, CIA and European Unity: The American Committee of United Europe, 1948–1960', *Diplomacy and Statecraft*, 8.1 (1997), 184–227.
  'Putting Culture into the Cold War: The Cultural Research Department (CRD) and British Covert Information Warfare', *Intelligence and National Security*, 18.2 (2003), 109–133.
Alomes, Stephen, *When London Calls: The Expatriation of Australian Creative Artists to Britain* (Cambridge: Cambridge University Press, 2000).
Al-Samahi, 'Abdel-qadir, "Hamlit"', *Al-Thaqafah*, 384 (1946), 18–21.
Al-Sayyid-Marsot, Afaf Lutfi, *Egypt's Liberal Experiment* (Berkeley, CA: University of California Press, 1978).
Al-Shetawi, Mahmoud F., '*Hamlet* in Arabic', *Journal of Intercultural Studies*, 20.1 (1999), 43–63.
Anderson, Benedict, *Imagined Communities* (London: Verso Books, 2006).
Anderson, Carol, 'The Histories of African Americans' Anti-Colonialism during the Cold War', in *The Cold War in the Third World*, ed. by Robert J. McMahon (Oxford: Oxford University Press, 2013), pp. 178–191.
Anderson, Perry, 'Components of the National Culture', *New Left Review*, 50 (1968), 3–57.
Annan, Noel, *Changing Enemies* (London: Harper Collins, 1996).
Anon, 'An Address to the Artists of the Old Vic Company by the President of the Federazione Nazionale Fascista' (Private Press: Milan, 1939).
Anon, 'The British Council: Speeches Delivered on the Occasion of the Inaugural Meeting at St. James's Palace on July 2, 1935' (London: British Council Private Press, 1935).
Anon, *Souvenir Programme for the Shakespeare Memorial Theatre, Stratford-upon-Avon, 1955* (London: Reinhardt & Evans, 1955).
Anthony, Scott, *Public Relations and the Making of Modern Britain: Stephen Tallents and the Birth of a Progressive Media Profession* (Manchester: Manchester University Press, 2012).
Armstrong, Gareth, *A Case for Shylock: Around the World with Shakespeare's Jew* (London: Nick Horn Books, 2004).
Ashcroft, Bill, Gareth Griffiths, and Helen Tiffin, 'Introduction to Diaspora', in *The Post-Colonial Studies Reader*, ed. by Bill Ashcroft, Gareth Griffiths, and Helen Tiffin (Abingdon: Routledge, 1995), pp. 425–427.
Aune, M. G., 'Importing Shakespeare: Tyrone Guthrie and British Cold War Cultural Colonialism', *Shakespeare*, 5.4 (2009), 423–440.

Badawi, M. M., 'Shakespeare and the Arabs', in *Cairo Studies of English* (Cairo: Al-Maktaba al-Anjlu al-Misriyya, 1966), pp. 181–196.
Bailey, John, *A Theatre for All Seasons: The Nottingham Playhouse* (Stroud: Alan Sutton Publishing, 1994).
Balme, Christopher B., 'The Bandmann Circuit: Theatrical Networks in the First Age of Globalization', *Theatre Research International*, 40.1 (2015), 19–36.
Banham, Martin, ed., *A History of Theatre in Africa* (Cambridge: Cambridge University Press, 2004).
Banham, Martin, Errol Hill, and George Woodyard, eds., *The Cambridge Guide to African and Caribbean Theatre* (Cambridge: Cambridge University Press, 1994).
Barker, Felix, *The Oliviers: A Biography* (London: Hamish Hamilton, 1953).
Bate, Jonathan, 'Shakespeare Nationalised, Shakespeare Privatised', *English*, 42 (1993), 1–18.
Beauman, Sally, *The Royal Shakespeare Company: A History of Ten Decades* (Oxford: Oxford University Press, 1982).
Belfiore, Eleonora, and Oliver Bennett, *The Social Impact of the Arts* (London: Palgrave Macmillan, 2008).
Belich, James, *Replenishing the Earth. The Settler Revolution and the Rise of the Anglo-world, 1780s–1920s* (Oxford: Oxford University Press, 2011).
Benedictis, Michele De, 'Crossing the Rubicon in Fascist Italy: Mussolini and Theatrical Caesarism from Shakespeare's *Julius Caesar*', in *Shakespeare and Tyranny: Regimes of Reading in Europe and Beyond*, ed. by Keith Gregor (Newcastle-upon-Tyne: Cambridge Scholars Publishing, 2014), pp. 105–126.
Berman, Edward H., 'The Foundations' Role in American Foreign Policy: The Case of Africa, Post 1945', in *Philanthropy and Cultural Imperialism: The Foundations at Home and Abroad*, ed. by Robert F. Arnove (Bloomington, IN: Indiana University Press, 1982), pp. 203–232.
Blakemore, Michael, *Arguments with England* (London: Faber and Faber, 2005).
Botman, Selma, *Egypt from Independence to Revolution, 1919–1952* (New York: Syracuse University Press, 1991).
Bourne, Richard, *Nigeria: A New History of a Turbulent Century* (London: Zed Books, 2015).
Boyce, Michael W., *The Lasting Influence of the War on Post-War British Film* (Basingstoke: Palgrave Macmillan, 2012).
Bradley, Mark Philip, 'Decolonisation, the Global South, and the Cold War, 1919–1962', in *The Cambridge Companion to the Cold War, Volume I: Origins*, ed. by Melvyn P. Leffler, and Odd Arne Westad (Cambridge: Cambridge University Press, 2012), pp. 464–485.
Brantlinger, Patrick, *Rule of Darkness: British Literature and the Imperialism, 1830–1914* (Ithaca, NY: Cornell University Press, 1988).
Brecht, Bertolt, 'Against Georg Lukács', in *Aesthetics and Politics*, ed. by Theodor Adorno, et al. (London: Verso, 1977), pp. 68–85.
  'The Popular and the Realistic', in *Brecht on Theatre*, ed. by John Willett (London: Methuen, 1964), pp. 107–114.

Bibliography

Brendon, Piers, *The Dark Valley: A Panorama of the 1930s* (London: Pimlico, 2001).
   The Decline and Fall of the British Empire 1781–1997 (London: Jonathan Cape, 2007).
Brent, Jonathan, and Vladimir P. Naumov, *Stalin's Last Crime: The Doctor's Plot* (London: John Murray, 2004).
Brian Vickers, *Shakespeare, Co-Author: A Historical Study of Five Collaborative Plays* (Oxford: Oxford University Press, 2002), pp. 150–152.
Brown, Ivor, and Anthony Quayle, *Shakespeare Memorial Theatre 1948–1950: A Photographic Record* (London: Reinhardt and Evans, 1951).
Brown, Judith, and Wm. Roger Louis, eds., *The Oxford History of the British Empire: Volume IV: The Twentieth Century* (Oxford: Oxford University Press, 1999).
Brown, Ross, *Sound: A Reader in Theatre Practice* (Basingstoke: Palgrave Macmillan, 2010).
Bush, Sophie, *Valerie West Interview Transcript* (London: British Library Theatre Archive Project, 2010).
Calder, Angus, *The Myth of the Blitz* (London: Jonathan Cape, 1991).
   The People's War: Britain 1939–1945 (London: Pimlico, 1992).
Caute, David, *The Dancer Defects: The Struggle for Cultural Supremacy during the Cold War* (Oxford: Oxford University Press, 2003).
Chambers, Colin, *Inside the Royal Shakespeare Company* (Abingdon: Routledge, 2004).
Charmley, John, *Lord Lloyd and the Decline of the British Empire* (London: Weidenfeld and Nicolson, 1987).
Coleman, Terry, *Olivier: The Authorised Biography* (London: Bloomsbury, 2005).
Collis, Robert, *To Be a Pilgrim* (London: Secker and Warburg, 1975).
Constantine, Stephen, "Bringing the Empire Alive': The Empire Marketing Board and Imperial Propaganda, 1926–1933', in *Imperialism and Popular Culture*, ed. by John M. MacKenzie (Manchester: Manchester University Press, 1986), pp. 192–231.
   Buy and Build: The Advertising Posters of the Empire Marketing Board (London: Public Records Office, 1986).
Conville, David, *The Park: The Story of the Open-Air Theatre, Regents Park* (London: Oberon Books, 2007).
Cooper, Artemis, *Cairo in the War, 1939–1945* (London: Hamish Hamilton, 1989).
Corse, Edward, *A Battle for Neutral Europe: British Cultural Propaganda During the Second World War* (London: Bloomsbury, 2014).
Courtney, Krytyna Kujawinska, 'Celebrating Shakespeare under the Communist Regime in Poland', in *Shakespeare in Cold War Europe: Conflict, Commemoration, Celebration*, ed. by Erica Sheen, and Isabel Karremann (Basingstoke: Palgrave Macmillan, 2016), pp. 23–35.

'Krystyna Skuszanka's Shakespeare of Political Allusions and Metaphors in Communist Poland', in *Shakespeare in the Worlds of Communism and Socialism*, ed. by Irena R. Makaryk and Joseph G. Price (Toronto: University of Toronto Press, 2006), pp. 228–245.

Croall, Jonathan, *John Gielgud: Matinee Idol to Movie Star* (London: Methuen Drama, 2011).

Sybil Thorndike: A Star of Life (London: Haus Books, 2008).

Cull, Nicholas J., *The Cold War and the United States Information Agency: American Propaganda and Public Diplomacy, 1945–1989* (Cambridge: Cambridge University Press, 2008).

Currey, James, *Africa Writes Back: The African Writers Series and the Launch of African Literature* (Athens, OH: Ohio University Press, 2008).

'Literary Publishing after Nigerian Independence: Mbari as Celebration', *Research in African Literatures*, 44.2 (2013), 8–16.

Curtis, Mark, *Web of Deceit: Britain's Real Role in the World* (London: Vintage Books, 2003).

Cushing, Peter, *The Complete Memoirs* (Cambridge: Signum Books, 2013).

Darian-Smith, Kate, and Patricia Grimshaw, eds., *Britishness Abroad: Transnational Movements and Imperial Cultures* (Melbourne: Melbourne University Press, 2007).

Darwin, John, 'A Third British Empire? The Dominion Idea in Imperial Politics', in *The Oxford History of the British Empire: Volume IV: The Twentieth Century*, ed. by Judith Brown and Wm. Roger Louis (Oxford: Oxford University Press, 1999), pp. 64–87.

The Empire Project: The Rise and Fall of the British World-System, 1830–1970 (Cambridge: Cambridge University Press, 2009).

Davis, Caroline, 'Creating a Book Empire: Longmans in Africa', in *The Book in Africa: Critical Debates*, ed. by Caroline Davis and David Johnson (Basingstoke: Palgrave Macmillan, 2015), pp. 128–152.

Creating Postcolonial Literature (Basingstoke: Palgrave Macmillan, 2015).

'Publishing Wole Soyinka: Oxford University Press and the Creation of 'Africa's own William Shakespeare'', *Journal of Postcolonial Writing*, 48.4 (2011), 344–358.

Davis, Caroline, and David Johnson, eds., *The Book in Africa: Critical Debates* (Basingstoke: Palgrave Macmillan, 2015), pp. 128–152.

Dawson, Anthony B., *Shakespeare in Performance: Hamlet* (Manchester: Manchester University Press, 1995).

Dean, Basil, *Theatre at War* (London: Harrap & Co, 1956).

Defty, Andrew, *Britain, America, and Anti-Communist Propaganda 1945–1953: The Information Research Department* (Abingdon: Routledge, 2003).

Delabastita, Dirk, et al., eds., *Shakespeare and European Politics* (Newark, DE: University of Delaware Press, 2008).

Dench, Judi, *And Furthermore* (London: Pheonix Press, 2010).

Dessen, Alan. C., *Titus Andronicus: Shakespeare in Performance* (Manchester: Manchester University Press, 1990).

Devlin, Diana, *A Speaking Part: Lewis Casson and the Theatre of His Time* (London: Hodder and Stoughton, 1982).
Dollimore, Jonathan and Alan Sinfield, 'History and Ideology: The Instance of Henry V'', in *Alternative Shakespeares*, pp. 210–231.
Donaldson, Alasdair, *All the World's: How Shakespeare Is Viewed around the Globe and the Role His Work can Play to Support the UK's Soft Power* (London: British Council Press, 2016).
Donaldson, Frances, *The British Council: The First Fifty Years* (London: Jonathan Cape, 1984).
Dowden, Oliver, 'We Won't Allow Britain's History to Be Cancelled', *The Telegraph*, 16 May 2021.
Drakakis, John, ed., *Alternative Shakespeares* (Abingdon: Routledge, 1985).
Drogheda Report Summary, *Report of the Independent Committee of Enquiry into the Overseas Information Services* (London: HMSO, 1954).
Eliot, T. S., *Notes Towards a Definition of Culture* (London: Faber and Faber, 1948).
Elsom, John, ed., *Is Shakespeare Still Our Contemporary?* (Abingdon: Routledge, 1990).
Engerman, David C., 'Ideology and the Origins of the Cold War, 1917–1962', in *The Cambridge Companion to the Cold War: Volume I: Origins*, ed. by Melvyn P. Leffler, and Odd Arne Westad (Cambridge: Cambridge University Press, 2012), pp. 20–43.
Esty, Jed, *A Shrinking Island: Modernism and National Culture in England* (Princeton, NJ: Princeton University Press, 2003).
Fawkes, Richard, *Fighting for a Laugh: Entertaining the British and American Armed Forces, 1939–1946* (London: Macdonald and Jane's, 1978).
Forbes Adam, Colin, *Life of Lord Lloyd* (London: Macmillan, 1948).
Forsyth, James, *Tyrone Guthrie* (London: Hamish Hamilton, 1976).
Friedman, Michael D., and Alan Dessen, *Titus Andronicus: Shakespeare in Performance* (Manchester: Manchester University Press, 2013).
Gallagher, John, and Ronald Robinson, 'The Imperialism of Free Trade', in *The Decline, Revival and Fall of the British Empire*, ed. by John Gallagher (Cambridge: Cambridge University Press, 1982), pp. 1–18.
Gay, Penny, 'International Glamour or Home Grown Entertainment? 1948–1964', in *O Brave New World: Two Centuries of Shakespeare on the Australian Stage*, ed. by John Golder and Richard Madelaine (Sydney: Currency Press, 2001), pp. 180–199.
Geertz, Clifford, *The Interpretation of Cultures: Selected Essays* (New York: Basic Books, 1973).
Gershoni, Israel, and James P. Jankowski, *Confronting Fascism in Egypt: Dictatorship Versus Democracy in the 1930s* (Stanford, CA: Stanford University Press, 2010). *Redefining the Egyptian Nation, 1930–1945* (Cambridge: Cambridge University Press, 2002).
Gillespie, Marie, 'Writers at Bush House', *Wasafiri*, 26.4 (2011), 1–3.
Gilroy, Paul, *After Empire* (Abingdon: Routledge, 2004).

Glenny, Misha, *The Balkans: Nationalism, War, and the Great Powers 1804–2012* (London: Granta, 2012).
Golder, John, and Richard Madelaine, *O Brave New World: Two Centuries of Shakespeare on the Australian Stage* (Sydney: Currency Press, 2001).
Goodwin, John, ed., *Shakespeare Memorial Theatre Annual Programme, 1957* (Eversham: Journal Press, 1957).
Gopal Priyamvada, 'On Decolonisation and the University', *Textual Practice*, 35.6 (2021), 873–899.
Goulding, Daniel J., *Liberated Cinema: The Yugoslav Experience 1945–2001* (Bloomington, IN: Indiana University Press, 2002).
Grafftey-Smith, Laurence, *Bright Levant* (London: Stacey International, 2002).
Gregor, Keith, ed., *Shakespeare and Tyranny: Regimes of Reading in Europe and Beyond* (Newcastle-upon-Tyne: Cambridge Scholars Publishing, 2014).
Guinness, Alec, *Blessings in Disguise* (London: Hamish Hamilton, 1985).
Guthrie, Tyrone, *A Life in the Theatre* (London: Hamish Hamilton, 1960).
  'Report on Australian Theatre', *The Australian Quarterly*, 21.2 (1949), 78–83.
Halpern, Richard, *Shakespeare among the Moderns* (Ithaca, NY: Cornell University Press, 1997).
Hamouda, Sahar, and Colin Clement, eds., *Victoria College: A History Revealed* (Cairo: The American University of Cairo Press, 2002).
Hankey, Julie, ed., *Richard the Third: Plays in Performance* (Bristol: Bristol Classical Press, 1988).
Hansen, Peter H., 'Coronation Everest: The Empire and Commonwealth in the 'Second Elizabethan Age'', in *British Culture and the End of Empire*, ed. by Stuart Ward (Manchester: Manchester University Press: 2001), pp. 57–72.
Harbage, Alfred, *Shakespeare's Audience* (New York: Columbia University Press, 1969).
Harwood, Ronald, *Sir Donald Wolfit: His Life and Work in the Unfashionable Theatre* (London: Secker and Warburg, 1971).
  The Dresser (London: Amber Lane Press, 1984).
Heller, Mikhail, and Aleksandr Nekrich, *Utopia in Power: The History of the Soviet Union from 1917 to the Present* (New York: Summit Books, 1986).
Hendley, Mathew C., 'Cultural Mobilisation and British Responses to Cultural Transfer in Total War: Shakespeare Tercentenary of 1916', *First World War Studies*, 3.1 (2012), 25–49.
Hewison, Robert, *Culture and Consensus: England, Art, and Politics since 1940* (London: Methuen, 1995).
Hindle, Maurice, *Studying Shakespeare on Film* (Basingstoke: Palgrave Macmillan, 2007).
Hixson, Walter L., *Parting the Curtain: Propaganda, Culture, and the Cold War, 1945–1951* (London: Macmillan, 1997).
Hoggart, Richard, *The Uses of Literacy: Aspects of Working-Class Life* (London: Chatto and Windus, 1957).
Holden, Anthony, *Olivier* (London: Little Books, 2007).

Holderness, Graham, *Shakespeare in Performance: The Taming of the Shrew* (Manchester: Manchester University Press, 1989).
Holland, Patrick, and Graham Huggan, *Tourists with Typewriters: Critical Reflections on Contemporary Travel Writing* (Ann Arbor, MI: University of Michigan Press, 2000).
Holland, Peter, 'Touring Shakespeare', in *The Cambridge Companion to Shakespeare on Stage*, ed. by Stanley Wells, and Sarah Stanton (Cambridge: Cambridge University Press, 2002), pp. 194–211.
Holm, Ian, *Acting My Life* (London: Corgi Books, 2004).
Hopkins, A. G., *American Empire* (New Jersey, NJ: Princeton University Press, 2018).
Horne, John, and Alan Kramer, *German Atrocities 1914: A History of Denial* (New Haven, CT: Yale University Press, 2001).
Hourani, Albert, *Arabic Thought in the Liberal Age, 1789–1939* (Cambridge: Cambridge University Press, 1983).
Howatt, A. P. R., and H. G. Widdowson, *A History of Second Language Teaching* (Oxford: Oxford University Press, 2004).
Huang, Alexander C. Y., 'Global Shakespeares as Methodology', *Shakespeare*, 9.3 (2013), 273–290.
Huggett, Richard, *Binkie Beaumont: Eminence Grise of the West End Theatre 1933–1973* (London: Hodder and Stoughton, 1989).
Hunt, Albert, and Geoffrey Reeves, *Peter Brook* (Cambridge: Cambridge University Press, 1995).
Ivie, Robert L., 'Metaphor and the Rhetorical Invention of Cold War "Idealists"', in *Cold War Rhetoric: Strategy, Metaphor and Ideology*, ed. by Martin J. Medhurst, et al. (Ann Arbor, MI: University of Michigan Press, 1997), pp. 103–127.
Jackson, Robert, *The Malayan Emergency and Indonesian Confrontation: The Commonwealth's Wars 1948–1966* (London: Pen and Sword Aviation, 2008).
James, C. L. R., *World Revolution, 1917–1937: The Rise and Fall of the Communist International* (London: Seeker and Warburg, 1937).
Jameson, Fredric, *Marxism and Form* (Princeton, NJ: Princeton University Press, 1971).
Jensen, Kenneth M., ed., *Origins of the Cold War* (Washington, DC: United States Institute of Peace Press, 1993).
Johnson, David, 'From the Colonial to the Post-Colonial: Shakespeare and Education in Africa', in *Post-Colonial Shakespeares*, ed. by Ania Loomba and Martin Orkin (Abingdon: Routledge, 1998), pp. 218–234.
Shakespeare and South Africa (Oxford: Clarendon Press, 1996).
July, Robert W., *An African Voice: The Role of the Humanities in African Independence* (Durham, NC: Duke University Press, 1987).
King, A. H., 'The Nature and Demand for English in the World Today, as It Effects British Universities', in *English Teaching Abroad and the British Universities*, ed. by H. G. Wayment (London: Methuen, 1961), pp. 22–25.
Knapp, Terence, *Hawaii's Adopted World-Class Actor* (Bloomington, IN: Xlibris Press, 2000).

Knightley, Phillip, *Australia: A Biography of a Nation* (London: Vintage Books, 2001).
Korsberg, Hanna, 'Creating an International Community during the Cold War', in Balme Szymanski-Düll, *Theatre, Globalization, and the Cold War*, pp. 151–163.
Kott, Jan, *Shakespeare Our Contemporary* (London: Methuen, 1964).
  Still Alive: An Autobiographical Essay (New Haven, CT: Yale University Press, 1994).
Kustow, Michael, *Peter Brook: A Biography* (London: St Martin's Press, 2005).
Lawrence, Mark Atwood, 'The Rise and Fall of Nonalignment', in *The Cold War in the Third World*, ed. by Robert J. McMahon (Oxford: Oxford University Press, 2013), pp. 139–155.
Lawrence, James, *Churchill and Empire: Portrait of an Imperialist* (London: Phoenix, 2013).
Layiwola, Dele, ed., *African Theatre in Performance: A Festschrift for Martin Banham* (Amsterdam: Harwood Academic Press, 2000).
Leavis, F. R., *For Continuity* (Cambridge: Minority Press, 1933).
Lee, Christopher J., *Making a World After Empire: The Bandung Movement and Its Political Afterlives* (Athens, OH: Ohio University Press, 2010).
Lee, J. M., 'British Cultural Diplomacy and the Cold War: 1946–1961', *Diplomacy and Statecraft*, 9.1 (1998), 112–134.
Leeson, Peter T., and Andrea Dean, 'The Democratic Domino Theory', *American Journal of Political Science*, 53.3 (2009), 533–551.
Levenson, Jill. L., and Robert Ormsby, eds., *The Shakespearean World* (Abingdon: Routledge, 2017).
Lieblein, Leanore, 'Jan Kott, Peter Brook and *King Lear*', *Journal of Dramatic Theory and Criticism*, 1.2 (1987), pp. 39–50.
Litvin, Margaret, *Hamlet's Arab Journey: Shakespeare's Prince and Nasser's Ghost* (Princeton, NJ: Princeton University Press, 2011).
Louis, Wm. Roger, 'The Dissolution of the British Empire', in *The Oxford History of the British Empire: Volume IV: The Twentieth Century*, ed. by Judith Brown and Wm. Roger Louis (Oxford: Oxford University Press, 1999), pp. 329–356.
Lucas, W. Scott, 'Beyond Freedom, Beyond Control: Approaches to Culture and the State-Private Network in the Cold War', in *The Cultural Cold War in Western Europe 1945–1960*, ed. by Giles Scott-Smith, and Hans Krabbendam (London: Frank Cass Publishers, 2003), pp. 40–56.
Lunn, Eugene, *Marxism and Modernism: An Historical Study of Lukács, Brecht, Benjamin, and Adorno* (Berkley, CA: University of California Press, 1992).
MacKenzie, John M., "In Touch with the Infinite': The BBC and Empire, 1923–1953', in *Imperialism and Popular Culture*, ed. by John M. MacKenzie (Manchester: Manchester University Press, 1986), pp. 165–192.
MacPhee, Graham, *Postwar British Literature and Postcolonial Studies* (Edinburg: Edinburg University Press, 2011).
Makaryk, Irena R., and Joseph G. Price, 'Introduction: When Worlds Collide: Shakespeare and Communism', in *Shakespeare in the Worlds of Communism*

and Socialism, ed. by Irena R. Makaryk, and Joseph G. Price (Toronto: University of Toronto Press, 2006), pp. 3–10.
Makaryk, Irena R., and Marissa McHugh, eds., *Shakespeare and the Second World War: Theatre, Culture and Identity* (Toronto: University of Toronto Press, 2012).
Mancewicz, Aneta, and Alexa Alice Joubin, eds. *Local and Global Myths in Shakespearean Performance* (London: Palgrave Macmillan, 2018).
Mangan, Richard, ed., *Gielgud's Letters* (London: Weidenfeld and Nicolson, 2004).
Marshall, Norman, 'Shakespeare Abroad', in *Talking of Shakespeare*, ed. by John Garrett (London: Hodder and Stoughton, 1954), pp. 91–110.
Martin, Daniel, 'Subtitles and Audiences: The Translation and Global Circulation of the Films of Akira Kurosawa', *Journal of Film and Video*, 69.2 (2017), 20–33.
Massai, Sonia, 'Networks: Researching Global Shakespeare', in *The Arden Research Handbook of Shakespeare in Contemporary Performance*, ed. by Peter Kirwan, and Kathryn Prince (London: Bloomsbury Press, 2021), pp. 114–131.
Mazov, Sergey, *A Distant Front in the Cold War: The USSR in West Africa and the Congo, 1956–1964* (Palo Alto, CA: Stanford University Press, 2010).
Medhurst, Martin J., et al., eds., *Cold War Rhetoric: Strategy, Metaphor, and Ideology* (Ann Arbor, MI: University of Michigan Press, 1990).
Monod, David, 'He Is a Cripple an' Needs My Love': *Porgy and Bess* as Cold War Propaganda', in *The Cultural Cold War in Western Europe, 1945–1960*, ed. by Giles Scott-Smith, and Hans Krabbendam (London: Frank Cass, 2003), pp. 300–312.
Mayhew, Christopher, *Time to Explain: An Autobiography* (London: Hutchinson, 1987).
War of Words: A Cold War Witness (London: I. B. Tauris, 1998).
McCullough, Christopher J., 'The Cambridge Connection: Towards a Materialist Theatre Practice', in *The Shakespeare Myth*, ed. by Graham Holderness (Manchester University Press: Manchester, 1988).
McKern, Leo, *Just Resting* (London: Methuen, 1983).
McMahon, Robert J., *The Cold War: A Very Short Introduction* (Oxford: Oxford University Press, 2003).
ed., *The Cold War in the Third World* (Oxford: Oxford University Press, 2013).
Merriman, Andy, *Greasepaint and Cordite: How ENSA Entertained the Troops During World War II* (London: Aurum Press, 2013).
Menzer, Paul, *Anecdotal Shakespeare: A New Performance History* (London: Bloomsbury, 2015).
Milne, Geoffrey, *Theatre Australia (Un)Limited: Australian Theatre Since the 1950s* (Amsterdam: Rodopi Press, 2004).
Murphy, Andrew, *Shakespeare for the People: Working-Class Readers, 1800–1900* (Cambridge: Cambridge University Press, 2010).
Murphy, E. Jefferson, *Creative Philanthropy: Carnegie Corporation and Africa, 1953–1973* (New York: Carnegie Corporation Publishing, 1976), pp. 164–167.
Neel, Boyd, and J. David Finch, *My Orchestra and Other Adventures: The Memoirs of Boyd Neel* (Toronto: The University of Toronto Press, 1985).

Neirick, Miriam, *When Pigs Could Fly and Bears Could Dance: A History of the Soviet Circus* (Madison, WI: The University of Wisconsin Press, 2012).
Nicholson, Virginia, *Among the Bohemians: Experiments in Living 1900–1939* (London: Penguin Books, 2003).
Niebur, Louis, *Special Sound: The Creation and Legacy of the BBC Radio-phonic Workshop* (Oxford; Oxford University Press, 2010).
Nowak, Jan, *Courier from Warsaw* (Detroit, MI: Wayne State University Press, 1982).
Nye, Joseph, *Soft Power: The Means to Success in World Politics* (New York: Public Affairs, 2004).
Obiechina, Emmanuel, *An African Popular Literature: A Study of Onitsha Market Literature* (Cambridge: Cambridge University Press, 1971).
O'Connor, Garry, *Darlings of the Gods: One Year in the Lives of Laurence Olivier and Vivien Leigh* (London: Hodder and Stoughton, 1984).
Olivier, Laurence, ed., *Five Seasons of the Old Vic Theatre Company: A Scrapbook Record of Production for 1944–1949* (London: Saturn Press, 1949).
Oguntoyinbo, Deji, 'Review of Ahmed Yerima's *Modern Nigerian Theatre: Geoffrey Axworthy Years, 1956–1967*', *California Linguistic Notes*, 37.2 (2012), 167–171.
Omotoso, Kole, 'Concepts of History and Theatre in Africa', in *A History of Theatre in Africa*, pp. 1–12.
Osman, Tarek, *Egypt on the Brink: From Nasser to the Muslim Brotherhood* (New Haven, CT: Yale University Press, 2010), pp. 56–83.
Parfenov, Alexandr, and Joseph G. Price, eds., *Russian Essays on Shakespeare and His Contemporaries* (Newark, DE: University of Delaware Press, 1998).
Paul, Kathleen, *Whitewashing Britain: Race and Citizenship in the Postwar Era* (Ithaca, NY: Cornell University Press, 1997).
Payne, George Stanley, *A History of Fascism, 1914–1945* (Abingdon: Routledge, 1995).
Peslin, Daniela, *Le Théâtre des Nations: Une aventure théâtrale à redécourir* (Paris: L'Harmattan, 2009).
Phillips, A. A., *The Australian Tradition: Studies in a Colonial Culture* (Melbourne: Cheshire Press, 1958).
Phillipson, Robert, *Linguistic Imperialism* (Oxford: Oxford University Press, 1992).
Poddar, Prem, and David Johnson, eds., *A Historical Companion to Postcolonial Literatures in English* (Edinburgh: Edinburgh University Press, 2005).
Potter, Simon J., *Broadcasting Empire: The BBC and the British World, 1922–1970* (Oxford: Oxford University Press, 2012).
Puddington, Arch, *Broadcasting Freedom: The Cold War Triumph of Radio Free Europe and Radio Liberty* (Lexington, KY: The University Press of Kentucky, 2000).
Prashad, Vijay, *The Darker Nations: A People's History of the Third World* (London: The New Press, 2007).
Pratt, Mary Louise, *Imperial Eyes: Travel Writing and Transculturation* (Abingdon: Routledge, 1992).

Quayle, Anthony, *A Time to Speak* (London: Barrie and Jenkins, 1990).
Raffer, Kunibert, and H. W. Singer, *The Economic North–South Divide: Six Decades of Unequal Development* (Northampton, MA: Edward Elgar, 2001).
Raw, Laurence, 'People's Theatre and Shakespeare in Wartime: Donald Wolfit's *King Lear* in London and Leeds, 1944–1945', *Shakespeare*, 12.1 (2016), 55–66.
Read, Donald, *The Power of the News: The History of Reuters* (Oxford: Oxford University Press, 1992).
Read, Piers Paul, *Alec Guinness: The Authorised Biography* (London: Simon and Schuster, 2003).
Rebellato, Dan, *1956 And All That: The Making of Modern British Drama* (Abingdon: Routledge, 1999).
Reese, Jack E., 'The Formalisation of Horror in *Titus Andronicus*', *Shakespeare Quarterly*, 21.1 (1970), 77–84.
Richmond, Hugh M., 'The Audience's Role in *Othello*', in *Othello: New Critical Essays*, ed. by Philip Kolin (Abingdon: Routledge, 2016), pp. 89–102.
Shakespeare in Performance: King Richard III (Manchester: Manchester University Press, 1989).
Rickard, John, 'John Alden (1908–1962)', *The Australian Dictionary of Biography Online*. www.adb.anu.edu.au/biography/alden-john-9323 [Accessed 13 November 2018].
Rose, Jonathan, *The Literary Churchill: Author, Reader, Actor* (New Haven, CT: Yale University Press, 2014).
Rosenthal, Daniel, *The National Theatre Story* (London: Oberon Books, 2013).
Rowell, George, and Anthony Jackson, *The Repertory Movement: A History of Regional Theatre in Britain* (Cambridge: Cambridge University Press, 1984).
Rowse, A. L., *An Elizabethan Garland* (London: Macmillan, 1953).
Rubin, Andrew N., *Archives of Authority: Empire, Culture, and the Cold War* (Princeton, NJ: Princeton University Press, 2012).
Said, Edward, *Out of Place: A Memoir* (London: Granta Books, 1999).
Salmon, Patrick, *The Control of the Past: Herbert Butterfield and the Pitfalls of Official History* (London: University of London Press, 2021).
Saunders, Frances Stonor, *Who Paid the Piper?: The CIA and the Cultural Cold War* (London: Granta, 1999).
Sawicka, Zofia, 'Jan Kott: The Road to Shakespeare', *Culture.pl*, March (2009). http://culture.pl/en/article/jan-kott-the-road-to-shakespeare [Accessed 10 May 2023].
Scheil, Katherine, 'Importing Stratford', *Critical Survey*, 24.2 (2012), 71–87.
Schwarz, Walter, *Nigeria* (London: Frederick A. Praeger Publishers, 1968).
Scott-Smith, Giles, and Hans Krabbendam, eds., *The Cultural Cold War in Western Europe, 1945–1960* (London: Frank Cass, 2003).
Senelick, Laurence, '"Thus Conscience Doth Make Cowards of Us All": New Documentation on the Okhlopkok *Hamlet*', in *Shakespeare in the Worlds of Communism and Socialism* (Toronto: University of Toronto Press, 2006), pp. 136–156.
Sheen, Erica, 'Mystery in the Soul of State: Shakespeare in Airlift Berlin', in *Shakespeare in Cold War Europe: Conflict, Commemoration, and Celebration*,

ed. by Erica Sheen, and Isabel Karremann (Basingstoke: Palgrave Pivot, 2016), pp. 9–22.

Sheen, Erica, and Isabel Karremann, eds., *Shakespeare in Cold War Europe: Conflict, Commemoration, and Celebration* (Basingstoke: Palgrave Pivot, 2016).

Shewring, Margaret, *Shakespeare in Performance: King Richard II* (Manchester: Manchester University Press, 1996).

Shore, Marci, *Caviar and Ashes: A Warsaw Generation's Life and Death in Marxism, 1918–1968* (New Haven, CT: Yale University Press, 2006).

Shostakovich, Dmitri, *Testimony: Memoirs as Related to Solomon Volkov* (London: Faber and Faber, 2005).

Sinclair, Andrew, *Arts and Culture: The History of Fifty Years of the Arts Council in Great Britain* (London: Sinclair Stevenson, 1995).

Sinfield, Alan, *Literature, Politics, and Culture in Post-war Britain* (London: Continuum, 2004).

'Royal Shakespeare: Theatre and the Making of Ideology', in *Political Shakespeare: Essays in Cultural Materialism*, ed. by Jonathan Dollimore, and Alan Sinfield (Manchester: Manchester University Press, 1985), pp. 182–205.

Smialkowska, Monika, 'Introduction: Mobilising Shakespeare during the Great War', *Shakespeare*, 10.3 (2014), 225–229.

Smith, Emma, *Henry V: Shakespeare in Production* (Cambridge: Cambridge University Press, 2002).

Smith, James, 'MI5 Surveillance and British Cold War Theatre', in *Theatre, Globalization, and the Cold War*, ed. by Christopher B. Balme, and Berenika Szymanski-Düll (London: Palgrave Macmillan, 2017), pp. 133–150.

Soyinka, Wole, *You Must Set Forth at Dawn* (New York: Random House, 2006).

Speaight, Robert, ed., *A Bridge-Adams Letter Book* (London: The Society for Theatrical Research Press, 1971).

Springhall, John, *Decolonisation Since 1945* (Basingstoke: Palgrave Macmillan, 2001).

Stark, Freya, *Dust in the Lion's Paw* (London: Arrow Books, 1990).

Sumner, John, *Recollections at Play: A Life in Australian Theatre* (Melbourne: Melbourne University Press, 1993).

Tallents, Stephen, *The Projection of England* (London: Faber and Faber, 1933).

Taylor, Gary, *Reinventing Shakespeare: A Cultural History from the Restoration to the Present* (New York: Weidenfeld and Nicolson, 1989).

Taylor, Gary, and Stanley Wells, eds., *William Shakespeare: The Complete Works* (Oxford: Clarendon Press, 2005).

Taylor, Philip M., *British Propaganda in the Twentieth Century: Selling Democracy* (Edinburgh: Edinburgh University Press, 1999).

The Projection of Britain: Propaganda during the Second World War (Cambridge: Cambridge University Press, 1981).

Taylor, Timothy D., *Strange Sounds: Music, Technology and Culture* (Abingdon: Routledge, 2001).
Thompson, Carl, *Travel Writing* (Abingdon: Routledge, 2011).
Tighe, Carl, 'Jan Kott: The Revisionist', *Journal of European Studies*, 26.3 (1996), 267–297.
Toulouse, Mark G., *The Transformation of John Foster Dulles* (Macon, GA: Mercer University Press, 1985).
Trewin, J. C., *Peter Brook: A Biography* (London: Macdonald, 1971).
Shakespeare on the English Stage, 1900–1964 (London: Barrie and Rockliff, 1964).
The Old Vic Company, 1914–1963 (London: Old Vic Trust Ltd, 1963).
Tutuola, Amos, *The Palm-Wine Drinkard* (London: Faber and Faber, 1952).
Tynan, Kenneth, *Alec Guinness* (London: Salisbury Square, 1953).
Theatre Writings (London: Nick Hern, 2008).
Vadney, T. E., *The World Since 1945* (London: Penguin Books, 1998).
Vickers, Hugo, *Vivien Leigh* (London: Hamish Hamilton, 1988).
Viswanathan, Gauri, *Masks of Conquest: Literary Study and British Rule in India* (London: Faber and Faber, 1990).
Von Eschen, Penny M., *Satchmo Blows up the World: Jazz Ambassadors Play the Cold War* (Cambridge, MA: Harvard University Press, 2004).
Walton, Calder, *Empire of Secrets: British Intelligence, the Cold War, and the Twilight of Empire* (London: Harper Press, 2013).
Ward, Stuart, *Australia and the British Embrace: The Demise of the Imperial Ideal* (Melbourne: Melbourne University Press, 2001).
Watanabe, Aiko, 'Cultural Drives by the Periphery: Britain's Experiences', *History in Focus*, 10 (2006). www.history.ac.uk/ihr/Focus/cold/articles/watanabe.html [Accessed 30 March 2021].
Webster, Wendy, *Englishness and Empire 1939–1965* (Oxford: Oxford University Press, 2005).
Weingärtner, Jörn, *The Arts as a Weapon of War: Britain and the Shaping of National Morale in the Second World War* (London: Taurus Academic Studies, 2006).
West, Nigel, 'ASIO Opens its Books', *International Journal of Intelligence and Counterintelligence*, 28.3 (2014), 620–629.
Westad, Odd Arne, *The Global Cold War* (Cambridge: Cambridge University Press, 2007).
Whaley, George, *Leo 'Rumpole' McKern: The Accidental Actor* (Sydney: University of New South Wales Press, 2009).
Whidden, James, *Egypt: British Colony, Imperial Capital* (Manchester: Manchester University Press, 2017).
Wiebe, Heather, *Britten's Unquiet Pasts: Sound and Memory in Post-war Reconstruction* (Cambridge: Cambridge University Press, 2012).
Williams, Raymond, *Politics and Letters: Interviews with the New Left Review* (London: Verso Books, 1981).

Wilson, Steve, *The Making of* Gone with the Wind (Austin, TX: University of Texas Press, 2004).
Wolfit, Donald, *First Interval* (London: Odhams Press Limited, 1954).
Wright, Patrick, *On Living in an Old Country: The National Past in Contemporary Britain* (Oxford: Oxford University Press, 2009).
Yerima, Ahmed, *Modern Nigerian Theatre: Geoffrey Axworthy Years, 1956–1967* (Ibadan: Kraft Books, 2005).

Index

ABC (Australian Broadcasting Corporation), 69, 75, 78
Abyad, George, 32
AETTF (Australian Elizabethan Theatre Trust Fund), 84
Agate, James, 22, 61
Alden, John, 84–85, 180
Allenby, Lord, 44
al-Haddad, Najib
  Martyrs of Love (1895), 32
American University in Cairo, 44
American University of Beirut, 48
Anglo-Egyptian Union, 39, 43
Arabic Theatre Company, 32
archives, 5–6
Arts Council, UK, 59, 67, 145
Ashby, Sir Eric, 120
Ashcroft, Peggy, 148
ASIO (Australian Security Intelligence Organisation), 56, 85
Atienza, Edward, 148, 161, 171
Atlee, Clement, 54
Australia, 3, 5, 10, 30, 50–54, 62, 64, 67–68, 71, 75–76, 80, 82–83, 109, 149, 169, 181
  Anglo-Australian relations, 53–54, 57, 64, 70, 77
  Anzac Day celebrations in, 64
  Australian accents in the theatre, 78, 180
  British Council in, 57, 83
  British Council withdrawal from, 84–85
  cultural cringe, the, 12, 66, 78
  Little Theatre scene in, 78
  National Theatre scheme for, 57, 65–66, 75–76, 78, 83–84
  playgoing in, 80–82
  projection of Greater-British culture via, 56
  recolonisation of, 5, 8, 53–58, 65–66, 77
  Shakespeare's educational role in, 77, 80
  Shakespearean actors from, 78
  Soviet penetration of, 56
  theatre scene of, 57–58, 65–66, 76
  White Australia Policy in, 70, 182
Australian Shakespeare Company, 84
Austria, 3, 13, 86, 90–91, 103
Axworthy, Geoffrey, 124–27, 141

Balfour, Lord, 80
Ballantine, Sheila, 163
Bangladesh, 3, 146, 173
Barton, John, 158, 163
Baynton, Harry, 146
BBC (British Broadcasting Corporation), 17–18, 24, 78, 85, 101, 153
  Empire Service, 18, 56
  Overseas Service, 18
  World Service, 18
Beatty, Chester, 34
Beaumont, Hugh 'Binkie', 40, 157, 171
Beaverbrook, 18, 20–21
Beckhoff, Hans, 31
Belgium, 37, 86–87
Benin, 142
Benn, Brian, 155, 173
Benson, Frank, 38, 146, 153
Benthall, Michael, 157, 167, 171
Berliner Ensemble, the, 87
Bernhardt, Sarah, 32
Beyer, Elsie, 84
BFBS (British Forces Broadcasting Service), 42
Biafran Civil War, the, 142
Bihar Arts Theatre, 156
Birmingham Repertory Theatre, 22
Bishop, Major General W. H. A. 140
BIS (British Information Services), 129, 168
Black Lives Matter, 183
Blakemore, Michael, 6, 55, 106, 147–48, 152
bohemianism, 26
Bolshoi Ballet, the, 87
Boyd Neel Orchestra, the, 54–55
Brecht, Bertolt, 87
Bridges-Adams, William, 21, 36

247

Index

Bristol Old Vic, 67
  1963 tour of Pakistan, India, and Sri Lanka, 118, 149, 171–72
British Council, the, 4, 17, 48, 88, 105, 128, 130, 138, 146–47, 169, 178–79, 181, 183, 185
  1964 Shakespeare quatercentenary and, 143–44
  2016 Shakespeare quatercentenary and, 182
  Archives of, 6–7
  in Australia, 53–54, 56–57, 62, 65–67, 77, 83–85, 180
  in Austria, 107
  Cultural Relations Department (CRD) and, 49, 103
  in Denmark, 40
  Drama Advisory Committee (DAC) and, 7, 24, 51, 118–19, 152, 157–58, 179
  Drogheda Report, the, 83, 85
  in Egypt, 43
  English Language Teaching (ELT) and, 123–24
  ENSA and, 36
  early history of, 15–21, 119
  in India, 149–50, 168–69
  in Italy, 27, 29
  in Malta, 128
  Near East Committee, 45
  New Shakespeare Company Equity Report and, 170–72, 174–76
  in Nigeria, 120, 122–23, 128, 136, 140–41
  in Pakistan, 150
  Paper on Theatre Export, 86
  in Portugal, 1, 21
  Soviet Relations Committee (SRC) and, 13, 87–88, 92–95
  in Yugoslavia, 105, 108
British Food Appeal, 55
British foreign policy, 2, 20–21, 55, 121, 177, 179
British Institute, 1, 26
British race patriotism, 80
British Treasury, the, 35, 51
British War Relief Fund, the, 39
British-Soviet Friendship Society, the, 92
Britten, Benjamin, 55
Brook, Peter, 99–100, 102–3, 108, 110, 115, 117, 124
  1955 tour of Russia, 95–97
  Jan Kott and, 89, 94, 110–11, 116
  production of *Titus Andronicus*, 13, 88, 94, 97–102, 107, 111–12, 114, 117, 182
Burgess, Christopher, 149, 171
Burgtheater, the, 88
Burma. *See* Myanmar

Cairncross, James, 119, 139
Cairo and Alexandria Drama Festival, the, 35, 40
Camões, Luís de, 1
Canada, 5, 22, 54, 86
Carnegie Foundation, the, 122
Carter, Simon, 119, 171
Casson, Lewis, 24–25, 28, 32, 169
CCF (Congress for Cultural Freedom), 91
CEMA (Council for the Encouragement of Music and the Arts), 11, 35
Ceylon. *See* Sri Lanka
China, 9, 55, 86, 185
Church, Anthony, 119
Churchill, Winston, 20, 62, 68, 160
CIA (Central Intelligence Agency), 91
Clark, J. P., 128
Cold War, the, 2–3, 8–9, 12, 41, 48, 53, 55, 57, 82, 88–93, 97–99, 102, 105–6, 109, 111, 115, 182, 186
  decolonisation and, 8–9, 56, 92, 121–23
  theatre and, 9–11, 86, 88
Cole, Cozy, 121
Commonwealth, the, 2, 8, 12, 36, 53, 55, 57–58, 67, 69, 71, 74, 76, 82–83, 119–20, 123, 127, 140, 178–79
communism, 3, 87, 90–91, 102, 182
Communist Party, the, 41, 89, 113–14, 116
Conville, David, 146–48, 152–53, 157–59, 164, 168–76
Cooper, Duff, 105
Copely, Peter, 61
Coward, Noël
  Blithe Spirit (1941), 36, 41
CRD (Cultural Relations Department), 12, 49, 103, 179
Cultural Cold War, the, 3, 5, 9, 87, 117, 120–21
cultural cringe, the, 66
cultural diplomacy, 2–5, 9, 11, 14, 16–19, 29–30, 34, 40, 44, 49, 54, 85, 89, 94, 102, 108, 138, 149, 177–79, 182, 184–86
Cyprus, 184

D'Abernon Report, the, 16, 18
Dalby, Peter, 171, 173, 175
Daneman, Paul, 119, 129, 135
Dean, Basil, 36–37, 40, 42, 44, 47, 49, 61
decolonisation, 3, 5, 8, 48, 56, 120–21, 123, 127, 144, 184–86
Deep England, 68
Dench, Judi, 119, 124, 129, 132, 135, 138–39
Denmark, 40, 96, 114
Dew, Peter, 129
Donald, Robert, 146
Doran, Charles, 146
Dunlop, Frank, 128–30, 139

Index

Eastern Nigerian Theatre Group, 128
Edgehill, Jane, 172
EEC (European Economic Community), 83
Egypt, 2–3, 8, 10–11, 15, 20–21, 30–31, 33, 36–37, 39, 41–42, 44–45, 47–48, 82, 169
  Anglo-Egyptian relation in 1945, 39–41
  Ango-Egyptian relations in 1939, 29–30
  suez crisis in, 90–91
  translations of Shakespeare in, 32
Elizabeth II, Queen, 103
Ekwere, John, 128
ELT (English Language Teaching), 19, 119, 121, 123
EMB (Empire Marketing Board), 17–18
Empire, 1–3, 8, 11–12, 16–17, 34, 42, 45, 52, 55, 64, 68, 77, 84, 123, 132, 138, 143, 150, 177, 181–82, 184–86
ENSA (Entertainment National Services Association), 11, 35–36, 38, 40, 42, 61, 149
Epstein, Jacob, 99
Equity, 170–71, 175
Eric Elliott Company, the, 150
Esher, Lord, 51, 64
Ethiopia, 18, 30–31
Europe, 2, 5, 9–10, 12, 15, 18–19, 25, 29–31, 54, 58, 82, 87, 90–91, 105, 109, 120, 123, 148, 181, 184
  Eastern Europe, 5, 86, 88, 92–93, 104, 109, 111, 179
Eyre, Charmaine, 80

Farell, Alfred, 119
fascism, 2, 15, 18, 31
Fenice, La, 88
Festival of Britain, the, 67, 167
Finch, Peter, 65
Finland, 86
First World War, the, 17, 20–21
Flower, Hersey Caroline, 79
Flower, Sir Fordham, 79
Ford Foundation, the, 122
Foreign Office, the, 6–7, 19, 21, 49, 54, 103, 105, 108, 119, 123, 169, 179
France, 13, 16, 19, 31, 37, 45, 62, 87–88, 91, 120
Franco, General Francisco, 19
From Russia with Love (1963), 149
Fuseli, Henry, 46

Gandhi, Mahatma, 18
General Montgomery, 37
Germany, 2, 9, 16–17, 28, 86, 90, 103, 185–86
Ghana, 118, 121, 123, 130
Gielgud, John, 3, 15, 22, 36, 40, 49, 72, 142, 148, 153
  1946 Egypt Tour, 40–48

Gillan, Sir Angus, 62
Goldsmith, Oliver
  She Stoops to Conquer (1773), 62
Goldwyn, Samuel, 51
Gomulka, Wladyslaw, 90
Gone with the Wind (1939), 109
Goonasena, Karl, 145
Grafftey-Smith, Laurence, 40, 49
Granville-Barker, Harley, 22
Greater Britain, 53–54
Greece, 21, 86
Greenridge, Terence, 106
Guinness, Alec, 21, 26, 34
Guinness, Merula, 24–28, 32–33
Guthrie, Tyrone, 3, 21–22, 24–25, 31, 35, 50–51, 59, 64–66, 180

Hall, Peter, 115
Hanley, Lord, 41
Harwood, Ronald
  The Dresser (1980), 37
Haymarket Theatre, the, 40
Head, Lord, 120–21, 140
Herman, Ronald, 167
Higazi, Shaykh Salama, 32
Hilar, Karel, 24
Hiley, Peter, 65
Hitler, Adolf, 31, 59, 61, 157
HMS Durban Castle, 37
Hobson, Harold, 22, 61, 102
Hofman, Vlatislav, 24
Holland, 86, 103, 138
Holm, Ian, 101, 106
Hong Kong, 3, 146, 163, 167, 172
House of Commons, the, 19, 143
Howard, Arthur, 167
Hungarian uprising, the, 6, 90–91, 94
Hungary, 90–91
Hunt, Hugh, 84

Ibadan University Travelling Theatre, 128, 141
  1962 tour of Nigeria, 124–27
Independent Theatre, Sydney, 78
India, 3, 18, 20, 22, 30, 40, 55, 86, 118, 129, 138, 146, 149–52, 156, 159, 164, 169–71, 173
  British Council in, 149
IRD (Information Research Department), 93
Italy, 2–3, 16–18, 21, 24, 27–31, 33–34, 86–87, 103
ITI (International Theatre Institute), 103, 144

Jackson, Barry, 22
James, Griffith, 171

Jamshed Memorial Theatre, Karachi, 173
Jefford, Barabara, 71
John, Augustus, 26
Jones, Brian, 48
Jonson, Ben
 Volpone, 36

Kanal (1956), 149
Kennan, George F., 9
Khan, President Muhammad Ayub, 169
Khedivial Opera House, Cairo, 29, 36
Khrushchev, Nikita, 90, 93–94, 110, 116
King Farouk, 39
King, David, 148
Knapp, Terence, 119, 138–39, 142
Komisarjevsky, Theodore, 99
Kott, Jan, 13, 89, 94, 100, 110–17, 151, 181
 Peter Brook and, 89, 110–11

Lampson, Sir Miles, 39
Lancashire, 36
Landen, Dinsdale, 148, 162
Laurence Olivier Productions, 65, 88
League of Nations, the, 31
Leeper, Rex, 16
Leigh, Vivien, 51, 105
Libya, 31
Lisbon, 1, 25, 31
Littlewood, Joan, 151, 155, 157, 180
Lord, Lloyd, 1–2, 18–21, 25, 27, 29, 45, 84
Loraine, Sir Percy, 44
Ludlow Festival, 153
Lukács, Georg, 112, 115, 117
Lyttelton, Olivier, 51

Macmillan, Harold, 123
Malayan Emergency, the, 56
Malaysia, 3, 56, 170
Malta, 3, 21, 34, 129–30
Maly Theatre, the, 97
Manilla, 160
Marshall, Norman, 149–50, 157, 171
Mayhew, Christopher, 93
Mbari Clubs, 127
McBean, Angus, 5
McKern, Leo, 72–74, 79, 82
Menzies, Robert, 54, 66
Michel, Keith, 78
Miller, Arthur
 Death of a Salesman (1949), 78
Mills, James, 84
Moiseiwitsch, Tanya, 71, 156
Morris, Wolf, 149, 167
Muhammad Ali Club, the, 39
musique concrète, 101

Mussolini, Benito
 Cesare (1939), 24
Myanmar, 55

Naguib, Soliman, 36, 43
National Archives, the, 7
National Theatre, 12, 21, 38, 40, 51–53, 57–58, 64–67, 76–78, 83–84, 88, 147, 149
nationalism, 29–31, 42, 70, 125, 152
Nazism, 59
Neville, John, 118–19, 129–30, 138–39
Nevinson, Nancy, 41
New Elizabethanism, 52, 66, 68, 79, 83
New Glover Hall Theatre, Lagos, 132
New Shakespeare Company, the (NSC), 14, 143–50, 152, 154, 156, 158–61, 163–65, 167–69, 171–72, 175
 1964–1965 tour of South and Southeast Asia (*Richard II* in India and Sri Lanka), 149–57
 1964–1965 tour of South and Southeast Asia (*The Taming of the Shrew* in Pakistan and The Philippines), 157–63
 1964–1965 tour of South and Southeast Asia (*The Tempest* in Hong Kong, Singapore, Malaya and Borneo), 163–68
New Theatre, the (London), 59
New Zealand, 5, 12, 51–54, 57, 67, 69, 78–79, 83
Nicholas, Doris, 119
Nigeria, 5–6, 8, 10, 118, 120, 122–23, 125–27, 130, 134, 136, 139, 141, 181
 British Council in, 122, 141
Nkrumah, President Kwami, 119
non-alignment, 91
Northcliffe, Lord, 21
Norwich, John Julius, 105
Nottingham Playhouse Company, 118, 124
 1963 tour of Nigeria, 3, 13, 118, 128, 130, 132–41, 164

Ogui Players, the, 128
Ogunde, Hubert, 125
Ogunmola, Kola, 125, 141
Okhlupov, Nikolay, 95
Old Vic Theatre Company, the, 20–22, 26, 28, 33–35, 40, 50–52, 58–59, 64–67, 78, 82, 84, 87, 95, 128–29, 147–49, 171, 180
 1939 Mediterranean Tour, 3, 15, 21, 24–35, 181
 1944 European Tour, 61
 1948 Commonwealth Tour, 3, 12, 51–52, 55, 57, 62–67, 69, 83–84
 1955 Australia Tour, 148
 1955 European Tour, 149
 1958 European Tour, 109

Index

Olivier, Sir Laurence, 12, 22, 51–52, 55, 58–59, 62, 64–65, 72, 76, 78, 80, 83, 88, 103, 105, 108–9, 132, 142, 148, 180
   playing Henry V, 58–59, 114
   playing Richard III, 59, 61
   playing Titus Andronicus, 107, 109, 114
Onitsha Market Literature, 125–26, 133
Orwell, George, 18
Osborne, John
   The Entertainer (1957), 89

Pakistan, 3, 55, 118, 129, 143, 146, 149–50, 153, 157, 159, 163, 168–71, 173
Pavolini, Contessa Marcella, 24
Peele, George, 98
Pétain, Marshal Philippe, 19
Philippines, the, 3, 146, 157, 160, 163
Poel, William, 22
Poland, 3, 86–87, 90–91, 103, 105–6, 109–10, 112–13, 116
Pope Pius XI, 28
Portman, Eric, 146
Portugal, 1, 3, 21, 24–26, 29, 86
propaganda, 2, 15–21, 25–27, 29–30, 43–44, 48, 55, 57–58, 86–87, 91–95, 106–7, 123, 178, 185

Quayle, Anthony, 25, 28–30, 52, 67–68, 70, 72, 74–78, 80–84, 103, 156, 169, 180, 182
   New Elizabethanism and, 68–69, 74–75, 83
   playing Othello, 71–72, 74, 182
Quayle, Dorothy, 78
Quentin, Robert, 84

race, 1–2, 33, 68, 80, 83, 182
Radio Free Europe, 90, 113
Radiophonic Workshop, 101
Rattigan, Terrence, 78, 169
   Flare Path (1942), 36
Ravenscroft, Edward, 98
recolonisation, 5, 8, 53–54, 83
Regent's Park Open Air Theatre, 146, 152, 157, 171
Reuters, 56
Richardson, Ralph, 59, 64, 146, 149
Rizq, Amina, 32
Robert College of Istanbul, 48
Rockefeller Foundation, the, 122
Rostand, Edmond
   Cyrano de Bergerac (1897), 51
RSC (Royal Shakespeare Company), 99, 111, 115, 124, 129, 147, 151, 155, 158, 163, 185
Ruggeri, Ruggero, 28

Rushdi, Fatima, 32
Russia, 9, 28, 41, 86, 90, 92–93, 95, 102–3, 106, 120, 149
Rydin, Vadim, 96

Said, Edward, 44–45
Samoylov, Yevgeny, 95
Sartre, Jean-Paul, 113
SBBA (Shakespeare Beyond Borders Alliance), 184
Scarlett, John, 79
Schofield, Paul, 95
Second World War, the, 8, 10, 15–16, 26, 35, 37, 48, 53, 59, 83, 93, 95, 98, 109, 112, 123
Shakespeare Birthplace Trust, the, 5, 150, 186
Shakespeare, William
   1 Henry IV, 69
   Anthony and Cleopatra, 183
   As You Like It, 69
   Comedy of Errors, The, 128, 160, 182
   Hamlet, 3, 15, 20–22, 24–26, 28–29, 31–32, 36–37, 40–42, 44, 46–47, 62, 93, 95, 97, 109, 114, 145, 181
   Henry V, 21, 25, 31, 58, 88, 114, 146, 152
   Julius Caesar, 24, 77
   King Lear, 37, 89, 111, 152
   Love's Labour's Lost, 147
   Macbeth, 3, 13, 28, 66, 77, 93, 97–98, 118, 120, 127–30, 132–34, 136–37, 139–40, 145, 152, 158, 164–65, 179
   Measure for Measure, 91, 116
   The Merchant of Venice, 37, 145, 149
   Merry Wives of Windsor, 160
   Midsummer Night's Dream, A, 147
   Othello, 3, 12, 51, 69, 71–75, 79, 182, 225
   Pericles, 182
   Richard II, 3, 14, 143, 149, 151–55, 157, 164–65
   Richard III, vii, 3, 12, 51, 55, 58–59, 62, 114, 181
   Romeo and Juliet, 32, 109, 145
   The Taming of the Shrew, 3, 14, 124–25, 143, 146, 149, 152, 158, 160, 162, 165
   The Tempest, 3, 14, 143–44, 158, 164–65, 167, 169
   Titus Andronicus, 3, 5, 13, 86–89, 91, 94–95, 97–103, 105–6, 110–12, 114, 116–17, 179, 182
   Troilus and Cressida, 183
   Twelfth Night, 34, 36, 39, 118, 136, 139, 147, 182
   Two Gentlemen of Verona, 152–53
   The Winter's Tale, 39, 182
Shakespeare's Globe Theatre, London, 184
Sheybal, Vladek, 149, 157–58, 161, 163

Shostakovich, Dmitri, 93
Sidky, Ismail, 43
Sierra Leone, 118–19, 123, 130
Singapore, 3, 62, 146, 161, 163, 174
SMT (Shakespeare Memorial Theatre), 50, 52–53, 58, 67–68, 83, 88, 94, 98, 103, 180
   1949 Australia and New Zealand Tour, 66
   1953 Coronation Tour, 3, 12, 53, 57, 69–82, 182
   1955 European Tour, 148
   1957 Eastern European Tour, 3, 13, 87, 105–10
Smuts, Jan, 17
Socialist Realism, 92, 104, 110
Society for Cultural Relations with the USSR, 92
soft power, 10, 14, 82, 177, 182, 184–87
South Africa, 17
South America, 16, 18, 149
South Pacific (1949), 79
Soviet Union, the, 5, 9, 13, 43, 87–89, 91–93, 95, 104, 109, 120
Soyinka, Wole, 124, 127
Spain, 19, 25, 86
Spanish Civil War, the, 19
Spears, Edward, 61
SRC (Soviet Relations Committee), 87–88, 92, 94–95, 103, 179
Staatliche Schauspielhaus Theatre, Hamburg, 61
Stalin, Joseph, 9, 12, 85, 90, 93–94, 103, 113, 116
Stalinism, 91, 117
Stark, Freya, 39, 43
state–private networks, 4, 10, 94, 102, 105, 177, 180
Statute of Westminster Commonwealth Act, 1931, 53
Stoll Theatre, London, 88
Stratford-upon-Avon, 5, 37, 39, 67–68, 70, 81
Sudan, the, 43
Suez Canal, 29–30
Suez crisis, 90
Sumner, John, 75
Swinton, Lord, 83

Tagore, Rabindranath, 150
Tallents, Stephen, 17, 19
Tearle, Geoffrey, 72, 74
Tennant, Cecil, 65, 95
Theatre Archive Project, the (British Library), 6
Théâtre des Nations, 88, 103, 144
Third World, the, 9, 90–91
Thomas, Brendon
   Charley's Aunt (1892), 40
Thomas, Stephen, 103
Thompson, Eric, 129
Thorndike, Sybil, 61

Thring, Frank, 105
Tito, Josip Broz, 91
Tivoli Theatre, Sydney, 71
Tree, Beerbohm, 38
Trewin, J. C., 88, 99, 101
Tutuola, Amos
   The Palm-Wine Drinkard (1952), 125
Tynan, Kenneth, 22, 97

UN (United Nations), 144
UNESCO (United Nations Educational, Scientific and Cultural Organisation), 103, 144, 185
United States, the, 5, 9, 41, 44, 48, 54, 56, 87, 109, 120–22
University of Ibadan, 13, 120, 122, 125, 141, 181
USIS (United States Information Services), 120

Vercoe, Rosemary, 129
Verdi, Giuseppe
   Aida (1871), 32
Victoria College, Cairo, 45–46

Wafd Party, Egypt, 19, 30, 41
Wahbi, Youssef, 32
Wales, 36
Wanigasuriya, D.B.
   Portia Nadagama (1884), 145
War Office, the, 37
Waters, Frank, 78
West End, the, 22, 35, 37, 40, 67
West, Valerie, 139
Westwell, Raymond, 79
Wilder, Thornton
   Skin of Our Teeth (1942), 62
Wilkie, Allan, 82
William, David, 143, 146, 149, 153, 165
Williams, Emlyn
   Night Must Fall (1935), 36
Williams, Tennessee
   A Streetcar Named Desire (1947), 109
Williams, Vaughan, 54
Williamsons, J. C., 66
Wolfit, Donald, 3, 15, 36, 48, 59, 61, 85, 146
   1945 Egypt Tour, 37–40
Wyse, John, 149–50, 164, 173

Yoruba travelling theatre, 125
Yugoslavia, 3, 13, 86–87, 90–91, 103, 105–6, 109

Zawistowski, Roman, 95
Zedong, Mao, 9
Zeffirelli, Franco, 109
Zhdanovism, 113